Passions Between Women

Phoebe initiating Fanny in the brothel, from John Cleland, Memoirs of a Woman of Pleasure *(1766 edition)*

Emma Donoghue

Passions Between Women

British lesbian culture 1668 - 1801

HarperCollins*Publishers*

Acknowledgements:
Some material from this book has been published before and is reprinted with thanks: 'The Female Husband' in *Corridor: the Cambridge Feminist Magazine* (summer 1992) and 'Imagined More Than Women: lesbians as hermaphrodites, 1671–1766' in *Women's History Review* (June 1993).

I would like to thank all those who encouraged my research at the 'Questions of Homosexuality' Conferences 1991 and 1992; National Bisexual Conferences 1991 and 1992; Lancaster University Centre for Women's Studies Open Seminar 1991 and 'Romance Revisited' Conference 1993; University of Sussex 'Mary Wollstonecraft: 200 Years of Feminism' Conference 1992; London Renaissance Seminar; Cambridge Young Lesbian and Gay Group; Anglia Polytechnic University Women's Group and Pink Soc; Cambridge University Women Studying Women Group, Queer Theory Group, and Women and Literature Seminar.

I am grateful to Vicky Wilson at Scarlet Press for commissioning and nurturing this book; to Ros Ballaster and Robbie Smith for advice and references; to my friend Lene Rubenstein for untangling Latin and Greek allusions; and particularly to Patricia Duncker, who has given generously of her time and passion for the past.

Finally, many thanks to the women of Paradise Co-op in Vic Road for putting up with endless anecdotes about our foresisters, and making a warm home for me to work in.

This book is dedicated, with love, to Debra Westgate, who has heard and questioned just about everything in it.

This book was originally published in Great Britain in 1993 by Scarlet Press. It is here reprinted by arrangement with Scarlet Press.

HarperCollins books may be purchased for educational, business, or sales promotional use. For information please write: Special Markets Department, HarperCollins Publishers, Inc., 10 East 53rd Street, New York, NY 10022.

FIRST U.S. EDITION

Designed by Chase Productions Services

Library of Congress Cataloging-in-Publication Data

Donoghue, Emma, 1969–
Passions between women : British Lesbian culture, 1668–1801 / Emma Donoghue. — 1st ed.
p. cm.
Originally published: Great Britain : Scarlet Press, 1993.
Includes bibliographical references and index.
ISBN 0-06-017261-4
1. Lesbianism—Great Britain—History—17th century. 2. Lesbianism—Great Britain—History—18th century. 3. Lesbians—Great Britain—Sexual behavior. 4. Lesbians in literature—Great Britain. I. Title.
HQ75.6.G7D65 1995
305.48′.9664′.0941 95-7777

---

95 96 97 98 99 RRD 10 9 8 7 6 5 4 3 2 1

Contents

Introduction

During their devoted partnership of over twenty years, Queen Anne sent Sarah Churchill, Duchess of Marlborough, endless loving letters. These tend to conclude with the words 'passionately' or 'most passionately and tenderly yours', or by assuring Sarah of Anne's 'sincere, passionate heart' or 'a most sincere and tender passion'.[1] But in 1709 Sarah sent the queen a brief review of a pamphlet (probably the anonymous *The Rival Dutchess*), commenting that it included 'stuff not fit to be mentioned of passions between women'.[2] Were these two uses of the word 'passion' – one describing a respectable friendship, the other a sexual perversion – entirely separate? Or can we find, between these two extremes, a wide spectrum of interpretations of passion between women?

Only a year before, Sarah Churchill had accused Queen Anne of allowing her favourite Lady of the Bedchamber, Abigail Hill Masham, too much political influence and personal intimacy. How can Anne keep harping on the purity of her reputation, Sarah asks in a letter, 'after having discover'd so great a passion for such a woman, for sure there can be noe great reputation in a thing so strange & unaccountable, to say noe more of it'?[3] This third kind of passion can be placed about halfway along the spectrum. Though Sarah cannot quite dare to call the relationship with Abigail a sexual affair to the queen's face, she implies that it is at the very least suspicious and damaging to Anne's reputation.

Lesbian history has often been impoverished by rigid divisions between friendship and sex, social acceptability and deviance, innocence and experience. This book sets out to discuss the full range of representations of lesbian culture in British print between 1668 and 1801, in a variety of discourses, from the poetic to the medical, the libertine to the religious. Although nowadays the word 'passion' tends to refer to sexual love, in the period between the Restoration and the nineteenth century it still retained multiple connotations of strong feeling, interest, anger, grief, enthusiasm, sexless as well as sexual love. Not every text discussed in this book presents passion between women as specifically sexual, or as invariably benevolent, but almost all highlight its intensity. Whether these early writers denounced it as a sexual crime or glorified it as a moral pinnacle, they tended to agree in marking it off from milder, more familial female bonds.

It should be possible, then, to broaden the meaning of 'lesbian history' to include a variety of concepts from previous centuries without diluting it into a study of all forms of sisterly affection. This book aims to explore the range of meanings given to 'passions between women' in late seventeenth- and eighteenth-century British publications.

What lesbians do in dictionaries

Eve Kosofsky Sedgwick has pointed out that one of the favourite arguments of academics who want to dismiss the history of same-sex relations goes like this: 'since there was no language about them, they must have been completely meaningless.'[4] Indeed, it is often claimed that there was 'no language' about erotic passion between women before the late nineteenth century. This argument usually calls on the *Oxford English Dictionary*, which traces 'lesbianism' back to 1870, 'lesbic' to 1892, and 'lesbian' as an adjective to 1890 and as a noun to 1925. Similarly, the entries for 'Sapphism' start in 1890, with 1902 given as the first date for 'Sapphist'.[5] These entries give the impression that only after the publications of late-nineteenth-century male sexologists such as Havelock Ellis did words for eroticism between women enter the English language. Some historians working on women's relationships before the nineteenth century – for example Judith Brown and George Haggerty – do use the word 'lesbian' for convenience and political impact, but (trusting the *OED)* worry that it might be anachronistic.[6] Brown comments resignedly: 'before the nineteenth century, women who engaged in sexual relations with other women were incapable of perceiving themselves as a distinct sexual and social group, and were not seen as such by others.'[7]

Passions Between Women sets out to show that generations of writers and commentators did indeed perceive some women who loved women as 'a distinct sexual and social group'. And to assume, as Brown does, that women-lovers were 'incapable of perceiving' that they belonged to such a group is to underestimate them. The lack of explicit acknowledgement in surviving personal papers is no proof of a lack of perception; the women's own discretion and desire for privacy, as well as the censoring actions of families and scholars, would have ensured that most passions between women were presented in letters and memoirs as harmless and innocent. A good example of such a veiled life, from a slightly later period than the one covered in this book, is Anne Lister (1791–1840), who lived, like many other women of the gentry, in a circle of passionate friendships. Only her diaries, decoded and published in part during recent years, reveal that these were sexual relationships and that she and her friends knew themselves to be (in Lister's words) 'too fond of women'.[8]

Passions Between Women is urgently committed to dispelling the myth that seventeenth- and eighteenth-century lesbian culture was rarely registered in language and that women who fell in love with women had no words to describe themselves. Silences can be interesting and significant, but this book is not about silence. What we are beginning to discover is that early texts are full of words the dictionary-makers have not noticed, specific labels for women who would be called lesbian or bisexual if they were living now. These seventeenth- and eighteenth-century words do not seem to refer only to isolated sexual acts, as is often claimed,[9] but to the emotions, desires, styles, tastes and behavioural tendencies that can make up an identity. Certainly, it was not until the late nineteenth century that the sexologists cemented a selection of such elements into the stereotype called 'the lesbian' (tall, flat-chested, intellectual, frustrated); however, a wide variety of lesbian types had been described in texts of the seventeenth and eighteenth centuries.

The compilers of the *OED* assume that early uses of the word 'Lesbian/lesbian', especially if the poet Sappho is mentioned, simply mean 'of or pertaining to the island of Lesbos'. Similarly, they gloss 'Sapphic/Saphic' as 'of or pertaining to Sappho the famous poetess of Lesbos' and give a list of examples, the adjective in every case describing the metre or quality of poems. But in 1732 William King's mock epic *The Toast* referred to sexual relationships between women as 'Lesbian Loves'[10] and the edition of 1736 called those women 'Tribades or Lesbians'.[11] So 'Lesbian' could be used both as an adjective and a noun to describe women who desired and pleasured each other more than a century and a half before the *OED*'s first entry for that meaning. Sappho's feelings for the women of Lesbos seem to have been well known among the educated. A 1762 translation from Plato describes two women as 'Sapphic Lovers' without needing to explain the adjective,[12] while a London magazine of 1773 indexes a discussion of sex between women under the simple phrase 'Sapphic passion'.[13] By 1790, in Hester Thrale's circle of intellectuals a 'Sapphist' was the label for a woman known to like 'her own sex in a criminal way'.[14]

'Tribade', another word of Greek origin, was adopted into both French and English by the sixteenth century.[15] Literally, it meant a woman who rubs, that is, one who would enjoy tribady or tribadism (rubbing clitoris on clitoris, pubic bone, leg, whatever) with other women. It is worth noting that 'tribade' could be used to describe any woman capable of enjoying sex with women, whether or not she ever acted on her desires; this was a word that hinted at identity, not just sexual acts.[16] The similar French words 'fricatrice'[17] and 'ribaude'[18] were also derived from Latin and Greek verbs for rubbing; they became diluted in meaning over the centuries and in English usually referred to any sexually loose woman.

A tribade was often described as having a 'female member' (imagined as either a prolapsed vagina or an enlarged clitoris) which allowed her to have penetrative intercourse with other women. This 'member' was seen as a phallic or male organ, making her double-sexed, or at least visually indistinguishable from the truly double-sexed. So it is under the words 'hermaphrodite', 'female hermaphrodite', or 'pseudo-hermaphrodite' that we often find discussions of lesbian desire in early modern Britain.[19] Randolph Trumbach has pointed out that if a woman was called a hermaphrodite, it often simply signified that she was unfeminine, with no implication of deviance in her choice of sexual object, whereas the word hermaphrodite used of a man was a euphemism for homosexual by the 1730s. However, women suspected of desiring other women as well as of being mannish were often accused of hermaphrodism.[20] 'Hermaphroditical' was not an exact synonym for 'lesbian', then, but a sister concept; the female hermaphrodite and the tribade were overlapping figures.

Spicy synonyms were provided by other European languages – for instance, 'that unnatural Act the *Spaniards* call *Donna con Donna*' (literally, woman with woman).[21] But the fact that British writers liked to show off their knowledge by sprinkling their texts with European and classical references does not mean that the concept of sexual passion between women was in any way foreign to the English language. Even when the word used was thought to be unfamiliar to those who knew only English, equivalents could easily be found. For example, one 1789 translation from a French text by Mirabeau uses the word 'tribade' for a notorious Parisian lesbian, but footnotes it for English readers as 'a woman-lover'.[22] Similarly, an English pamphlet of 1741 denounces certain women as 'Lovers of their own Sex'.[23] This is an example of a phrase which could sound harmless, as when Mary Astell signed her feminist treatise 'a Lover of her Sex' in 1694 (see pp. 122–3), unless the context made its sexual meaning clear. To avoid linguistic ambiguity, and to highlight the sexual aspect of this kind of passion between women, writers often compared it to heterosexuality; in a footnote to *The Toast* William King explains, 'she loved Women in the same Manner as Men love them; she was a Tribad.'[24]

We also find some specifically English slang. 'The Game of Flats' is how a satirical pamphlet of 1749 describes the practice of sex between women.[25] 'Tommy' seems to have been a home-grown slang word for a woman who had sex with women. The first such use I have found is in a satire of 1773. The anonymous writer threatens to expose particular deviants in print:

> Woman with Woman act the Manly Part,
> And kiss and press each other to the heart.
> Unnat'ral Crimes like these my Satire vex;
> I know a thousand *Tommies* 'mongst the Sex:
> And if they don't relinquish such a Crime,
> I'll give their Names to be the scoff of Time.[26]

'Tommy' may derive from 'tom boy', 'tom lad' or 'tom rig', all names for boyish, uncontrollable girls, or indeed from other phrases in which 'tom' suggested masculinity. By the mid-nineteenth century, 'tom' meant 'a masculine woman of the town' or prostitute; by the 1880s it referred to a woman 'who does not care for the society of others than those of her own sex'.[27] 'Tom(my)' is just one example of how an unbroken slang tradition can go unrecorded by the *OED*.

Each of these words was used in a different context, and in some cases survives only in one or two sources, so it is very difficult to work out why a writer would choose one term rather than another. Randolph Trumbach asserts that Sapphist and tommy were 'the high and low terms for women, as sodomite and molly were for men',[28] but we need more examples of their use to be sure of this distinction. What is suggested by the fact that there was a variety of explicit words for lesbianism in this period is that there was no consensus on the meaning of women's passion for each other. Pockets of knowledge about possibilities for eroticism between women seem to have been scattered right across British culture, but the words, the stories, were isolated from each other. Attitudes varied wildly; the same woman could be considered by different observers an innocent 'romantic friend', a 'pseudo-hermaphrodite' or 'tribade' with partial responsibility for her abnormal anatomy, or a sinful 'Lesbian', 'Sapphist' or 'tommy'.

As well as these explicit labels, and rather abstract phrases such as 'feminine congression'[29] or 'accompanying with other women,'[30] we find many euphemisms. Suggestive adjectives include 'irregular', 'uncommon', 'unaccountable' and (still popular today) 'unnatural'. John Cleland refers to 'vicious Irregularities',[31] Delarivier Manley to 'unaccountable intimacies'.[32] Robert James discusses tribades' 'uncommon and preternatural Lust',[33] Jonathan Swift mentions 'unnatural Appetites in both Sexes',[34] and Henry Fielding denounces women's 'unnatural affections' and 'abominable and unnatural pollutions'.[35] Metaphors of soiling and pollution were quite common: William King, for instance, refers to tribades as 'the Dames, who pollute their own Sex'.[36] Lesbianism was often associated with art and invention rather than nature; a dialogue of 1699 calls it a 'new Crime' and 'new Sort of Sin' discovered by Sappho of Lesbos.[37] Though Britain had no explicit law against sex between women, writers often described it as a crime against nature or society in phrases such as 'criminally amorous of each other'[38] or 'attempts to converse in a criminal manner with other Women'.[39]

These phrases were all fairly explicit about the deviant nature of this sexuality. But many writers preferred to use general derogatory terms, making the nature of the act clear only by the context. 'Lewd women',[40] 'lustful elves',[41] 'abominable women'[42] and 'female Fiends'[43] may sound vague on their own, but in the texts from which they are taken each makes a perfectly clear reference to women-lovers. Euphemisms for bisexuality included a 'secret bias'[44] and a 'more extensive taste'.[45]

Lesbians have been badly served by dictionaries, whose authors keep misreading or ignoring our culture. We find that long before the late nineteenth-century publications of the sexologists there was a variety of terms for sexual passion between women, as well as specific labels for the type of woman considered likely to love and have sex with another. A study of this vocabulary suggests that eroticism between women in the seventeenth and eighteenth centuries was neither so silent and invisible as some have assumed, nor as widely tolerated as others have claimed. Inconsistency and contradiction marked this space in British thought, probably because love between women could be seen as either supporting or threatening the patriarchal status quo. Even those writers who condemned lesbianism could find themselves reacting to individual women-lovers with fascination and grudging respect, and many writers who officially disapproved of passion between women nonetheless surrounded it with deviant glamour. Some of the descriptions sound startlingly modern, for example, Alexander Pope's phrase about Sappho in 1712, 'guilty love', could have come from a 1950s lesbian pulp novel.[46]

Lesbian, the term I will be using as comprehensible shorthand for this subject in this book, may be the rarest of those early words, since I have found it used in this period with an undeniably erotic meaning only once, in William King's poem of 1732. But that is precisely why it is most useful. Lesbian does not have the specific connotations of such terms as tribade, hermaphrodite, romantic friend, Sapphist and tommy, and so can encompass them all. Generally in this book I use the word lesbian as an umbrella term for those seventeenth- and eighteenth-century concepts, rather than as the more strictly defined modern label.[47] Following Bonnie Zimmerman, I could point out that words for heterosexual concepts such as 'marriage' and 'wife' have changed their meanings radically over the centuries, but nobody is accused of anachronism when they refer to seventeenth- and eighteenth-century 'marriages' and 'wives'.[48] Similarly, our foresisters who loved women probably differed in many crucial respects from those of us who love women in the 1990s, but it seems fair to use 'lesbian culture' as an umbrella term for both groups.

While many of us make a useful erotic and political distinction between the labels 'lesbian' and 'bisexual' today, I have found little evidence of any such distinction in seventeenth- and eighteenth-century texts. Occasionally a writer remarks on the exclusivity of a woman's devotion to her own sex (see pp. 82–3); even more rarely, a woman's sexual interest in men as well as in women is mentioned as unusual (p. 236). But usually what writers comment on is the quality of passion between two women, not their personal histories.

Lesbian culture seems to have been understood as a matter of relationships and habitual practices rather than self-identifications. Whether or not a woman also had loving relationships with men, her passionate connections with women were worthy of comment.

In an essay called 'Who Hid Lesbian History?', Lillian Faderman has exposed hostile biographers' strategies of 'bowdlerization, avoidance of the obvious, and *cherchez l'homme*' (look for the man).[49] But who hid bisexual history? Lesbian historians must take some of the blame; redressing the wrongs done by lesbian-hating biographers, they have often edited the lives of women who loved both sexes into exclusively lesbian histories.[50] In this book I have made some distinctions between women who seem to have loved only women and those whose lives could be called bisexual, and I point out the very different economics and status of women's relationships with women and with men, but I have tried not to treat bisexuality as a side issue; it is woven right through our history. Indeed, it seems to me an impossible task, and a narrow-minded one, to divide seventeenth- and eighteenth-century women's history into bisexual and lesbian components. As a lesbian and a feminist, I offer *Passions Between Women* as a shared history for all women who love women.

About this book

Gay historians have had access to a mass of evidence, particularly court records, on the networks, clubs and cruising grounds that formed a subculture for male 'mollies' in the eighteenth century. Because there was no British law against lesbianism, and because documents by and about women have never been preserved with the same care as those used in men's history, I expected this study to be constrained by a lack of evidence. Certainly, relative to the endless commentary about male same-sex acts in publications of this period, there is less said about women's love. At its most simple, the difference seems to have been that sodomy between men was exposed and publicised as a crime, to scare off any men who might be considering it, whereas lesbianism was generally treated as what church authorities called 'the silent sin', the assumption being that if it were kept out of the news it would not occur to women to try it.[51]

This vague policy of silence had many loopholes. Some indignant writers thought that, like sodomites, lesbians should be denounced in print to warn off imitators. Others seem to have considered it acceptable to write about passion between women in a discreet, satirical or otherwise oblique way. Anonymous writers exploited the topic for all the sensation and titillation it could provide. Certain genres, such as medical treatises and erotica, were not constrained by the usual etiquette about content. Many writers do not seem to have understood what they were writing about; they offered the facts of a case in isolation, having no conceptual framework about passion between women to help them interpret the story. For instance, some writers repeated without comment stories of women who ran away with women or who married other women in disguise; we can only deduce that the writers did not identify such behaviour as deviant, never put these anecdotes of eccentricity side by side, never saw the pattern they made. And finally, many women and some men wrote about love between women in the lofty terms of romantic friendship, admitting no connection between this and sexual passion.

As I anticipated, in researching this study I had to trawl widely, follow hunches and browse almost at random in a variety of genres, since mentions of lesbian love in seventeenth- and eighteenth-century texts are hardly ever signalled as such by their authors, and most twentieth-century critics are slow to point them out. What I did not expect was quite how much material there was – not just the literature of romantic friendship, resurrected in Lillian Faderman's *Surpassing the Love of Men* (1981), but a substantial body of writings on lesbianism as a matter of hermaphroditical anatomy, crossdressing, sex between women and a secret Sapphic tradition.

So the evidence turns out to be rich, if we look with an open eye at texts about women rather than hunting for exact equivalents of gay men's sources. Many studies of sexuality have suffered from treating women as an afterthought to men. Even gay men's histories tend to treat lesbian culture as a pale shadow of the gay prototype, reducing us to a couple of token paragraphs or footnotes.[52] In 'gay and lesbian studies', a potentially fruitful collaboration, the agenda has often been set by gay men. Lesbian historians can exhaust themselves looking for lesbian equivalents to particular aspects of gay history, for example sodomy trials or an early urban bar culture. A study like this one, which looks at lesbians without comparison with gay men, can let us establish our own priorities and ask our own questions.[53]

Since the sources turned out to be so plentiful, I have limited this study to texts published in English in the British Isles (including my own country, Ireland, the English-speaking parts of which were effectively run by Britain throughout this period), between the markers of 1668 (Margaret Cavendish's play *The Convent of Pleasure*) and 1801 (Maria Edgeworth's novel *Belinda*). Texts published before and after these dates, and private papers not published until later, are mentioned only when they are crucial to the development of a theme. I focus on texts published, rather than written, during this period, because I am less interested in a couple of hundred writers than in tens of thousands of readers. Stories printed, sold and read in the seventeenth and eighteenth centuries influenced and participated in British culture of that time, rather than merely describing it to later readers. Secondly, a practical consideration: most early published texts are available in copyright libraries, whereas the lesbian history hidden in private journals and letters, or in the unpublished records of institutions such as prisons and convents, will take many decades to bring into the light.

I chose this period, the 'long eighteenth century', for several reasons. Though it was a time of intense and fairly open debate on female sexuality, it has been under-researched by lesbian historians. Only in this period did women became professional writers in large numbers, providing me with plenty of texts written from a female perspective.[54] Perhaps most importantly, from the late seventeenth century onwards, a boom in literacy and publishing brought printed texts into the lives of a significant percentage of the population of the British Isles.

Many of the texts discussed here are ephemeral newspaper reports or pamphlets which have long been forgotten. Others, such as works by Marvell, Pope, Swift, Defoe and Richardson, have been enshrined in the literary canon, and can be illuminated by a specifically lesbian reading. Classical texts are crucial to this study because they were frequently translated and reprinted in the seventeenth and eighteenth centuries and because scholars and schoolteachers looked to ancient Rome and Greece for examples of every human vice or personality. Important French texts are used at various points; these were often translated for readers in English within a year or two of their appearance and can be seen as part of British print culture.

Certain changes in writing habits over the period can be discerned: for example, it undoubtedly became more difficult for women writers to be frank about lesbian sex,[55] and physical affection between women seems to have been represented less and less on stage.[56] But generally I have found consistent numbers of texts about lesbian culture in every part of the period, though certain genres or points of enquiry seem to have been more popular at certain times. The first half of the eighteenth century saw a vigorous printed debate on female hermaphrodites, for instance, while gossip about networks and clubs of Sapphists was rife in the closing decades of that century.

My first priority has been to bring this mass of little-known material to the attention of a general, as well as academic, readership. I want to provide ample quotes and interpretation for the reader-for-pleasure, as well as precise references for the scholar. This dual task, and the book's wide scope, has meant that I have had to focus on the lesbian content of texts, making only brief reference to their genres, authors and social context. There has not been room to probe certain women writers' use of male personae, eroticised personifications or other strategies for veiling lesbian meaning. Nor could I spare the space to follow some interesting tangents, such as the links between lesbian culture and revolutionary politics, religion or prostitution. At this early stage in the pursuit of lesbian history, what seemed to me most urgently needed was an accessible study of the extraordinary variety of early writings about love between women.

To make such diversity manageable, *Passions Between Women* is structured around four primary topics which I see as central to lesbian culture: gender blurring, friendship, sex and community. This is not to imply that the topics or the women can be isolated from each other; romantic friends are not necessarily distinct from crossdressers or women who had sex with women, and certain key women or texts could have been placed in any of several chapters. An accusation of lesbianism in this period usually came not as a direct labelling but in the form of a juxtaposition of several elements which on their own would not seem criminal: for example, the combination of romantic friendship, spinsterhood and masculine/feminine role play in the case of a 1790 newspaper report on the Ladies of Llangollen, two Anglo-Irish cousins who eloped together in 1778 (see pp. 107, 129). The mixture was all; no one act or attribute was seen as a sure symptom of a lesbian identity. The purpose of this book's chapter divisions, then, is not to isolate women into distinct types, but to explore lesbian culture from different angles.

The first three chapters are concerned with gender, which I see as the central problem for writers trying to understand the desire of a woman for a woman. 'Female hermaphrodites' explores the links made between same-sex lust and what doctors and writers saw as genital abnormality. Chapter 2 presents texts which discuss 'Female husbands', women who passed as men in order to live in fraudulent or conspiratorial marriages with women. A chapter on less extreme anomalies of gender, 'The breeches part', probes the eroticism of women who crossdressed in order to get a job, for a limited period or only on occasion, as well as women whose masculinity was seen as residing not in their clothes but in their minds and manners.

Texts which present passion between women as a matter of friendship are the subject of Chapters 4 and 5. Even if the women's bond is not portrayed as explicitly sexual, their connections are shown to challenge what Janice Raymond has called 'hetero-reality', a state in which 'most of women's personal, social, political, professional, and economic relations are defined by the ideology that woman is for man.'[57] The women in these chapters are passionately 'for' each other in a variety of ways. 'A sincere and tender passion' takes a fresh look at romantic friendship, exploring key topics such as spinsterhood, relationships with both sexes, class divisions and suspicions of the sexual element of such friendship. 'The truest friends' follows this up by offering a close analysis of some female partnerships.

Stories hinting at seduction or describing sex between women are the subject of the sixth chapter, 'What joys are these?', which asks what specific pleasures and powers were ascribed to female same-sex practices in erotic writings of this period. 'Communities' ends the book by bringing together texts about groups, either rooted in a time (convents, social networks) or over time (the lesbian tradition stretching from Sappho to eighteenth-century Britain).

Readers

Passions Between Women is a history not of facts but of texts, not of real women but of stories told about women, stories which reflected and formed both attitudes to lesbian culture and lesbian culture itself. But who had access to these texts and how did these ideas circulate?

There are no agreed figures for women's literacy during the seventeenth and eighteenth centuries; all we know is that it was generally much lower than the rate for men. Estimates of the percentage of all English women able to sign their names vary from between 10 and 20 per cent around 1700 to almost 50 per cent at the close of the eighteenth century;[58] this improvement is probably due to the rise of charity schools. But there seem to have been massive variations across Britain, depending on place and class. For rural and working-class women, the rates were generally far lower than for urban and middle-class women, and in some groups female literacy rates stagnated or fell during the period, especially in areas where child labour was on the increase.[59]

However, there were many women on the margins of literacy whose lives were touched by printed texts. Since girls were usually taught to read but (unlike boys) not to write, many of those unable to sign their names would still have had reading skills, though they do not show up in the literacy statistics. The technical term for this is 'passive readers', an inappropriate description for such resourceful, hardworking women. Even women who were completely illiterate would have had indirect access to print culture as listeners. At this time, British culture was in transition between oral and written communication, which meant that there would be no shame in a woman asking a literate neighbour to read something to her. Novels were read aloud at firesides and ballads were sung in the streets; the gist of scandalous stories, for example tales of female husbands, would have been passed on through gossip.[60]

It is often assumed that the price of literature kept the poor from any contact with it. That may have been true for epic poetry, but not for the more popular genres. Those who could not read but went to the theatre had access to plays months or years before the scripts were published. Theatre was relatively cheap; a woman could see a play for the price of a drink, whereas the price of a novel would feed her family for a week.[61] Chapbooks (literally, cheap books), costing a couple of pence each, were hawked around villages. A woman who could not afford half a crown for such a book as Charlotte Charke's narrative of crossdressing and female friendship had only to wait until it was serialised in the newspapers at a penny or two per paper. Circulating libraries, increasingly popular after 1740, were an invaluable resource for women.

Where time was the missing ingredient, reading aloud could save it; Hannah More complains in 1801 that working-class girls sometimes shared the work of one of their group among themselves, freeing her to read bawdy books aloud to the circle.[62]

It cannot be denied that most of the poor did not have the time, money or education to read for pleasure during this period. But what I want to emphasise is that stories were circulated in a variety of ways and an eager reader or listener could pick up quite a lot about a subject that interested her.

Only the leisured women who read friendship literature tended to leave evidence of their reading experiences. Where women recorded reading books with overtly lesbian content, they almost never commented on it. Eleanor Butler, one of the Ladies of Llangollen, made a note in 1788 of having read Anthony Hamilton's *The Memoirs of Count de Grammont*, without commenting on the lesbian character Mistress Hobart. Lillian Faderman cites this as evidence that the Ladies had no sense of their sexuality as deviant: 'It is probable', she asserts, 'that one who was concerned with the difficulties that female homosexuals might encounter would have noted the case'.[63] But I find it far more probable that any woman reader of *The Memoirs of Count de Grammont* who recognised herself as (like Mistress Hobart) liable to persecution if her sexuality were exposed, would have kept her thoughts on the matter out of a book journal that friends might see. Records of reading experience, then, cannot be taken at face value.

It has often been assumed on slim evidence that women did not read erotica. (I am not talking about hard pornography here; none of the texts I will be dealing with features the violent rape, mutilation and murder which are the stuff of modern porn, and to emphasise this distinction I use the milder term erotica.[64]) Of course women did not record their readings of explicitly sexual material – to do so would have been beyond the pale of female modesty – but we have no reason to believe that they shut their eyes to such material. Literary classics of this era were full of bawdy, occasionally including stories of lesbian encounters. I have no doubt that the kind of explicit sex stories discussed in my sixth chapter, though aimed primarily at men, were read by some women too. To satisfy their curiosity about sex, women might have taken knowledge wherever they found it, especially if they were aware of longings they found hard to explain. In our search for textual evidence of awareness of lesbian culture, we cannot afford to be disdainful of the male-centred genre of erotica.

Compared with the nineteenth and twentieth centuries, the period dealt with in this book saw very little censorship of literature. The banning of books was rare, a measure reserved for the most shocking of French pornography. Nor were they abridged for children's use; schoolgirls were encouraged to read uncut editions of Richardson's *Pamela* and Swift's *Gulliver's Travels*, two classics which include mentions of lesbian desire. One librarian, Mrs Lord, was accused by certain Dublin men of lending obscene novels to their daughters; she responded by assuring them that she underlined all the dirty bits so the girls would know what to skip.[65] Though a minority of editors, especially in Scotland, did attempt to prune (or 'castrate' or 'mutilate', as they would say) books that offended them, this had no general impact. Only in the early nineteenth century, as literacy began to spread widely, did upper-middle-class writers like Harriet Bowdler begin to censor books, in an attempt to control the ideas that reached the working class.[66]

Even when occasional efforts were made to bowdlerise texts, readers fought back. Girls were considered particularly active and resourceful in this. In a book on education of 1797, Erasmus Darwin advises governesses to express disapproval of bawdy passages in books read at school but by no means to cut them out, since censorship might only 'raise curiosity, and induce young people to examine different copies of the same work, and to seek for other improper books themselves'.[67] His tone of resignation suggests that schoolgirls of the day were not passive recipients of conduct books, but active hunters of sexually informative texts.

Though *Passions Between Women* is not concerned with visual materials, it is worth mentioning that access to images was fairly easy and did not depend on a special skill like literacy. London was full of print shops which, as well as renting pictures to well-off customers, put displays in the windows that anyone could see for free;[68] complaints were made that these displays included explicit pictures of what went on in brothels.[69] A printseller of the 1780s called Mrs Roach was accused of opening a portfolio of obscene pictures 'to any boy or to any maidservant' who asked her.[70] The asking, the expression of interest, is crucial; I think it likely that in seventeenth- and eighteenth-century Britain anyone wanting to know how to interpret passion between women could have had access to stories about it, even if many other readers averted their gaze.

Who knew what

Though we can conclude that in general knowledge about lesbian possibilities spread with the boom in textual production in the late seventeenth century, it is impossible to tell exactly who knew or did not know about these possibilities. Information about lesbian existence, once heard, might quickly become a secret to be kept from others. For a woman, to admit to such knowledge could be to risk being thought immodest or having her own friendships suspected. For a man, one fear was that to pass on such knowledge, even in a spirit of condemnation, might advertise and promote lesbian culture by planting ideas in innocent female minds. That something was not stated does not mean it was not known. Writers often betrayed an embarrassed half-knowledge, such as an awareness that 'bad' women could do such things, hand in hand with a refusal to suspect 'good' women. Sometimes they wrote so coyly that it is difficult to tell how much they knew, how much they were censoring and how much was tongue-in-cheek.

This paradoxical state of knowledge is illustrated by two moments in the same literary periodical, only a couple of years apart. In early 1760 the *Critical Review* took to pieces Elizabeth Nihell's book about midwifery, in which she protests against the intervention of 'man midwives' in a woman's profession. At one point in her book Nihell explains that many women in pain can be comforted if the midwife chafes or strokes them with her hand, something they would be ashamed to ask of a man. The (presumably male) reviewer quotes this passage with amusement, commenting, 'How far Mrs. Nihell's shrewd, supple, sensitive fingers, may be qualified for the art of titillation, we shall not pretend to investigate.' This sentence suggests that he has discovered a lesbian motive in Nihell and/or her patients, a dangerous intimacy between women. But he goes on to protest that surely women in labour would prefer a man-midwife to stroke them, 'unless our author has talents that way which we cannot conceive.'[71] This joke assumes that normal women have nothing to stimulate each other with, unless Mrs Nihell has some hidden parts or 'talents' which provide only a barren pleasure, unable to make anyone (literally) 'conceive'. The wit relies on a protestation that the reviewer knows nothing, that he will not 'pretend to investigate' possibilities of lesbian sex, that he 'cannot conceive' of such a thing. This also saves him from having to be explicit; his unknowing readers can take his words at face value and not be shocked, while the more sophisticated can laugh at the in-joke.

Two years later, in a review of a book on gynaecological disease, the same periodical mentions calmly that women's 'furor uterinus' (a sort of nymphomania) can be caused by either 'self-pollution' or 'the titillations of their own sex'.[72] The repetition of the word 'titillation' may even suggest that this is the work of the same reviewer. In one context, then, he must be coy and veiled about lesbian possibility; in another, in the same periodical, he feels free to mention lesbian sex bluntly.

In many of the texts discussed in this book, references to sex between women and to innocent female friendship coexist uneasily. Where they touch, we find double entendres, truths pretending to be jokes and convoluted disclaimers along the lines of 'others say, but I don't understand what they mean,' 'others say, but they're paranoid, I don't believe it,' 'it could be, but not in this country,' or 'I say it, I believe it, but I'd rather not think about it.'

Another complicating factor is that what is concluded by the writer may not always be the same as the impression left on the reader. Numerous paramedical tracts and manuals describe lesbianism in attractive terms, then warn their readers not to try it; such literature contains the most exciting documentation of the very vices it was apparently trying to stamp out. So to say that most of the texts discussed in *Passions Between Women* are hostile to lesbianism is not to say that their message was effectively offputting, or that these prejudices would have been reproduced in their readers. At many points I give a positive interpretation of rather brutal stories, because I am convinced of the possibility of subversive readings. For seventeenth- and eighteenth-century women isolated in a new knowledge of their desires, I suggest, any texts about those desires would have been better than none.

The knowledge whose circulation through British culture I want to explore is not some eternal truth about lesbian existence, but rather theories, stories, possibilities. For example, most feminist historians have had little time for male writers' stories of giant clitorises, disdaining them as phallocentric fantasy. By contrast, I devote my first chapter to this idea because it is so central to popular impressions of lesbian sexuality in the seventeenth and eighteenth centuries and because it raises fundamental questions about how same-sex desire bends gender. The same goes for bisexuality, group sex and sado-masochism. These are not just male libertine fantasies but the stuff of real women's lives, and they deserve a place in our history. As well as hunting for truths about our foresisters, *Passions Between Women* is a study of some of those learned, powerful ignorances discussed by Eve Kosofsky Sedgwick, ignorances 'in which male sexuality receives careful education'.[73] One such educated ignorance is a male writer's refusal to admit that women could give each other significant pleasure; another is a respectable woman writer's resistance to knowledge about the tastes of her role model, Sappho. My subject is whatever was known, thought and fantasised in Britain about passions between women.

Gay male historians often use the laws of a given period as evidence of widespread knowledge of same-sex practices. For some eras and places in lesbian history this is a useful source. Throughout medieval and Renaissance Europe and in the European colonies of North America, laws based on Christian Roman edicts treated sex between women as a crime deserving execution or at least severe punishment. In continental Europe, women were occasionally executed or exiled for affairs with each other as late as the eighteenth century.[74] In the British Isles, however, the laws against sodomy were interpreted as applying only to acts between men or between women and men; the legal silence on sex between women seems to have been uniquely British. This lack of a specific law does not imply that, like Queen Victoria at the end of a very different century, seventeenth- and eighteenth-century British people did not believe in lesbian sex, or that they were generally tolerant of it. It suggests rather that law-makers preferred to keep it unthinkable, while going ahead and punishing women who loved women on vaguer charges of lewdness and fraud.

Sex between women is only one part of the combination of behaviours called lesbian culture. Lesbian history has often centred on the question of whether women's passion for each other used to be seen as acceptable or deviant. Lillian Faderman devotes most of *Surpassing the Love of Men* to romantic friendship, which she sees as the typical form of pre-modern women's love. She argues that in the English upper and middle classes until the late nineteenth century, romantic friendship was seen as harmless or silly at worst and at best as the most edifying of social bonds.

Faderman's theory is a useful rebuttal of the mid-twentieth-century assumption that passion between women has always been a matter of a small, sick or sinful minority. For its celebratory tone and reassuring picture of a golden age when it was possible for women who loved women to be considered valuable (and ordinary) members of society, *Surpassing the Love of Men* was widely welcomed in lesbian communities.

Today, Faderman's thesis still helps to make sense of the many early texts which present female friendship, even its jealousies and embraces, as sexless and innocent. But there are other texts that this theory distorts or simply fails to address: texts about 'tribades' and 'Sapphists' masquerading as romantic friends, or texts in which sex between women takes place in a context of female social friendship. Also, Faderman's argument that women were only suspected of sexual deviance if, as transvestites for instance, they were seen to be usurping a male prerogative, does not explain why some women who passed as men were given royal pensions, while some romantic friends were attacked in print.

I have found no simple answer to the question of whether women who loved women were socially acceptable. It seems always to have depended on the details of a particular woman's story, on the way her life was told. Robbie Smith has hypothesised, with regard to the seventeenth century, that lesbianism was unthinkable unless linked to other symptoms or concepts, such as Spain, Roman Catholicism or witchcraft.[75] For the eighteenth century, the suspicious characteristics seem to me to have included spinsterhood, aristocracy, crossdressing or mannish style, general sexual looseness and a theatrical or artistic career. But it is impossible to predict on the basis of these elements alone how a woman was likely to have been treated; the attitudes of commentators, judges and writers introduced a large measure of unpredictability.

Another crucial question is whether women who felt passion for women experienced this as an identity and were seen by outsiders as playing a definite lesbian role. Much has been said in histories of sexuality about the differences between 'essentialists' and 'social constructionists'. Yet most of us working in this field are somewhere in the middle, and would agree that in any age it is possible for one woman to love another, but that the way that she and others might interpret that love would vary according to prevailing concepts of sexuality and morality. We should remember that a century's dominant ideals or the attitudes of its rulers are not the same as the private thoughts of its people. Asexuality was an ideal for Victorian women, for example, but that does not prove that particular women were in reality sexless or thought of themselves in that way. Similarly, it seems that many seventeenth- and eighteenth-century writers were beginning to be aware of lesbians as a group with a distinct identity, but I would be wary of setting any date on that development, since some women could have had such a sense of themselves millennia before. I am dubious about any attempts to tie such a profound shift in attitudes to a particular decade or half-century. I suspect that the change from a concept of sex acts between women to a concept of lesbian identity was very gradual, and that these ideas overlapped for several centuries. When seventeenth- and eighteenth-century texts are full of woman loving each other and playing a variety of roles, it makes no sense to try to track down the birth of a single 'lesbian role'.

Besides, as soon as such a date is suggested, further research pushes it backwards. For example, Randolph Trumbach's essays on male sodomy, written in the late 1980s, tend to include generalisations about lesbians not having a 'third sex' role equivalent to that of gay men until the late nineteenth century.[76] But after a closer look at the evidence on women, Trumbach in his more recent essay on 'London's Sapphists' finds a role parallel to the male molly role in London beginning slowly in the mid-eighteenth century and well established by the century's end. This is a persuasive essay; however, because of his focus on the few infamous and visible Sapphists in late-eighteenth-century London, Trumbach gives little weight to earlier texts which concentrate on lesbians as deviants of biological sex rather than gender. Also, though almost all his evidence is in the form of literary records of people's perceptions of lesbianism, Trumbach makes some unsupported generalisations about real women's sexual practices. 'In the first half of the eighteenth century', he claims, 'women who had sex with women also had sexual relations with men and were likely to use their hands for stimulation and to avoid penetration.' He goes on to admit that perhaps some women did use dildos, but never questions his assumption that all these woman-lovers had sex with both women and men. The exclusive lesbians, and the women who liked thighs or tongues or penetration with anything but hands, are edited out, as they are not part of what Trumbach sees as the norm. Trumbach also tries to establish a development not just in what women did but in how they were understood.

He argues that lesbianism was originally seen as 'a wicked sin to which any woman might be brought', until certain far-seeing (male) writers of the mid-century such as Henry Fielding and John Cleland began to interpret it psychologically as 'a corruption of the mind', so that by the time London's Sapphists began behaving mannishly to attract women in the late eighteenth century their sexuality was widely understood as 'the perversion of a minority'.[77]

By contrast, I see these theories of lesbian sexuality as sin or perversion as overlapping throughout this period. Several texts published in England before Fielding and Cleland present lesbianism as a psychological peculiarity of a minority: examples include references to a 'genius' for desiring women rather than men, in 1709 (p. 234), the 'Singularity' of loving only women, in 1714 (p. 93), and the exceptional 'Cast' of personality found in female 'Lovers of their own Sex', in 1741 (p. 186). And what Trumbach sees as the old explanation, that lesbian sex was a sin any woman might be brought to, can be found to linger throughout this period in other texts. I can discern no point at which one explanation gave way to another.

This question of knowledge is so important because many historians assume that women at this time were wholly ignorant of lesbian possibilities and therefore did not know how to conceive of themselves as lovers of women. Lotte van de Pol and Rudolph Dekker's rich study of transvestism, for instance, suffers from some startlingly unwarranted conclusions:

> Most people at the time were ignorant of the existence of the phenomenon of tribady. No lesbian networks or subculture existed; tribady was far less known than sodomy; and the taboo on it was at least as great. Practically no woman did know any examples of sexual relations between women and few, at any rate of the common people, had even heard of them ... Therefore, it is logical that those women would think: if I covet a woman, I must be a man.[78]

Given that few of 'the common people' ever had an opportunity to record their thoughts freely, how can Dekker and van de Pol be so convinced of working-class ignorance? How can they assume that 'most people' in seventeenth- and eighteenth-century Europe remained ignorant of the existence of sexual passion between women when there were songs, court cases, pornographic pictures, medical and literary books and endlessly retold anecdotes about that very subject? Van de Pol and Dekker also claim to know that there were 'no lesbian networks or subculture', when, logically, secrecy would have characterised such networks and judges would have tended to hush them up in order to deny publicity to 'the silent sin'. Since everyone seems to have heard of sodomy, plenty of people could have been aware of tribady too. Where there is a taboo, there must be enough knowledge for that taboo to arise. The last sentence in the Dekker and van de Pol passage quoted above makes the wildest of leaps; assumed to be unable to interpret her feelings any other way, the lesbian is converted to an early transsexual. Once more we are offered a single typical form of lesbian selfhood rather than the range that exists in any era. (This kind of historical argument might identify the 1990s lesbian as an urban dyke in lipstick and leathers, ignoring the other, less visible lives we lead.)

Though gender is central to *Passions Between Women*, I see same-sex desire as disrupting the conventions of femininity rather than denying womanhood itself. By contrast with van de Pol and Dekker, I would guess that there was so much underground knowledge circulating that it would be a rare woman whose desire for a woman would make her think, 'if I covet a woman, I must be a man.' She may have thought herself odd, sinful, unwomanly, even monstrous; she may have been ready to pass as a man, crossdress, or send out some signals of masculinity; but she would surely not simply have equated her desire for women with maleness. Dekker and van de Pol go on to hypothesise, in a section entitled 'From Tribades to Lesbians', that crossdressers who thought of themselves as men were replaced by nineteenth-century woman-lovers in skirts.[79] It is possible that certain styles were more commonly reported by writers in some eras than in others; perhaps some practices really did die out; but it is nonsense to represent the variety of lesbian culture as a parade of types, each one replacing the last.

It could be that because our own era is so marked by identity politics, we focus too exclusively on questions of identity when we read seventeenth- and eighteenth-century texts. I do want to show that for a woman to see herself or someone else as a lover of women in a forbidden way was quite possible in this period. But *Passions Between Women* is not just about those women who seem to have perceived themselves as sexual deviants or rebels; it also includes many texts about spinsters, romantic friends and even women who passed as men, who may have seen their emotional lives as entirely respectable. There is more to lesbian culture than lesbian identity, just as 'British culture' includes many of us who are living here at the moment and take part in this culture but for various reasons do not identify ourselves as 'British'. *Passions Between Women* is not just about the relatively small percentage of women who might have had the knowledge and courage to admit to themselves that they were (in Anne Lister's phrase) 'too fond of women'; it is also concerned with stories of women's passionate fondness for women, whether or not the characters or authors seem to think this fondness excessive or deviant.

Lesbian history is a very new subject; it has seen some excellent resurrection of sources, but often conclusions have been drawn too prematurely. The critics I find most helpful are not those who have offered generalisations about women's love in each period, but those who stress the variety of representations of such love. Martha Vicinus, for instance, points out in an essay of 1982 that lesbian history does have a 'dual nature' but has suffered from being polarised by rival camps of scholars interested in romantic friendship or in butch/femme roles. 'Romantic friendships and a conscious lesbian subculture do not always intersect', Vicinus argues, 'but they are more closely related, I believe, than has yet been recognized.'[80] The example she gives is from the late nineteenth century, but quite a few eighteenth-century texts discussed in this book display such 'intersections' too. Vicinus' approach is refreshingly open-minded; in this and a later essay she warns against researchers who 'ransack the past to find women who fulfil current expectations', hunting for heroines rather than accepting our 'fragmentary and confusing history'.[81]

In the face of such recently discovered and seemingly contradictory evidence, several of us have adopted the strategy of reading side by side texts from very different discourses. Elaine Hobby's essay on Katherine Philips, for example, does not simply put her in the context of mid-seventeenth-century poetry; it also adds Quaker testaments, and comments on female hermaphrodites from a midwifery manual and a German history, to tease out the strands of early modern thought on lesbian desire.[82] Similarly, George Haggerty concentrates on one literary text about romantic friendship, Sarah Scott's *A Description of Millenium Hall* (1762), but illuminates it by bringing in references to sex between women from the same era.[83] Lisa Moore goes even further to break down the hierarchy of genres by structuring her essay on early-nineteenth-century romantic friendship around a triangle of texts: Maria Edgeworth's novel *Belinda*, Anne Lister's diaries, and the Woods–Pirie law case.[84] These essays, along with work by Ros Ballaster and Robbie Smith, do not seem to be promoting any one agenda or definition of lesbianism; instead, they pay close attention to the clashing interpretations of love between women in the last three centuries. It is this kind of lesbian history that seems to promise to be most fruitful in the coming decades.

Passions Between Women has not been written simply to increase our understanding of seventeenth- and eighteenth-century Britain. Many readers will be more interested in lesbian existence today, and one aim of this book is to illuminate the different elements that have gone to make up our far from unified 'community'. In the past few decades it has proved difficult to make connections across ideological barriers; perhaps we can make them across time instead. Celibate friends, SM dykes, women who get mistaken for men whether they like it or not, singles and couples and threesomes, separatists, prostitutes, in-your-face activists, respectable closet-cases, those of us who also like orgies or weddings or study groups or men or domestic bliss: we can all find our origins here. If we take the long view, learning that we all have a share in the past and none of us can own it, perhaps we will not fight so bitterly over the present.

Tribady, an activity that is rarely discussed, provides a stimulating metaphor for the business of doing history. The researcher is not so much penetrating the past to find what she wants as making contact with it, touching the surface of her present interests to the details of the past; the more she touches, the more she will become sensitised to the nuances she is exploring. This friction between centuries can bring us a sense of intimacy with our foresisters, as well as great pleasure, and laughter when things fail to fit. *Passions Between Women* is primarily intended to get the stories to the women, so that we can all take part in this never-ending act of tribady that is lesbian history.

1 Female hermaphrodites

In seventeenth-century Britain the female and male sexes tended to be defined in part though their desire for each other and the roles they played in reproductive sex, which begged the question: if a woman wanted a woman, was she no longer a woman herself? Did her desire turn her into a man, stem from or cause the growth of a phallic member, require a phallic dildo or lead to cross-dressing? These deviations could be interpreted as helpless strayings from femininity, conscious rebellions against it or a range of positions in between, with women held more or less responsible for what they did with the bodies and desires nature gave them. This chapter focuses on lesbianism as gender deviation, with its source in the body. From the mid-seventeenth through to the mid-eighteenth century, probably the most common strategy for explaining away women who desired each other was to accuse them of having abnormal or double-sexed genitals.

In recent years some excellent work has been done on the figure of the hermaphrodite. Michel Foucault has focused on historical changes in the interpretation of sexual anatomy;[1] Anne Rosalind Jones and Peter Stallybrass have placed the hermaphrodite at the heart of Renaissance constructions of gender;[2] Lynne Friedli's article on 'Women Who Dressed as Men' touches on the mid-eighteenth-century medical debate about hermaphrodism in England and France.[3] What concerns me here is not hermaphrodism in general, but the ways in which discussion of hermaphroditical anatomy (and by extension psychology) was used to attack women who loved women. By the late seventeenth century most writers were calling the 'perfect hermaphrodite' a myth, but they still insisted on the existence of the 'pseudo-hermaphrodite', 'female hermaphrodite' or 'tribade', different names for an overgrown woman with some similarities to a man, chief of which was a desire for women.

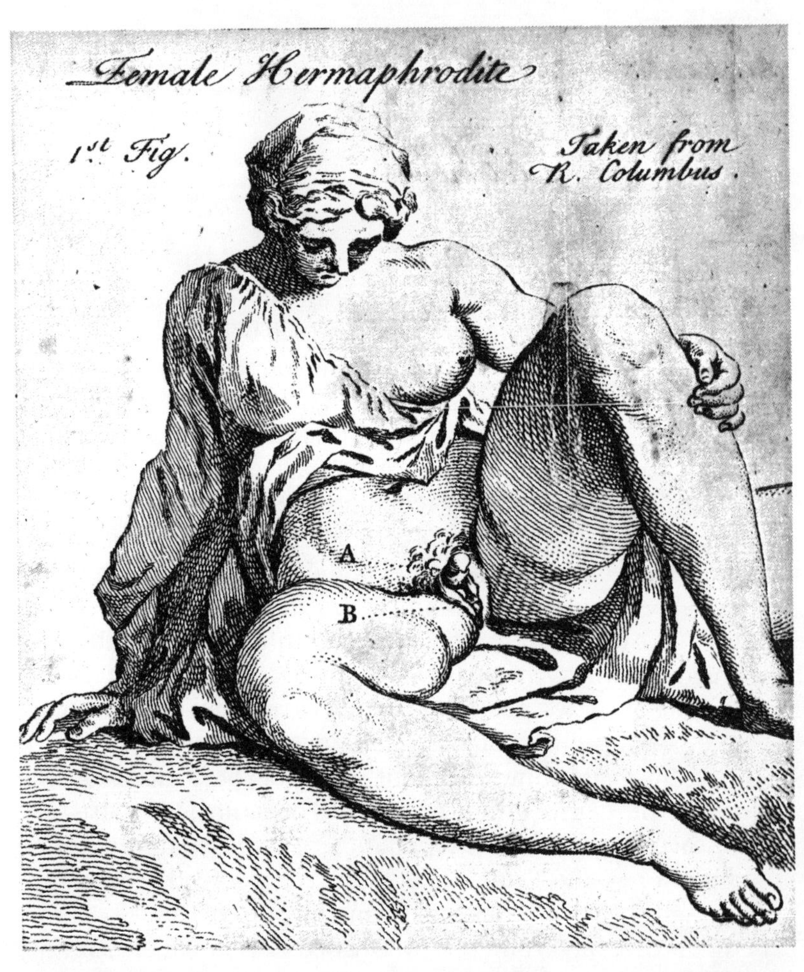

Female hermaphrodite from George Arnauld, A Dissertation on Hermaphrodites *(1750)*

Michel Foucault argues in *The History of Sexuality* that theories of sexual wrongdoing did not distinguish clearly between 'natural' and 'unnatural' acts until late in the nineteenth century; before that time, such vague terms as 'sodomy' and 'debauchery' covered a multitude of heterosexual and homosexual sins. This hypothesis ignores the 'molly', an eighteenth-century man treated as unnatural in much the same way as the 'homosexual' was later. Also, Foucault's focus on men means that his conclusions are of questionable value for the historian of female sexuality. While the 'sodomite' may have been simply a person (almost always male) who had committed one or more of a miscellany of 'forbidden acts', as Foucault puts it,[4] my research on the 'female hermaphrodite' suggests that this was a much more specific label which coupled the ideas of sex between women and double-sexed anatomy. Within the narrow chamber of female sexuality, it seems, 'natural' desire was distinguished from 'unnatural' long before the nineteenth century.

The female hermaphrodite, pseudo-hermaphrodite or tribade was generally understood to be a woman whose 'member' enabled her to rub another woman's vulva and/or penetrate her vagina. This tribadic member could be explained, in the Galenic medical tradition, as a vagina which prolapsed or popped out because of increased body heat or sudden motion. Alternatively, the female member could be seen as an enlarged clitoris; this explanation was dominant throughout the second half of the seventeenth century and seems to have replaced the vagina theory by the early years of the eighteenth. Either way, the penis was the model for imaginings of what a female member, a lesbian source of potency, could be.

How seriously are we to take these stories of six-inch erect female members? They are useful, I suggest, not as factual sources but as cultural fantasies; they were certainly far too common and influential in their day to be disregarded now. The popularity of the notion of the lesbian as hermaphrodite proves nothing about the size or shape of real women's genitals in the early modern period, but it does tell us a lot about social fears of female sexuality. When a woman was reported as having a six-inch member, factors which contributed to establishing the story could have included her doctors' assumptions about the small size of a normal clitoris,[5] their expectations that any woman said to have sex with women would be abnormal, the effects of exaggeration every time the story was passed on by translation, plagiarism or word of mouth, and also, of course, the reporter's capacity for sheer invention. What matters most about the concept of lesbians as hermaphrodites is not its accuracy, but its function: this theory served the interests of those who wanted to frighten women into heterosexual passivity. By cutting off lesbians from their own femaleness, writers could reduce them to exceptional (and therefore harmless) freaks of nature.

This chapter follows the figure of the hermaphroditical tribade through translations from influential classical sources, anecdotes in medical and pseudo-medical writings and literary texts. Although the writers are generally male and hostile to their tribade subjects, their debates over anatomy and motivation and the ambiguities in their treatment of these scapegoat heroines make these texts rich sources for lesbian history. While these writers generally condemn eroticism between women, they also attribute to it an incomprehensible power.

Classical sources

Starting with the premise that when a woman makes love to a woman she is imitating a man, male classical writers played with versions of the tribade as man. The three texts I examine here, by Ovid, Martial and Lucian, were available in Britain in the original and in translations throughout the seventeenth and eighteenth centuries. As respectable scholarly sources, yet titillatingly explicit, they were widely read and had incalculable influence on early modern writers' conceptions of lesbian desire.

The only time passion between women is faced head on in the *Metamorphoses* of the Latin poet Ovid (43 BC–AD 17) is in the story of Iphis and Ianthe in the ninth book. To avoid having her baby girl killed, Iphis' mother brings her up as a boy; at the age of 13 Iphis and her friend Ianthe fall in love and are engaged to be married. Iphis knows she is risking exposure and punishment; only a miracle can save her.

Perhaps the liveliest of the English versions is the verse translation of 1717 by Samuel Garth, John Dryden and others. The translator is frank about the nature of Iphis' feelings as the wedding approaches:

> Ev'n her Despair adds Fuel to her Fire;
> A Maid with Madness does a Maid desire.

Iphis has realised that her love for a woman is contrary to nature's plan for heterosexual mating in all mammals:

> Nor Cows for Cows consume with fruitless Fire,
> Nor Mares, when hot, their Fellow-Mares desire ...
> Her females Nature guards from Female Flame,
> And joins two Sexes to preserve the Game.

Notice that nature has to 'guard' women from the 'Flame' of lust for each other, which is always threatening to break through and spoil the reproductive 'Game'. Lesbian desire is not so much impossible as forbidden. This poem is particularly interesting for its psychological analysis of Iphis. Unable to ignore or deny her feelings, she begins to think of herself as a freak:

> Wou'd I were nothing, or not what I am!
> *Crete,* fam'd for Monsters, wanted of her Store,
> 'Till my new Love produc'd one Monster more.

She does try to redirect her attention towards men, but finds it impossible. As the wedding night nears, her panic grows. Then the day before the wedding, the repentant prayers of Iphis' mother to the goddess Io cause a miracle – Iphis is granted a masculine body:

> The latent parts, at length reveal'd began
> To shoot, and spread, and burnish into Man.

Ovid's Latin original describes only the outward signs of masculinity, such as sharper features and strength; by contrast the translator feels obliged to specify a genital sex change. In his pseudo-scientific explanation, the vagina is imagined as a 'latent' penis, which in exceptional cases can suddenly grow, like a seedling, out of its hiding place. A footnote speculates further on what is really going on in this story:

> Had the Poet a mind to shew us by it, a Disguise carried on even to the Point of Marriage? Or one of those extraordinary Appearances mentioned in the Books of Physic; or did he only intend to let us know that the Gods recompense Piety? Whatever it be, that Fable may have its Foundation in Nature itself: Sexes have often been hard to distinguish 'till several Years after Birth.[6]

This mishmash of theories is typical of discussions of sex change and hermaphrodism in the seventeenth and eighteenth centuries. Wary of both absolute credulity and absolute cynicism, the translator keeps his options open, showing awareness of all the possibilities – that Iphis is a metaphor for piety, a female husband, a boy with delayed growth or a truly 'extraordinary' hermaphrodite as mentioned in medical books.

However the ending of Ovid's story was interpreted, its beginning was an influential testament to the possibility that one girl (especially if she had a confused gender identity) could fall in love with another. The writer Hester Thrale, always on the lookout for sexual perversion, records in her diary for 10 January 1779 that a certain man she knows, although so effeminate that he is nicknamed 'the It', is very attractive to the ladies. Thrale wonders anxiously whether if women are not looking for masculinity in their partners, perhaps they are no longer even looking for men. 'What will not a Wench fall in Love with!' she exclaims. 'Ovid's Iphis & Ianthe no longer seems out of Possibility.'[7] So heterosexuality depended on rigid gender distinctions; once gender was upset, same-sex desire could emerge. Ovid's story did not just function as a myth or an anecdote from a long-dead civilisation; for suspicious readers like Hester Thrale, it represented the anarchic passion between women which was always lurking around the corner.

A text even more commonly cited by early writers on lesbian desire is Epigram 91 (book 1) of the Latin poet Martial (*ca.* 40–104). The epigram is reproduced in full by a French surgeon, George Arnauld, in *A Dissertation on Hermaphrodites*, published in London in 1750. This simple prose translation reads:

> I own, Bassa, I had all along taken you for a virtuous person; but, O infamous! you played the whore-master, and had the impudence to act the part of a man with your own sex, and make yourself pass for one; a prodigy worthy the Theban riddle, that adultery may be committed without the intervention of a man!

Arnauld explains that the historical personage Bassa must have been a female hermaphrodite, just like Sappho of Lesbos.[8]

James Elphinston's more elaborate version of 1782, entitled 'To Bassa', adds details that reveal his own preoccupations:

> That with the males thou ne'er wast known to mix,
> Nor e'er gallant did envious slander fix;

That thine officious sex thee homag'd round,
And not a man durst taint the hallow'd ground;
What less than a LUCRETIA could'st thou be?
Ah! what was found? Th'adulterer in thee.
To make the mounts collide emerg'd thy plan,
And monstrous Venus would bely the man.
Thou a new Theban torture could'st explore,
And bid adultery need a male no more.[9]

The first five lines detail Bassa's claims to female sexual virtue. She does not mix with men socially, has never been rumoured to have a 'gallant' (male lover) and has earned the homage of her own sex, so she seems to be another Lucretia (the legendary woman who killed herself after being raped). But in line six, the poet discovers an 'adulterer' hanging about, not near Bassa, but 'in' her self. Where Martial gives no details of lovemaking, Elphinston tries to: Bassa's technique or 'plan' is explained rather vaguely as 'to make the mounts collide'. This sounds like tribadic rubbing, but there is also an implication of penetration with a female member, because 'monstrous Venus' reminds the classically educated reader that Theophrastus described the Roman goddess of love as a hermaphrodite. ('Monstrous' is a heavily derogatory word for Elphinston to use here; Martial's phrase, *prodigiosa Venus*, suggests something strange or astonishing rather than monstrous.) Using this hermaphroditical anatomy, then, Bassa will 'bely the man', that is, counterfeit or pose as a man. Where Arnauld refers to a 'Theban riddle', Elphinston describes a 'Theban torture'; this makes lesbian sex sound tortuously difficult. But at least it is presented as serious enough to count as adultery. Whatever Bassa and her partners do with their 'mounts', suspicion has been cast on the spinsterhood and female friendships of the first lines, phenomena very common in Britain at the time of Elphinston's translation.

Perhaps the best-known classical source on lesbian desire is the fifth dialogue of the courtesans by the Greek author Lucian (born around AD120; died after 180). Here the secret at the heart of tribadism, explored briefly in Martial's epigram, becomes even more elaborate and mysterious. 'A Dialogue Between Cleonarium and Leana' (a translation of 1684–5) begins with a frank question: Cleonarium asks her friend and sister courtesan to explain the 'strange rumours' that 'that Rich Lady of *Lesbos*, caresses thee as a Man would do.' Leana expresses embarrassment and will only comment that the woman in question, Megilla, is 'a strange Female'. As is typical in early texts about lesbian desire, the questioner affects complete ignorance; Cleonarium insists that she has no idea 'to what all these Caresses tend'. Yet her very next remark betrays her knowledge: 'I can't imagine what you mean, unless she's a *Tribadian*, as there are said to be many in that Island, who will not have to do with men, and only commit with Women.' To tantalise the reader and make sex between women sound wildly unusual, Cleonarium must be ignorant; however, to provide titillating details she must suddenly understand what women can 'commit with Women'. After teasing her friend with these declarations of incomprehension, Cleonarium settles down to enjoy the story, asking Leana how Megilla 'declar'd her Passion, the Returns you made, and the rest of that Adventure'.

At this point Leana takes control of the conversation. She tells how she was hired as a minstrel by Megilla and Demonassa. After they got rather drunk, she explains, the rich women 'honoured' her by asking her to get into bed between them. (Commonly in the initial stages of tales of lesbian seduction, the innocent girl accepts caresses as tokens of friendship from superior women.) But soon their technique makes her question their gender:

> They began to toy, kissing me as Men are wont, not barely applying the Lips, but opening the Mouth, biting and pressing my Bosom, with all other Testimonies of a violent Passion, whereat I was strangely amaz'd, as not being able to guess the matter.

Suddenly Megilla pulls off her headgear, revealing a shaved head like a champion's, and declares, 'I am not called *Megilla* but *Megillus*, and there's my Wife', pointing to Demonassa.

Leana's first reaction is amusement, then she asks Megilla if 'you have deceived us all this while, being a Man, and passing for a Woman.' She can only understand Megilla's claim to a masculine role literally, as a claim to biological maleness. Suspiciously, she questions Megilla about her 'virility' and asks 'can you like a Man perform with *Demonassa*?' 'Like a man' is Leana's only point of reference; she still has no idea of any other standard for lovemaking or sexual identity. Megilla's reply is interesting in its rejection of the male standard. 'No, said she, there's no need of that; and if you'l try, you'l find I want nothing for the accomplishing thy and my Desires.' Rather than claiming to have a penis or any kind of penis substitute, Megilla concentrates on the mutual pleasures she can offer; the source of female 'virility' can only be understood by a woman who takes part in female lovemaking. Still desperate to find a physical basis for such promises, Leana asks whether Megilla has had a miraculous sex change like Tiresias, or whether she is a 'Hermophrodite' (sic). But once again Megilla refuses to reduce her power to a phallus: 'No, said she, but I've all the Passions and Inclinations of Men, and something of Manhood.' After giving Leana a necklace and some linen (presumably as a bribe), we are told, Megilla 'kist and satisfied her Passion'. The pronoun does not make clear whose passion was satisfied, but the quality of the satisfaction is not in any doubt.

Cleonarium intervenes in the dialogue once more to demand information on the lovemaking, but Leana clams up and tells her, 'Enquire no further; for it's neither handsome for me to say, nor you to hear it.'[10] This ending is so evasive that it was used by lawyers in the 1810 court case involving the Scottish schoolteachers Miss Woods and Miss Pirie to prove that sex between women must be a physical impossibility, since even Lucian did not know how it was done.[11] However, to readers of this translation in the late seventeenth century, aware of women's capacity for lust, Lucian's dialogue would have been proof that women could do something together, something fully satisfying, even if few were willing to say quite what they did.

Lucian's dialogue was most influential in the strong link it made between lesbian desire and gender rebellion. Of course, Leana and Demonassa are both shown as enjoying sex with women without being in any way unfeminine, but it is Megilla who is put in the spotlight as the instigator of these activities; though she denies being a literal hermaphrodite, she does claim to have 'something of Manhood' both psychologically and in her mysterious sexual technique.

The enduring popularity of these three classical texts can be attributed to this focus on the discourse of the hermaphroditical. They discussed sexual preference, that strange new concept, in the familiar terms of gender.

Case histories

The majority of references to lesbians as hermaphrodites are found in texts that could be described as paramedical. They deserve the term not because they were all written to inform doctors or patients – in fact many of them are clearly designed to titillate – but because their structures are those of scientific or medical treatises. Arguments are supported by anecdotes and lengthier case histories; evidence is weighed up; the lesbian hermaphrodite is stripped bare, taken apart piece by piece in a textual post mortem. There are surprising similarities between the attitudes expressed in the most high-minded of medical treatises and the smuttiest anti-masturbation pamphlet. I have found nothing more pornographic in eighteenth-century literature than the fold-out at the back of Dr James Parsons' respectable medical treatise of 1745, which features a huge centrefold-style engraving of the vulva of a 'hermaphroditical' Angolan woman sold into slavery in America.

What follows is a roughly chronological survey of how (pseudo)medical writers made the link between female same-sex desire and what they saw as abnormal female anatomy. Ideas about anatomy varied or alternated over the period rather than developing in any one direction; a particular writer's assumptions could be quoted with scorn by one successor, yet revived by another. Nor was there any consensus on attitudes to the female hermaphrodite; she could be denounced as a monster, pitied as a patient, given a freakish heroine status or celebrated (tongue-in-cheek) as a sexual prodigy.

Generations of readers would have got their first ideas on the subject from Nathaniel Wanley's *Wonders of the Little World* (1678), a giant compendium of oddities and a popular book for children right up to the nineteenth century. Wanley's succinct chapter on 'such Persons as have changed their Sex' gives twenty-four examples of magical sex change from a mixture of classical and contemporary sources. Twenty-three of them are female-to-male, a metamorphosis Wanley clearly considers more logical, since every creature in the great chain of being is thought to aspire to a higher state. (Judith Brown finds this true of texts about sex change before the seventeenth century; as she explains drily, 'perfection was not likely to degenerate into imperfection.')[12] Also, for Wanley's phallocentric readers the change from female to male makes a better story than vice versa, since the magic member is mysteriously discovered or created rather than being lost or replaced with the nothingness of the vulva. The new female member has great narrative potential because it brings economic power and begins an adventure.

Opinions varied on the question of whether a female hermaphrodite's 'member' was a prolapsed or inverted vagina, or an enlarged clitoris, both female organs being described in gynaecological handbooks as versions of the penis. The vagina theory seems to have been dominant in the sixteenth and early seventeenth centuries, but during the period with which I am concerned it was gradually overshadowed by the idea of the tribadic clitoris.

For Wanley in 1678 the hermaphroditical member is clearly a prolapsed vagina; in several cases the change happens on the wedding night when the breaking of the hymen lets the woman's hidden member slide into view and 'those parts which were inverted and conceal'd, began to appear, and she rose in the Morning of a contrary Sex.' In another example, this time clearly a lesbian situation, a sixteenth-century French teenage girl is described as 'wantoning in bed with a Maid that lay with her' when 'the signs of a man brake out of her'.[13]

After Wanley, such stories tend to concentrate not on sex change but on women who turn out to have always possessed a 'member', or who gradually develop one but still remain women. In *The Midwives Book* (1671), a popular work which reached four editions by 1725, Jane Sharp suggests warily that 'Hermaphrodites' may be just 'women that have their Clitoris greater, and hanging out more than others have'. She goes on to explain how physical abnormality can lead to sexual deviance: 'Sometimes it grows so long that it hangs forth at the slit like a Yard [penis], and will swell and stand stiff if it be provoked, and some lewd women have endeavoured to use it as men do theirs.'[14] In this version, anatomy precedes desire; sex between women seems to be opportunistic, a matter of open-minded 'lewd women' (for whom Sharp can find no more specific name) taking advantage of a new anatomical toy.

British writers in general admit to the existence of only the occasional female hermaphrodite in their own 'civilised' nation, while claiming that vast numbers are found in Asia and Africa. As Sharp puts it, 'in the Indies and Egypt they are frequent, but I never heard of but one in this country.' Not only the clitoris but the labia ('nymphae' or 'wings') are described as abnormal: 'Some Sea-mem [sic] say that they have seen *Negro* Women go stark naked, and these wings hanging out.'[15] Nakedness is used here to heighten the voyeuristic appeal, to make the black woman into a living illustration of abnormality. As Barbara Bush points out, early European travellers' accounts of the Caribbean describe the indigenous women as just as tall and muscular as their men.[16]

No doubt this served to justify overworking black women as slaves. It also reinforced the idea that gender distinctions were a feature of a more civilised, refined society; gender blurring and the resultant sexual perversion were blamed on the 'natives'.

Egypt was a particular target for accusations of female hermaphrodism. Rumours of a common practice of genital mutilation there were twisted into proof that women must have had something big that needed cutting off.[17] As Sharp explains with relish in *The Midwives Book*,

> In some Countries they [the wings] grow so long that the Chirurgion cuts them off to avoid trouble and shame, chiefly in *Egypt*; they will bleed much when they are cut, and the blood is hardly stopt; wherefore maids have them cut off betimes, and before they marry.[18]

Though Sharp is vague about the 'trouble and shame' such genitals can cause, she makes it clear that the operation facilitates marriage in some way.

The mid-seventeenth-century Latin folio of Joannes Benedictus Sinibaldus reached many editions in English throughout this period, although its content was sometimes seen as objectionable, as in 1707 when John Martin was prosecuted (then acquitted) for publishing his translation of it.[19] Richard Head's 1687 translation, entitled *Rare Verities*, includes a section on 'Whether females may change their Sex'. If the clitoris is stimulated by another person, we are told, it may 'chance to grow over-much' until it 'may stand in stead of a mans members'. Neither Sinibaldus nor his translator makes clear whether this is a real change of sex or merely an addition to female anatomy. What the text is explicit about is the consequent potential for same-sex relations: 'Wherefore heretofore there hath been laws enacted against feminine congression, because it is a thing that happens too too common and frequent.' If the sex had really changed, this would no longer be a matter of 'feminine congression' (sex between women); the overgrown woman is placed uneasily on the borders of her sex.

Like Sharp, Sinibaldus claims that many Egyptian women have to be operated on 'by reason of their untamed lust'; this comment shows that the point of the mutilation is to reduce female desire and keep it in the tame channel of heterosexuality.[20] So the British were not alone in using Egypt as a handy dumping ground for rumours about lesbianism; it seems that the West always liked to displace its anxieties to the east. And of course this displacement gave fresh fuel to pseudo-scientific theses about the inferiority and animality of women of colour; racism and hatred of lesbians endlessly reinforced each other. This easternisation of lesbianism seems to have gained strength in the nineteenth century. At the Woods–Pirie trial in 1810, Lord Meadowbank insisted over and over again that no woman 'in this country' (Scotland, or the United Kingdom) would have a big enough clitoris to commit the kind of penetrative tribadism he had heard was so common in India.[21]

For medical writers like Sharp and Sinibaldus, the primary interest is anatomy; lesbian desire is discussed only as a consequence of a physiological change. By contrast, clergymen tend to focus on sin, and on anatomy only as it can facilitate that sin. The Italian Franciscan monk Ludovico Maria Sinistrari developed the theory of penetrative tribadism in a section on 'Sodomia' in his treatise on criminal law, *De Delictis et Poenis* (1700). Since for sodomy to occur, genitals have to enclose each other fully, he reasons, a finger or dildo is not enough; they merely represent 'pollution'. Sinistrari explains that for true sodomy between women to occur, one partner needs a huge clitoris with which she can not just stimulate but actually penetrate the other.[22] This crucial text does not seem to have been translated into English in this period, though Sinistrari's theories do appear to have filtered, via other medical texts, into Britain.[23]

The French surgeon Nicholas Venette's treatise on sex in marriage, written in the late seventeenth century, was very popular in eighteenth-century England. One full translation was *The Mysteries of Conjugal Love Reveal'd* (second edition, 1707). The preface makes it clear that this book is aimed not just at doctors but at bridegrooms, priests, philosophers, mothers, virgin girls – anyone, in fact, who needs to be advised on marital sex and warned off the illicit sorts. Venette admits that he has been criticised before for discussing unnatural sexual vices, but he insists that frankness is best: 'by exposing it to all the World, I cry down unlawful pleasures, that they may be shunned and abhorred.' *The Mysteries of Conjugal Love Reveal'd* certainly exposes lesbian possibilities 'to all the World'. After a description of the clitoris, we are informed bluntly that 'this part, lascivious Women, often abuse.' In the very next sentence, Venette gives 'the Lesbian Sappho' as one example of a woman inclined to vice by her large clitoris. So does a woman abuse her clitoris, making it grow, or does she abuse it because it is large already? Venette slides away from this puzzle. Later, genital anomaly is displaced on to other races and we are told that 'African Maids' are so often overgrown and in need of genital mutilation that men walk through the streets bawling, 'Who wants to be cut?' French women, Venette concludes regretfully, would be too shy to undergo such an operation.[24]

At the end of his book Venette writes about sexual eccentricities such as the hermaphrodite – or rather, five classes of hermaphrodites. The first three are basically 'real Men' with slits between penis and anus or late-dropping testicles, the fifth are described as 'perfect Hermaphrodites' with confused, impotent genitals of both sexes, and the fourth are our old friends the 'Women who have the Clitoris bigger and longer than others'. The Greeks call them tribades, Venette tells us, 'whence the *French* have formed the name *Ribandes* [Ribaudes?].'[25]

Venette debunks some myths about how hermaphrodites are conceived and offers his own theory of prenatal development. In the case of the fourth class, the female hermaphrodites, he explains that on about the forty-fifth day after conception, the 'intelligence' or 'soul' finds that there is an excess of 'matter', so decides to put it into the clitoris rather than spoil the internal genitals, which might some day be necessary for reproduction. These are real women, not half men, and stories of their impregnating other women are nonsense; many 'have abused their Clitoris, but never, engendred with it on another'. Venette insists that this is not about sex change:

> Women who sometimes pass for Men, who have a beard on their chin, and hair on their Body, and have a big and strong voice, are also true Women, though they may divert themselves with their Companions with their Clitoris.[26]

So no matter how many traditionally masculine attributes a woman may have, no matter how much her sexuality is directed at other women, she remains female. Liberating news for any woman reader having doubts about her own gender.

For Venette, the important part of sex is reproduction. He does not call lesbian sex futile or pathetic, only barren:

> Tho' they make use of this part to play the wag with other Women, to whom they give for the most part as much pleasure as Men do, yet there is no hopes that any generation will ensue ... Witness *Daniel de Bantin*, who only sported

> with his Wife, but was got with Child himself by one of his Comrades.

Venette's logic for using the vocabulary of 'play' and 'sport' to describe sex between women is that it is non-reproductive; within that category, he presents it as just as satisfying as heterosex. Only at one point does he become alarmed at the potential for lesbian seduction, when he is wondering whether overgrown women should be allowed to enter convents. The answer is a provisional yes, 'provided they are not of such a lascivious temper, as to tempt and debauch the most holy and most reserved Virgins' or as 'lascivious as that *Bassa Martial* makes mention of'.[27] Even without the means of impregnation, lesbians have the power to 'tempt and debauch'; in a religious setting, the 'sport' and 'play' of sex between women take on dreadful significance. No matter how calmly patronising this doctor sounds while analysing the different classes of hermaphrodites, finally the spectre of Bassa, the predatory hermaphroditical seductress in Martial's epigram, comes to haunt his text.

These ideas about giant clitorises were not experimental notions on the borders of medicine; they became part of the common stock of knowledge handed down through the medical mainstream. The London doctor Thomas Gibson published an introductory textbook on anatomy for medical students in 1682; his section on the clitoris includes, as a matter of course, an explanation of sex between women:

> In some it grows to that length as to hang out from betwixt the Lips of the Privity: yea, there are many stories of such as have had it so long and big as to be able to accompany with other Women like unto Men, and such are called *Fricatrices*, or otherwise Hermaphrodites, who it is not probable are truly of both Sexes.[28]

In his popular treatise on venereal disease, which ran to half a dozen editions in the early 1700s, Dr John Marten credits Gibson as his source for anatomical details. However, he alters Gibson's paragraph on the tribadic clitoris a little:

> In some Women, especially those that are very Lustful, it is so vastly extended, that it hangs out of the Passage externally, and so much resembles the *Yard* of a Man, that by some they have been called *Fricatrices*, and accounted Hermophrodites [sic], and we have read that such have been

> able to perform the Actions of a Man, in accompanying with other women.[29]

Marten has added an explanation of why this happens only to 'some' women, the most 'lustful' ones, and expanded and rearranged the phrases to emphasise the vast, phallic, active 'member'. Compared with Gibson's dry description, Marten's paragraph provides more drama.

John Marten also adds more anecdotes. Genital mutilation is common, he claims, in 'Arabia' and 'AEthiopia', and the women of the Cape of Good Hope voluntarily submit to it for ornamental and religious reasons. We are informed of a 'nation' of hermaphrodites in Florida and Virginia who are despised and enslaved by the native 'Indian' population, and are told the story of a hermaphrodite serving-maid who impregnated her master's daughter and was buried alive in a Scottish city in 1461.[30]

Another popular story was that of the two nuns in Rome. Dr Richard Carr devotes one of his *Medicinal Epistles* (published posthumously in 1714) to this case. A clergyman friend of his has written to tell him a story going the rounds in Rome, about two nuns in a convent who 'were changed in such a manner, as to be suspected of Virility'. The report finally reaches the Pope, who sends some cardinals to examine the nuns. The cardinals pronounce that the nuns have 'grown in such a manner, as to have changed their Sex' and order them to leave the convent; the nuns take to wearing men's clothes and working in men's jobs. Commenting on the story, Carr expresses amusement that cardinals, so unqualified by their holy modesty and ignorance of women, were chosen to carry out the examination. But he can believe that the women's clitorises had grown to the point where they might look like men; this 'wonderful Phenomenon' is just about within 'the Bounds of Nature', he explains. 'Frequent Irritations' of an unspecified sort must have caused the clitorises to grow. Tongue in cheek, Carr urges his reader not to accuse holy nuns of perversion, or to 'suspect their Lasciviousness should prompt them to an unusual Exercise of those Parts; by which they might encrease their Bulk', as is mentioned in Martial's epigram on Bassa. It can happen in babies, he admits, so it is not a definite proof of 'wanton Practices'. In adult women, underclothes can chafe the clitoris while walking or taking exercise, causing these women to experience 'extravagant Desires'; this is known as 'Furor Uterinus' (an early name for what men saw as excessive sexual desire in women, which came to be known as 'nymphomania' from the late eighteenth century onwards). With obvious approval, Dr Carr reports that the 'skilful Chyrurgeons [surgeons]' of 'some Eastern Countries' have discovered how to cut the enlarged clitoris off brides, 'lest it should be a hinderance in Coition'.[31]

It was not just respectable medical texts which included such stories; they were a feature of the anti-masturbation manuals that sold so well in eighteenth-century Britain. The war on 'self-pollution' began much earlier in Britain than in France; it was launched by *The Onania* (1708) and its sequels, which have been attributed to the quack clergyman Balthazar Beckers. The *Onania* texts went through at least nineteen editions, tripling in size and selling up to 38,000 copies.[32] *The Supplement to the Onania*, published around 1710, is full of references to sexual acts between women, most of them borrowed from earlier publications. The author reprints in full Carr's epistle on the two Roman nuns, and quotes a line in Latin from Martial's epigram on Bassa to imply that the nuns were lovers. Then he includes his own version of the paragraph which John Marten adapted from Thomas Gibson:

> It is certain, that in some Women, especially those who are very salacious, the *Clitoris* is so vastly extended, that by hanging out of the Passage, it is mistaken for a Penis, such have been called *Fricatrices*: By *Caelius Aurelianus*, *Tribades*: By *Plautus*, *Subigatrices*, and accounted Hermophrodites [sic], because, as said before, they have been able to perform the Actions of Men with other Women.

The main change in this third version of the passage is that two more words for lesbians have been added – tribades and subigatrices. The author of the *Onania* seems to be trying to make up in scholarly detail for what he lacks in understanding of this strange phenomenon. The sheer range of his references suggests not that he has read these source texts (because his Latin words are often garbled), but that he has borrowed brief allusions from several other medical or anecdotal publications. For example, in the paragraph quoted above he cites a treatise on the passions by the fifth-century physician Caelius Aurelianus and refers to Plautus on 'subigatrice', the French for 'subigatatrix', a vague term for a woman who indulges in illicit intercourse.[33] The author goes on to borrow from John Marten the stories about the enslaved race of hermaphrodites in North America, and the Scottish hermaphrodite executed in 1461. He mentions pairs of women punished for sexual relationships in Turkey and Lisbon, and repeats hearsay about genital mutilation in Arabia and French hermaphrodites being allowed to choose their own true sex.

It is rarely made clear which comes first: the women's desire for sex with each other, or the anatomy that permits it. Nor is the author of the *Onania* sure whether to blame these women as strongly as he blames masturbators; he comments at one stage that although many women develop a giant clitoris because of 'excessive Lust and abuse of the Parts', others must be considered innocent because they are 'born with it, both to their Trouble and Shame'.[34]

The Supplement to the Onania borrows the following detailed case history of a pseudo-hermaphrodite from an unnamed author:

> A certain young Woman at *Thoulouse*, had a relaxation of the vagina, resembling a Man's *Penis*, and some pretended that she abused it that way, it being six inches in length, and four in Circumference in the middle, where it was very hard. It gradually encreas'd from her Childhood: She was searched by the Physicians there, who gave their Opinion, it was a real *Penis*; upon which the Magistrates of the Town, ordered her to go in Man's Habit. In this Equipage she came to *Paris*, where she got Money by showing herself, till upon other assurances that she was a Woman, and a promise of being cured, she was brought into the *Hôtel Dieu*, where the descent was soon reduc'd, and she forc'd to resume her Female Dress, to her great regret.[35]

This brief account exhibits the typical features of stories of lesbians portrayed as hermaphrodites. First, the setting is emphatically non-English; France, at a safe but imaginable distance, was a favourite location for British stories of sexual transgression. Next, notice the vagueness about anatomy: though in the *Supplement*'s general description of female hermaphrodites (quoted above) the female member is identified as a huge clitoris, this time the member is 'a relaxation of the vagina'. (This is the last text I know of which uses the vagina theory.) The change is described, quite unlike the lofty erection of the penis, as a 'descent' – the moral fall of the female genitals, perhaps.

Next it is suggested – coyly, with the safe formula 'some pretended' – that this ambiguous member is used sexually, presumably with other women, though whether this is the cause or the consequence of the genital growth is far from clear. Gossip brings doctors who make what is presented in retrospect as a misdiagnosis; this is another common element of such stories. Typical, too, are the various solutions offered: for her appearance to match her sexual identity, her outside to fit her inside, the hermaphrodite must be recast as a whole man. Because she desires women and can make love to them with what the doctors honour as 'a real Penis', the magistrates order her to play the role (and wear the clothes) of a man.

A similar assumption of universal heterosexuality was made in eighteenth-century Grenoble in the case of Anne Grandjean, whose confessor reacted to her teenage confession of desire for girls by advising her that she must therefore dress as the boy she clearly was.[36] In fact, even the criteria used to determine sex were based on compulsory heterosexuality; the ever-popular *Aristotle's Book of Problems* explains that a hermaphrodite should be considered a man or a woman depending on 'in which member it is fittest for the act of copulation'.[37]

In the *Supplement*'s anecdote of the Toulouse woman, we notice that with the change in clothes comes a move to the big city; this represents a fresh start, a new life in urban anonymity. But it is also significant that Paris, as the centre of commerce, offers the unnamed female hermaphrodite new rewards for the very abnormality from which she is running. Rejecting the safety of passing as a whole man, and thus resisting the story's closure, she finds that the status of freak can be made profitable through self-exhibition. Once again, however, the medical establishment intervenes, turning her into a patient and offering her, perhaps bullying her into, a stable female identity. Her 'descent' having been 'reduc'd' (whether fully or partially, we are not told, nor how), she is expected to reclaim her womanhood with gratitude. The sting in the tail is that the woman regrets having to slot back into a female role; it is implied that she misses a man's social freedom and access to (and perhaps capacity for) sexual relations with women.

Perhaps the most remarkable text in *The Supplement to the Onania* is the letter from 'Mrs. E.N.' This comes after a long stream of letters from men thanking the author for his *Onania*, which showed them the error of their masturbatory ways, together with follow-up letters thanking him for his patent medicines, which have cured all their alarming symptoms. These letters are so enthusiastic and so formulaic that they are probably creations of the author; however, it is just about possible that he adapted letters from real readers. The last letter, dated 16 October 1725, is supposed to be from a rich girl aged 18, who sounds rather proud of her remarkable history. First her mind was 'debauch'd' by reading 'Martial, Juvenal, Ovid, &c.', she explains, and then she was seduced by an older woman:

> I began, Sir, the folly at 11 Years of Age, was taught it by my Mother's Chamber Maid, who lay with me from that Time all along till now, which is full seven Years, and so intimate were we in the Sin, that we took all Opportunities of committing it, and invented all the ways we were capable of to highten the Titillation, and gratifie our sinful Lusts the more. We, in short, pleasured one another, as well as each our selves.

In the seventeenth edition of the *Supplement* a sentence is added, letting us know that the girls were 'prompted to' this sexual experiment by reading a text of Aristotle's which mentioned that women could give themselves an amazing sensation 'cum Digitis, vel aliias Instrumentis' (with fingers or other instruments).[38] The details are left in Latin, so that readers literate only in English cannot gather information and repeat the cycle of reading, experimentation and corruption.

In this story, desire precedes hermaphroditical abnormality. E.N.'s lust leads to sex, which leads to enlargement of the genitals, which in turn heightens desire, in an endless cycle of arousal. Though it involves a 20-year-old maid seducing a pubertal middle-class girl – an ideal opportunity, we might expect, for the author to execrate the evil of servants – the relationship is described in startlingly appreciative terms:

> Whether by the hard usage of my Parts by her, or my self, or both, or whether from any thing in Nature more in my make, than is customary to the Sex, I don't know, but for above half a Year past I have had a swelling that thrusts out from my Body, as big, and almost as hard, and as long or longer than my Thumb, which inclines me to excessive lustful Desires, and from it their [sic] issues a moisture or slipp'riness to that degree that I am almost continually wet.

This vivid description is ostensibly included to warn readers off sexual experimentation, but the effect is quite otherwise, because it is narrated from E.N.'s point of view; despite her ill health, she comes across as a confident, pleasure-filled woman. Her lover/maid sounds tenderly supportive, for example when she goes to consult a midwife about E.N.'s symptoms – without, we are assured, telling her what they have been up to. After reading the *Onania* the women have given up sex, but there has been no quarrel; they are obviously still united in their affection and in their hope of obtaining 'God's Grace'.[39]

We are never told exactly what are 'all the ways' the girls invent to satisfy each other, but it is clear the author thinks that penetrative tribadism is involved. He explains that E.N. has a 'relaxation of the *Clitoris*', just like the two nuns in Rome and the many other women punished for sexual acts with each other in various countries. At the end of his miscellany of anecdotes about pseudo-hermaphrodites, he comes back to the case of E.N.:

> beyond the *Nasamones*, and about *Matchlies*, there are ordinarily found Hermophrodites, which so much resemble both Sexes, that they have carnal knowledge one of another by turns; and this, by an Expression in the young Lady's Letter aforegoing, and which introduced all this Discourse about the Clitoris, seems to be part of the Practice between her, and her Bedfellow the Chambermaid.[40]

Here the myth of a monstrous race in an exotic setting and the prosaic vices of chambermaids are brought together in the discourse of the hermaphroditical. The context for the E.N. story may be an anti-onanistic manual, yet the lovemaking between the women is described not merely as shared masturbation but as 'carnal knowledge one of another by turns'; they are taken seriously as lovers as well as deviant sinners.[41]

Another crucial early text is *A Treatise of Hermaphrodites* (1718), which has been attributed to Giles Jacob. This author assumes that anatomy comes before desire. A woman who finds herself to be a female hermaphrodite can use her vagina for intercourse with men (unless her member is longer than three inches, in which case it would get in the way), or use her member to have penetrative sex with women, giving them more satisfaction than she gets herself:

> Women well furnish'd in these Parts may divert themselves with their Companions, to whom for the most part they can give as much Pleasure as Men do, but cannot receive in any proportion the Pleasure themselves, for want to

> Ejaculation, the Crisis of Enjoyment to the Male in the Intrigues of *Venus*.

It is noteworthy here that the size and pleasure-giving power of the female member is taken for granted (Jacob may be echoing Venette), and the only worry is whether the female member can feel enough. Although the clitoris was known to be the primary site of female pleasure, it seems that the author has stopped considering the member as a clitoris and regards it only as a pseudo-penis which lacks the capacity for ejaculatory orgasm and therefore true release.

Despite the unequal pleasure, Jacob presents sex between women as very common: 'many Lascivious Females divert themselves one with another at this time in the City' (London). 'Masculine Females' are not necessarily lesbian in their tastes, he explains, nor do 'Large Appurtenances' alone always signal same-sex erotic behaviour; however, the body and the mind do correspond in many cases. Because he presumes that such lovemaking is based on anatomical eccentricity, he is sure that it cannot be taught. Anticipating criticism for spreading such filth in his *Treatise*, Jacob insists:

> my Design in the following Sheets is meerly as an innocent Entertainment for all curious Persons, without any Views of inciting Masculine-Females to Amorous Tryals with their own sex; and I am perswaded there will not be one single Hermaphrodite the more in the World, on account of the publishing this Treatise.[42]

Professing to believe the 'female hermaphrodite' theory that limits lesbianism to anatomy allows writers like Jacob to defend their titillating works by insisting that they will have no effect on women's behaviour. However, his language does covertly imply that some 'Masculine-Females' will not have thought of 'Amorous Tryals' with women until they read this.

A Treatise of Hermaphrodites also includes poems and stories about sex between women. A 'Song' by one Mr Rowe, for instance, emphasises the mutuality of pleasure women can give each other. The regular metre and simple rhyme scheme reinforce the ideas of role-swapping and balance.

> While Sappho, with harmonious Airs,
> Her dear Philensis charms,

> With equal Joy the Nymph appears,
> Dissolving in her Arms.
>
> Thus to themselves alone they are,
> What all Mankind can give;
> Alternately the happy Pair
> All grant, and all receive.

By contrast with John Donne's 'Sappho to Philaenis' (1633), which presents lesbian desire as entirely narcissistic, this song describes Sappho and Philaenis as getting 'equal Joy' from their lovemaking. But Rowe can only understand this joy as a male or female pleasure; though they alternate roles, the women can never escape the model of heterosexuality. He describes them as feeling 'the Joys of either Sex in Love', turn by turn, and his final couplet makes the roles even clearer: 'Sucessive each, to each does prove,/Fierce Youth, and yielding Maid.'[43]

A prose story included in Jacob's text uses the same pattern of two women alternating masculine and feminine roles. The 'Masculine-Females' Margureta and Barbarissa come from aristocratic Italy and France respectively. Their story is told from the point of view of a curious manservant, Nicolini, who has bored a peephole in their wall to watch them having sex. After kissing and touching each other, 'one of the Females threw herself down upon the Bed, and displaying her self commodiously, the other immediately began the amorous Adventure, covering her Companion so effectually, that *Nicolini* could not possibly discover any further Particulars.' The closeness of the bodies hides what brings them together; tribadism is the mysterious act that can never be fully witnessed. But the reader's curiosity must not be frustrated too long; conveniently enough, Margureta happens to get up and walk towards the light, so Nicolini can observe 'something hang down from her Body of a reddish Colour, and which was very unusual'.

In the second session, after some refreshing wine, the penetrative role is passed to Barbarissa, who being 'not so Masculine' is having difficulty with the 'erection of her Female Member'. Pornographic pictures and mutual spanking have little effect; finally, Margureta whips her with a birch rod:

> Upon this, something appear'd from the Privities of *Barbarissa*, like unto what *Nicolini* had observ'd of *Margureta*, and they instantly put on their loose Gowns, and ran to

> the Bed, where *Barbarissa* embracing her Companion, did her Work effectually.[44]

There is no name for Barbarissa's member; it can only be described as a 'something' similar to Margureta's reddish 'something'. The author comprehends it only through its 'work', in which he assumes it will function exactly like a (rather tired) penis.

Giles Jacob's tribades are not always exclusively lesbian; the hermaphroditical heroines of the last story in his *Treatise*, Diana and Isabella, seem to be bisexual, since he says they 'not only frolick'd with each other, but with both Sexes in general'. This is a more troubling story than the others; when the hermaphrodites seduce anyone (male or female) they are shown to be punished. Sharing a bed with Diana, a certain parson's wife thinks little of the initial kisses and embraces, supposing Diana to be drunk, and is 'pretty easy' (which suggests how acceptable fondling was among women) 'till at last *Diana* threw her self upon her, and began an Adventure, very displeasing, which surpriz'd her to that degree, that she cried out vehemently.' The parson bursts in, but only when he has examined Diana's genitals does he take the attack seriously, as attempted rape, and throw her out of the house.

A similar disaster befalls Isabella in her relationship with a man. The Count and she have a pleasant affair until he reaches down in the post-coital darkness and is outraged to discover that his lover is 'a Monster'. 'In his passion,' Jacob tells the readers cheerfully, 'he pull'd out a sharp Penknife, and cut off the external Members of *Isabella*.' When she has healed, all she can do is retire to live with Diana 'as Man and Wife'. But they are not allowed even that refuge. In case readers have missed the point that hermaphrodites both deserve and need castration, the same thing is shown to happen to Diana. The next time she tries to seduce a woman, she is punished by having her member cut off. 'After which,' Jacob reassures his readers, 'both of them liv'd to be harmless old Women.'[45]

Many texts pass on the received wisdom about lesbians as hermaphrodites, but add nothing new. For example, Dr John Quincy's medical dictionary of 1719, which went into ten editions by 1787, mentions briefly that the growth of hermaphroditical female members does 'frequently happen from lascivious Titillations, and Frictions, as in the celebrated Instance of the two Nuns at *Rome*'.[46] Quincy does not say exactly what frictions these are, but the conjunction of the 'two Nuns' and the word 'Frictions' (with its hint of 'fricatrice') makes his meaning clear. Another dictionary published by Ephraim Chambers in 1738 describes the normal clitoris, then comments, 'some women are apt to abuse it'. Here, 'abuse' does not depend on abnormal size; any clitoris can be used in a sexually deviant way. Chambers goes on to say that in some women the clitoris is very long, almost penis-size, and so these women frequently 'pass for hermaphrodites'; he may mean that they are accused of being hermaphrodites, but there is a hint that these women deliberately exploit their genital anomalies by 'passing' for something more than they are. Speculating on the nature of hermaphrodites, Chambers quotes Quincy's opinion that clitoral enlargement, in cases such as that of the nuns in Rome, is caused by 'lascivious frictions, and titillations', but he adds 'on what grounds he asserts this we do not know.'[47] Ephraim Chambers' tone is wary; he offers the opinions of several medical experts but is unwilling to make a firm judgement himself.

Not afraid to make judgments, Dr James Parsons published *A Mechanical and Critical Enquiry into the Nature of Hermaphrodites* in 1741. Mocking old superstitions, Parsons' commonsense treatise makes a comprehensive case for what earlier writers had suggested, that there are no real hermaphrodites, only 'Macroclitorideae' – Parsons' term for women with large clitorises. He also calls them tribades, which, as he defines the word, means all those 'capable' (both physically and emotionally) of 'that Action from whence the Name arose, whether they perform it or not' – so a woman can be a tribade even if she never has sex with a woman. Such women should not be hounded as monsters, Parson urges, but only mutilated, following the practice in Africa and Asia: 'the People knowing that the Length of them produces two Evils, *viz.* the hindering the Coitus, and Womens abuse of them with each other, wisely cut or burn them off while Girls are young.'[48] Where most writers only hint that the custom of genital mutilation in some way facilitates marriage or tames women's lusts, Parsons is frank about the fear of 'Womens abuse of them with each other'. Heterosexuality, usually presented as natural and universal, is here shown to need the aid of surgery. I know of no case of clitoral mutilation performed in Britian before the mid-nineteenth century; earlier doctors seem to have been content to examine, comment in print, hypothesise and wait for post-mortem dissection. But the fact that they mention the operation with such approval demonstrates their wish that unruly female desires could be simply pruned away.

Parsons gives women's desire for each other a central place in his discussion of their anatomy. Tribades are not pseudo-men, he insists, and their tastes do not de-sex them. Their desire for women makes sense, though it is immoral; he suggests that their main reason for choosing women is 'fear of that Accident, that is the necessary Consequence of dealing with Men' – that is, pregnancy and subsequent ruin. Parsons also stresses the pleasure involved: lesbian sex is not just a matter of making do. Only one of the women needs to be a tribade for satisfying penetrative sex to take place: 'by an overlong Clitoris in one, both find their accounts answer'd.'[49] These women may be sinful – and Parsons implies that it would certainly be better for society if they were disabled by surgery at an early age – but he presents them as sensible, sensual people who are wholly women.

There is no clear development to be found in these texts. Robert James' *Medicinal Dictionary* (1745), for example, takes the traditional point of view that anatomy precedes desire. In an entry under 'Tribades', James describes women who happen to have grown to the point where, suddenly noticing their pseudo-phallic capacity, they make experimental 'attempts to converse in a criminal manner with other Women'. Only when these acts have become habitual, James implies, do the women become 'fonder of associating themselves with Women than with Men'.[50] It is interesting here that experience is shown to reinforce a desire until it hardens into a definite sexual preference and thus an identity called 'tribade'.

James goes on to tell the story of Hendrikje Verschuur, a woman who passed as a man in early seventeenth-century Holland.[51] 'Henrica Schuria' is described as a rebellious woman 'of a masculine Turn of Mind' who becomes 'weary of her Sex', crossdresses and enlists as a soldier. On her return home she lets her disguise slip and her relationships with a number of women, including a widow, cause her to be 'accus'd of uncommon and preternatural Lust'. On examination, she is reported to have a large clitoris ('half a Finger long') with which she has been pleasuring the Widow, 'of whom she was excessively fond, so well, that, if the Laws of the Land had permitted, [the widow] would have married her'. They are both whipped, James records with satisfaction, and Henrica (presumably as the masculine, sexually 'active' and so guiltier party) is banished.[52]

This passage offers two readings of the same problem. On the one hand, lesbian desire goes with having (or being accused of having) a giant clitoris. On the other, lesbian desire leads to cross-dressing. To any contemporary woman reader who felt alienated from the feminine role yet drawn to other women, this passage would suggest one solution: since the 'Laws of the Land' did not permit her as a woman to marry another woman, perhaps she could bypass them by converting herself first into an eligible bachelor and then into a female husband.

George Arnauld's *A Dissertation on Hermaphrodites* (1750) divides hermaphrodites into perfect, imperfect, predominantly male and predominantly female. He explains that many women have a swollen clitoris, but only in the female hermaphrodite does it free itself from the labia and become erect. Such women – 'rare in Europe ... common in Egypt' of course – are like 'eunuchs, who can enjoy coition without the perfect consummation of the venereal act'. Bassa in Martial's epigram and Sappho of Lesbos were both obviously 'of this species'. (Michel Foucault argues that only the nineteenth-century 'homosexual' was thought of as a 'species',[53] but note that in 1750 Arnauld is referring to the 'species' of tribades.)

Arnauld offers two case histories. The first is the story of the woman from Toulouse, which has been told in greater length in *The Supplement to the Onania* (see pp. 42–3). The second is an account of 'two young persons' in mid-seventeenth-century Spain who, soon after their marriage, are both found to be 'pregnant women'. Convicted of 'the most abominable crime' (presumably sodomy between women), they are sentenced to be burned alive. At the last minute, a doctor saves them by insisting that they are not women but hermaphrodites, who (once married) are lawfully allowed to use their four sets of genitals to impregnate each other.[54] So the discourse of hermaphrodism may be insulting to its subjects, but can sometimes save them from having to bear the full moral weight of their 'crimes'. Being exiled from womanhood can be an advantage, if as an unnatural 'woman' you have been sentenced to death.

The Swiss doctor Samuel Tissot published one of the most vehement anti-masturbation treatises in 1760. One of the English translations, *Onanism* (1766), went into five editions by 1781. After masturbation or 'manual pollution', Tissot goes on to consider 'another kind of pollution, which may be called *clitorical*'. Tissot claims that this originated with Sappho of Lesbos and he quotes (in Latin) Ovid's description of Sappho's companions (see pp. 244–5). He also describes this vice as 'too common amongst the Roman women, at the time when all morality was lost', and quotes four lines (again in the original Latin) from the women's orgy scene in Juvenal's *Sixth Satire* (see pp. 212–14).

For an explanation of this practice, Tissot must call on the discourse of hermaphrodism. He agrees with earlier writers that the 'hermaphrodite' is only a 'chimera' based on the fact that Nature has given certain women 'a semi-resemblance to man'. Of those few, a smaller percentage take the matter further: 'some women who were thus imperfect, glorying, perhaps, in this kind of resemblance, seized upon the functions of virility.' It is one of the ironies of sexuality in this period that Tissot can present these women's abnormal 'imperfection' as something to take perverse 'glory' in; he cannot help admitting that even a 'semi-resemblance' to men is an honour. Though, as freaks, they are less than whole women, Tissot presents them as in some sense more than women too. In a Latin footnote he calls them 'Tribades' or 'Ribaudes' and quotes from Juvenal again. Tissot sees these women as partly helpless, partly criminal. The 'supernatural size' of their clitorises causes 'all the miracle', he decides, but their 'shameful abuse of this part' brings 'all the evil'.

Reaching a moral high ground again, he reminds us that this kind of 'pollution', like the others, leads to 'emaciation, languour, pain, and death'. However, he cannot quite fit sex between women into his scheme of 'sorts of masturbation'; he comments uneasily that 'this last species deserves the greater attention, as it is frequently practised at present.' Not only is it common, but (unlike private masturbation) it is associated with relationships which disrupt heterosexual society:

> Women have been known to love girls with as much fondness as ever did the most passionate of men, and conceive the most poignant jealousy, when they [the girls] were adressed by the male sex upon the score of love.

At this point Tissot breaks off, announcing that he is 'weary' of providing such 'shocking details'. He has already charted dangerous waters. An eighteenth-century girl given *Onanism* to warn her away from masturbation could learn from it that desire between women was not just a matter of lust or anatomical abnormality, but of 'love' that rivalled anything 'the most passionate of men' could offer.[55] Although medical and pseudo-medical texts on female hermaphrodites were probably intended to mock and marginalise lesbian desire, many of them ended up putting it centre stage.

Randolph Trumbach claims that the idea of the lesbian as hermaphrodite died out after the mid-eighteenth century; as a social role for tommies and Sapphists became more visible, there was no longer any need to place such women in that biological category which Parsons called 'macroclitorideae'.[56] Yet these theories seem to me to have coexisted and overlapped, rather than one simply replacing the other. The works of these eighteenth-century doctors sold many editions after the mid century and the biological explanation appears to have endured in some form throughout the nineteenth century (seen particularly clearly in the Woods–Pirie trial) and into the twentieth. Perhaps there will always be some commentators who want to limit our difference to anatomy.

Literary games

The discourse of hermaphrodism spilled over from medical texts into other genres. Here I look at three texts – an anecdotal biography, a mock epic, and a love lyric – in which the ideas of hermaphroditical anatomy and passion between women are strongly linked.

A Scots/Irishman, Anthony Hamilton, published *Memoirs of the Life of Count Grammont* (his brother-in-law) in French in 1713 and in multiple English editions from 1714 on. This rambling, bawdy saga of the English court of Charles II was for a long time considered polite reading even for ladies; in 1796 Edward Gibbon called it 'a favourite book of every man and woman of taste'.[57] It includes the tale of a senior maid of honour, Mistress Hobart. Along with ugliness, vivacity and an '*irregular Fancy*', Miss Hobart is known to have 'a *tender Heart*, whose *Sensibility*, some pretended, was in Favour of the *Fair Sex*'. (Note the 'some pretended' formula, which was common in discreet references to lesbianism.) Her attempts to draw several young women into intimate friendship lead to rumours; Hamilton plays with multiple interpretations of her behaviour:

> 'Twas not long before the Report, whether true or false, of this *Singularity*, spread though the whole Court, where

> *People* being yet so uncivilíz'd as never to have heard of that kind of *Refinement* in *Tenderness* of *ancient Greece*, imagined that the *illustrious H_t*, who was so fond of the *fair Sex*, was something more than she appear'd to be.[58]

It is a measure of the persistence of the lesbian-as-hermaphrodite motif that such an author, considering himself too sophisticated to believe the myth himself, still chooses to allude to it to colour his satire. Hamilton's double-edged mockery undercuts the 'uncivilised' bigots who have never heard of Greek homosexuality, while making sure that the taint of abnormality still clings to Mistress Hobart. Rather than being more than the woman she appears to be, he hints, she is less; the tribade has lost her power to threaten the 'civilised' reader.

Hamilton goes on to explain that only when satirical ballads compliment Mistress Hobart on her 'new Attributes' do her companions 'begin to be afraid of her'; his implication is that court ladies have no real objection to lesbian affairs so long as they are not risking pregnancy. The poet Lord Rochester manages to lure the timid Mistress Temple away from Hobart by telling her that the latter has impregnated her own maid. What terrifies Mistress Temple is not the discovery that Hobart desires her, but the ambiguous danger posed by a hermaphrodite in her circle.

> After what she had just learnt concerning her, she look'd upon her as a *Monster* injurious to the *Virtue* of the *Fair Sex*, or what *Sex* soever she might be; and blush'd at the *familiarities* she had with a Creature whose *Woman* was with *Child*.[59]

Miss Temple's credulity is presented as laughably naive. Rochester, like his author Hamilton, is making use of tales he has outgrown. Without really believing that women can impregnate each other, he perpetuates the myth for his own purposes. (The Hobart–Temple seduction is discussed in more detail on pp. 187–90.)

Probably the most elaborate attack on a woman in terms of hermaphrodism was *The Toast* (second edition, 1736) by the Oxford don William King. During his stay in Ireland, King took the widowed Duchess of Newburgh (Lady Frances Brudenell) to court for several thousand pounds that she owed him, and lost.[60] In revenge, he wrote a mock-epic poem in four books of English and Latin, attacking the Duchess as 'Myra', a bisexually promiscuous witch and hermaphrodite ruling a social circle of tribades in Dublin. Popular among the educated, *The Toast* went into four editions by 1754.

Showing the misogyny characteristic of men's Augustan poetry, King places his heroine outside, not just femaleness, but humanness:

> With a toothless wide Mouth, and a Beard on her Chin,
> And a yellow rough Hide in the Place of a Skin;
> Brawny Shoulders up-rais'd; Cow-Udders; Imp's Teat;
> And a Pair of bow'd Legs, which were set on splay Feet.

Rather than dwelling on Myra's genital anatomy to prove that she is literally a hermaphrodite, King creates around her an atmosphere of abnormality, using language associated with animals and witchcraft. A footnote helpfully explains that all witches have a 'masculine appetite' for women, particularly Horace's sorceress Folia. Another footnote gathers all the hints together into a fact: unsated by three husbands and an estimated 200 male lovers, Myra daily practises 'that unnatural Act the *Spaniards* call *Donna con Donna*'. King is coy about the details, for example in this meeting between Myra and her lover Ali (Lady Allen):

> Then impatient she rush'd to a closer Embrace.
> Let the rest be untold! – And thus ever forbear,
> Lest thy Numbers ... offend the chaste fair.[61]

The real danger is not that women, 'the chaste fair', will be offended, but that they will be educated about lesbian possibilities. Any woman literate in Latin could find the details in the footnote; with the intellectual snobbery common to his age, King assumes that the highly educated are morally strong.

Though Myra is introduced in the preface as 'the principal Hero or Heroine (for she was both a Man and a Woman)', and is described as experiencing 'alternate Joys', there is no attempt at doubling pronouns. For most of the poem she is presented not as a literally two-sexed being but as a tribade, with a potent character and clitoris but no phallus. It is her pride in sexual prowess that lets her rival men, not her anatomy; for most of the poem her hermaphroditical identity is psychological rather than physical. Myra is shown as being proud of her gender anomaly; she quotes from Megilla's speech in Lucian's Dialogue (see pp. 31–3), claiming to be 'all over man'. When towards the end of the poem Venus decides to make Myra 'more fit for her sex' (fit to satisfy her sex, that is, not to be a member of it), what she gives her is a penis:

> Let her thus be erect! (Here she held out her Fan.)
> And be superindu'd all the Virtues of Man! ...
> Let her Passions be strong, as her Form is Compleat,
> And her Name of Distinction be FRIGA the Great!

A footnote explains that Venus, counterpart of the Scandinavian goddess Friga (Frigg or Freyja, wife of Odin), is often worshipped as an idol with a beard, a divinely hermaphroditical female rather than a true hermaphrodite.[62]

Apollo, furious, decides to restrict the contagion by forbidding Myra access to men and to innocent 'Nymphs': ''Tis my Will, since to wayward Amours she's inclin'd,/She be only permitted to mix with her Kind.' (This is a startlingly early version of the sexologists' theories that lesbians or inverts belong to a certain 'kind', and should make sexual connections with each other rather than corrupting ordinary women into 'pseudo-lesbianism'.) Myra, however, has no problem with this; she seems to have lost interest in all lovers but Ali. Basking in Venus' patronage, she enjoys a brief and illusory period of glory with her new penis. When her cheated husband Mars bursts in on her and Ali and comments scornfully, 'Pretty Lambkins at play!', Myra tells him, 'I am ripen'd to Man' and announces that she can now cuckold both him and Ali's husband in a single act. Soon, however, King explains with relish, Myra is blinded by powder from Mars' wig and threatened with castration: 'shall your Manhood as smooth, as black Eunuch's, be made.' She gives in, and surrenders her money and freedom to avoid that fate – the irony is that by surrendering she is symbolically emasculated anyway, reduced to a female eunuch.[63]

Lillian Faderman has claimed that texts such as *The Toast* accuse women of bisexuality 'primarily as a metaphor' for assertiveness in other areas of life.[64] But it seems clear to me that the focus of King's hatred is Myra's sexual identity, her freedom from the rules of womanhood. His tongue-in-cheek use of the discourse of the hermaphroditical is an elegant way of attacking lesbian pretensions to social and sexual power. Plenty of Augustan poems denounced women for assertiveness; this one focuses specifically on lesbian desire and potency as something that is out of the control of men. (There is further discussion of social structures in *The Toast* on pp. 258–61.) Paradoxically, as well as mocking his enemy, King's employment of hermaphroditical terms also glamorises her; at many points in the poem she comes across as supremely powerful. Perhaps it was safe to describe the female hermaphrodite in heroic and seductive terms so long as her impotence was established by the end of the text.

It would be a mistake to assume that the discourse of hermaphrodism could be used only to demean women's sexuality. Celebratory texts are rare but telling; one example is Aphra Behn's fantasy of 1688, 'To the Fair Clarinda, Who Made Love to Me, Imagined More than Woman.' Often heralded as the first professional woman writer, Behn was a hugely productive playwright, novelist and poet, as well as a spy. This poem plays with the idea that a woman whom the speaker desires (and who desires her) is a hermaphrodite. Though the topic, the personal voice and the appreciative tone are all risky, Behn is safely situated within literary tradition; for example, the name 'Clarinda' is that of an Amazon in Tasso's sixteenth-century epic poem. Behn describes her beloved Clarinda as combining the best of both sexes:

> Fair lovely maid, or if that title be
> Too weak, too feminine for nobler thee,
> Permit a name that more approaches truth:
> And let me call thee lovely charming youth.

Behn's theme is not the exotic delights of loving a hermaphrodite, but the convenient escapes from various guilts provided by a female lover who is alternately recognised as a woman and a man. The speaker explains that addressing a man would 'justify my soft complaint', but the fact that the object is a fellow woman does 'lessen my constraint'. She avoids the forwardness of being seen to pursue a man and takes refuge in the fact that it is aesthetically suitable (even for a woman) to want to look at a woman: 'And without blushes I the youth pursue,/When so much beauteous woman is in view.' However, in case anyone might accuse her of pursuing the woman sexually, Behn's speaker, tongue in cheek, denies that such a thing could exist in the absence of a penis:

> In pity to our sex sure thou wert sent,
> That we might love, and yet be innocent;
> For sure no crime with thee we can commit;
> Or if we should – thy form excuses it.
> For who that gathers fairest flowers believes
> A snake lies hid beneath the fragrant leaves.[65]

Behn here cleverly takes society's ignorance and waves it in its face. Having admitted in the title that Clarinda is a woman and not a hermaphrodite, Behn is hinting that a sexual 'crime' is indeed being committed, but that society is too blind to see it. She knows the snake – not a phallic, but a seductive power – lies beneath the leaves. Like modern jokes about lesbianism being the safest form of contraception, this poem contrasts the idea of wholesomeness with a hint of delightful wickedness.[66]

The idea of lesbians as hermaphrodites was an enduring one, nor has it quite died out. Nowadays, instead of measurements of lesbians' clitorises there are studies of our brain structure, our chromosomes, our hormones. The twentieth-century terms of investigations into the biological 'causes' of lesbianism may be subtler, less overtly hostile, but the motive is generally the same as in those seventeenth- and eighteenth-century texts: the need to exile us from womanhood.

2 Female husbands

Another way of interpreting erotic bonds between women in terms of gender anomaly was to see one of them not as a pseudo-man but as a woman deliberately disguised as a man to get access to another woman. In this chapter I deal with stories of female husbands – women who passed as men, enabling them to court and/or marry women – and female husbands' wives.

A startling number of stories of 'passing women' emerged in the 1980s. Their motives for disguising their sex were many: escape from home, patriotism, the need for a job, crime, following men to sea or war, leaving men behind, avoiding rape, preserving virginity, and love and desire for women. I make no claim that this last reason, the subject of this chapter, was the most common motive, but it does seem to have been a crucial one in many cases and has received little attention. Studies by Julie Wheelwright (on women passing as men in the military) and Dianne Dugaw (on the figure of the warrior woman in popular culture) have brought to light many stories of such women, but they play down lesbian motives, and their focus on soldiers effectively excludes tales of women who crossdressed specifically in order to marry women.[1] Female husbands do not sit comfortably on pedestals as early feminist rebels, nor can they be claimed by lesbian historians as wholesome women-loving women. Researchers can be made uneasy by female husbands' profound deceptions (sometimes, it seems, even of their wives), by their misogyny and exploitation of male privilege, and by those worryingly phallic dildos.

From records of sixteenth- and seventeenth-century law cases across continental Europe, we find that sex between women was considered a greater crime when one woman penetrated the other with an object.[2] What mattered in such cases, I suggest, was not the act of penetration (which after all could be done by female fingers), but the use of what lawmakers saw as a substitute penis. Judges were particularly outraged by women's attempts to usurp

A 'passing woman' goes courting, from Giovanni Bianchi, The True History and Adventures of Catherine Vizzani *(1755)*

the legal privileges of husbands. In seventeenth-century Holland, most of the handful of women charged with sodomy lived as marital-style couples and had tried (and sometimes managed) to go through a legal wedding.[3] Several historians have minimised the sexual element of these stories by arguing that the real crime was passing as men.[4] In Britain, where there were no laws against sex between women or women dressing as men, a female husband's crime tended to be described in terms of vagrancy or financial fraud.[5] Yet we do not have to look far below the surface to see that lawyers and judges did not want to publicise sex between women; a word like 'fraud' in a female husband case might suggest men's fear of being usurped by uppity women, but it can also be taken as a euphemism for lesbian seduction. The female husband's crime seems to have been neither purely social nor purely sexual: as Rudolph Dekker and Lotte van de Pol put it, what threatened the lawmakers was 'not so much lesbian relationships or cross-dressing in and of themselves, but their combination'.[6]

Did 'passing women' have sex with other women? Did they want to? Randolph Trumbach, arguing that the Sapphist role was invented only in the late eighteenth century, thinks that the main motives of earlier crossdressers were economics and safety. 'It is likely,' he claims, 'that most women who dressed and passed as men for any length of time, did not seek to have sexual relations with women, and this was probably true even of those who married women.'[7] Trumbach offers no evidence for this claim. Of course we rarely have proof of desire or of sexual acts between two women in a female marriage, any more than we have proof about most marriages between women and men. When a woman passed as a man and married a woman, it seems fair to me to assume that one of her primary motives was erotic. (Women who married men in this period, on the other hand, were often clearly motivated by financial need.)

Looking at marriage between women from another angle, we can ask why a woman who loved women would want to pass as a husband. It has been argued that this was a way of recasting herself, of turning a deviant desire into pseudo-heterosexuality. Lotte van de Pol and Rudolph Dekker see the 'passing woman' in early modern Europe as wearing an inner disguise that let her think of herself as a man and 'psychologically enabled [her] to court another woman'.[8] Considering the many other models for woman–woman desire circulating at the time, however, I cannot agree that a woman who loved women would have had to think of herself as a man. I see practical considerations as primary in most cases; the disguise was assumed for the world, and sometimes (at least initially) for the wife, rather than for the female husband's psyche.

Marriage was a refuge that seemed to offer so much: social status, domestic privacy, economic convenience, a sense of emotional stability, a 'No Trespassers' sign for any man casting an eye at the female husband's wife. Even today, the institution of matrimony has its attractions: in a phone-in survey conducted by Channel 4's *Out on Tuesday* in the early 1990s, lesbian and gay viewers registered by an overwhelming majority that they would marry a same-sex partner if they could. In the seventeenth and eighteenth centuries, when marriage was a more popular and secure institution, many lesbians must have longed for its cover.

The paucity of research on female husbands is not due to any lack of evidence. It is true that we have no reliable autobiographies or memoirs, but we do have a variety of reports, ranging from paragraphs to entire volumes, about more than a dozen suspected cases of female marriage in Britain in this period, and several more abroad.

Before extrapolating from the evidence, we should remember that it is fragmentary and unrepresentative. A woman who was completely successful in passing as a man was recorded (if at all) as a man, and so wrote herself out of history. We only know about the few female husbands who were found out and exposed in print – that is, the more vulnerable or unlucky ones. This means that many of our first impressions could be false. For example, most recorded female husbands were working class, and so female marriage has become known as the working-class branch of lesbian history. But perhaps upper-class female husbands used their privileges of travel and relative privacy to avoid being found out. Also, it seems from the recorded cases that most female husbands fooled their fiancées or wives about their gender. It could be argued, however, that cases of such fraud, or marriages in which a lesbian relationship broke down into hostility, would be most likely to end in exposure, whereas a wife happy to be married to a woman would have helped to keep the secret, laying out her husband's body herself if 'he' died.[9] For each wife who turned her female husband over to the police as a fraud, I suggest, there may have been some who never knew the difference in the dark, some who found out and were not discontented, and others who knew from the beginning and preferred it that way. Before looking in close up at two detailed biographies of female husbands as lovers of women, I want to examine the many short reports that appeared in a variety of sources, from private letters, to marriage registers, to newspapers.

Short reports

Nathaniel Wanley's *Wonders of the Little World* (1678) includes the story of an impoverished Spanish woman, battered by her husband because she cannot have children. She escapes in a suit of his clothes and eventually (perhaps influenced by her masculine social role, perhaps having grown genitally) 'she who had been a wife, desired to perform the offices of a husband.' Her happy marriage to a woman is not interrupted by exposure; Wanley explains that he only knows the story because the female husband told it to a male acquaintance who passed it on. In the context of a section on miraculous sex changes, Wanley recounts this story without judging the women's behaviour.[10]

Perhaps the most popular anecdote circulating in Britain about a female husband was a story set in Turkey – thus reinforcing the links the British made between sexual perversion and Mediterranean and Moslem cultures. The story seems to have originated in the sixteenth-century travel accounts of A.G. Busbequius, a Romanian diplomat. An English translation of Busbequius in 1744, called *Travels into Turkey,* explains that in the popular public baths the beauty of girls is 'exposed Naked to the view of other Women', causing these 'other' (older, less beautiful, less womanly?) women to 'fall in Love with them, as young Men do with us, at the sight of Virgins'. One old woman visits the baths and falls in love with a poor girl; the contrast of youth and age is meant to be funny. Woman-to-woman overtures fail: 'when neither by wooing nor flattering her, she could obtain that of her which her mad Affection aim'd at, she attempted to perform an Exploit almost incredible; she feigned herself to be a Man'. 'Mad affection' here suggests that lesbian desire is a kind of mental illness, perhaps an early symptom of senility.

Disguised as a high official, the woman lodges near the girl's father and persuades him to let her marry his daughter. On the wedding night, however, she makes no attempt at fooling the girl; perhaps she tries another direct appeal? 'After some Discourse, and plucking off her Head-geer', we are told, 'she was found to be a Woman.' When the judge reproaches her for letting her old age be disrupted by beastly, unnatural love, her answer is spirited: 'Away, Sir, says she! You do not know the Force of Love, and God grant you never may.' The authorities pack her in a barrel and drown her.[11]

This cautionary tale seems to have appealed to many readers. It crops up again in the French baron J.B. Tavernier's *Collections of Travels Through Turkey* (1684).[12] When an anonymous author put together a lipsmacking catalogue of vices called *Satan's Harvest Home* in 1749, he warned that an epidemic of lesbianism had spread across Europe, as far as London; however, his chief example was nothing uncomfortably close to home but the female husband story from the Busbequius translation.[13] *Satan's Harvest Home* was sold nationwide in snuffshops as well as bookshops, while the travel books appealed to a more scholarly audience; one way or another, the Turkish female husband anecdote must have reached readers and listeners all over Britain.

Most British female husbands from the end of the seventeenth century are presented in print as eccentric minor criminals. With a mixture of denunciation and amusement, authors reduce complex life-stories to the elements of crossdressing, fraud, discovery and punishment. The Oxford antiquarian Anthony à Wood includes this anecdote in a letter to a friend in 1694:

> Appeared at the King's Bench in Westminster hall a young woman in man's apparel, or that personated a man, who was found guilty of marrying a young maid, whose portion he had obtained, and was very nigh of being contracted to a second wife. Divers [several] of her love letters were read in court, which occasioned much laughter. Upon the whole she was ordered to Bridewell to be well whipt and kept to hard labour till further order of the court.[14]

As is usual in such reports, we are told the place of trial, but not the woman's name or anything much about her except for her crime. Wood makes an interesting slip; he says that she was 'in man's apparel', then recollects that women sometimes crossdress for fun rather than disguise (like a girl he had heard about who had been arrested for dancing in an inn in breeches),[15] so he pauses to explain that she actually 'personated a man', a much more serious business. Watch the pronouns: Wood slides from 'a young woman' to 'he' to 'her' to 'she' within a couple of sentences. This grammatical ambiguity is typical of stories about female husbands;

depending on what aspect of the personality the writers are discussing, or perhaps for comic contrast, a mixture of female and male names and pronouns is used.

The female husband's motive is assumed to be a financial scam: though all Wood knows for sure is that she married one woman, he implies that she hoped to marry several times, each time stealing the bride's dowry or 'portion' before deserting her. The legal language steers us away from sexuality towards theft. The anarchy of the women's act is defused into comedy; their love letters are read aloud to laughter, not rage. The punishment too sounds mild, in the context of the period, when pickpocketing and rape were hanging matters. Though reports of European female husbands tend to end in execution, there is no record of such executions in Britain or America. When British female husbands received any punishment, it was typically a matter of six months in jail and a symbolic exposure, either a public whipping – to mar those seductive, boyish good looks – or a session in the pillory, to warn off other women from imitating them. Since they could be belittled so effectively, perhaps there seemed no need to wipe them out.

A London prison list records that in 1720 one Sarah Ketson called herself John and tried to defraud one Ann Hutchinson into marriage; predictably enough in the context of a prison list, the motive is assumed to have been financial.[16] Marriage registers, on the other hand, generally do not interpret motives but simply record the clerk's perceptions, speculating on the appearance of the bridegroom. There are two very strange entries in a marriage register in Taxal, Cheshire:

> Hannah Wright and Anne Gaskill, Parish of Prestbury, 4th September 1707.
> Ane Norton and Alice Pickford, Parish of Prestbury, 3rd June 1708.[17]

No comment is made on the apparent womanhood of all four partners. Reactions to marriages between women, then, seem to have been wholly at the discretion of the clergymen who married them.

Debt-ridden clergymen living in or near the Fleet prison in London were known for their unscrupulous approach to weddings. Male fortune-hunters made a practice of eloping with heiresses, buying quick 'Fleet weddings' that entitled them to all their wives' money, then deserting them. But these no-questions-asked weddings were also ideal for women marrying each other. The Fleet registers include several hints about female husbands which show that there were some attempts to prevent marriage between women, but no shock or fury at such marriages is recorded. On 15 December 1734, for example, a clergyman refused a marriage certificate to John Mountford, a tailor, and Mary Cooper, a spinster, both from Soho; 'Suspected 2 Women, no Certif', he noted briefly. A fuller note comes on 20 May 1737, when a clergyman married two Londoners, John Smith and Elizabeth Huthall, but recorded his doubts on the matter:

> By ye opinion after matrimony my Clark judg'd they were both women, if ye person by name John Smith be a man, he's a little short fair thin man not above 5 foot. After marriage I almost co[ul]d prove [the]m both women, the one was dress'd as a man thin pale face & wrinkled chin.

Such a note shows that both clerk and clergyman found it conceivable that women would want to marry each other, and that, despite their suspicions, the officials went ahead with the ceremony and seem to have made no attempt to have the couple punished. A similar note of 1 October 1747 concerns the marriage of another pair of Londoners, John Ferren and Deborah Nolan: 'The supposed John Ferren was discovered after [th]e Ceremonie were over, to be in person a woman.'[18] How was she discovered, and what happened next? The note suggests that, the ceremony being over before discovery, the clergyman took no further action.

Lord Hardwicke's Marriage Act of 1753, which was intended to end Fleet weddings, increase parental control and keep the privileges of marriage more exclusive, should have made illicit weddings between women more difficult. Not only was parental consent now needed if the bride was under 21, but all weddings had to be publicly registered, so fraud would be easier to trace. However, reports of female husbands continue throughout the rest of the century.

A series of fairly brief accounts in a popular newspaper, the *London Chronicle*, treats female marriage with surprising indulgence, more often viewing it as an eccentricity than as a crime. In late May 1759, for example, the paper reports that a soldier being treated in Edinburgh Royal Infirmary has been discovered to be a woman. She has served most patriotically for three years, and 'managed matters so dexterously, that though she lately married a wife, her story was still kept a secret from the regiment'.[19] The writer makes no comment on whether or how the soldier kept the secret from her wife; he seems interested only in how she was perceived within the army.

The following January in York, one John Brown tried to enlist but was recognised by an old acquaintance as Barbara Hill, a York woman who had disappeared, leaving nothing but her feminine clothes, fifteen years before. The *Chronicle* describes the jobs her male role has enabled her to hold, from apprentice stonecutter to London postchaise driver. Around 1755, the report claims, Barbara Hill married a woman 'with whom she has lived very agreeably ever since'. This report is unusual in commenting on the quality of the marriage and in giving some idea of the wife's reaction to her husband's exposure as a woman: 'On her sex being discovered after her enlisting, her supposed wife came to town in great affliction, begging that they might not be parted.'[20] This line suggests either that the wife knew all along about her husband's gender or that her love was not diminished by the discovery; the reporter's tone is appreciative, almost approving.

Only two months later came a case which the *London Chronicle* did treat as criminal. The handsome, hardworking Samuel Bundy was exposed as a woman and committed to Southwark Bridewell 'for defrauding a young woman of money and apparel, by marrying her'. The report, claiming to be based on her own account, tells how the defendant was coerced into boy's clothes by a male abducter when she was 13. Giving up a life at sea in her mid-teens, she worked as a painter and 'was taken notice of by a young woman' whom, at the age of 19 or so, she married. The only strains on their marriage seem to have been economic:

> Quitting her master upon some dispute between them, she was obliged to depend upon her wife for support, who expended her money and pawned her clothes for her mate's maintenance, which is the fraud she is charged with: the adopted husband says, the wife soon discovered the mistake she had made, but was determined for some time not to expose the matter.

The logic here is hard to follow. The wife, we are told, discovered that her husband was a woman, but did not intend to prosecute. Only when she found herself bearing the financial burdens did she go to the courts. But surely the female husband's crime was being female, not being a bad provider? If the wife's financial sacrifice was voluntary, then how could she claim she was defrauded? This report gives more detail than most about the participants' emotions. The husband, we are told, enlisted as a sailor to escape poverty, but ran away from ships twice, first to escape discovery and the second time simply 'to return to the wife, whom (she says) she dearly loves'. It is not quite clear at what point the wife became exasperated and had her husband sent to jail. But she seems to have changed her mind again at once: 'there seems a strong love, or friendship, on the other side, as she keeps the prisoner company in her confinement.'[21] Notice that the word 'love' can be used easily to describe what the husband feels for the wife – an active desire – but the reporter shies away from attributing an equal passion to the wife, and suggests it may have been more like 'friendship'. Even when both are biologically female, the wife's feminine role means that such strong and deviant passion must not be attributed to her. Another point of interest is that the husband prides herself on the fact that 'she never knew any other man than her seducer'; despite her having married a woman, she presents herself as sexually virtuous because of her avoidance of men.

A follow-up report two weeks later adds some details: the unnamed woman is made into a fictional-sounding heroine, becoming 'Samuel Bundy, alias Sarah Paul, the female husband'. The reporter describes how the case came before the justice, but 'the prosecutrix, Mary Parlour, her bride, not appearing against her, she was discharged'. So the court depends on the ill-will of the female husband's wife; where a wife, even at the last minute, decides that she is happy in the marriage, the state (it seems) cannot pass sentence. All the judge can do is burn Sarah Paul's masculine clothes, and warn her 'never more to appear in that character'.[22] He must know from the behaviour of the wife as well as the husband that women can love each other, but it is hard to prove and there is no British law against it; all he can destroy are the clothes that facilitate such courtship and marriage.

In February 1764 the *London Chronicle* reported the death in Middlesex of John Chivy, a woman who had passed undetected as a male farmer until the end of her life. 'Notwithstanding she had been married upwards of 20 years, her sex never discovered till her death.'[23] Does this mean that the wife – from whom Chivy separated a few years before her death – never knew her husband was a woman, or does it suggest that she knew but never, even after separation, let that knowledge out? Like most of the *Chronicle* reports, this one leaves much unsaid but is startlingly calm about female marriage. Despite the 1753 Marriage Act, then, female marriage seems to have flourished in the mid-eighteenth century. Though the reports tend to treat each case on its own, the similarity in phrasing gives a sense that the female husband is not a one-off freak but quite a common social phenomenon.

Two cases reported in the 1770s were given the minimum of publicity and presented as simple financial fraud. In June 1773 the *Gentleman's Magazine* gave an account (later picked up by the *Annual Register*) of the satisfactory foiling of a young crossdresser who married a richer, older woman. 'The old woman was possessed of 100l [£100], and the design was to get possession of the money, and then to make off; but the old lady proved too knowing.'[24] On 5 July 1777 the *Gentleman's Magazine* mentioned a woman sentenced to six months in jail 'for going in man's cloaths, and being married to three different women by a fictitious name, and for defrauding them of money and effects.'[25] The woman's name was Ann Marrow. She was sentenced to sit in the pillory before beginning her jail sentence; the rubbish thrown at her by an incensed crowd left her blind.[26] Unlike the *London Chronicle* reports, which concentrate on the affectionate aspects of female marriage, these brief accounts in the *Gentleman's Magazine* and *Annual Register* are about exploitation and punishment. It is hard to tell whether it is the cases that are different, or the reporters' attitudes.

There is also a tradition of broadsheets telling, in verse or comic prose, of female marriage; here the emphasis is usually on the wife's uncomprehending irritation with her husband's incapacity. 'The Counterfeit Bridegroom' is a one-page publication from around 1720 that tells the story of a woman in Southwark who in an advertisement of 1695 offered £200 to any man who would marry her daughter. The lucky husband is described as 'a Young Smock fac'd [pale] pretended Youth, lately arrived from *Ireland*, under the disguis'd name of Mr. K_ a Squires Son'. On the wedding night there is no 'real Performance, excepting now and then a kiss or two'; the wife mopes around for some time before investigating with a curious hand and finding that her husband is a woman. On discovery, this 'cheating Female Jilt of *Salisbury-Court* Society' escapes with the £200.

'The Female Husband, A New Song' was sung and sold in the late eighteenth century; this ballad offers a comic contrast between the young wife's eagerness and her husband's apparent coldness on the wedding night. 'The poor innocent Bride' pouts for six months, until by chance her hand 'discover'd her husband was of her own sex':

> Provok'd very much to a justice she went,
> And told him the cause of her discontent,
> Who granted a warrant unto you I tell,
> And the sham husband sent unto Southwark bridewell.

The mention of Southwark Bridewell (prison) may suggest that this ballad is based on the case of Sarah Paul, alias Samuel Bundy, who was sent there in 1760; however, the song is full of conventional elements and may be pure fiction.

One female husband case that was treated quite differently was that of Mary East, reported in the July, August and October 1766 issues of the *Gentleman's Magazine*. Unlike the other female husbands, she was not accused of deceiving her wife or of making love to her with any bodily or artificial 'female member'. But in her outrageously successful attempt to live for decades as a respectable married man, East can be said to have stolen more male power than the more flamboyant female husbands did.

In the first report, on 10 July 1766, readers of the *Gentleman's Magazine* are told that in the English town of Poplar, 'two women had lived together for six and thirty years, as man and wife, and kept a public house, without ever being suspected.' In case anyone might jump to a cynical conclusion, the writer hurries to add that sad circumstances forced this strange choice: 'Both had been crossed in love when young, and had chosen this method to avoid farther importunities.'

A full-length article in the August issue expands this hint – on the basis of further evidence, or (more likely) wishful thinking – into a step-by-step explanation. In this colourful version, the 16-year-old Mary East (fictionalised into 'our heroine') loses her beloved suitor, who has been discovered to be a highwayman and sentenced to transportation. It just so happens, according to the report, that Mary's best friend, aged 17, has been similarly crossed in love. They decide to shut their hearts to other men, and to pose as wife and husband.

I find this story most improbable. Even if we believe that two teenage girls would make such an absolute decision about the rest of their lives, why would that decision entail a disguise? Though the field of employment for single women had certainly narrowed in the eighteenth century, it was not entirely closed, especially at the levels below the upper and upper-middle classes. Mary East and her friend could have farmed, done needlework or run a small shop; it was considered acceptable for spinster friends to live together and they would not have come under special attack. If these two women had lived together as spinsters, they could have kept a sexual relationship secret. Bearing all that in mind, their decision to pose as a married couple must have been less a matter of economics than of love. Living in disguise as a husband and wife could have enabled desire, giving them a heterosexual model for their erotic life. Most importantly, perhaps, it would have been the only way for these two women to be treated as a couple, to receive the validation and respect of their neighbours. And if, as the *Gentleman's Magazine* report claims, their main motive was to keep themselves safe from male advances, then that surely implies something about the exclusivity of their devotion too.

But the tone of the August account continues firmly businesslike, leaving no room for commentary on romantic friendship or suspicions of unnatural passion. 'Having consulted on the most prudent method of proceeding', we are informed, 'it was proposed that one of them should put on man's apparel.' Though the emotions are vague, the financial details are precise: they toss a halfpenny to decide on roles (Mary East becoming the husband, 'James How'), they have a combined fortune of £30, out of which they buy East a man's suit, and in thirty-six years of innkeeping they save over £3,000. Mr and Mrs How become pillars of the community. He serves in almost every town office, ignoring the odd comment on his 'effeminacy'. Neighbours find them scrupulously punctual, honest and respectable.

All goes well until an old acquaintance from their home town, Mrs Bentley, recognises the Hows and decides that they are worth blackmailing. She obtains £10 in 1750, then leaves them alone for another peaceful stint of fifteen years; falling on hard times again in 1765, she demands more money. When it fails to arrive she hires two men – one described as 'mulatto', the other presumably white – who drag East/How into the fields, and accuse her of theft and impersonation, with threats like 'you b—-h had you not better give us the 100l [£100] than be hanged?'

At the time of the attack, Mrs How is staying with her brother in Essex in an attempt to improve her health. Feeling death to be imminent, she sends for her 'husband', who for some reason fails to come. Perhaps James How is preoccupied with Mrs Bentley's threats, or maybe the relationship is going through a bad patch? Feeling deserted, the 'wife' tells her brother everything before she dies, and makes a will leaving to her relations half of what she estimates the How business is worth.

Harassed by Mrs Bentley's thugs, East/How confides in a male friend, who brings the blackmail case to the magistrates. When the dead wife's brother turns up, we are told, Mary East 'at first endeavoured to support her assumed character, but being closely pressed, she at length owned the fact'. This suggests that she would prefer to live on in a male role, even after the death of her wife. But her options are limited. She changes back into skirts, to the relief of everyone concerned; the *Gentleman's Magazine* reports with satisfaction that now 'she appeared to be a sensible well-bred woman, though in her male character she had always affected the plain plodding alehouse-keeper'. In court, however, 'her awkward behaviour in her new assumed habit, caused great diversion to all'. No doubt this shames her, but at least she is not the one on trial.

Despite the mockery Mary East endured, what could she be charged with? Not deception of 'Mrs How', since the women had planned the disguise together; not a fraudulent marriage, since they had never aspired to a legal wedding ceremony. Even if a crime called lesbianism had been on the English statute-books, it is most unlikely that Mary East would have been accused of it, as she was a respectable, prosperous, ageing member of a loyal community which sent witnesses to attest to the Hows' characters. At the trial, and in every British writer's analysis of their case until well into the twentieth century, the Hows were given the benefit of the doubt.

Mrs Bentley and the 'mulatto' man were brought to court; the white man had escaped. The only record we have of a sentence, mentioned in the *Gentleman's Magazine* on 21 October, is that William Barwick got four years in Newgate for blackmail. (Since his role was minor, we can deduce some racist scapegoating here.) Mary East won her case but lost her status and community; she gave half the fortune to her wife's brother and retired to another part of Poplar until her death in 1781.

My version of the case is a composite of the three *Gentleman's Magazine* reports and a piece in *Kirby's Wonderful and Eccentric Museum* of 1820.[27] However, these accounts are full of ambiguities and missing details. For example, different texts offer different explanations of Mary's exposure; sometimes it is said to have been due to blackmail, sometimes to the wife telling her brother. Much of the evidence cited sounds as though it was invented to pad out the little that was known about the Hows' life together. Though the story endured, writers seemed content to add layers of conventional speculations rather than going back to look for details that might disrupt their safe, sexless reading of this female marriage.

A further account by a clergyman in 1825 paints a bleak picture of the couple's strategies to ensure secrecy: 'They were never known to cook a joint of meat for their own use, to employ any help, or to entertain private friends in their house.'[28] Despite their public roles as innkeepers, these women seem to have lived in isolation because they could not risk letting servants or friends too close. Even if we imagine a secret, romantic and sexual bond between Mary East and her wife for thirty-six years, the price of deception must have been high. Perhaps that shows how much they needed to live as a couple – the strength of desire and will that led such women to become female husbands, and female husbands' wives.

Mary Hamilton

One story that has survived in some detail in a fictional form is that of Mary Hamilton. We know few facts about her except that she was arrested in Glastonbury on 13 September 1746, accused of posing as a physician (Dr Charles or George Hamilton) and of duping Mary Price of Wells into marriage two months earlier. As usual in such cases, no appropriate title could be found for her crime. Instead she was charged, under a clause in the vagrancy act, with 'imposing on His Majesty's subjects', and was sentenced to four public whippings and six months' hard labour.

The case received relatively little publicity, just a couple of accounts in provincial papers that were eventually picked up by the London magazines. But it did catch the eye of Henry Fielding, writer and brother of the novelist Sarah Fielding. At that time he was working on a translation of Ovid concerned chiefly with the quirks of 'Women's raging Desires'.[29] He quickly turned the brief newspaper accounts of Mary Hamilton into an anonymous pamphlet, *The Female Husband*, which has been an embarrassment to Fielding scholars ever since. It sold rapidly in two editions of 1,000 each in November 1746; at sixpence, it would have been just within the reach of shopkeepers, apprentices and domestic servants with a little cash to spare. The story lingered on and was turned into a more elaborate anonymous chapbook called *The Surprising Adventures of a Female Husband* (1813). It is noteworthy for being one of the only tales in which marriage between women is presented explicitly as a matter of love and desire.

Though Fielding claimed the story was 'taken from her own Mouth', there is no evidence that he had even read Mary Hamilton's court deposition. He seems to have scanned a few newspaper reports, reduced the number of Hamilton's wives from the rumoured fourteen to the more credible three, and woven his own version around the bare bones of her story; one scrupulous critic has estimated that the end product is 13 per cent fact.[30] Fielding could have had access to the facts had he wanted, since his cousin David Gould was a lawyer working on the case, but he evidently preferred having room to fictionalise. As Terry Castle sees it, this process silences deviance: 'Making Hamilton over into a "fictive" personage is a way of transferring the troubling historical facts of female transvestism and homosexuality into the safe realm of literature.'[31] That may have been Fielding's motive, but I would argue that the effect was quite otherwise. Without *The Female Husband*, the little-known 'troubling historical facts' of Mary Hamilton's life would have been forgotten within weeks; there was no evidence that her case was shaking society, or that she would ever have been allowed to tell her own story. Within the not-so-safe realm of literature, however, she became a memorable 'fictive' character and taught several thousand readers that a woman could fall in love with women and satisfy them sexually and emotionally, even if she had to find a rather roundabout way of doing it. Though parts of Fielding's text are deeply hostile to Hamilton and other parts are clearly intended as titillation for heterosexual readers, *The Female Husband* can (and could in 1746) be read as an adventure story, a saga of lesbian survival.

In his attempt to show that anyone can fall to such moral depths, Fielding emphasises what a normal and likeable girl Mary Hamilton is. She causes no trouble to her mother, a sergeant's widow, 'nor did she in her younger years discover the least proneness to any kind of vice, much less give cause of suspicion that she would one day disgrace her sex by the most abominable and unnatural pollutions'. Fielding is calling same-sex desire abominable, yet he is also showing that it can happen to anyone, that lesbians are not aliens. With refreshing bluntness, he explains that Mary Hamilton 'was first seduced by one *Anne Johnson*', a Methodist who 'converts' Mary Hamilton to her religion and sexuality simultaneously. This seduction is presented as a kind of brainwashing, but the delights of being converted are clear. Sexual innuendo is played out through religious vocabulary: Anne Johnson is described as 'no novice in impurity, which, as she confess'd, she had learnt and often practiced at *Bristol* with her methodistical sisters'. Fielding's main motive for linking the two seductions is to mock Methodism, but the connection also functions to suggest that women's love for each other is an 'Enthusiasm' in the religious sense, a deep idealism that may finally overflow moral boundaries.

Economic manipulation is presented as another factor in the seduction. When they have become 'inseparable companions', we are told, '*Molly Hamilton* was prevail'd on to leave her mother's house, and to reside entirely with Mrs. *Johnson*, whose fortune was not thought inconsiderable.' So the seductress uses her financial autonomy to gain access to the dependent Hamilton as a bedfellow. Next she moves the household to Bristol, cutting Hamilton off from her mother. Trying to explain desire as a divergence from friendly love rather than the logical extension of it, Fielding shows his readers that the cooler Anne Johnson is the sexual initiator, and that the one who lusts most loves least:

> Young Mrs. *Hamilton* began to conceive a very great affection for her friend, which perhaps was not returned with equal faith by the other ... As *Molly Hamilton* was extremely warm in her inclinations, and as those inclinations were so violently attached to Mrs. *Johnson*, it would not have been difficult for a less artful woman, in the most private hours, to turn the ardour of enthusiastic devotion into a different kind of flame.

This opposition is unconvincing. Hamilton's warm affection and violent ardour already sound like the sexual love into which they will be perverted; the flames are not so 'different' at all. The implications are startling; though Fielding's conscious intention seems to have been to isolate and attack lesbians, what he is suggesting is that any intimate friendship can be twisted towards the unnatural if even one of the partners is moderately 'artful'. So no one is safe; the spectre of the tribade stands behind every loving friend.

Fielding's attitude to sexual details is similarly ambivalent. He can be frank and witty up to a point, but then retreats into the stern clichés of euphemism: 'Their conversation, therefore, soon became in the highest manner criminal, and transactions not fit to be mention'd past between them.'[32] Terry Castle suggests that the tone swings in this way because the text is aimed at two distinct audiences – male libertine readers wanting titillation and virtuous women seeking a moral lesson.[33] As for rebellious women readers, I suggest it is for fear they might learn too much about the strategies and techniques of sexual deviance that the text must pause to censor itself as it goes along.

Female readers are allowed to identify with Mary Hamilton only up to a point. If the early lesbian experience described in *The Female Husband* sounds attractive, then Anne Johnson's story represents the correct escape route. Wooed in secret by a handsome Methodist called Rogers, she opts for heterosexual married bliss. On her wedding day she writes a note of smug repentance to Hamilton:

> Follow my example now, as you before did my temptation, and enter as soon as you can into that holy state ... in which, tho' I am yet but a novice, believe me, there are delights infinitely surpassing the faint endearments we have experienc'd together.

But there was nothing 'faint' about the affair from Hamilton's perspective. When she gets the note, she is shown responding with the ritual gestures of a wronged spouse: 'she tore her hair, beat her breasts, and behaved in as outrageous a manner as the fondest husband could, who had unexpectedly discovered the infidelity of a beloved wife'. The marital vocabulary is used to mock Hamilton, but it also has the effect of giving credence to her spouse-like feelings and hinting at her future career as a female husband.

In her fury, we are told, Hamilton decides to disguise herself as a man, in order to make a living as a travelling Methodist teacher (and, it is implied, to have male status and access to women). Though her decision is presented as unprecedented and eccentric, Fielding does not call her a monster or a hermaphrodite. Subtler comic effects can be achieved by depicting her as a slightly effeminate and 'most beautiful youth' going by the name of Charles Hamilton. Her next attempt at pairing up with a woman is a failure. In Dublin she lodges with a widow and quickly forms a plan of 'gaining the lady's affection, and then discovering herself to her, hoping to have had the same success which Mrs.

Johnson had found with her'.[34] It is most unusual for a text about a female husband to show her intending to call a halt to the deception and to woo and seduce a woman in complete honesty. It doesn't work for Mary, however; the widow mocks 'Charles Hamilton's' effeminacy and marries an Irish cadet instead.

By the time of her next attempt, also in Ireland, Hamilton is less optimistic about finding an open-minded lover but more confident in her ability to maintain her masculine disguise, even in bed. When the wealthy Widow Rushford falls for her boyish figure, it occurs to Hamilton to marry her – for her money rather than for her 67-year-old body, we are assured. Fielding assumes that sexual desire is not a motive for Hamilton this time, since 'with this old lady, whose fortune only she was desirous to possess, such views would have afforded very little gratification'. Their merry public wedding is described with contempt for the sexuality of older women. Hamilton's secret unsuitability as a husband is paralleled by the impropriety of the old bride, who dresses like a girl and will not let the parson omit the prayer for fruitfulness. They are both described as unnatural; as the great-grandson comments, though the bridegroom has no beard, the bride does.

For a while, all is well. The resourceful female husband may be (technically speaking) fooling the bride, but the sexual satisfaction she offers is not illusory. Hamilton's lovemaking pleases the widow far more than her previous heterosexual experiences; after a few days of marriage she is 'so well satisfied with her choice, that being in company with another old lady, she exulted so much in her happiness, that her friend began to envy her, and could not forbear inveighing against effeminacy in men.' The wife defends her virile husband as 'the best man in *Ireland*'.

Hamilton's more-than-phallic sexual power comes and goes, however, since she does not always have her dildo in place. One crudely comic scene shows that when on one occasion the wife gets lusty, 'our poor bridegroom ... having not at that time *the wherewithal* about her, was obliged to remain meerly passive, under all this torrent of kindness of his wife'. Fielding casually compares this to male impotence – which begs the question, if all men are liable to drops in potency, is maleness itself a matter of flux, of luck? For Mary Hamilton at least, a masculine identity is never secure. One night the widow's curious, fondling hand discovers the significant absence: 'Undone! I am married to one who is no man.'[35] Her hysteria gives Hamilton a chance to run away and return to England.

We next meet her at Totness as 'Dr. Hamilton', who manages to cure and elope with a Miss Ivythorn. After a happy fortnight of marriage, Hamilton is woken one night by her wife weeping. 'Have you not married me a poor young girl, when you know, you have not ... you have not ... what you ought to have.' At this point Hamilton makes a last brave attempt to convert a pseudo-heterosexual marriage to a lesbian partnership by shifting the attention from what she ought to have and has not, to what she does have to offer. 'The Doctor endeavoured to pacify her, by every kind of promise, and telling her she would have all the pleasures of marriage with none of the inconveniences.' The miserable wife refuses to be persuaded, and Hamilton has to escape before morning.

Her third marriage, to a reputedly lovely 18-year-old, Mary Price, takes place in Wells, Somersetshire. Though Fielding introduces this development by telling us that Hamilton goes to Wells 'in quest of new adventures', he soon drops the terms of gallantry and admits that this love is real. 'With this girl, hath this wicked woman since her confinement really declared, she was really much in love, as it was possible for a man ever to be with one of her own sex.' Considering the general understanding of lesbian desire as wickedness, this grudging testimony that the two were 'in love' is suprisingly positive. Class is an element in the seduction; as the rich Anne Johnson once manipulated the impressionable Molly Hamilton, now the apparently professional 'Dr. Hamilton' courts the humble Molly Price by arranging a 'dancing among the inferior sort of people' and sending eloquent letters to which Price returns misspelled answers. Price thinks herself the unqualified one for such a marriage, because of her lowly origins; in her naive devotion to the doctor she ignores all rumours of his effeminacy and she even manages to forget a fight in which the doctor's torn shirt reveals a curvaceous breast. During the first few months of marriage, the happy bride recounts her husband's sexual prowess in terms which no one can credit: 'she asserted some things which staggered her mother's belief, and made her cry out, O child, there is no such thing in human nature'. These indirect descriptions may be intended to titillate male readers, but they actually serve to inflate the unmentionable dildo to the point where it far outdoes the penis it is meant to imitate.

But Hamilton's confidence is her downfall. Despite the rumours about effeminacy, gossip from her last adventure in Totness, and her being pelted with mud by a suspicious mob, she stays on in Wells. Lulled by Mary Price's devotion, she cannot think of herself as a criminal: 'as to danger, she was not sufficiently versed in the laws to apprehend any'. *The Female Husband* reaches a crisis when Price's mother turns in her false son-in-law, producing as evidence 'something of too vile, wicked and scandalous a nature, which was found in the Doctor's trunk'. This is an interesting divergence from the known facts of the court case, for the real Mary Price reported her husband herself. Fielding's characterisation of Mary Price is an odd mixture of opposites. She is humble and virginal, yet boasts of sexual fulfilment; gullible, yet firm in resisting interference from friends. 'She said she had chosen for herself only, and that if she was pleased, it did not become people to trouble their heads with what was none of their business.'[36] However, Fielding is unwilling to contemplate that she might have known exactly what she was doing when she married a woman.

The real Mary Price reported Hamilton while they were travelling, far from any relative who might have bullied her. It was clearly her choice to do so. According to her deposition,

> the said pretended Charles Hamilton ... entered her Body several times, which made this Examinant believe, at first, that the said Hamilton was a real Man, but soon had reason to Judge that the said Hamilton was not a Man but a Woman.[37]

'Soon' was in fact two months. Could it be that Mary Price discovered her husband's sex as quickly as the other wives had done, but held her peace and only reported her when their relationship turned sour? (This was the sequence of events which led to the execution of a German female husband, Catharina Linck, in 1721.)[38] Fielding clearly wanted to present their marriage as more idyllic than it was in real life – possibly for dramatic suspense, more likely to stress the innocence and ignorance of the 'normal' woman, the female husband's wife.

As for Mary Hamilton, she was whipped in four towns, her androgynous beauty sacrificed to the public view: 'so lovely a skin scarified with rods, in such a manner that her back was almost flead'. In case this might sound like a heroic love story, Fielding reassures us that the bleeding Hamilton played the rake in Bridewell, trying to bribe the jailer 'to procure her a young girl to satisfy her most monstrous and unnatural desires'. The ending is cynical, the moral stern; as with earlier criminal biographies such as Daniel Defoe's *Moll Flanders* (1722), Fielding claims that this text is a warning, intended 'to deter all others from the commission of any such foul and unnatural crimes'. But determent is an interesting concept; it implies that the readers are capable of, or even thinking of committing, the crime in question. So lesbian transvestism can be situational; it is a crime within any woman's scope. Fielding's conclusion is less morally ambiguous than the rest of the story: 'unnatural affections', he trumpets, 'are equally vicious and detestable in both sexes'.[39] In his sympathy for his heroine, however, he has shown her to be neither vicious nor detestable. A lesbian reader of *The Female Husband* would learn that she was not monstrous, only immoral, at times distinctly heroic – and, most importantly, that there were 'others' out there whom nothing could deter.

Catherine Vizzani

A text which has received far less critical attention is the largely conjectural biography of a 'passing woman' and lesbian, Catherine Vizzani, written in 1744 by Professor Giovanni Bianchi of the University of Siena, who had performed her autopsy. Translated by John Cleland as *An Historical and Physical Dissertation on the Case of Catherine Vizzani* (1751), it was reissued as *The True History and Adventures of Catherine Vizzani* in 1755.[40] Despite Cleland's outraged interjections, Bianchi's basic liking for his heroine shines through the work. *Catherine Vizzani* is an example of the many translations from liberal continental authors which reached British readers and widened the margins of moral judgement.

The text is startlingly calm about lesbian sexuality; from the frontispiece, which shows her in men's clothes courting a gentlewoman, to the final details of the post mortem, this book is frank about Catherine's exclusive, passionate interest in women. (This so shocked a journalist in the *Monthly Review* for March 1751 that he refused to mention any more than the book's title, being 'sure that the female part' of his audience would appreciate the tact of this omission.) As in Fielding's *The Female Husband*, the tone swings frequently, from condemnation of Catherine, to an irrepressible admiration for her 'masculine' attributes of courage and persistance, and back to disapproval.[41]

According to Bianchi – though we must remember that this is probably guesswork, since he claims to have only a few secondhand reports of her – Catherine Vizzani was born in 1718 or 1719, the daughter of a carpenter in Rome. Despite her artisan origins and lifelong career as a servant, she is described on the title page as 'a young Gentlewoman'. This could have been a deliberate lie to help sell the book, or it could reflect her anomalous position on the margins of classes and genders. By the age of 13 – the conventional time for sexual maturing – Catherine is a lesbian. Bianchi knows which tradition to fit her into; he describes her as surpassing '*Sappho*, or any of the *Lesbian* Nymphs, in an Attachment to those of her own Sex'. Catherine is not seduced or influenced by an older woman; in fact, Bianchi has no interest in producing a 'cause' for her sexual orientation.

> When she came to her fourteenth Year, the Age of Love in our forward Climate, she was reserved and shy towards young Men, but would be continually romping with her own Sex, and some she caressed with all the Eagerness and Transports of a Male Lover.

Bianchi quickly hones in on her partiality for one girl: 'above all, she was passionately enamoured with one *Margaret*, whose Company she used to court, under Pretence of learning Embroidery'. Instead of the tomboy background we might expect in a transvestite biography, we learn that Catherine exploits the customs of feminine society, such as unsupervised sewing lessons, to get what she wants. Similarly, she starts crossdressing not for the thrill of it but as a means to an end, so that she can spend her nights underneath Margaret's window. It is clear that Margaret approves of the costume and returns the love, though Bianchi does not think it was sexually consummated. 'In all Appearance, her Pleasure must be limited to the viewing *Margaret*'s captivating Charms, and saying soft Things to her. This whimsical Amour went on very quietly for above two Years.' Words like 'whimsical' and 'pranks' reflect the author's amused attitude rather than that of the girls, who take their love seriously – as does Margaret's father, who finds Catherine serenading his daughter with 'fervid Expressions of Love' one night and threatens to report her to the city governor.[42] We are not told what he says to his daughter; Margaret is not given a voice in the story and soon drops from view.

Catherine flees in disguise as 'Giovanni Bordoni' and charms a series of churchmen into giving her help and jobs. Restless and unsatisfied in the world of male camaraderie, she moves from employer to employer. Her passion for women, which becomes more general after the loss of Margaret, irritates her masters. One unusual aspect of the story is the support she receives from her parents. Her mother is loyal throughout; having heard the whole story in a letter from Catherine, she marches off to obtain references for 'Giovanni's' first job. When a churchman complains to Peter Vizzani about his lecherous 'son' the reader expects a shock dénouement, but instead it gradually becomes clear that the father is in the know too and is just as wryly accepting as his wife. Trying not to laugh at the pompous clergyman, Peter comments of his 'son' that 'since such was the Case, and the Vigour of his Constitution not to be repressed by Words or Blows, Nature must e'en take its Course.'[43] This defence of 'Giovanni's' high libido as a product of 'Nature' hints, by analogy, at Peter's acceptance of his daughter's lesbianism.

Catherine is described as 'incessantly following the Wenches, and being so barefaced and insatiable in her Amours'; she gets venereal disease twice, as well as a stabbing from a jealous male rival. It sounds as if she has a series of short or overlapping relationships with women, though this is never made clear. Catherine uses a strap-on dildo, described in a roundabout way as 'several delusive Impudicities'; apparently it deceives, and profoundly pleases, all the women she has sex with. Her fame spreads and 'within a short Time, it was whispered about that *Giovanni* was the best Woman's Man, and the most addicted to that alluring Sex'. Proud of her reputation, we are told, 'she hugged herself with such Pride and Delight'. It is difficult to know how to read this part of the biography. Could so many sexually experienced women have been fooled by a dildo in the dark, when many female husbands seem to have been found out, even by timid and naive wives, within a few weeks? It seems much more likely that at least some of her lovers knew her to be a woman and that her fame was based on coded recommendations. As for Bianchi, he is baffled by Catherine's success. Later in the book he calls her foolish for trying 'to amuse [women] with passionate Addresses; to kindle in them Desires, without the Power of Gratification'.[44] However, his own narrative has shown that she has no difficulty in gratifying women; the traditional mockery of lesbian impotence fails to fit the story.

Another thing that puzzles the author is Catherine's utter lack of interest in even the most handsome of men. Bisexuality he could just about comprehend, but not this exclusive devotion to women. Catherine often shares a bed with male servants, Bianchi comments in puzzlement, yet never makes 'any advances to her Bedfellow, though he were an *Adonis*'. He finds it odd, and rather admirable, that Catherine holds out 'against any Inclination or Love for a Man, though living continually in the utmost Freedom with them'. Heterosexuality is described as 'a Passion universally natural to young Women', but Bianchi begins to question the universality of something that is never triggered in his heroine.[45]

Catherine Vizzani goes almost all the way to being a female husband. Giovanni, we are told, has 'the Presumption to offer his Addresses to a very lovely young Gentlewoman, Niece to the Minister of the Village ... they both grew passionately in Love with one another'. This gentlewoman, Maria, agrees to elope and be married in Rome; we are not told whether she knows her future husband is a woman, but her commitment is clear. However, she is indiscreet enough to tell her younger sister Priscilla, who insists they bring her too, or else she will tell her uncle. Giovanni willingly takes them both, but this slows the party down and the uncle's chaplain and servants catch up with them on their journey. Outnumbered and, like Mary Hamilton, over-optimistic about the lawyers' ignorance of lesbianism, Vizzani decides to give in. She is sure that 'one Girl's running away with two others might, in a Court of Justice, if it should go that Length, be slightly passed over as a Frolick, rather than severely animadverted upon as a Crime'.

The case never gets to court, but for a more horrifying reason. Just as Vizzani is surrendering, the spiteful chaplain forces the servant to fire and both Catherine and a passing boy are shot in the legs. Maria and Priscilla are hurried into 'a Conservatory of recluse Ladies', while the boy and Catherine lie in hospital dying of gangrene. As her body swells, Vizzani has to unstrap and remove her 'leathern Contrivance, of a Cilindrical Figure'. It is found under her pillow by the trainee surgeons, who, never having seen a dildo before, 'immediately were for ripping it up, concluding that it contained Money, or something else of Value, but they found it stuffed only with old Rags'.[46] They can discover no solid core to her phallic power; it takes an educated eye to see in Catherine's dildo anything more than old rubbish.

On one level a virile stud, on another Catherine Vizzani is presented as the epitome of purity. Before her death at the age of 24 she confesses everything to a kind woman, in order that 'she might be buried in a Woman's Habit, and with the Garland on her Head, an honorary Ceremony observed among us in the Burial of Virgins'. Her virginity is evidently very important to her, as a symbol not of sexual innocence but of being untouched by men. Others value it too – some religous people call her a saint for preserving her 'chastity', which the author finds rather ironic. But even he is impressed by the evidence of her intact hymen. The other thing that strikes Bianchi during the autopsy is the normality of Catherine's genitals, the lack of any hermaphroditical oddity. Banishing the myth that tribadism depends on having a giant member, he explains that her clitoris is in fact on the small side. As her father insisted more simply many years before, Catherine is 'as truly, in all Respects, a Female, as the Woman who bore her'.[47]

At this point our translator, John Cleland, can bear no more of Bianchi's sympathetic commentary. Cleland has already intervened on several occasions to explain why he is censoring unnecessary and 'nauseous' sexual details, which, 'if agreeable to the *Italian Goût*, would shock the Delicacy of our Nation'. At the end, he reproaches Bianchi at length for failing to offer an origin for Catherine's lesbianism. It seems not to be the usual anatomical defect, Cleland reasons, but it could be due to the Italian climate, since 'in a warm Country like theirs, where Impurities of all Sorts are but too frequent, it may very well happen that such strange Accidents may, from Time to Time, arise'. The explanation Cleland likes best is a psychological one: Catherine must have 'had her Imagination corrupted early in her Youth, either by obscene Tales that were voluntarily told in her Hearing, or by privately listening to the Discourses of the Women, who are too generally corrupt in that Country'. Gathering confidence, the translator constructs a chain of causality in which hearing 'obscene Tales' leads to masturbation, which eventually causes 'a preternatural Change in the animal Spirits, and a Kind of venereal Fury'.[48] Behind the vague terms his message is clear: desiring women drives a woman mad.

Cleland reinforces this link with another anecdote of a female husband, this time an apothecary's wife. She runs away with her husband's money, lives as a gentleman, marries a lady and is promptly found out. Like the Vizzani story, this one ends bleakly; the shamed bride frets herself into a fever and early death, while the female husband is sent back to her apothecary husband who has her 'confined as a Lunatic' in an asylum where she dies within a few years. Cleland concludes with satisfaction that 'there is an amazing Violence in these vicious Irregularities'. But any reader could work out that in this case, as in Vizzani's, the deaths are caused by the punishment, not the crime.

Cleland was ahead of his time in concluding, in *Catherine Vizzani*, that lesbianism is a taste which originates not in the genitals but in the imagination. He ends by warning readers not to talk about perversions in front of children and not to let them near 'scandalous books', in case their sexual tastes become corrupted. But is *Catherine Vizzani* not one of these 'scandalous books'? Early writers always faced the fear that by describing, even by explicitly condemning lesbian sexuality, they were unwittingly advertising something that might never have occurred to readers. Cleland ends *Catherine Vizzani* in a state of paranoia; even women's mannish riding habits begin to seem sinister to him, and he warns that one of the 'ill Consequences' of the fashion of occasional crossdressing is lesbianism.[49] For this writer, who was so casual about playful lesbian sex in his popular erotic novel *Fanny Hill* only a couple of years before (see pp. 202–6), a single would-be female husband has filled the world with danger.

From the end of the eighteenth century, there certainly seems to have been less said about female husbands. In Holland, prosecutions of crossdressers for living in marital-style partnerships with women during the seventeenth century contrast with the trials of tribades for sodomy or 'dirty acts' with each other in the 1790s. All this proves is that lawyers and writers began to concentrate on a different aspect or interpretation of lesbian culture, though it has been read as evidence that female marriage was dying out.[50] Van de Pol and Dekker conclude that, with the increase in publicity about female sodomy at the end of the eighteenth century, lesbians no longer needed to think of themselves as husbands and wives to each other, so female marriage quickly became 'anachronistic'.[51] As I have not looked for cases beyond 1800, I cannot prove that it endured as a practice. However, cases brought to light in the 1980s, such as that of Billie Tipton, the twice-married jazz musician and adoptive father discovered to be a woman at death, show not only that it is still possible to pass for a lifetime and not be discovered, but that for some lovers of women in a hostile society, the husband role is the only one that offers enough privacy and dignity. As for the issue of gender fraud, that one is alive and well. The case of Jennifer Saunders, jailed in the early 1990s for having consensual sex with two women who afterwards claimed they had thought she was a man, raises many of the same issues as accounts of female husbands do. Lawmakers are still ready to believe that the non-crossdressed, 'normal' woman is innocent of lesbian desire, and there is still infinite resentment against the woman who usurps what heterosexual men see as their clothes, their role, their access to women.

3 The breeches part

Female crossdressing was central to British culture in this period, but it was a site of contradiction and double standards. While female husbands such as Mary Hamilton were being whipped and jailed for male impersonation, women were playing 'breeches parts' in roughly a quarter of all plays. Individual attitudes too were inconsistent and unpredictable; as Terry Castle has pointed out, Henry Fielding could denounce female transvestites in his translation of Juvenal's *Sixth Satire*, yet as a theatre manager hire the crossdressing actress Charlotte Charke to play male roles.[1] Hostility to female crossdressing does not seem to have borne any relation to the completeness of the disguise; some female soldiers who successfully passed as men were lauded for it, while other women were attacked for wearing unfeminine riding habits. The figure of the crossdresser was read in many different ways, depending on the circumstances, what her motives were thought to be, and how much she seemed to threaten the powers of men over women.

A rhyme about the actress Margaret (Peg) Woffington, who played both male and female roles, is often quoted to show the transparent, titillating quality of the breeches part:

> That excellent Peg,
> Who showed such a leg,
> When lately she dressed in men's clothes.

The second stanza, which shows her appeal to have been rather more complex, is less well known:

> A creature uncommon
> Who's both man and woman
> And chief of the belles and the beaux![2]

What is shown to be attractive here is not just Woffington's visible leg but her almost hermaphroditical glamour, which

'Anne Bonney [sic] and Mary Read convicted of piracy', from Daniel Defoe, A General History of the Robberies

appeals to both men and women. A breeches part actress may have been hired to show 'such a leg' and titillate men in the audience, but her effect (on women, for example) may have been quite different. Playing heterosexual male heroes, actresses like Woffington were licensed to court women on stage, and audiences seem to have loved watching them do it. Kristina Straub has argued persuasively that such actresses were increasingly seen as objects of desire for women, and that as the public became more aware of the threat posed by 'Sapphists' and 'tommies' towards the end of the eighteenth century, the breeches part was condemned and died out.[3]

There were other dramatic conventions that presented eroticism between women as a spectacle. Many plays of the late seventeenth and early eighteenth centuries feature assertive female characters who are crossdressed (on slim pretexts) for most of the action and flirt with other women in scenes of humour and erotic tension. Critics have assumed that such hints of lesbianism tantalised men in the audience;[4] what has received less attention is the response of women spectators. Examples of plays that feature this motif include Aphra Behn's *The Widow Ranter* (1689), Thomas Southerne's *Sir Anthony Love* (1690) and *Oroonoko* (1695), Colley Cibber's *The Lady's Last Stake* (1707) and Eliza Haywood's *A Wife to be Lett* (1723). Richard Steele's *The Tender Husband* (1705), which includes a scene of a female transvestite wooing another woman, was so popular with women that it played on Ladies' Nights (dates on which women could request the performance of a particular play) on average every two years during the first half of the eighteenth century.[5] The most uncomfortable moment in one such play is when Sylvia, the crossdressed heroine of George Farquhar's *The Recruiting Officer* (1706) flirts and eventually spends a night with her nurse's daughter, Rose, who emerges next day in bewilderment, complaining 'I don't know whether I had a Bedfellow or not.'[6] Neither do we. The obvious joke is that, though Rose doesn't know it, she has not had a 'Bedfellow' in the sense of a male heterosexual partner. But the audience cannot be sure what is being implied; what has happened to Rose in the night to make her so unsure about the nature of sex, about what being 'Bedfellows' means?

Randolph Trumbach claims that whereas male crossdressing was linked to sodomy after the early eighteenth century, the link was not made in the case of women until the end of that century. 'Most cross-dressing women did not dress as they did as a means of attracting other women. Some Sapphists began to do that only at the end of the eighteenth century.'[7] How can Trumbach know what were the intentions of women as they chose their clothes? And even if we leave aside the question of intention, we can find evidence that others saw a link between lesbian culture and cross-dressing in a variety of seventeenth- and eighteenth-century texts that hint at a connection between crossdressed (or even more subtly mannish) women and same-sex attraction.

Warnings against masquerades often hinted at the danger of cross-gender practices for women. For instance, the *Freethinker* cautioned in 1719 that the practice of women going to masquerades in masculine costumes blurred 'the Distinction of Sexes' and could lead to accidental (or intentional) lesbian seduction when 'a Countess listens to the Gallantry of a Chamber-Maid'.[8] Terry Castle has pointed out the horror of same-sex possibilities that often underlay attacks on crossdressing; these were mostly directed at men, but sometimes the capacity for exploitation of dress confusion in both sexes was noted. For example, on 14 December 1728 the *Universal Spectator* commented that every culture differentiated the sexes by dress for the sake of 'decency', and specifically 'in order to prevent Multitudes of Irregularities, which otherwise would continually be occasion'd'.[9] Exclusive heterosexuality could only be maintained by rigid costume codes; blur the lines between breeches and skirts and sexual 'Irregularities' would be sure to follow. Female crossdressing, then, could be indulged or condemned in British society, but in texts that mention it most uneasily, we often find the fear that crossdressing was expressing, facilitating, or in some way connected to lesbian desire.

In the first section of this chapter, 'Acting the lover as well as the soldier', I look at biographies of military women. Generally these texts insist on their subjects' loyalty to fiancés or husbands, but they also include intriguing episodes of flirtation with and commitment to women. Next I focus on two crucial texts about crossdressers, Charlotte Charke's autobiographical *Narrative* (1755) and Maria Edgeworth's novel *Belinda* (1801). Finally, in 'Amazons in petticoats', I broaden the discussion to look at texts featuring women who do not technically crossdress but who encroach on manhood with their voices, movements, manner, skills and passion for women. This chapter covers the spectrum of women for whom crossing gender lines was one central element, a 'breeches part' of their lives – something they did for half their time, as a disguise for some years, a leisure frolic, a stage career, or part of their daily dress. What I want to emphasise is the flexibility of their choices of sartorial signals to communicate resistance to heterosexual norms.

Women who loved women and who crossdressed or mixed gender signals have often been read as simply wanting to be men. As Marjorie Garber points out in *Vested Interests*, some modern psychologists still find female-to-male transsexualism a logical ambition but deny the existence of female transvestism, the specific and erotic thrill for a woman of wearing men's clothes.[10] This chapter is not about women wanting to live as men, but about women dipping in and out of masculine disguises, roles and styles, and the ways in which this influenced erotic expression between them, both practically and psychologically.

Acting the lover as well as the soldier

Memoirs of women passing as men in the military almost invariably include flirtation with or courtship of women. These episodes draw heavily on mistaken-courtship scenes in drama; their conventionality suggests we need not read them as fact. As Julie Wheelwright points out, they may have been intended to titillate heterosexual readers or to mock the crossdresser for aspiring to manhood.[11] However, we should not underestimate the way these scenes undermine the plots of marital loyalty, nor should we ignore the veiled hints they give us of the erotic adventures that female soldiers and sailors may have enjoyed.

Those who wrote or copied down these women's memoirs usually present encounters between women as amusing tests of the crossdresser's disguise; the challenge is for her to imitate male heterosexual behaviour with a naive girl or a lust-crazed older woman. But we need not read such episodes in the terms in which they are offered. In April 1692 the *Gentleman's Journal*, edited in London by the French-born Peter Anthony Motteux, gave an appreciative description of a beautiful Englishwoman in her 20s who served with the French army in Piedmont until, 'playing with another of her Sex, she was discover'd'.[12] Any kind of 'playing' which reveals anatomical sex, I suggest, deserves an erotic reading.

The soldier memoirs are full of such 'playing'. The anonymous *The Female Soldier* (1750) tells the story of Hannah Snell. Daughter of a Worcester hosier, Snell was born in 1723 and married a

Dutch sailor, James Summs, in 1744. He stole her possessions to finance his use of prostitutes and finally ran away, leaving her pregnant and facing his debts. After the death of her baby, motivated by a mixture of love and hatred, Hannah followed Summs to war. She cut her hair and used the name of her brother-in-law, James Gray.

At this point, the narrative begins to introduce other women as love objects. When her sergeant, Davis, confides in 'James Gray' his plans to rape a certain young woman, Hannah secretly warns the victim,

> which Act of Virtue and Generosity in a Soldier, gained her the Esteem and Confidence of this young Woman, who took great delight in her Company; and seldom a Day passed but they were together, having cultivated an Intimacy and Friendship with each other.

It is not clear what the writer thinks of this relationship. His approving tone, and use of words like 'Friendship', make it sound like a virtuous bond. Yet the young woman is reported as being surprised by such generous behaviour 'in a Soldier', which implies that she has no idea that Hannah is female. Crossdressers' memoirs tend to highlight scenes of discovery or revelation, but there is no such scene here. Yet the writer treats this daily intimacy with appreciation, not suspicion.

Spurned by the young woman, Sergeant Davis suspects that 'James Gray' is acting as his rival and has 'him' savagely whipped for neglect of duty. Hannah bears all this with dignity and is rewarded with the tender gratitude of her 'Female Friend'. To avoid discovery when an old acquaintance turns up, and to escape further punishment from Davis, Hannah decides to desert; 'tho' loth to lose the Company of such a Friend and Companion', we are told, the young woman helps 'James Gray' with money for the flight. We might suspect that Hannah is glad to escape from this ambiguous courtship, but the writer insists that the difficulty of army life is her only motive for flight. The whipping incident, he reminds us, chained Hannah and the young woman together 'in the strictest Bonds of Love and Affection, which never quitted its hold, till forced thereto by a hard Fate'.[13] Using the rhetoric of friendship rather than cynical flirtation, Snell's biographer presents this courtship in positive, but safely virtuous, terms.

In Lisbon, according to our narrator, Snell has to engage in intense flirtation to keep up her image as a military man. In one episode 'James Gray' and her male friend Jeffories are courting two women, 'the handsomest of which was the favourite of our Heroine'. However, when Jeffories offers to toss a coin for the right to pursue the handsomer woman, Snell agrees and loses, 'not caring how soon she should be rid of such a Companion'. So Snell desires the other woman, yet wants to be rid of her; courts her just as a man would, then panics and wants to escape. 'Gray' and Jeffories socialise with these two women as their 'sweethearts' all the time they are in Lisbon; as the sailors leave, the women ask to be let on to the ship, but Snell, afraid of one of them penetrating her disguise, makes sure they are refused permission.

As time goes on, and Snell keeps having to drop out of the courtship game, she seems to become increasingly cynical about both women and men (especially after she discovers that her worthless husband has been executed for murder). In Portsmouth she becomes very friendly with Catherine, the drum major's sister-in-law; instead of drinking with her mates she spends all her time with Catherine, who falls in love with this friendly soldier. 'Finding this young Woman had no dislike to her', we are told, Snell 'endeavoured to try if she could not act the Lover as well as the Soldier'. Only when they have become engaged does Snell run away again, promising to return for a formal marriage.[14] This rather cruel episode shows Snell acting out the sexually predatory side ('the lover') of the soldier role. Julie Wheelwright generally reads encounters between women in such memoirs as heartless macho games: 'The need to prove their masculinity forced these women to mimic male power relations, flirting with, mocking or flattering their admirers ... There appeared to be no room for any real sexual intimacy.'[15] In Snell's flirtation with Catherine there is certainly little intimacy, but her earlier relationships, especially with the first unnamed 'Female Friend', are described with more warmth and leave more room for interpretation. And her adventures have an intriguing ending. When Snell moves in with her sister's family, her brother-in-law asks their female lodger if she is willing to have his sister as her bedfellow. The woman agrees, but is taken aback to see a soldier undressing in her room; only after a visual 'Demonstration' will she believe that Hannah is a woman. Not only is the lodger willing to share a room, but a throwaway remark reveals that she travels as Hannah's 'supposed Wife' as long as Snell stays in uniform. To outside observers this intimacy looks clearly sexual: 'ever since they have been Bedfellows, which made the Neighbours report

... that the young Woman was married to a Soldier'.[16] In a very real sense, she is; despite the writer's tone of calm humour, it is clear that this operates as a female marriage.

By contrast, *The Life and Adventures of Mrs Christian Davies, the British Amazon* (1741) probes the eroticism of such courtships rather than assuming their virtue. This book, which has been attributed to Daniel Defoe, claims to be taken down from Davies' own dictation. It begins with her childhood as the tomboy daughter of a Dublin brewer. Married at a young age to a servant, Richard Davies, Christian is happy until her husband is pressganged into the army, at which point she dresses up in one of his suits and follows the army to Flanders, leaving her children with her mother. The silver 'urinary instrument' she straps on to complete her disguise, we are told, was something she found in her teens in the guest bed after the visit of a colonel who was discovered at her death to be a woman.[17]

So Christian is taking part in a secret tradition of 'passing women', wearing an instrument inherited from her earliest role model. Julie Wheelwright reads Christian's instrument as a 'clumsy, mechanical device' which eighteenth-century readers would have perceived as hollow in every sense, and concludes: 'since only a phallus could bring another woman the "real" sexual pleasure of penetration, the female soldier's flirtations were rendered harmless and pleasingly erotic in the popular imagination'.[18] But fictions about 'female husbands' and erotic stories of dildo-users (see pp. 206–12) must have spread the knowledge that a dildo could give women as much pleasure as a penis could. If Christian Davies could strap on a urinary instrument she could strap on a dildo too, and readers could only find her flirtations with women totally 'harmless' if they shut their ears to all the stories about dildos that were circulating in the 'popular imagination'.

Despite her ostensible motive of marital loyalty, from the beginning Davies' career includes flirtation with women. Unable to find her missing husband, she explains, 'in my Frolicks, to kill Time, I made my Addresses to a Burgher's Daughter, who was young and pretty'. In this game Christian parodies all the clichés of heterosexual courtship – sighs, squeezings of hands, foolish looks – the very devices men used to trap her. Along with masculine power, she begins to pick up misogyny: she applies the double standard of sexual behaviour, despising women for showing desire, yet exploiting the licence the male role gives to express desire herself.

Christian tries to make a move on the burgher's daughter, taking an 'indecent freedom', then claims to be gratified when the girl virtuously rebuffs her and only lets Christian take her into her arms – which begs the question, what would Christian have done if the girl had not said no? The issue is evaded, as the author has Christian explain away the strength of her feelings: 'Indeed, I was now fond of the girl, though mine, you know, could not go beyond a platonick Love.' But the 'Frolicks' are becoming serious. When a man tries to rape the burgher's daughter, Christian challenges him to a duel, furiously demanding 'how he durst attempt the Honour of a Woman, who was, for aught he knew, my Wife; to whom he was sensible I had long made honourable Love'. Is this all a pretence, or has Christian really found some way to court this woman 'honourably'? At this point, realising how emotionally and socially entangled she is, Christian begs her beloved to postpone engagement until she obtains a commission, then escapes. 'Thus I got off from this Amour without Loss of Credit', the text concludes, a flippancy that jars with the deep emotions Christian has been displaying.[19]

The masculine role she has been playing has changed, or simply widened, her sexuality; it allows her to be assertive in her desires, to set the rules of love herself. Thus when she finally locates her husband after twelve years and finds that he has a mistress, she cannot face being a wife again; she bullies him into letting her live platonically as his 'Brother' until the war is over. Nor can Christian break herself of her taste for women. On a trip to Rotterdam, her flirtation with a Dutch girl is cut short when she is repulsed by the girl's easiness: 'When she threw her Arms around my Neck and would have kissed me, I pushed her rudely off, saying, *I had mistaken a Fiend for an Angel.*' Once again, desire makes her try to obtain sexual favours, but misogyny (and perhaps fear of exposure) makes her repulse any response. Her continued liking for the male sexual role is shown when, having rejected a certain woman's advances, she is accused of paternity of that woman's child and does not deny it. Even after she has been exposed as a woman and forced back into wifehood, Christian slips off for the odd adventure in masculine clothes. The next time she courts a woman, we are told, it is just to spite the woman's fiancé, a cadet who has been rude to Christian. Our heroine charms the woman at first meeting, offering marriage and 'an

Affection which no Time should have force to alter'; she effectively humiliates the cadet, but also betrays the woman.[20]

As with the biography of Hannah Snell, this text shifts its crossdressed heroine between fairly loving relationships with women and apparently cold flirtations. Perhaps the most fascinating aspect of both women's stories is how they manage to combine bonds with women and with men in one identity. The object of desire seems to switch with their clothes, allowing them a flexible bisexual preference. Neither Davies' nor Snell's biographers express much anxiety about the matter, nor – apart from the brief assurance about Christian's love for the burgher's daughter being 'platonick' – do they seem to expect readers to be shocked. It is as if wearing men's clothes gives certain women the temporary right to woo women, so long as the game ends when they put their dresses back on.

A different sort of encounter between women is acted out in *A General History of the Pyrates* (1724), another text attributed to Daniel Defoe. The story is not one of a crossdressed woman and a 'normal' one, but of two crossdressers, the famous female pirates Mary Read and Anne Bonny. Their story is retold in many subsequent versions; here I will deal only with the 1724 account.[21]

Born in England and Ireland respectively, Read and Bonny are both described as having been brought up as boys, for various convoluted economic reasons; this means that their adult decisions to pass as men are never questioned. After marriages and liaisons with men, they both happen to end up in masculine clothes on the ship captained by Anne's lover Rackam. Their relationship is described from Mary's point of view:

> Her Sex was not so much as suspected by any Person on board till *Anne Bonny*, who was not altogether so reserved in Point of Chastity, took a particular Liking to her; in short, *Anne Bonny* took her for a handsome young Fellow, and for some Reasons best known to herself, first discovered her Sex to *Mary Read*.

This is presented as a simple matter of heterosexual attraction; Anne, the sexually unreserved one, exposes her own sex as a way of attracting the 'Fellow' she thinks Mary to be. But Mary,

> knowing what she would be at, and being very sensible of her own Incapacity that way, was forced to come to a right

> Understanding with her, and so to the great Disappointment of *Anne Bonny,* she let her know she was a Woman also.

Here the potentially explosive intimacy between two 'passing women' is made safe, explained away as a matter of accident, misconception and the inherent 'Incapacity' of one woman to satisfy another. It is assumed that the women's only response to the mutual exposure could be 'Disappointment'.

However, their relationship seems to have remained very close – so much so that 'this Intimacy so disturb'd Captain *Rackam* ... that he grew furiously jealous, so that he told *Anne Bonny,* he would cut her new Lover's Throat, therefore, to quiet him, she let him into the Secret also'.[22] Though the author goes out of his way to deny any possibility of a sexual relationship between the two women, he shows their friendship to be so intimate as to look to an outsider like an affair. The famous engraving of Read and Bonny (p. 88) shows them standing in parallel positions, but at a distance; perhaps they were too unnervingly similar in their resistance to norms of femininity to be pictured as a close couple.

Charlotte Charke

Charlotte Cibber Charke, who published *A Narrative of the Life of Mrs. Charlotte Charke* (1755) for money at the age of 42, is probably the best known of early crossdressers. The facts of her life, and the details of her *Narrative,* have been argued over in several modern publications.[23] What I want to offer here is an analysis of how Charke's 'breeches part' – the masculine clothes and behaviours she adopted at various points in her life – influenced her encounters with women.

Charke's *Narrative* includes a most vivid account of growing up as a tomboy. She describes her early gender rebellion in detail to 'raise a Laugh' among her readers. But the clever thing about her accounts of early 'mad pranks' is that they mock men rather than her sly imitations of them. As a hunting, riding, gardening, doctoring 19-year-old, for example, she is equipped with all the accessories of manhood: a pruning knife, a halter, and a big bacon sandwich, as well as 'a Shrug of the Shoulders and a Scratch of the Head, with a hasty Demand for Small-beer'. By rebelling against femininity, Charlotte earns, alternately, the pride and disgust of her parents. When her father (the actor-manager Colley Cibber) sees her riding past his office on a donkey, we are told, his face shows a 'strong Mixture of Surprize, Pleasure, Pain, and Shame'. 'An Ass upon an Ass!' he exclaims, and Charlotte's actress mother dehumanises her further by tying her leg to the table with a 'packthread'. However, her mother's feelings seem to be ambivalent too. In the absence of her husband, terrified of burglars, she is only too glad to hand over the family guns to her teenage daughter who, as Charke puts it, 'most heroically promised to protect her Life, at the utmost Hazard of my own'.[24] So this tomboy's parents give her the mixed message that masculine attributes are valuable, but should be out of her reach.

Charke goes on to describe 'indiscreetly plumping into the sea of Matrimony' and the misery of the year she spends pursuing her husband through the brothels of London. Having 'agreed to part', and gradually freed herself of his financial demands, Charke finds herself bringing up her daughter Kitty alone. She makes her stage debut in 1730; by 1732 she is playing a mixture of female and breeches roles, though her *Narrative* dwells only on the female ones, downplaying her tendency to crossdress at every opportunity. When she is first arrested for debt, the bailiff finds her easily because of her distinctive silver-laced man's hat, she being 'for some substantial Reasons' dressed as a man; this coyness about her 'secret' reason for crossdressing continues throughout the book.[25]

Tripping from job to job, Charke always relies on the kindness of women. Having escaped from her exploitative husband, she runs a shop under the name of a widow friend of hers, so that he cannot claim the profits that eighteenth-century law allows him. On the occasion of her first arrest for debt she turns to a group of London brothel- and coffee-house owners, who go bail 'for the relief of poor Sir *Charles*, as they were pleased to stile me'; these women seem to have treated her as a sort of transvestite mascot. Next, Charke's attempt at being a meatseller fails when a dog eats her stock of pork, but she is saved by a young woman, who 'though not in the highest Affluence, supported myself and Child for some Time, without any View or Hopes of a Return, which has since established a lasting Friendship between us'.[26]

During nine gruelling years as a strolling player, Charke crossdresses on and off stage, travelling as 'Mr. Brown' and never, she claims, 'making the least Discovery of my Sex by my Behaviour', except on one occasion when Kitty is having a fit and observers consider Charke's wild grief 'Lunatick' behaviour for a father. This impenetrable disguise – as well as Charke's natural charm – leads several women to fall in love with her. One of the incidents is described as purely comic. Her employer in a pub, Mrs Door, takes a liking to the handsome young 'Mr. Brown' and when at last she has been persuaded of Charke's womanhood, Mrs Door blames her for having led her on. '*No truly; I believe,* said she, *I should hardly be 'namour'd with one of my own Sect*: Upon which I burst into a Laugh.'

On a different occasion, Charke does not find the situation funny at all. She becomes, 'as I may most properly term it, the unhappy Object of Love in a young Lady', an orphan heiress to £40,000. 'Unhappy' is the key word here; throughout this episode Charke is clearly uneasy, not knowing how to 'properly term' this accidental attraction between women. 'This was a most horrible Disappointment on both Sides', Charke comments briskly at first, 'the Lady of the Husband, and I of the Money'. But the story does not end here. Her troupe of players persuade her to court the lady; they plan to substitute a man for the wedding night. Though tempted by the money, Charke explains, she cannot bring herself to pose as a female husband. Feeling 'how unfit I was to embrace so favourable an opportunity', she becomes increasingly troubled about her betrayal of the young lady. 'I own I felt a tender concern', she admits, describing how she backs out of the plot at the last minute. In a final scene with the lady, Charke admits her sex and tells the lady that she is 'sorry for us both, that Providence had not ordained me to be the happy Person she designed me'.[27]

Lynne Friedli uses the fact that Charke did not persist in this courtship as proof that she had no 'erotic inclination towards women'.[28] But it can be read quite the other way; rather than callously arranging a trick marriage to steal this woman's money, Charke tells her the truth, in a scene of honesty and tenderness. (As for other evidence of Charke's passion for women, her long partnership with her friend 'Mrs. Brown' is discussed on pp. 164–6).

Charke's last scene with the heiress also hints at a shadow of insufficiency behind her bravado. Even at her most confident, she is always self-deprecating, mocking herself for some lack or oddity. With subdued grief she describes herself as 'an Alien from the Family'; blocked parental and filial relations are a running theme in this book. She insists, for example, that she can only handle a sewing needle 'with the same clumsey Awkwardness a Monkey does a Kitten, and am equally capable of using the one as Pug is of nursing the other'.[29] Here, feminine skills are equated with the ability to breastfeed; even though Charke has given birth to and raised a daughter, she still feels excluded from maternal (female) power. The *Narrative* shows the precarious rewards of a social and sexual identity based on part-time crossdressing.

Lillian Faderman's work on eighteenth-century crossdressers is primarily concerned with the punishment of those whom society took most seriously as criminals. She has little time for what she sees as privileged, unrepresentative part-timers such as Charlotte Charke, whom she calls 'a stage personality ... not a "real-life" human being'.[30] Similarly, Lynne Friedli is disdainful of the upper-class or actress 'eccentric personality' who bent the rules and in some senses got away with it.[31] But I suggest that it is time to take these women just as seriously as the apparently more extreme cases of female husbands, precisely because they lived on the margins between worlds. Charke may have been shielded from punishment by her background in the theatre and as a daughter of a famous theatre manager, but that does not make her story any less 'real'. As a famous crosser of sexual boundaries, Charke could have been a living fantasy of lesbian possibilities for women readers.

Harriot Freke

Crossdressing woman are rarely found in non-autobiographical fiction in this period; their rebellious activity and ambiguous characterisation must have been hard to fit into the structure of a domestic novel. As heroines such women were inappropriate; as villains, however, they had potential.

Maria Edgeworth's novel of 1801, *Belinda*, makes crossdressing the key to the characterisation of Mrs Harriot Freke, one of the most memorable of fictional lesbians. 'Freke' was a real eighteenth-century surname, but Edgeworth clearly chose it as a pun on 'freak', since Harriot is an exception to every 'natural' characteristic of womanhood. Her oddity is located not in anatomy but in body language. When she stands 'leaning with her bold masculine arms on the coach door', the arms are only masculine because of their bold position. Similarly, Freke's 'stentorian voice' and 'horse laugh' are not inborn characteristics but simply bad manners; the same goes for her restless habit of 'stretching herself so violently that some part of her habilments [clothes] gave way'. Our heroine Belinda's older friend Lady Delacour, trying to explain Harriot's fascination for her when they met many years before, mentions her 'assurance', 'impudence' and 'brass'. Far from being a social reject, Harriot is a leader of fashion, popularising 'harum scarum manners', especially with a set of young men about town, and this status protects her from other people's disapproval.[32]

Lady Delacour's reaction to Harriot is nervous and erotically charged:

> She struck me, the first time I saw her, as being downright ugly; but there was a wild oddity in her countenance which made one stare at her, and she was delighted to be stared at, especially by me; so we were mutually agreeable to each other – I as starer, and she as staree.

The erotic gaze is reversed one night as Lady Delacour is getting into her carriage with a male admirer, Lawless. '"A smart-looking young man, as I thought"', she tells her friend Belinda, '"came up close to the coach door, and stared me full in the face"'. Terrified when the fellow jumps into her carriage, she is most relieved when a familiar laugh reveals the intruder to be Harriot. '"Who am I? only a Freke!" cried she: "shake hands." I gave her my hand, into the carriage she sprang.' Desire between the women can only be expressed negatively, as veiled hints of rape. '"I verily believe you are afraid to trust yourself with us,"' Harriet murmurs to Lady Delacour. '"Which of us are you afraid of, Lawless, or me, or *yourself*!"'[33]

Harriot crossdresses, we are told, because men's clothes suit her figure. But they also enable her to seize male privilege, for instance when she disguises herself in order to get into the House of Commons. Duelling is another such privilege; in fact Harriot bullies Lady Delacour into challenging another woman to a duel, using a mixture of macho intimidation and sisterly encouragement. As Lady Delacour explains helplessly:

> I had prodigious deference for the masculine superiority, as I thought it, of Harriot's understanding. She was a philosopher, and a fine lady – I was only a fine lady ... Harriot offered to bet any wager on the steadiness of my hand, and assured me that I should charm all beholders in male attire.

Such a seductive invitation leads to disaster. The duel is prevented by a furious mob which will allow gentlewomen in breeches no class privilege. In discharging her pistol into the air, Lady Delecour thumps her breast; this develops into an abcess which she assumes is breast cancer – her foolish trust in her friend has become a festering sore. When, as a concession to the husband she hates, Harriot switches political sides, Lady Delacour realises how many times her friend has betrayed her.[34]

After this point in the novel, there is a long silence about Harriot Freke, broken only by a mention of a manuscript being passed around that compares her to the Chevalier d'Eon (a famous diplomat who was thought to be either a woman or a hermaphrodite). Evidently the fashion for Harriot is waning; from now on she is the butt of everyone's humour and the Jamaican servant/slave Juba is allowed to deride her as a 'man-woman'. Eventually Harriot meets the young heroine of the novel, Belinda. Harriot's characterisation has slipped from the intriguing to the ludicrous – now she speaks in bluff masculine clichés like '"Hail, fellow! well met!"' Whereas she used to entice Lady Delacour with subtle eroticism, now she bluntly praises Belinda's figure and tells her, '"I swore to set the distressed damsel free, in spite of all the dragons in Christendom; so let me carry you off in triumph in my unicorn."' Such hamfisted appeals only amuse our quiet heroine. Freke's threats, too, ring hollow; it is almost as if she is parodying herself, playing the lesbian vampire. '"I stop at nothing," repeated she, fixing her eyes upon Miss Portman, to fascinate her by terror. "Friend or foe! peace or war! Take your choice."' For Belinda, there is little attraction to overcome.[35] Like the female soldiers we have looked at, Harriot can be seen as both feminist and misogynist; she calls herself 'a champion for the Rights of Woman', yet treats young ladies with condescension and contempt.[36]

Though Belinda is invulnerable to Harriot's badgering, a certain Miss Moreton is not. Mrs Freke persuades her to run away and live with her; most of Miss Moreton's relations make no protest, since Harriot is so fashionable, and the one cousin who objects (a clergyman) is harassed and tricked out of a job by the furious Harriot Freke. Belinda hears this story when, on an outing to some famous rocking stones, she and her friends see what looks like a man with a gun on top of a swaying stone, laughing and hauling up a screaming girl in a riding habit. Mr Percival explains that Miss Moreton has been lured by Mrs Freke into 'all kinds of mischief and absurdity', including crossdressing and an affair with an army officer. (It seems likely that Edgeworth introduced this last detail to distract from the more obvious interpretation of Miss Moreton's elopement.)

We never hear what becomes of Miss Moreton, but Harriot Freke comes to the predictable sticky end. Obsessed with hurting Lady Delacour, she goes in male disguise to spy through Lady Delacour's bedroom window at night. When she is caught in the gardener's mantrap and badly mangled, her virtuous enemies are most satisfied. The punishment is suitable, since it prevents her crossdressing any longer: 'She grew quite outrageous when it was hinted, that the beauty of her legs would be spoiled, and that she would never more be able to appear to advantage in man's apparel.'

It is a paradox of eighteenth-century sexuality that those women who loved women within the respectable culture of romantic friendship could see no kinship with their sisters in breeches. Perhaps it was precisely because Maria Edgeworth was a spinster and romantic friend that she had to police the boundaries of such friendship, mark the unacceptable friend (Harriot Freke) off from the merely passionate (Lady Delacour), and prove herself to be on the side of the angels.

What is most fascinating about the characterisation of Harriot Freke is the details. Rather than generalising about mannish women, Edgeworth dwells on significant words, postures and accessories, the stolen trappings of masculinity. As Mr Percival comments sternly of Harriot Freke's tall boots:

> These are trifles; but women who love to set the world at defiance in trifles seldom respect its opinion in matters of consequence ... They defy the world – the world in return excommunicates them – the female outlaws become desperate, and make it the business and pride of their lives to disturb the peace.[37]

'The female outlaws' in Britain during the seventeenth and eighteenth centuries, I suggest, acted out their rebellion in the tiniest details of clothes and manner as well as in the important choice of who to love.

Amazons in petticoats

In Aphra Behn's play of 1682, *The False Count*, old Francisco is shown becoming more and more uneasy whenever he finds his young wife Julia talking to her sister or her maid. When the women finally ask him whether he is jealous even of a petticoat (a woman), he reveals his nightmare: 'I have known as much danger hid under a Petticoat, as a pair of Breeches. I have heard of two Women that married each other – oh abominable, as if there were so prodigious a scarcity of Christian Mans Flesh.'[38] The danger is quickly glossed over – the maid jokes that male flesh is easily available – but the point has been made. There is more than one way for a young wife to cuckold her husband, and the flesh hid under a petticoat is no less alluring to a woman than the breeches of transvestites. The privilege men guard most closely is the right to be lovers of women; the crossdresser's breeches are most threatening as a symbol of that sexual role.

Several texts from the second half of the eighteenth century make the question of gender-bending more subtle, internal and psychological. They focus not on literal breeches but on the masculinity breeches can represent. In this section I look at characterisations of mannish or unsexed women who rebel against femininity not through actual crossdressing but in the subtleties of manner, speech and particularly their passionate behaviour towards other women. Certain novelists were writing discreetly of the 'mannish lesbian' a century and a half before Radclyffe Hall.

Most critics have turned a blind eye to Miss Barnevelt, one of the comic characters in Samuel Richardson's last novel, *Sir Charles Grandison* (1753–4), which was widely read and admired among his vast circle of fans, especially women. She may be the prototype for Harriot Freke and later examples of the brusque, male-identified, misogynist lesbian. Barnevelt's style is not a product of fashion: her physical and mental oddities are assumed to be a genetic package. The heroine Harriet Byron describes her initially in a letter as 'a lady of masculine features, and whose mind bely'd not those features; for she has the character of being loud, bold, free, even fierce when opposed'. 'Masculine' here does not just mean assertive; we are given clear hints of her almost transsexual identity and her desire for women: 'No-body, it seems, thinks of an *husband* for Miss *Barnevelt*. She is sneeringly spoken of rather as a *young fellow*, than as a woman; and who will one day look out for a *wife* for herself.' But until that day arrives – until Miss Barnevelt makes a move and claims male status – all such talk can remain on the level of sneering innuendo.

The hostility of Harriet Byron's description makes sense when we see her become the unwilling object of Barnevelt's overbearing advances, which are disguised as the hyperbolic compliments acceptable between lady acquaintances:

> Miss Barnevelt said, she had from the moment I first enter'd beheld me with the eye of a Lover. And freely taking my hand, squeezed it. – Charming creature! said she, as if addressing a country innocent, and perhaps expecting me to be covered with blushes and confusion.

At their second encounter, Barnevelt cleverly takes advantage of public acceptance of physical affection between women: 'Clasping her mannish arms round me, she kissed my cheek', Harriet Byron tells a friend in a letter, and comments 'I was surpris'd, and offended.' Her reaction has little effect: 'Miss Barnevelt only laughed at the freedom she had taken with me. She is a loud and fearless laugher.'[39]

By now Harriet is becoming fascinated by Miss Barnevelt's confidence. She starts to blame herself, giving the female harasser the same guilt-free status as a man. Harriet practises in her mirror 'a solemnity of countenance, that, occasionally, I might dash with it my childishness of look; which certainly encouraged this freedom of Miss Barnevelt'. The fault is no longer Barnevelt's aggression, but Harriet's provocative childishness. As Harriet gets drawn into the fantasy of Miss Barnevelt as an abductor/rapist, she sees herself as more and more helplessly infantile and miniature. For example, in a letter to a friend she imagines how Miss Barnevelt would drool over her, Harriet, to a male correspondent:

> 'Tis the softest, gentlest, smiling rogue of a girl – ... and I wish'd twenty times as I sat by her, that I had been a man for her sake. Upon my honour, Bombardino, I believe if I had, I should have caught her up, popt her under one of my arms, and run away with her.

Which tells us far less about Miss Barnevelt than about Harriet's fearful longing to be run away with.

It makes sense that Miss Barnevelt's imagined correspondent should be male, because she is wholly male-identified. In the course of an argument on manhood, she announces her contempt for 'milk-sops' who stay at home with their women, by contrast with the military 'brave man' she likes. In this kind of gender polarity, there is no room for her, a 'brave man' in a woman's body, attracted to the very women she despises. As Richardson sees it, lesbians, having rejected womanliness, must reject women; Miss Barnevelt reveals 'such airs of contempt of her own sex, that one almost wonders at her condescending to wear petticoats'. He adds a quip borrowed from Lady Mary Wortly Montagu, which takes on a more sinister force in Barnevelt's mouth: 'One reason indeed, she every-where gives, for being satisfied with being a woman; which is, *that she cannot be married to a* Woman.' Is this a joke, Barnevelt playing the clown to deflect male resentment? Or is she supposed to despise women so much that she denies all love for them even while she is courting them?

Wisecracking, Miss Barnevelt stands outside the system of heterosexual romance, and takes part only in games of flirtatious intimidation. As she tells the whole party, '"it is my glory, that I never knew what Love was"'.[40] Though Richardson probably means this as sour grapes, the withered lesbian despising what she can't have, it can also be read as a strategy for survival. Notice that Miss Barnevelt is asked to parties as long as she provides entertainment, puts up with men's mockery of her impotence and does nothing more to the ladies than kiss them. Love would be impossible under such conditions, in such a public arena, so she makes it her glory that she has never lost herself in it.

Though Richardson describes Miss Barnevelt as the incarnation of masculinity, a more common fictional strategy was to divide unfemininity into distinct types, each linked to one quality or pastime. For example, in Charlotte Lennox's novel of romantic friendship, *Euphemia* (1790), the paired caricatures of the Amazon and the Bluestocking are briefly introduced. The first is 'the Diana of our forests, the fearless huntress Miss Sandford, who, at the age of forty-five, declares her fixed resolution never to marry'. Her romantic friend is 'the learned and scientific Lady Cornelia Classick', who pretends to classical knowledge and pedantically hogs conversations.[41] Each claims a masculine area of expertise and each shows an unwomanly self-confidence. Though they are comic figures, they undermine male expectations and make the heroine's fiancé most uneasy, as he explains:

> 'A Man makes a silly figure,' said Mr Harley, 'in company with so learned a Lady, and her Amazonian friend ... When Lady Cornelia declaims in Greek, and Miss Sandford vaults into the saddle like another Hotspur, I forget I am in company with women: the dogmatic critic awes me into

> silence, and the hardy rider makes my assistance unnecessary.'

Lennox hints that their unnaturalness extends to their passionate friendship: Miss Sandford 'does not accompany Lady Cornelia in the carriage, but mounts her steed with most masculine agility, to escort her female friend.'[42] It is interesting here that although Miss Sandford plays the male role in the ritual of rider-escorting-lady's-carriage, the two are not described in any terms equivalent to butch and femme, but rather as a similar pairing of two types of unfemininity, united in oddity.

A similar pairing is described in a local Welsh newspaper of the same year. The *General Evening Post* for 24 July 1790 includes an article on the 'Ladies of Llangollen', the Irish cousins Eleanor Butler and Sarah Ponsonby who had eloped to Wales in 1778. Entitled 'Extraordinary Female Affection', the article makes no explicit accusations about the nature of their relationship, but simply juxtaposes several elements – chosen spinsterhood, romantic partnership and mannish dressing – which, though harmless on their own, might sound suggestive in combination. The Ladies must have picked up the innuendo, because they wrote to Edmund Burke (who had fought innuendos about his own sexuality in court) for advice on sueing the author.

Two sentences in the article contrast the Ladies' personal styles:

> Miss Butler is tall and masculine, she wears always a riding habit, hangs her hat with the air of a sportsman in the hall, and appears in all respects as a young man, if we except the petticoats which she still retains. Miss Ponsonby, on the contrary, is polite and effeminate, fair and beautiful.

The fact is that in 1790 Eleanor Butler was short, plump and 51 years of age, yet this writer has recast her as a mannish young deviant. Without claiming that she goes so far as to wear breeches, he makes her sound as unfeminine as he can. Sarah Ponsonby, by contrast, is turned into a paragon of femininity. We are even told that she looks after the housework, while Eleanor Butler supervises the garden and grounds. Altering the realities of shape, age, costume and behaviour, the journalist is clearly trying to interpret the Ladies' enduring bond as an imitation of heterosexual marriage.[43]

In conclusion, it seems that crossdressing was one way for women who loved each other to give expression to those feelings, whether by passing as men or by developing a personal style that allowed behaviours characteristic of both sexes and sent out mixed messages. In many texts of the seventeenth and eighteenth centuries, crossdressing is the frame of interpretation for passion between women.

But in giving it a central place in lesbian history, I do not want to fall into the common trap of presenting the crossdresser as the true, real, daring lesbian. Hers was only one of a range of strategies for survival. Besides, how can there be a female husband without a female husband's wife, a flirting soldier without another woman to flirt with? It is the enterprise of crossing gender lines that I find most interesting, and every woman who read a crossdresser's signals and related passionately to her took part in that enterprise. I find crossdressing most important not for itself but for the space it gave women to recognise each other.

4 A sincere and tender passion

The term 'romantic friendship' was widely employed in the eighteenth century to refer to a loving relationship (usually between women of the middle or upper classes) of varying degrees of romance and friendliness. Since the 1970s many historians have used it as a label for any passion between pre-twentieth-century women about which no hard evidence of genital sexual activity survives. But there are problems with this usage. First, it makes these relationships sound like slightly more fervent versions of ordinary friendship, whereas often they were lifelong emotional partnerships, more like marriages than friendships. Also, because the term is often used in opposition to a phrase like 'lesbian love', for example by Lillian Faderman,[1] the two are assumed to be incompatible, when in fact many of the romantic friends of the seventeenth and eighteenth centuries might have shared sex, 'genital' and otherwise. It is crucial to distinguish between the dominant ideology's explanation of romantic friendship – that it was sexless, morally elevating, and no threat to male power – and the reality of such bonds between women. A sensible point made by Chris White is that no matter how often society informed women that their friendships were purely spiritual, their bodies could have taught them otherwise: 'it seems hardly credible that simply because women did not have penile erections they would not have recognized how sexual arousal felt and what it meant'.[2]

Elizabeth Mavor resurrected the phrase 'romantic friendship' in 1971 specifically to shield the Ladies of Llangollen from being called lesbians.[3] It has become a popular term among historians, often invoked to neutralise and de-sexualise textual evidence. Many use it, as Bonnie Zimmerman points out, 'with an audible sigh of relief, to explain away love between women, instead of opening our eyes to the historical pervasiveness' of that love.[4] Because so many women were passionate friends, they argue, passionate friendship between women must have been nothing more than

'Sincerity the Tie of Female Friendship', from The Lady's Magazine *(1783)*

a fashion and could have no connection with sexual identity. An extreme example of this viewpoint is provided by Jean Hagstrum, whose favourite euphemisms for lesbian are 'morbid' and 'irregular'; he manages to conclude that the famous romantic friendship at the heart of Samuel Richardson's novel *Clarissa* (1747–8) may be somewhat 'homoerotic' but has nothing to do with 'consummated lesbianism (from which both girls would have recoiled)'.[5] Such godlike insight into the hypothetical sexual practices of fictional characters is not rare among critics who hate lesbians.

Some feminist critics wear similar blinkers, assuming, for example, that the word 'chaste' in a poem of romantic friendship means the participants never did anything we would consider sexual – when in fact all it may mean is that the romantic friends considered their physical embraces to be pure in motive, or free of men. Germaine Greer, Susan Hastings, Jeslyn Medoff and Melinda Sanson complain, with regard to the seventeenth-century poet of romantic friendship, Katherine Philips, that 'some of her champions' (that is, lesbian critics) 'choose to ignore her own stipulation that such friendship be free from carnal interest'.[6] These editors read Philips in a wholly straightforward manner, ignoring the pressures of a seventeenth-century closet which could have demanded such a 'stipulation', the reasons why a woman poet would have to insist on her own sexual purity. It is also worth bearing in mind that we have no idea exactly which body-to-body caresses a woman of Philips' era would have considered 'carnal' (literaly, 'bodily'). She may have thought of sex as penetrative intercourse with men, which was a sin outside marriage, whereas women's embraces were allowed. Narrow definitions of 'eroticism', and of 'lesbianism' as a matter of genital sex between abnormal women, mar otherwise useful feminist studies of the literature of female love.[7]

Another problem with the phrase 'romantic friendship' is class. Study of the phenomenon has tended to focus on those who used its terminology – literary, leisured women of the upper strata of British society – and has ignored the more down-to-earth accounts of partnerships between actresses, prostitutes, and other less respectable women. In *Surpassing the Love of Men*, Lillian Faderman presents romantic friendship as the primary form of passionate love between women before the twentieth century, but many critics have questioned this. Lynne Friedli claims (rather prematurely, I think) that the conventions of romantic friendship 'only ever applied to a small number of upper class women',[8] while Myriam

Everard draws a rigid distinction between Dutch middle-class women who had romantic friendships, and working-class women who had sex.[9] But the problem seems to be one of different kinds of evidence. In general, middle-class women's romantic friendships were described in pious poems and novels, which did not give sexual details, whereas working-class women's lives were represented in the bawdier and more hostile genres of medical treatises and criminal biographies. I have found no reason to believe that friendship was limited to the upper classes of women-loving women, nor sex to the lower. Rather than segregating our history on the basis of class, I suggest that we stretch the concept of female friendship to include more than the handful of upper-class romantic friends who usually get written about.

From the beginning, some of those friends were themselves unhappy with the word 'romantic', which made their friendships sound, as Samuel Johnson's *Dictionary* of 1755 defined the word, 'wild', 'improbable' and 'fanciful'. Mary Granville Pendarves complained to her beloved sister that 'romantic' was quite the wrong description for female friendship, which tended to be based on clearsighted, solid devotion.[10] Instead of using one standard term to cover the whole range of their feelings for each other, these women employed a wide vocabulary, saying they were 'in love' or 'dazzled' with each other, had a 'deep affection' or a 'sincere and tender passion' (Queen Anne's pet phrase) for each other. They emphasised what they saw as the particular strengths of female relationships – sincerity, depth, tenderness, generosity, commitment – rather than using the word 'romantic', which tended to be defined by heterosexual norms, then as now.

In 1928 Virginia Woolf could not think of a single strong female friendship in literature.[11] The body of texts she was mentally scanning was 'English Literature' – the traditional canon constructed by predominantly male critics who seem not to have found female friendship interesting. Woolf's ignorance is understandable; more depressing is the 1991 *Oxford Book of Friendship*, whose male editors assure us that they regret the slimness of the chapter on female friendship, which is due not to their bias but to the paucity of examples, especially among women writers. They include Katherine Philips (1631–64) and Jane Austen (1775–1817), but no woman from the period of this study – perhaps the single richest era for the literature of passionate friendship between women.[12]

I have made no attempt to establish a canon of the best of this literature, nor to offer new readings of its handful of fictional 'classics', such as Samuel Richardson's *Clarissa* (1747–8) or Sarah Robinson Scott's *A Description of Millenium Hall* (1762). Instead, I begin with a brief selection of little-known poems of romantic friendship, in elegaic, complaining or celebratory modes. Next I study such key issues as spinsterhood, reconciling relationships with both sexes, and class divisions; I am less interested in the ideal of romantic friendship than in its contradictions. Finally, I look at rumours circulating about particular friends in late eighteenth-century England, gossip that linked this apparently respectable phenomenon to Sapphist culture.

Seven poems of romantic friendship

Anne Killigrew was a spinster and Maid of Honour to the Duchess of York. She died of smallpox at the age of 25, leaving a collection of poems that was edited and published by her father in 1686. The last three are startlingly erotic addresses to a woman called Eudora; Dr Killigrew introduces them by claiming that, though he found them among his daughter's papers, they cannot be hers.[13] The simplest and perhaps the most effective is the last, entitled 'On the Soft and Gentle Motions of Eudora'. Such poems of praise commonly dwell on the female beloved's looks, singing, painting or writing skills; Killigrew breaks with convention by focusing on the way Eudora moves.

The speaker begins by comparing the beloved's motions to the gentlest of notes from a lute, or:

> The silent gliding of the Howers [hours],
> Or yet the calmer growth of Flowers;
> Th'ascending or the falling Dew,
> Which none can see though all find true.

After this series of similes the poem speeds up, its short, fluid lines and assonance contributing to the impression of Eudora's sensuality:

> How downie, how smooth,
> Eudora doth Move,
> How Silken her Actions appear,
> The Aire of her Face,
> Of a gentler Grace
> Than those that do stroke the Eare.

Elegy was a form in which women could often express their most passionate appreciation of their friends. Jane Barker was a Lincolnshire Catholic who worked as a herbalist and Jacobite spy; despite going blind, she published five novels as well as a collection of poems. Her role model, whom she read in a spirit of worship, was 'Orinda', Katherine Philips, who in the mid-seventeenth century had adapted the conventions of male heterosexual poetry (such as John Donne's) to fit passionate female friendship.[14] Unmarried and proud of it (for her writings on spinsterhood see pp. 124–5), Barker structured her life around a triangular devotion to her God, books and friends. One of her most moving poems is called 'On the *Death* of my Dear Friend and Play-fellow, Mrs. E.D. having Dream'd the night before I heard thereof, that I had lost a Pearl' (1688).

Barker begins with a passage of rather abstract praise of friendship, which is worth more than pearls:

> Friendship is that mysterious thing alone,
> Which can unite, and make two Hearts but one;
> It purifies our Love, and makes it flow,
> I' th' clearest stream that's found in Love below;
> It *sublimates* the Soul, and makes it move
> Towards Perfection, and *Celestial* Love.

What is interesting here is how explicitly Barker states the need to raise, purify and sublimate the basic 'Love' that draws two people together. This passion between women is straining to lift itself out of the grubby everyday world into some heaven untouched by circumstances. Yet paradoxically their love is rooted in those circumstances; the next sixteen lines are quite specific about the growth of Barker's friendship with E.D. from childhood in 'the Wilsthorp-Fields' in Lincolnshire:

> Where we indulged our easie Appetites,
> With Pocket-Apples, Plumbs, and such delights:
> Then we contriv'd to spend the rest o' th' day,
> In making Chaplets, or at Check-stone play;
> When weary, we our selves supinely laid
> On Beds of Vi'lets under some cool shade,
> Where th' *Sun* in vain strove to dart through his *Rays*;
> Whilst *Birds* around us chanted forth their *Lays*.[15]

What makes this poem fresher than most scenic poems of romantic friendship is the realism of its setting. After the apples, plums and daisy chains, the 'Beds of Vi'lets' sound like real violets rather than just a cliché, and there is humour in the image of the masculine sun trying to penetrate the shade where these sensually loving girls lie. So though Barker insists at the start on the need to sublimate and purify mere human love, the second part of the poem shows such love to be wholesome and beautiful in itself.

A poem by Aphra Behn published in 1692, 'Verses design'd by Mrs. A. Behn to be sent to a fair Lady, that desir'd she would absent herself to cure her Love. Left unfinish'd', imagines the beloved as Diana/Artemis, the virgin goddess of the forests and the hunt. The title is startlingly bold, not only in presenting 'love' between women as a disruptive passion that needs 'curing', but in identifying the speaker as Aphra Behn herself, rather than its author hiding behind a conventional romance name. The poem begins with her vain attempt to find a pastoral refuge from her passion for this 'fair Lady':

> In vain to Woods and Deserts I retire,
> To shun the lovely Charmer I admire,
> Where the soft Breezes do but fann my Fire!
> In vain in Grotto's dark unseen I lie,
> Love pierces where the Sun could never spy.

The calm shady landscape of Barker's poem of 'sublimated' friendship is disrupted in Behn's text by the unsettling attraction between adults. Without being explicit about the sexual nature of this attraction, Behn does make it sound troubling, passionate and a long way from innocence:

> Distance, alas, contributes to my Grief
> No more, of what fond Lovers call, Relief
> Than to the wounded Hind does sudden Flight
> From the chast Goddesses pursuing Sight:
> When in the Heart the fatal Shaft remains,
> And darts the venom through our bleeding Veins.[16]

Behn casts the beloved as Diana the huntress and herself as the animal prey. 'Hind', a female deer, sounds like a feminised version of Actaeon, the man who spied on Diana bathing and was punished by being turned into a stag and torn apart by his own hounds. Thus the poem lesbianises a myth of heterosexual conflict. The most conventional images – the speaker 'disarmed' by a ray from the beloved's eyes, then struggling in 'Cupid's Chains' like 'Birds in Nets' – are made new by this central couple of the female animal and the female deity. Behn offers this poem as a declaration of agonised passion, very much like an ode from a male suitor to a heartless mistress, rather than as a conventional poem of female romantic friendship.

One woman poet who has never been quite forgotten is Anne Finch, Countess of Winchilsea. Known as 'Ardelia', she was a Maid of Honour to the Duchess of York, in company with her fellow poet Anne Killigrew. Her work was circulated among aristocratic friends in manuscript, but little was published in her lifetime. One dramatic lyric with an erotic charge is 'The white mouses petition to Lamira the Right Honble the Lady Ann Tufton now Countess of Salisbury'. Winchilsea speaks as a mouse (a symbol of female lust)[17] who has the run of the beloved's body:

> I sue to wear Lamira's fetters
> And live the envy of my betters
> When I receive her soft caresses
> And creeping near her lovely tresses
> Their glossy brown from my reflection
> Shall gain more lustre and perfection
> And to her bosom if admitted
> My colour there will be so fitted
> That no distinction cou'd discover
> My station to a jealous Lover.[18]

The mouse does not scamper merrily; it is well aware of the dangers. Although its surreptitious advances into the Countess' hair and then bosom are rewarded with caresses, it must watch out for the jealous suspicion of her male suitors. This is a poem about camouflage. It is the sameness of colour that allows the mouse to revel, unseen, between the lady's breasts, and it is the sameness of sex, combined with the whimsy, that allows the female poet to write such an erotic poem to a woman and get away with it.

Pastoral poetry – set in idealised landscapes – provides some of the most uninhibited poems of female passion. One of its countless practitioners is Elizabeth Singer Rowe, daughter of a prosperous preacher/clothier, who grew up in a circle of intellectual, aristocratic friends and was briefly married to a history student thirteen years her junior. Anne Finch, Countess of Winchilsea was one of her literary friends; Frances Thynne, Countess of Hertford was her romantic friend and patron. Although Rowe later became known as a religious writer of meditations and Scripture paraphrases, her poems of the 1690s are exuberant pastoral lyrics, in many of which it is impossible to tell whether the 'you' addressed is male or female.

'Love and Friendship: A Pastoral' is an early poem taken from her *Miscellaneous Works* (1739) which went into at least six editions by 1820. The nymph (pastoral code for a woman) Amaryllis begins the poem by describing the lovely evening, a perfect time for her and her friend Sylvia to sit under a tree and tell their 'am'rous secrets' without fear of being overheard by any 'swain' (shepherd, that is, a man). What follows is not so much a discussion as a set of alternating speeches; Rowe gives almost exactly the same number of lines to each viewpoint. Sylvia speaks first, upsetting Amaryllis' preconceptions from the start by insisting that she needs no hiding place in which to confess her 'am'rous secret', because she is proud to reveal that her beloved is not a man but a woman, Aminta:

> To ev'ry shepherd I would mine proclaim;
> Since fair Aminta is my softest theme:
> A stranger to the loose delights of love,
> My thoughts the nobler warmth of friendship prove.

Here love and friendship do not appear to mean different intensities of relationship, but a passion for men and for women respectively; this becomes clear as we see the fervour of Sylvia's 'friendship' with Aminta.

With much more reluctance, Amaryllis admits that she is in love with the swain Alexis. The only obvious differences between the sexualities of Amaryllis and Sylvia so far is that relations with men are presumed by Sylvia to be sexually 'loose', compared with 'nobler' female friendship, and that conventions of female modesty make it difficult for Amaryllis to be proud of her passion for a man. But more stress is laid on the similarity between the two experiences, and their equal value, than on their difference. It seems to be a matter of personal taste and identity; Amaryllis focuses on men and prays to Eros, 'propitious god of love', whereas Sylvia is vowed to virginity and female friendship in the service of Diana, 'chaste goddess of the groves'.

In her first speech about her beloved Alexis, Amaryllis describes him in conventional terms as attractive to all women ('for him each virgin sighs') and beating all men in competition. Yet we have already met one virgin, Sylvia, who sighs for no man; this passion for friends disrupts the generalisations about universal heterosexuality usually made in pastoral poetry. By contrast, Sylvia describes Aminta as attractive not just to one sex but to everyone:

> When she is near, all anxious trouble flies;
> And our reviving hearts confess her eyes.
> Young love, and blooming joy, and gay desires,
> In ev'ry breast the beauteous nymph inspires.

The effect Aminta has is not just to make people 'sigh' for her, but to make them brighten up; she belongs to no one person, but has a metamorphosing effect on many. Faced with this image of Sylvia's beloved as a goddess figure who makes everyone happy, Amaryllis stops generalising about Alexis' attractions. What she does know is her own reaction to him: when her 'dear, lovely youth' is absent, she wanders 'lonely' through 'some obscure retreat'. Sylvia, on the other hand, profits by absence from Aminta by seeking out 'flow'ry banks' and writing poetry, inspired by her beloved muse: 'Tis she that does my artful notes refine:/With fair *Aminta*'s name my noblest verse shall shine.' Though neither woman gives any signs of having listened to the other, by the end of the poem Amaryllis has clearly decided to change her strategy: she announces that she is going to 'twine fresh garlands' for Alexis, offer him 'eternal vows' and (like Sylvia) be inspired to poetry by her beloved. But the mention of vows makes a jarring contrast to Sylvia's passion for Aminta. Where Amaryllis acts possessively in the heterosexual economy, hoping to win Alexis to be her own, Sylvia concentrates on Aminta's glories and how happy such love makes her.[19]

Elizabeth Hands, who was a domestic servant before her marriage, published an epic about incest, *The Death of Amnon*, in 1789. As an appendix she included shorter poems, some of which praise female friendship. In 'The Rural Maid in London', the speaker explains how she misses her beloved friend and home. More difficult to interpret is 'An Epistle', which describes the romantic friendship of two upper-class women so fervidly that – in a collection by a woman of working-class origins – it sounds almost tongue-in-cheek. In her superb study of poetry by eighteenth-century labouring women, Donna Landry reads this poem as 'subtle parody'.[20] However, 'An Epistle' sounds to me no more melodramatic than many another poem of absence, from one romantic friend to her faraway beloved; Hands may simply be taking part in a tradition which was formed by the assumptions of upper- and middle-class women who had time to droop on sofas. What I find most remarkable about 'An Epistle' is not its potential to be read as parody, but Hands' documentation of the devastating psychological effects of absence from the object of obsessive love.

Belinda addresses her long-absent Maria in the form of a verse letter that both uses and questions pastoral conventions:

> Let love-sick nymphs their faithful shepherds prove,
> Maria's friendship's more to me than love;
> When you were here, I smil'd throughout the day,
> No rustic shepherdess was half so gay.

She goes on to describe the symptoms of breakdown:

> But now, alas! I can no pleasure know,
> The tedious hours of absence move so slow;
> I secret mourn, not daring to complain,
> Still seeking for relief, but seek in vain.

Romantic friendship generally enjoyed a large measure of social acceptance in the late eighteenth century, but here Elizabeth Hands describes Belinda's mourning as 'secret'; her passion seems to have become so overwhelming that she cannot 'dare' to express it.

Belinda now details her day. Her morning walk is always to the top of a hill from which she can see the spire of Maria's village church, where, she tells Maria, she can 'sigh to you, and languish with desire'. By noon she has retired to a shady grove, where she experiences hallucinations of her friend:

> In search of you, my wand'ring fancy roves
> From shade to shade, pleas'd with the vain delight,
> Imagination brings you to my sight;
> Fatigu'd I sink into my painted chair,
> And your ideal form attends me there.

By evening Belinda is walking through the garden, where all the flowers droop and weep as she does. At night she cannot sleep; she paces up and down, is momentarily distracted by the beautiful moonlight, then remembers her absent beloved, and the moon clouds over again.

After this detailed account of the effects of absence, the poem ends with a simple plea:

> 'Tis you, Maria, and 'tis only you,

That can the wonted face of things renew:
Come to my groves; command the birds to sing,
And o'er the meadows bid fresh daisies spring:
No! rather come and chase my gloom away,
That I may sing like birds, and look like daisies gay.[21]

The pastoral convention, that the beloved makes birds and flowers come to life, is abandoned in the last couplet; Belinda brings the focus back to her own mind, and realises that she can provide her own music and beauty if she is nourished by Maria's presence.

The last poem I want to look at is by Anna Seward (pronounced like 'seaward'). A lame and scholarly spinster, daughter of a clergyman poet, Seward's most passionate attachments were to women. Generally her happier poems are bland, as are her addresses to her friends the Ladies of Llangollen; one ends with the wish that when Eleanor and Sarah die, it will be together, under a single bolt of lightning.[22] But Seward's grief-stricken sonnet sequence, which she began before the marriage of her beloved Honora Sneyd to Richard Edgeworth (Maria Edgeworth's father) in 1773 and went on writing until many years after Honora's death in 1780, is extraordinarily powerful. One of the most moving is Sonnet X, written in April 1773. In one long, relentless sentence, Seward expresses her sense of betrayal, and her dread of further alienation from her beloved and greater unbearable loss.

Honora, should that cruel time arrive
When 'gainst my truth thou should'st my errors poise,
Scorning remembrance of our vanish'd joys;
When for the love-warm looks, in which I live,
But cold respect must greet me, that shall give
No tender glance, no kind regretful sighs;
When thou shalt pass me with averted eyes,
Feigning thou see'st me not, to sting, and grieve,
And sicken my sad heart, I could not bear
Such dire eclipse of thy soul-cheering rays;
I could not learn my struggling heart to tear
From thy loved form, that thro' my memory strays;
Nor in the pale horizon of despair
Endure the wintry and the darken'd days.[23]

Whereas slightly later sonnets on the marriage attack Honora and her husband with self-righteous scorn, in this one Seward admits that some 'errors' were mixed in with the 'truth' of her friendship for Honora. This is a poem not of blame but of grief; it focuses not on the circumstances of the betrayal but on anticipation of the daily, petty losses of Honora's love. The hackneyed metaphor of sunlight/darkness is anchored by Seward's precise imagining of a social encounter with a future, cold Honora.

In half a dozen lyrics, then, we see that this kind of poetry does not endlessly repeat the ideals of romantic friendship, but adapts many different conventions for expressing and justifying love between women.

Spinsterhood

The primary contradiction within romantic friendship, and one which has received almost no attention from historians, is its threat to marriage. Generally the official story in texts of the seventeenth and eighteenth centuries was that women's passionate bonds prepared them for, coexisted with and even took the pressure off their marriages. However, there was also a strand of misogamist (marriage-hating) women's writing throughout this period that linked the love of friends to a revulsion for marriage; it is these writings which convince me that spinsterhood was central to lesbian culture. Spinsters were a core group of man-free women whose lives and writings inspired other women to put themselves, and the women they loved, first.[24]

In this period, every opportunity was taken to promote marriage – both to increase the population and to tame women into wives. During the eighteenth century other career options for women were closed off one by one. Yet despite these pressures, marriage rates fell sharply from the end of the seventeenth century onwards; Laurence Stone estimates that at least one fifth of the daughters of the landed gentry were old maids throughout the eighteenth century, peaking at a quarter around 1725. Stone assumes that these women were unlucky, consigned to spinsterhood by economic factors, because the system of primogeniture (inheritance by the eldest son) reduced their dowries and impoverished their potential suitors. He even speculates that some of the men stayed bachelors because they were homosexual – but he suspects no lesbian motives among the women![25]

By contrast, I see this high rate of spinsterhood not merely as an economic phenomenon but as an index of women's choices. Chosen spinsterhood is sometimes discussed as an upper-class luxury, though in fact many rich women were pressured into marriage to make alliances of property, whereas poor women sometimes managed to support themselves in single life. In every class, the freedom to live without men was available to some women – perhaps a random set, perhaps to those who wanted it enough. We find women choosing spinsterhood at every point along the economic scale, from the upper-middle-class spinster writers who subsisted in genteel dependence on their families and friends, to a Welsh maid-of-all-work, Elizabeth Davis, who earned just enough to allow her to refuse twelve proposals of marriage because she 'preferred seeing more of the world'.[26]

Texts from the seventeenth and eighteenth centuries often sneered at the sexuality of the 'old maid', using arguments popular among lesbian-baiters in our own era. It is ironic that one particularly bitter rant, 'Advice to Silly Maids', was featured in a miscellany of verses by university men, published with and meant to promote the *Poetical Recreations* (1688) of the spinster poet Jane Barker. Among the claims of the anonymous 'Advice to Silly Maids' are the arguments that choosing not to marry is a sign of madness, and that unmarried women are uglier and have more 'wrinkled Skins' than wives. The author invokes a superstition which, however bizarre it may seem now, persisted well into the twentieth century: the idea that women's bodies need regular doses of semen. 'Who can expect the Body e'er should thrive/And lack its natural preservative?' The tone becomes even sterner in the last verse, which is a warning to independent women such as Jane Barker:

> But if you will continue proud and coy,
> And slight those *Men* who court you to enjoy,
> Here you in wretched *Ignorance* shall dwell,
> And may deservedly *lead Apes in Hell*.[27]

Leading apes in Hell was the proverbial fate of spinsters; the apes can be read as representing male lust, which the women would not be able to avoid in death as they had in life.[28]

Far from accepting this doom, a series of women writers throughout this period argued for the advantages of spinsterhood. The prototype of the spinster as a respectable public figure, and the first to theorise this issue, was Mary Astell. A political and religious writer from a family of wealthy Newcastle coal merchants, Astell published two controversial feminist treatises, *A Serious Proposal to the Ladies* (part I 1694, part II 1697, 'by a Lover of her

Sex') and *Some Reflections upon Marriage* (1700). Though they quickly dropped out of print, these treatises had enormous influence, particularly on later women writers. Astell's life was spent loving women and God, and the rumour that she had been jilted by a clergyman cannot be substantiated by any evidence.[29]

The readers of *A Serious Proposal* are told not to be 'terrified with the dreadful name of Old Maid'. Once women dare to break the 'enchanted circle' of heterosexual femininity, Astell explains, we can become 'absolute Monarchs in our own Bosoms'.[30] Her furious *Some Reflections upon Marriage* works more indirectly to advocate spinsterhood. The first two editions are anonymous; the preface to the third admits that the author is a woman, but denies any rebellious feminist motive: 'far be it from her to stir up Sedition of any sort ... she did not in any manner prompt them to resist, or to Abdicate the Perjur'd Spouse'.

Astell's strategy here is a clever one: rather than pleading for reform of the oppressive institution of marriage, or inciting rebellion against it, she insists on its traditional form – subordination of the wife – in order to discourage her women readers from trying it. The coy phrase 'far be it' recurs in Astell's ambiguous defence of marriage: 'it is the institution of Heaven, the only Honourable way of continuing Mankind, and far be it from us to think there could have been a better'. After a scathing account of common marital problems, she wonders: 'if Marriage be such a blessed State, how comes it, may you say, that there are so few happy Marriages?' She cannot make such a suggestion herself, but 'you' can; Astell rarely poses dangerous questions in the first person. She uses another neutral pronoun to draw the obvious conclusion: 'It may be said, if a Wife's case be as it is here represented, it is not good for a Woman to Marry.' However, Astell has to draw back from this revolutionary suggestion and content herself with a warning that a woman 'has no reason to be fond of being a Wife, or to reckon it a piece of Preferment when she is taken to be a Man's Upper Servant'.[31]

An unbroken tradition of such misogamist writings can be traced running throughout the eighteenth century. They often link disdain for marriage with the female friendship for which there is room in a life of spinsterhood.[32] An anonymous poem of 1720, 'Cloe to Artimesa', crows:

> We, whom a nicer taste has raised above
> The dangerous follies of such slavish love,

Despise the sex, and in our selves we find
Pleasures for their gross senses too refined.[33]

This poem's tone of smug satisfaction with the morally lofty 'pleasures' of women's love is characteristic of much of the literature of romantic friendship.

Nor were all such texts by women; male writers took an occasional interest in this subject. On 17 September 1709, Richard Steele's periodical the *Tatler* included a letter purporting to be from two women who, fearing that marriage would break up their friendship, were considering both marrying the same unappealing man so that they could stay together. In his introduction and reply, Steele mocked the women for their calm approach to bigamy, but not for their passionate friendship which was presented as a fact of female life.

Some blistering attacks on marriage early in the century came from the spinster writer Elizabeth Thomas and her unhappily married friend Lady Mary Chudleigh. The most important early writer on spinsterhood, however, must be Jane Barker. The rare literary historians who notice her at all assume that, like her heroine Galesia, she chose single life after being jilted by a suitor. This 'early jilting' motif was such a conventional and acceptable reason for being an old maid that it could function as a cover for a woman's basic disdain for heterosexuality. Barker's triumphant poem 'On the Apothecary's Filing my Bills amongst the Doctors' explains, in the voice of her persona Galesia, that the consequences of desertion were wonderful, since after being jilted by her fiancé she found a career as a professional healer.

Barker's writings often entwine ideals of spinsterhood and romantic female friendship in what she celebrates in one poem as 'A Virgin Life'. But most important are her four patchwork-style fictions, which form the first sustained account of a spinster heroine in English fiction. Having been jilted by Bosvil in *Love Intrigues* (1713), Galesia soon recovers her cheerful independence. In *A Patch-work Screen for the Ladies* (1723), we find her living in the country, rapturously reading and imitating the friendship poetry of Katherine Philips. A virtuous adventurer, Galesia swaps stories with strangers in a stagecoach, falls in rivers and is befriended by women at every point. Several other suitors propose marriage, but Galesia either finds moral reasons to refuse them or, in one case, stalls until the suitor is hanged as a highwayman.

Meanwhile, in the tiny garret she thinks of as 'Paradise', Galesia studies medicine and writes poetry. She has a troubled, erotic relationship with her female Muse: 'Sometimes I wou'd repel her Insinuations, and sometimes again accept her Caresses.' Galesia's mother, dismayed by her daughter's spinster lifestyle, tells her that 'we, in a manner, frustrate the End of our Creation, to live in that uncouth kind of Solitude.' Galesia can see her point, but confesses to 'a secret Disgust against Matrimony', and it is clear that she is not suffering from 'frustration'. When her next troublesome suitor happens to shoot himself, Galesia is not at all disconsolate; she remarks with tongue firmly in cheek that she 'endeavour'd to be resign'd'. With relief she announces that 'Providence had ordain'd for me a *Single Life.*' Her mother can only agree: 'if there be a fatal Necessity that it must be so, e'en go on, and make thyself easy with thy fantastick Companions the Muses'.[34]

A key text for misogamy in the mid-century period is the body of letters between the Bluestocking writers Elizabeth Carter and Catherine Talbot, recording their lifelong romantic friendship, most of which were published by 1809. Elizabeth Carter seems to have been much more deliberate than her friend in her choice of spinsterhood and her resistance to marriage as an institution.[35] On 24 May 1744, for example, she took up her pen at four in the morning to tell Talbot why she had been depressed recently. Carter's letter explains that she had suspected another dear friend was going to be married, and was terrified of losing her, having 'read in a book, that people when they marry are dead and buried to all former attachments'. (The book could have been Katherine Philips' *Letters from Olinda to Poliarchus,* published in 1705, but by the mid-century marriage was fairly commonly described as the funeral or grave of friendship.) Carter goes on to say that her depression lifted only when the friend guessed what was on her mind and reassured her that she was not engaged. Using whimsy to veil her intense anxiety, Carter tells Talbot that, without this reassurance, 'you might have heard of my being run wild into a wood, and hopping about from tree to tree like a squirrel, and feeding on nuts and acorns'. What worries her is not just the possible loss of the friend, but her dawning realisation that she is not like most other women; more possessive and impassioned than friends are supposed to be, she feels like a greedy wild animal among humans. Fearing reproach, Carter asks for advice on how to tame herself; here she exposes her vulnerabilty to Talbot in a characteristic act of friendship. 'Whether you will laugh at, or pity me most for this strange delicacy of friendship I cannot tell', she concludes shyly, 'but as I have so honestly confessed all my weakness, I hope you will have the charity to give me your advice how to conquer it.'

Talbot's reply of 27 June 1744 offers several suggestions of varying degrees of flippancy. Perhaps Carter could avoid such a loss by being the first to marry? Or (equally unlikely) convert to Roman Catholicism and enter a convent 'where you may have a whole sisterhood of friends secluded from the rest of the world'? The third, and only feasible option, is resignation:

> we must e'en lower our ideas of friendship to the pitch of common life, and be content with loving and esteeming people constantly and affectionately amid a variety of thwarting, awkward circumstances, that forbid all possibility of spending our lives together.

Notice that she has moved from 'you' to 'we', and made herself a participant in this predicament. Complete fulfilment, Talbot adds, is 'inconsistent with such a world as this'. She ends more reassuringly by explaining that when another close friend of hers married, their affection continued unchanged and she managed to rise above jealousy: 'I have no notion of monopolies in friendship; and provided people love me with sincerity, in the moderate degree I deserve, they are welcome to love as many more as they please.' But Carter is not satisfied. Her answer of 20 July 1744 insists rather defensively that she does not want to possess her friend entirely, just to keep the bond they have, 'for her favourites always become mine, and could I flatter myself the case would be parallel to what you describe, I could bear it with tolerable tranquillity, but I am persuaded it would be quite different'. Her message is clear: other female friends will probably not get in the way, since friends expect to share each other, but a husband makes such primary demands on a wife's attention and energy that a romantic friendship has little chance of surviving. For Carter, spinsterhood is not only the enabling factor for her independent lifestyle and professional writing career; it is a fundamental requirement for her love relationships with women as well.

Elizabeth Carter was writing a private letter; in public print, it would have been difficult for her to be so frank. Whereas the early defenders of Mary Astell's theories attacked marriage boldly and proclaimed the joys of spinsterhood, the next few generations seem to have felt the need to tone down their enthusiasm. Texts published in the mid-eighteenth century, such as Frances Brooke's twopenny weekly *The Old Maid* (November 1755 to April 1756) and Sarah Fielding's novels, generally show a more wary and sometimes tongue-in-cheek attitude; they are supportive of spinsterhood only in particular cases. Jane Spencer has argued that mid-century women writers tended to muffle their feminist voices because they were becoming respectable members of the male-dominated writing community.[36] Also, there was increasing social pressure to marry and produce children for the British Empire; by the mid-eighteenth century it would have been considered shockingly unpatriotic as well as unfeminine to advocate spinsterhood in general. A good example of this is found in the semi-autobiographical utopian fiction *A Description of Millenium Hall* (1762) by Sarah Robinson Scott, who left her husband after less than a year of marriage and settled near Bath with her beloved Lady Bab Montagu. *Millenium Hall* features a group of widows and spinsters who form a community for scholarship and good works. Presumably to shield herself from accusations of misogamy, Scott shows her heroines going out of their way to help poor girls of the parish to marry. One of them offers this coy explanation of the paradox: 'according to all ancient tenures, those obliged to perform knight's service, might, if they chose to enjoy their own firesides, be excused by sending deputies to supply their places'.[37] Scott is comparing marriage to war – because they are both social institutions which cannot be openly attacked in the mid-eighteenth century, and also perhaps because both have damaging or fatal effects on the human beings involved. The tone of the remark is light and self-deprecating, but the half-hidden message is serious: let us enjoy our own firesides as long as we can.

It was often assumed, with charitable condescension, that spinsters were women whom no man wanted to marry. One writer who set up a milliner's shop in her teens, Mary Chandler, had a crooked spine, which many commentators have identified as the bar to her marriage. But in several witty poems Chandler makes it clear that spinsterhood, like vegetarianism, is her choice. 'A True Tale' tells the comic saga of an unromantic proposal of marriage that she received late in life, while 'A Letter to the Right Honourable the Lady Russel' explains that 'Friendship's the sweetest Joy in human Life:/'Tis *that* I wish – and *not* to be a Wife.'[38] A Midlands poet of the 1770s, Priscilla Pointon, had a similar alibi: she was blind from childhood. Under the veil of disability, she could publish poems of assertive misogamy such as 'The Maid's Resolution', which ends with a cheerful spinster telling a taunting bachelor that if there are apes in hell, he is one of them.[39]

The strange thing is that this literature by women in praise of the single life attracted little or no attention from men. Did men tend not to read such texts, or did they read them as insincere? Male writers – a typical example is Francis Douglas in his *Reflections on Celibacy and Marriage* (1771) and *Considerations on the Causes of the Present Stagnation of Matrimony* (1772) – continued to assume that men were at fault for choosing roving bachelorhood, whereas women were only to be pitied for their consequent inability to catch husbands. The poet William Hayley devoted three volumes to a flippant analysis of the subject in *Essay on Old Maids* (1785), which was dedicated with mock-reverence to Elizabeth Carter, much to her annoyance. Hayley admits to knowing some old maids who claim it is 'the condition of their choice, and what every wise woman would chuse', but he interprets any such claim as 'a kind of ill-constructed rampart, raised very hastily by mistaken pride, to defend an uneasy situation'. Since any woman who really does not want to marry would be 'utterly devoid of tenderness', he would rather believe that these spinsters are lying. The only good reasons for a woman not to marry, as Hayley sees it, are devoted nursing of a brain-damaged brother, or being disappointed in love and helping your romantic friend to rear her children instead.[40]

I have found only a couple of texts from an outsider's perspective which admit that a woman's tendency to love women can turn her away from marriage. The first, a brief mention in Charlotte Lennox's novel *Sophia* (1762), makes the combination of romantic friendship and spinsterhood sound somewhat sinister. The gentle Dolly explains why Mrs Gibbons is so tyrannical as to forbid the marriage of her nephew William to Dolly:

> When she was a young woman, a great lady took a fancy to her, and kept her as her companion a great many years, and when she died, she left her all her cloaths and jewels, and a prodigious deal of money: she never would marry, for she was crossed in love they say in her youth, and that makes her so illnatured and spiteful.[41]

The 'crossed in love' explanation is brought in at the end, to obscure the pattern of this woman's life; the love and money she gets from a woman enable her to stay a spinster.

Another text that makes this link is the *General Evening Post*'s report of 24 July 1790 on the 'Extraordinary Female Affection' between the Ladies of Llangollen. Eleanor Butler, we are told, rejected several offers of marriage; since Sarah Ponsonby, 'her particular friend and companion, was supposed to be the bar to all matrimonial union, it was thought proper to separate them, and Miss Butler was confined. The two Ladies, however, found means to elope together.' In this exceptional text, romantic passion between women is seen as similar to heterosexuality (leading to 'elopement') and rivalling it.

George Elers, an army captain who wrote his memoirs in his 60s, remembered with amused nostalgia how as a teenager he tried to court his cousin Sophia Colston. It was 1791, when the cult of romantic female friendship was at its height; Sophia laughed at all his professions of love. In retrospect, Elers is convinced that he 'never made the slightest impression upon her, or ever should have done', and has 'since been informed' of this 'by ladies who knew her well'.

At the age of 16, when she became the object of George's desire, Sophia was not yet in a female couple. However, she was already so likely to form such an attachment – so clearly situated in this category of women we have no specific name for, these women who wanted nothing but to live as beloved friends – that 'ladies who knew her well' were sure, even then, that she would never marry. Sophia, as it happened, found happiness early:

> After I went abroad she formed a most romantic attachment to a young lady by the name of Arabella Ross. At that time Lady E. Butler and the Hon. Miss Ponsonby lived in Wales together. Their affection, I presume, was founded on similar principles.

Elers' diffidence is endearing; he cannot take it upon himself to specify what those principles of female affection might be, but he never questions that they are more important to Sophia than the marriage her entire education had trained her for. Clearly women's romantic partnership was such a reality when Elers was growing up – with the Ladies of Llangollen representing only the most famous, public example – that it does not occur to him now to challenge or pry into it. He concludes by telling how Sophia Colston died, aged 25, of rapid consumption, and left her entire fortune to Arabella Ross.[42] We should not assume that stories like hers, of complete emotional and financial partnership outside the frame of marriage, were exceptional, just because the dominant British culture was understandably reluctant to record them.

Divided hearts

Much of the literature of passionate female friendship describes not spinsterhood but a double life, shared between a male lover/husband and a beloved woman. In many cases a female character goes through a marriage of convenience which proves nothing about her feelings; in other texts, however, women do seem to relate passionately to both women and men. I hesitate to use the adjective 'bisexual' in all these cases, because it suggests that the women's relations with men and with women were equivalent and parallel, when in fact legal marriages and female friendships had very different economic privileges and social status, and also because many women would probably not have thought of their friendships as sexual in the same way as their marriages were supposed to be.

In this section I look at some texts that treat the problems and joys of combining love for both sexes. As Janet Todd has pointed out, 'literary female friendship is rarely allowed to exist in a pair'.[43] Triangles of two women and one man, focused not on the man but on one of the women, are common in literature of this period; for example, many stories end with one heroine marrying her romantic friend's brother.

A poem of Aphra Behn's, 'To Mrs Harsenet' (1692), describes how one women can come to desire another via a man. The female speaker expects to be jealous of Mrs Harsenet, about whom she has heard so much, but when she sees her, hostility dissolves in worship. 'I wish'd to see, and half a lover grew/Of so much Beauty, though my Rival too.' Although her faithless swain Amyntas is pursuing Mrs Harsenet, the speaker cannot blame him, since his response now seems natural to her. 'And whilst I Blame him, I Excuse him too;/Who could be innocent that looks on you?' She does not just sympathise with his desire, she shares it. Behn's speaker ends the poem by hinting that she herself is a worthier suitor than Amyntas with all his stale professions, and that what Mrs Harsenet deserves is (note the neutral gender) 'a Virgin-heart'. The wit of this poem lies in the switch of love objects. Amyntas having betrayed the speaker by turning to Mrs Harsenet, the speaker does not bewail her loss but betrays him in her turn, rivalling him for Mrs Harsenet's attention. It is amusing to note that the economical Aphra was in a similar emotional triangle eight years earlier, when she published an almost identical poem under the title 'To my Lady Morland'.[44]

The playwright Catharine Trotter (later Cockburn) was Behn's heir in her focus on passionate friendship between women who are also emotionally committed to men. In her fictional autobiography, *Olinda's Adventures*, allegedly written when she was 14, Trotter describes her love for the untrustworthy 'Clarinda' as well as for a series of men.[45] Her romantic friend and patron was the poet Lady Sarah Piers; their troubled, convoluted letters hint at a sexual connection,[46] and a contemporary satire called them lovers (see pp. 237–8).

At the age of just 16, Trotter wrote the first tragedy by a woman to be produced on the London stage since the plays of Aphra Behn. *Agnes de Castro*, based on Behn's translation of a French novel, was performed with considerable success in 1695 and published the following year. The heroine, Constantia, loves her husband the prince and her friend Agnes equally and ecstatically. The two passions are expressed in parallel; Agnes is Constantia's 'Souls best Comfort', and Constantia loves the prince 'better than my Life'. She explains in the first act:

> For you are both so equal dear to me,
> So closely wove by Fate to my fond breast,
> That neither can be sever'd from my love,
> Without unravelling this Web of Life

This declaration sets the scene for the action, which is to test Constantia: can she hold on to both, can the web hold firm? For her there is no question of choosing between them, as she can no longer see where one passion ends and the other begins. Agnes and the prince, she insists, 'share my divided Heart/So equally, I cannot tell my self/To which I have given most.'[47] Notice that they don't split or tear her divided heart, they share it.

Constantia remains loyal to both friend and husband, despite all the attempts of the villainess Elvira to fracture the happy triangle. When she discovers that the prince has fallen in love with Agnes, she cannot blame him, since (as in the Behn poem quoted above) she feels the same: 'For I myself, prefer her to my self,/And love her too, as tenderly as he.' Agnes, horrified to be the cause of grief in their marriage, asks permission to leave court, but Constantia cannot do without her and pleads: 'Fate has depriv'd me but of half my blessing;/And you wou'd tear the other half away.' Constantia's dividedness has now become a doubleness, giving her emotional stability, since although she no longer comes first with the prince she is growing even closer to Agnes. Elvira, who had hoped to break up the women's friendship by revealing the prince's feelings, now discovers how little she understood the women. A servant reports seeing Constantia and Agnes, who 'mingled Kisses with the tend'rest Words,/As if their Rivalship had made 'em dear'.[48] Elvira resorts to murder. Slowly dying of a stab wound, Constantia begs Agnes to marry the prince and be a foster mother to their child. Trotter ends this play rather ambiguously: Agnes talks herself into a half-consent – telling the prince that she will think of him as a future husband, but only 'for her [Constantia's] sake' – before she too is murdered.

Kathryn Kendall's essay on this play hails Agnes as the first lesbian stage heroine, yet barely mentions Constantia. She ignores the evidence of Agnes' final speech, assuring the reader that Agnes is revolted by or indifferent to all men and does not marry the prince but dies instead.[49] Edna Steeves, by contrast, ignores the women's friendship and focuses on this last speech, in which Agnes (she imagines) 'hovers on the verge of a confession of true and passionate love' for the prince.[50] Both these readings – from a lesbian feminist and heterosexist viewpoint respectively – seem to be distortions of what Trotter's play actually shows. Making the best of a tragic situation, Agnes does seem to find in herself the potential to love a man as well as (though coming after) a woman.

The codes of heroic friendship, then, were often used by early women playwrights to explore love for both sexes. Catharine Trotter's *The Unhappy Penitent* (1701) deals with the 'strict Friendship' between Ann of Brittany and Margarite of Flanders – so 'strict', in fact, that Margarite can preserve her honour in the eyes of her stern friend only by giving up the man she loves and becoming a nun.[51]

Trotter's colleague Mary Pix wrote two tragedies in which the famous actresses Mrs Barry and Mrs Bracegirdle played pairs of romantic friends. In *The Double Distress* (1701), Cytheria and Leamira make great sacrifices to try to save each other from evil fates; at one point Leamira tells her friend:

> And while *I* hold thee thus, my *Cytheria*,
> The Crown upon my Father's Head is not

> So priz'd, as is this Gemm within my Bosom.
> What Monster, bred beneath the frigid Zone,
> But wou'd, like me, thus open wide it's Arms,
> And burn with ardent Fires for her Reception.[52]

The 'ardent Fires' are more agonising to the pair of friends in Mary Pix's *Queen Catharine* (1698), which is set in a siege during the Wars of the Roses. Isabella is planning to elope, but cannot bear to desert her beloved guardian Queen Catharine; as in *Agnes de Castro*, 'divided' is a key word.

> O my divided Soul,
> Can I leave the dear indulgent Queen;
> O draw me, Heaven, thro' this Labyrinth!
> For Love and Friendship pull me several ways,
> Like Cords upon the Rack.

Her devotion is returned; the queen tells her fiancé Tudor that Isabella is the 'Dearest object of my Friendship; nay she/Almost Rivals you.' But it is Isabella who seems most passionate, continuing to use the imagery of bondage in her unspoken addresses to the queen.

> Can you not find in my disordered looks,
> The tumults of my Soul, and Chain me
> Near ye?

A mistake made during Isabella's elopement opens the castle to invasion by enemy forces. Isabella reproaches herself in language of a sado-masochistic intensity which suggests that what she is really guilty about is having transferred her loyalty from a beloved woman and mother figure to a man:

> Let the injur'd Queen punish me, let her
> Spurn me, trample on me, print me with a
> Thousand wounds, I'll not complain.

But when the queen sees Isabella's dead body, she forgives her at once, concluding 'Love was her only crime'.[53] This principle of respect for love in any form allowed early women playwrights to integrate the theme of passion between women into the tradition of heroic love.

Sarah Fielding, an impoverished spinster from the professional classes, wrote some of the most perceptive novels of the period. Several of her fictions include triangles, composed of two women whose friendship is tested and ultimately strengthened by the invasion of a man. It was common in eighteenth-century fiction for a self-sacrificial woman to give up a suitor to her beloved friend, but Fielding charged the motif with new intensity by concentrating on the complex psychology of the women's friendship, its 'secret springs'.[54]

Familiar Letters (1747) includes the story of Priscilla, an orphaned child who is reared with her slightly older cousin Harriot. Their similar personalities make for a blissful partnership: 'Continually being together, appeared the greatest Pleasure, that even their Imagination could form.' The friendship is marked by unselfconscious generosity: 'instead of quarrelling and fighting for the best Play-thing, their only Dispute arose from the Fear each of them felt, lest her Companion should have any thing worse than she herself had'. When the girls grow up, the 'best Play-thing' turns out to be a man, their distant cousin Publius, with whom (being so well matched in every taste) they both fall in love.

> They acted as Friends should do, and confessed to each other the whole Truth, as soon as they knew it themselves. Great as their Distress was, they found some sort of Refuge from it in their own Goodness, and artless Sincerity; and agreed, that, if the Object of their Love should seriously make choice of either of them, the other should give him up.

Rather than letting heterosexual rivalry triumph over female friendship, Fielding shows that the honest confession, practical plans and sense of collusion draw Harriot and Priscilla closer together.

Publius quickly shows a preference for Harriot, who is too distressed by her cousin's pain to respond very gratefully. Priscilla generously urges on the wedding but disappears two days after the ceremony, leaving her friend a note to say she will return when she can overcome her sorrow. For two years Harriot misses Priscilla, who finally comes back as a cheerful spinster: 'she spent the Remainder of her Life (for she would never hear of Marrying) with her dear *Harriot*.'[55] Poor Publius, though he shares a house with them, never hears a word about any of this. Though the women's lives are organised around their social and emotional need of a husband, he is completely excluded from their intimate communication.

Sarah Fielding tells a more disturbing version of this story in *The Governess*, the first novel for and about schoolgirls.[56] Celia and Chloe are cousins, both orphaned and brought up together by a rich spinster aunt who delights in their fond friendship. They turn out alike in beauty and goodness: what can divide them, distinguish between them, make them reveal themselves to each other as individuals? Until the age of 22 the girls refuse proposals of marriage, preferring to stay with their aunt in a stable triangle of female love, 'perfectly happy in their own little Community'. But then Sempronious, an army friend of their dead fathers', comes visiting. He cannot decide which he prefers, and is particularly charmed by their lack of spite in this situation of rivalry:

> With Pleasure he observed, that they made use of none of those Arts which Women generally do to get away a disputed Lover: and this sincere Friendship which subsisted between them raised in him the highest Degree of Love and Admiration. However he at last determined to make the following Trial.

Fielding's irony is powerful here: Sempronious only admires their friendship insofar as it represents a worthy challenge to his charm. He wants to put it on 'Trial' so that it will fail.

Taking Chloe aside, he asks whether she knows of anything bad in Celia's character which should prevent him from marrying her. Strongly tempted to win him herself, Chloe says that Celia is a little artful and envious. When he puts the same question to Celia, she sighs and assures him that Chloe would make him very happy. However, Sempronious is not just trying to discover which is the most morally impeccable; he clearly wants to kill the friendship too. 'Could you believe it?' he asks Celia; 'this Friend of yours is false. I have already put her to the Trial.' He expects Celia to be overjoyed at having won, but she bursts into tears and cannot be comforted unless he promises to forgive Chloe's lie. The triangle cannot be simplified into the heterosexual line; Celia may feel betrayed by her beloved friend, but she is not prepared to give her up. She refuses to accept Sempronious as her husband until she is reconciled to Chloe.

At this point Chloe's character must undergo an equivalent growth. She repents her lie instantly, but, overhearing the couple in the garden, knows that it is too late to apologise. Sempronious cuts her dead; confusion silences her and Celia.

> They were both afraid of speaking. Shame, and the Fear of being (and with too good Reason) suspected of Insincer-

> ity, with-held *Chloe*; and an Unwillingness to accuse or hurt her Friend with-held the gentle *Celia* ... She knew that her Friend's Passions were naturally stronger than hers; and she therefore trembled at the Consequences of coming to an explanation.

Yet unless they dare the explanation, the mutual exposure of their desires and regrets, their friendship will wither away. The strain sends Chloe into a serious fever, which allows her to have Celia's constant attention as a nurse for three days. Knowing she will be believed on her deathbed, Chloe's tongue is loosened; she confesses, is forgiven and recovers. For three weeks they spend every hour together, never mentioning Sempronious, renewing their bond. At last Chloe has got the better of herself and can announce that she is looking forward to their wedding. Sempronious gets both more and less than he bargained for; he wins both women, in a sense, but knows that the marriage tie will always come second to their friendship. If everyone behaves well, such an arrangement can work, Sarah Fielding assures her young readers: 'They all lived together, and separate Property was not so much as mentioned or thought on in this Family of Harmony and Peace.'

Alongside tales of rivalry come plots of consolation; these often feature triangles in which primary energy is transferred from the heterosexual to the lesbian lines. Women come awake to each other with startled appreciation, and sometimes consolation is followed up by commitment. The men in these triangles can be shadowy to the point of invisibility; for example, the bestselling novelist Eliza Haywood structured *The British Recluse* (1722) around a missing, faceless man. The two heroines, Belinda and Cleomira, are shown confiding in each other about the men who broke one's heart and seduced the other; when these turn out to be one and the same man, the women's passionate friendship is sealed. They decide to live together, not just to continue mingling their tears but to grow into a new and tranquil life. Eve Sedgwick has argued that seemingly heterosexual plots by men are often really about 'male homosocial desire' being sent on a detour through women.[57] Perhaps in women writers' stories of consolation, such as *The British Recluse*, we can begin to spot the opposite structure: women bonding with each other through men.

An anonymous poem of 1688 addressed to Aphra Behn, entitled 'To Mrs. B. from a Lady who had a desire to see her, and who complains on the ingratitude of her fugitive Lover', speaks in the voice of 'Cleone'. Having been betrayed by 'Strephon', she now redirects her passion to Behn, telling her:

> You may act miracles if you'll be kind,
> Make me true joys in real sorrows find;
> And bless the hour I hither did pursue
> A faithless Swain and found access to you:
> Accept the heart I here to you present,
> By the ingratitude of Strephon rent ...
> As large as once, as uncontroul'd and free,
> But yet at your command shall always be.[58]

The speaker is more than consoled, she is invigorated; her heart is as independent and expansive as before it was wounded. This time, she concludes hopefully, love will not damage her heart, because Behn is so much kinder and more rewarding than the missing man.

The movement in this kind of story is not always from opposite-sex to same-sex commitments. In the controversial feminist Mary Wollstonecraft's early autobiographical novel, *Mary, a Fiction* (1788), the heroine moves the other way. Though this has often been claimed as the first lesbian novel, *Mary* describes the heroine's search for 'an object to love', the gender of the object being much less important than the freedom to love. Her first choice is Ann, with whom she forms an instant passionate bond. They are physically intimate, though this is carefully justified in case any readers are suspicious: 'Mary always slept with Ann, as she was subject to terrifying dreams, and frequently in the night was obliged to be supported, to avoid suffocation.' Unfortunately, Ann is described as having an 'exhausted heart', being still preoccupied with the man who jilted her. This only rouses Mary's pity more and she becomes addicted to helping her consumptive beloved, going so far as to marry a man she loathes in order to be financially secure enough to take Ann away to a warmer climate. The tragedy in this story is the gap between Mary's passion for Ann and Ann's cooler response.[59]

To begin with, Mary has no interest in men: we are told 'her friendship for Ann occupied her heart, and resembled a passion. She had had, indeed, several transient likings [for men], but they did not amount to love.' But Henry, the dying musician she befriends in Lisbon, slowly begins to matter to her. At first it is an intellectual friendship: Mary tells us that in his company her mind expands. Far from being jealous of Ann, Henry tries to entertain her and is in awe of the women's friendship. Mary begins to find conversation with him a welcome relief: 'This divided attention was of use to her, and prevented her continually thinking of Ann.'[60]

At this point we might expect a crisis of jealousy, but Wollstonecraft refuses to do the usual thing. The relationships are cleverly paralleled rather than contrasted, and one follows the other rather than clashing with it. When Ann dies, we are told, Mary needs someone else to love: 'Her heart longed to receive a new guest; there was a void in it.' Sometimes she feels guilty for forgetting Ann even for a moment; at other times her love for Henry dominates. Wollstonecraft is realistic about Mary's motivation: 'had Ann lived', we are told, 'it is probable [Mary] would never have loved Henry so fondly'. Yet the fact remains that she has loved them both, at least briefly. The relationships are similarly platonic, and Mary nurses Henry in his final illness, just as she did Ann. She tells him that her only comfort will be 'in heaven with thee and Ann', and the novel ends with Mary waiting for her own early death as an escape from her loathed husband, 'hastening to that world *where there is neither marrying*, nor giving in *marriage*'.[61] Only outside the economic institution of heterosexual matrimony, Wollstonecraft suggests, can relationships with men and with women be chosen with anything resembling free will. Unlike the many heroines who choose either romantic friendship or heterosexual romance, Mary has it both ways in her short life. Wollstonecraft's book expresses a remarkably clear vision, almost a philosophy, of love for both sexes.

These tales of happy bisexual triangles should not be read too literally. Women writers often used a heterosexual plot as a framework for a safe discussion of women's love for each other; if at least one of the heroines ended up married, the writer could not be accused of being misogamist or anti-social. Texts in which a woman switches her heart from a man to a woman, such as 'Cleone's' poem to Aphra Behn, take place on a lofty emotional plane, telling us little about the everyday world in which Cleone's feelings for a man could bring status, family and fortune, whereas her love for a woman would create only poetry. Wollstonecraft manipulates the plot in *Mary* to make sure the heroine cannot marry the male beloved any more than she can the female beloved, and that she never has to choose between them because they both die. This can be read as an idealistic author's attempt to escape from the way things are, the constraints of 'marrying and giving in marriage', into an imaginary world of free bisexual choice.

The distance between us

The most formulaic stories of female friendship in this period tend to concentrate on similarity: two girls grow up together, one perhaps a little livelier than the other, and they enter society side by side. However, some of the more interesting texts highlight difference, investigating the ways women can be friends across social chasms, particularly of class.

Texts on schoolgirl friendship often warn of the dangers of choosing an unsuitable friend. In the popular conduct book *Letters on the Improvement of the Mind* (1773), Hester Mulso Chapone advises her niece that age gaps can be beneficial in friendship, but differences in rank are dangerous. If the well-born niece chooses a social inferior for a friend, she will fall prey to flattery, while the friend will forget her lowly place and become arrogant.[62] As for servants, they are presented in most educational treatises as dirty, ignorant corrupters of middle-class youth. Unable to face the idea that nice schoolgirls might guess how to give pleasure to themselves and each other, pedagogical writers often blamed servants for spreading the contagion of masturbation.[63] This implausible idea, that overworked maids would industriously set about teaching their juvenile charges sexual techniques which they had somehow picked up themselves in a spare moment, lasted throughout the century. In her founding feminist text *A Vindication of the Rights of Woman* (1792), Mary Wollstonecraft's comments on the educational system include a warning that 'as many girls have learned very nasty tricks, from ignorant servants, the mixing them thus indiscriminately together, is very improper'.[64]

Occasionally a text in this era presents servants as victims of middle-class children – which, again, renders them unavailable as friends. In Sarah Fielding's schoolgirl novel *The Governess* (1749), Sukey Jennet confesses that she abused a friend from the age of 4:

> I had a little Play-fellow, in a Child of one of my Papa's Servants, who was to be intirely under my Command. This Girl I used to abuse and beat, whenever I was out of Humour

> ... For my Governess always told her, that she was but a Servant's Girl, and I was a Gentleman's Daughter; and that therefore she ought to give way to me, for that I did her great Honour in playing with her. Thus I thought the Distance between us was so great, that I never considered that she could feel.

Here, a class divide has become a gulf between species. Stretched over 'the Distance between us', the erotic bond has lost its element of friendship and become wholly sadistic.

Though the other girls in *The Governess* are shown to disapprove of such viciousness, they cannot escape the milder cruelties of the class system. When the oldest girl, Jenny Peace, has to leave school suddenly she weeps, but the only comfort she can offer her distraught companions is this: 'I hope a Friendship, founded on so innocent and so good a foundation as ours is, will always subsist, as far as shall be consistent with our future Situations in Life.'[65] There can be no forevers here; these girls are about to enter the marriage market, and their differing successes will segregate them according to 'Situations in Life', that is, their husbands' incomes and occupations. The fervour of their friendships, as Jenny knows, cannot bridge the class divides.

Many texts emphasise the chasm of distrust between adult women in different ranks. As a washerwoman – the first rural labouring woman to publish poetry – Mary Collier knew from experience how little the friendliness of employers could be trusted. In her poem *The Woman's Labour* (1739), the mistress who comes at mid-morning to put a cup of ale into the bleeding fingers of her laundresses has a double purpose: 'To cheer our Hearts, and also to inform/Herself, what Work is done that very Morn.'[66] Motives are always suspect; condescension and benevolence masquerade as true friendship. Ann Yearsley's 'Address to Friendship' ends abruptly and sadly:

> yet not to you,
> Bounty or Charity, or Mercy mild,
> The pensive thought applies fair Friendship's name;
> That name which never yet cou'd dare exist
> But in equality.

Like Collier, Yearsley spoke from experience. When she had worked as a milkseller, her customers had included the Bluestocking writer Hannah More, who 'discovered' her, lent her dictionaries and arranged for the publication of her poems. All the profits, however, were put in a trust fund for the Yearsley children, administered by Hannah More and Elizabeth Montagu; Ann Yearsley found that she had no access to this money, nor any say in how it was to benefit her children. Her subsequent battle in print with her former patron More made this one of the most notorious examples of the difficulties of forming friendships across class lines.[67]

Yet much of the literature of female friendship glosses over these problems, particularly stories that idealise the relation between a kind mistress and a humble, faithful maid. Typically the maid will follow her mistress through thick and thin, often without pay, offering masochistic devotion and never aspiring to equal friendship. Listen to Dorissa from *The Fair Moralist* (1745), a romance by the Irish writer Charlotte MacCarthy. Asking as payment only a smile from her employer Emilia, she insists:

> I'll wander with thee any where, content with every Thing but thy Distress; at Noon I'll seek thee out the coolest Shade, at Night the safest Spot to lay thee on; there will I watch thee till the Morning peep, then trudge the Forests with a chearful haste, to find thee somewhat to refresh thee with; I will do every Thing thy Need requires; let me go with thee.[68]

The servant speaks not from duty but from passion; her speech echoes the famous Biblical declaration of Ruth to her beloved mother-in-law Naomi, which in an English Old Testament of 1668 reads:

> Intreat me not to leave thee, or to return from following after thee: for whither thou goest, I will go; and where thou lodgest, I will lodge: thy people shall be my people, and thy God my God: Where thou diest, will I die, and there will I be buried.[69]

But there is one clear difference: Ruth addresses Naomi as an equal, wanting a shared life, whereas Dorissa offers Emilia submission and servitude. Notice that in the twenty-four-hour schedule Dorissa plans, she herself gets no sleep.

The American-born Charlotte Lennox included a similarly devoted (but more critical) servant in her third novel, *Henrietta* (1758). The heroine is befriended by her aunt's personal maid, Mrs White, who runs messages and eavesdrops to gather news for the girl. But when Henrietta is planning to run away, it does not occur to her to confide in someone who is so many social levels beneath her; instead she tells her shallow lady friend Miss Woodby, who betrays her at the first opportunity. Having been sacked by the aunt, Mrs White meets Henrietta again later in the novel and rebukes her for confiding in Miss Woodby: 'you made no scruple to trust her, miss, though you was so reserved to me.' Despite her hurt, Mrs White is still devoted to the young woman: 'I love you, miss, and must tell you every thing, whatever it cost me.'[70] The criticism is swallowed up in another wave of masochistic sentiment.

Most of these stories are written by middle-class women and reflect their certainties about the class system. One interesting exception is Jane Wiseman. A serving-maid in Oxford, she educated herself in her employer's library and wrote a successful tragedy, *Antiochus the Great* (1702); it was performed on and off until 1721, making her enough money to rise to the status of innkeeper. The heroines are Leodice and Berenice; each has a personal maid or 'favourite', called Cypre and Irene respectively, who have small but significant roles in the drama. Unable to stop Leodice from drinking poison, Cypre begs for some too, so that she may follow her mistress into the next world. Berenice ends the play as a grieving widow, retiring into the country with her beloved attendant Irene, who vows 'To the Worlds utmost Limits I would wander,/To follow you in Power or Distress.' This play is almost unique in the period in ending not with a marriage but with a female friendship.[71]

Wiseman's working-class perspective is demonstrated by her giving the two maids some role in the action; however, their devoted loyalty to their mistresses is never questioned. Passion between women in such plots serves only to reinforce certainties about the 'natural' social hierarchy. Only in a couple of fictional texts, such as Daniel Defoe's *Roxana* and Jane Barker's 'The Unaccountable Wife' (discussed on pp. 174–6, 176–80), does the love between mistress and maid seem to change the balance of power.

An interesting variation on the mistress–maid story is found in Samuel Johnson's fantasy, *The History of Rasselas, Prince of Abyssinia* (1759). When Prince Rasselas and his sister Princess Nekayah set off on their travels, we are told, 'The Princess was followed only by a single favourite, who did not know whither she was going.' The royal siblings visit one of the pyramids, but Nekayah's female attendant Pekuah is too scared to go in; by the time they return to fetch her, she has been kidnapped. The conventional maid–mistress bond is broken apart at this point and grows more complex. Guilt-racked, the Princess Nekayah tries every 'improbable' method to find her friend and then sinks into 'hopeless dejection': 'She sat from morning to evening recollecting all that had been done or said by her Pekuah, treasured up with care every trifle on which Pekuah had set an accidental value.' In retrospect, the princess' condescending appreciation of her lost 'favourite' becomes an obsessional love; Nekayah forgets her royal status and becomes merely Pekuah's grieving friend. First she wants to die and rejoin her beloved, whom she presumes has been killed; gradually she recovers, limiting her mourning to a certain time every day, but 'her real love of Pekuah' is not diminished and she has sealed herself off from other friendships. 'I shall henceforward fear to yield my heart to excellence however bright, or to fondness however tender', she explains, 'lest I should lose again what I have lost in Pekuah.'

In fact Pekuah is not dead; a huge ransom is paid and the women are reunited. Pekuah, still loving her mistress, has grown up; she has found enough courage to venture even into the catacombs and at one point she confesses that she has 'almost forgotten to bow down' before Nekayah. But their friendship is not lost. Both the women declare that they would like to live in women-only colleges, and the experience seems to have made them more sure of the unique value of their friendship. Only the enforced geographical distance of the kidnap allows them to re-evaluate the distance of status between them.[72]

Suspecting impossibilities

Most of the texts on female friendship examined so far treat it as something which may have social or emotional dangers, but is safely non-sexual. Lillian Faderman asserts that only certain categories of women were open to accusations of sexual activity with each other in this period. If passionate friends were not transvestites, actresses, prostitutes or members of the decadent aristocracy, she reassures us, they were protected from suspicion.[73]

I want to question this claim and to show that the polarised concepts of pure friendship and impure lust did touch. The same pair of women could be idealised as romantic friends by one observer and suspected of unnatural acts by another, or even in some cases idealised and suspected by the same person. This section is a study of texts which were not published until the twentieth century, but which record rumours that were circulating in the public sphere in the eighteenth. A fuller study of letters, diaries and memoirs of the time could produce many more examples of such gossip, especially now there are scholars scrupulous enough not to censor it.

For example, until the Yale edition of Horace Walpole's letters, every previous editor had omitted the two references to women whom Walpole thought of as lesbians. A letter of 1749 mentions that Lady Pomfret is setting out for Florence, 'trailing along with her' not her husband 'but a Miss whom Winnington used to call *filial piety*, for imitating her father, in bearing affection to her own sex'. The 'Miss' is probably Catherine Shelley, eldest daughter of a lord. It is clear that rather than directly accusing women of lesbian acts, Walpole's circle prefers to make delicate, sarcastic allusions to their possible tastes. Head-on attack would be rude and would raise too many dangerous issues, such as, perhaps, Walpole's own feelings for men. In a letter of 1755 Walpole makes a rather bawdier crack, this time about Mrs Elizabeth Cavendish: 'Lady Dysart is dead too, and Mrs Cavendish *in-cun-sole-able.*' The pun seems to hint at special abilities, of which Elizabeth Cavendish is the 'sole' possessor, in the vulva (cunny, cunt). As background to this hint, Walpole's editor quotes a letter from another of Elizabeth Cavendish's acquaintances telling a friend that 'the natural richness of her [Elizabeth Cavendish's] constitution seems more wickedly inclined than any young fellow here, and if Lady Betty Spencer is not sent away, I believe she will by force go in unto her and know her'.[74] Malicious amusement, not outrage, is the tone; it seems that lesbianism is nothing new. The joke lies in the parody of biblical vocabulary and the apparently comical idea of women raping each other.

As Martha Vicinus sees it, in the eighteenth century the typical romantic friend accused of lesbianism was a member of the aristocracy or royalty, such as the French Queen Marie Antoinette, and it was not until the nineteenth century that actresses and artists became the targets for such sneers.[75] Certainly, many texts target the gentry, but a significant number, from the very beginning of the eighteenth century, focus on women working in the arts and suggest that a bohemian lifestyle leads to sexual irregularity. Singers, artists, writers and actresses were accused of being lesbians long before the shift Vicinus notices around 1800.[76] Most common, I have found, is the motif of an aristocrat pursuing an actress.

Trusting these sources, some historians have assumed that lesbianism was a fashion confined to actresses and aristocrats, who were privileged in different ways. But satirical gossip proves nothing about which types of women had sexual relationships with each other, any more than the publicised 'outings' of the early 1990s targeted a representative cross-section of queers. Just as the actress Jodie Foster and the aristocrat Prince Edward are famous enough to attract rumours about their sexuality today, so in eighteenth-century London all slurs tended to be directed the stars and nobs of the time.

Anne Conway Damer (1749–1828) was both an aristocrat and an artist, independent and successful – the perfect target for accusations of lesbianism. A loveless marriage to John Damer ended in less than a decade when they separated before his notorious suicide in a tavern in 1776. As a wealthy widow in her late 20s, Anne was free to return to her childhood talent for sculpture; she exhibited thirty-two times at the Royal Academy, as well as being a scholar, book collector, amateur actress, diarist and novelist. Though some men enjoyed her personality – Horace Walpole praised her highly, and left her his gothic mansion Strawberry Hill – others were quick to resent her independence and ambition.

Most texts that refer to Anne Damer present her as fairly respectable. Even the cartoon prints that attack her artistic ambition cast no aspersions on her sexuality. Sir Herbert Croft's mock-epitaph of her in 1780 was much gentler than most of the others he wrote: as he saw it, it was 'her unsuspicious Gaiety of Sentiment' which made her liable to 'Foibles which rigid Virtue censures'.[77] Did he consider lesbianism an aristocratic 'foible', or had rumour of her sexual tastes not spread by 1780? The famous actress Sarah Siddons, who apparently thought of lesbians as 'female Fiends',[78] was still a close friend of Anne Damer's at this time. Other friends included Georgiana, Duchess of Devonshire (living in a notorious and happy ménage-à-trois with her husband the duke, and his mistress and her romantic friend, Elizabeth Foster),[79] Caroline Petersham Harrington (rumoured in the 1760s to get more than friendship from the actress Elizabeth Ashe),[80] and Emma Hamilton (Nelson's mistress, whom Napoleon had reportedly accused of having an affair with Queen Maria Carolina during her stay in Naples).

By the late 1780s Anne Damer was close friends with London's leading comic actress, Elizabeth Farren (1749–1828), the daughter of a Cork surgeon. Though several prints and caricatures of the

1780s and 1790s mock the unhappily married Lord Derby for his craven pursuit of Elizabeth Farren, none of them mentions Mrs Damer; it is only in a few written texts that we hear the gossip circulating about this pair. The hostess and writer Hester Lynch Thrale (later Piozzi) chose Anne Damer as an example of a modern 'Sapphist' for her denunciation of that sin in her diary of 17 June 1790:

> Mrs. *Damer* a Lady much suspected for liking her own Sex in a criminal Way, had Miss Farren the fine comic Actress often about her last Year; and Mrs. Siddon's Husband made the following Verses on them.
>
> Her little Stock of private Fame
> Will fall a Wreck to public Clamour,
> If Farren leagues with one whose Name
> Comes near – Aye very near – to *Damn her*.[81]

As in the Walpole letters, we see that oblique puns, rather than direct name-calling, are the fashionable way of mocking women who desire women. Notice that in this claustrophobic social circle it is Mrs Damer's dear friend's husband who pens the lampoon.

But this was not a private matter; several years later the same accusation appeared in print. *The Whig Club* (1794) is a satirical pamphlet mocking prominent supporters of the parliamentary Whigs, such as Anne Damer. The author (probably Charles Pigott) explains that Lord Derby wants to marry the lovely Elizabeth Farren, but though this appeals to her vanity and ambition:

> her amorous passions are far from being awakened by the idea. Superior to the influence of MEN, she is supposed to feel more exquisite delight from the touch of the cheek of Mrs. D_r, than from the fancy of any *novelties* which the wedding night can promise with such a partner as his Lordship.

Nor is this presented as strange or unique. In fact, the same pattern – a boring old man being no match for the charms of a woman – crops up elsewhere in *The Whig Club*. Discussing the 'cold' wife of drunken Sir William M_r, Pigott hints that:

> there is another reason assigned for Lady M_r's indifference to the caresses of Sir William; and by those who are intimate at N_n she is supposed to be a formidable rival to Mrs. D_r for the affections of Miss F_n.[82]

Pigott's tone is casual, almost blasé; he reports heterosexual and lesbian passions in the same breath. Unlike modern tabloids, his insinuations about sexual choices do not appear under screaming headlines.

Ultimately, Mrs Damer seems to have lost the competition 'for the affections of Miss F_n', not to 'Lady M_r' but to 'his Lordship'. In the early 1790s Lord Derby's desperate courtship speeded up; the rumours about Anne Damer clearly began to bother him and he seems to have put pressure on Elizabeth Farren to save her own reputation by breaking with her friend. Probably tempted by a title, Elizabeth obeyed, leaving Anne Damer to be laughed at by her social circle. By 9 December 1795 Mrs Thrale was reporting, "tis now grown common to suspect Impossibilities – (such I think 'em) – whenever two Ladies live too much together'. The words 'suspect' and 'Impossibilities' almost cancel each other out; Thrale's fear of widespread Sapphism makes her see perversion in the most committed romantic friendships, but in this sentence she projects that fear on to others and will not admit that she herself thinks such 'Impossibilities' possible. In a footnote she comments: "tis a Joke in London now to say such a one visits *Mrs Damer*. Lord Derby certainly insisted on Miss Farren's keeping her at a Distance'.[83] In 1797 his wife's death left Lord Derby free to marry Elizabeth Farren after a bare six weeks. The scandalous gossip seems to have been been forgotten within a few years, because the anonymous writer of *Memoirs of the Present Countess of Derby (late Miss Farren)* (1797), while accusing Farren of impoverished origins, a cold character and affairs with men, makes no more than a passing reference to Mrs Damer; if the Damer–Farren connection was widely rumoured to be sexual, the *Memoirs* would almost certainly have included some innuendo.

The real love of Anne Damer's life, on the evidence of her notebooks, was the writer Mary Berry.[84] It is this relationship which comes under suspicion in another report on Anne Damer, this time by Joseph Farrington, an artist whose diaries often reveal his resentment of Damer's pretensions to genius. In 1798 he identified and linked two suspicious qualities: her partial crossdressing and her fervent friendship.

> The singularities of Mrs Damer are remarkable – She wears a Mans Hat, and Shoes, – and a Jacket also like a mans – thus she walks ab[ou]t. the fields with a hooking stick ... The extasi[e]s on meeting, and tender leave on separating,

> between Mrs Damer and Miss Berrys, is whimsical. On Miss [Mary] Berry going lately to Cheltenham, the servants described the separation between Her and Mrs Damer as if it had been parting before death.[85]

This brief note shows the contradictory state of knowledge about passion between women in this period. On the one hand, expressions of fervent love continued to be acceptable enough for Anne Damer and Mary Berry to behave that way without being ostracised; on the other hand, such passion (especially when combined with crossdressing and ambition) was suspicious enough to make an enemy like Joseph Farington go so far as to interrogate the servants about it. For some, suspicions were certainties; a comic *Sapphick Epistle* of the late eighteenth century addressed Damer as a well-known modern 'tommy' (see pp. 262–4).

But Anne Damer was not the only target of these rumours; rather, she provided an example of what any romantic friend might become. Having had her eyes opened to sexual deviance among apparently respectable women, Hester Thrale began to suspect her own best friend, (Penelope) Sophia Weston (1752–1827). A spinster friend of Anna Seward's (see p. 120), Sophia Weston moved from Shropshire to London in 1787 with her widowed mother, and got to know Hester Thrale there. She was also in an intimate triangle with Miss Anna Powell and the Honourable Elizabeth Trefusis, as well as being a friend and confidante of Mrs Siddons' daughters, Maria and Sally. Left penniless at the age of 40 by her brother's misappropriation of her mother's money, Sophia Weston faced a bleak future. Anna Powell had married, gone to America and died in childbirth; Elizabeth Trefusis was being courted by Colonel Barry. Sophia received a proposal from an American friend, William Pennington, but she clearly did not want to marry him or anyone else. As Hester Thrale saw it, Sophia's 'romantic Friendship' for women should naturally give way to its reward, 'romantic Love' from a man;[86] her letters of the winter of 1792 keep urging Sophia to accept this excellent offer with gratitude. Asking 'How can you be so cold to him?', Hester rushes to conclude that it must be due to 'illness'. Her advice begins to strike a warning note: 'Reject not Heaven's offer of temporal happiness in its *natural form*: that of a good husband.'[87]

Sophia eventually married Pennington in December 1792, to Hester's delight. Their marriage was dogged by his gout and rheumatism and their poverty – the very fate she had married to escape. By 25 January 1794, Hester Thrale's suspicions had formed: in another discussion of Sapphists masquerading as romantic friends, she mentioned that 'Colonel Barry ... had a good Escape of Miss Trefusis if all be true', which suggests that Elizabeth Trefusis was one of those accused by rumour. In a footnote, Thrale speculated about Sophia Weston Pennington, the friend she and Elizabeth Trefusis had in common:

> Why was Miss Weston so averse to *any Marriage* I am wondering ... and why did Miss Weston make such an *Ado* about little Sally Siddons' Wit & Beauty & Stuff? The Girl is just like every *other* Girl – but Miss Weston did use to like *every Girl* so.[88]

The characteristics which suggest Sapphism to Mrs Thrale, it seems, are an especially determined choice of spinsterhood and a fervent appreciation for the physical and mental qualities of particular young women.

Despite these suspicions, Thrale wrote just as usual to her 'dear Friend' Sophia a few days later. Certain questions, it is clear, could not be asked. She remained close to Sophia, supporting her throughout her miserable marriage; in 1799 she addressed Sophia as 'first of friends in every sense of the word'.[89] How could Hester Thrale reconcile her furious suspicions and her warm affection? Mentioning certain men she thought of as homosexual, she swung between damning the sin and liking the sinner.[90] But possible perversion among women was closer to home and made Thrale even more uncomfortable.

To emphasise how socially acceptable love between women was in this period, Lillian Faderman points out that Hester Thrale was a close friend and visitor of the Ladies of Llangollen. She suggests that Thrale must have made a clear distinction between their virtuous love and the illicit passions between women which she attacked in her diary, because the Ladies 'seemed to follow to the letter the prescriptions for romantic friendship', including scholarliness, retirement from corrupt society and a spiritual communion with nature.[91] Randolph Trumbach argues that, because Hester Thrale does not seem to have suspected them of the Sapphism she was so aware of, the Ladies must have been considered as having a friendship which, to the most suspicious eye, only 'approached sapphism in some regards'.[92] Recently, however, Liz Stanley has unearthed an unpublished diary in which Hester Thrale describes the Ladies of Llangollen as 'damned Sapphists' and claims that women were reluctant to stay the night with the Ladies unless accompanied by men.[93] So it seems that romantic friendship had no symbolic refuge, not even Llangollen Vale, in which to hide from occasional suspicions of Sapphism. Hester Thrale is a fascinating example of the doublethink that made it possible to be aware of lesbian possibilities, yet defend romantic friendship as the epitome of moral purity. Mostly she hid away in the back of her mind the suspicion that some of her best friends were Sapphists.

But these and other texts which make an explicit link between romantic friendship and sexual relationships between women are not the only ones which make me question the idea that female friendship was considered entirely acceptable and harmless. Other stories, in this and the next chapter, are written in such a way as to betray their authors' unease with the sheer intensity of devotion between women. Martha Vicinus suggests that 'a fear of excess – whether of learning or of emotion – may well have been the cover for opposition to the erotic preference implied by a close friendship'.[94] As the subject is such a dangerous one, we cannot expect every attack on romantic friendship to come in the explicit form of an accusation of lesbian sex. Hatred of woman-lovers, I suggest, shows up most often in the form of sneers about spinsters and intellectuals, mockery of women-only living spaces, and disapproval of what writers see as the excessive political, practical and emotional influence some women have over their friends.

5 The truest friends

In this chapter I offer readings of a selection of prose texts, mostly auto/biographies and fiction, chosen for their success in describing particular partnerships between women. Rather than focusing on novels that idealise friendship, my bias is towards complexity. So the texts in this chapter are concerned with the gritty, day-to-day details of long-term partnerships between women who differ in religion, politics, wealth, moral standards, attitudes to men, and conceptions of what love between women can be.

Sister souls

A special kind of emotional triangle is formed when women pair up to worship a male god. Theological and auto/biographical writings within the various Christian traditions are a rich source of evidence of such impassioned partnerships. The radical sects formed in the seventeenth century, in particular, often allowed women to pull their friendships with each other to the centre of their lives. Quaker women such as Katherine Evans and Sarah Cheevers left husbands and children to travel and be imprisoned together.[1] In 1676 Theophilia Townsend wrote in memory of her friend Jane Whitehead:

> Oh thou dearest unto me of many and never to be forgotten by me ... oh thou blessed of the Lord, how often hath my heart been broken into tears of true sorrow because of the want of thee, as to thy bodily presence, because of thy tender Care over the Family of God.[2]

Notice how the context of religious elegy allows her to express passion for her friend and even a sense of loss of her 'bodily presence'; God's love for Jane, and Theophilia's love for her, can be wound together phrase by phrase.

Queen ANNE was very Graceful & Majestic in her Person: Religious, without Affectation. She always meant well. She had no false Ambition; which appear'd by Her never complaining at King Williams being preferred to the Crown before Her, when it was taken from the King Her Father, for following such Counsels, & pursuing such Measures, as render'd the Revolution necessary. It was Her greatest Affliction, to be forced to act against Him, even for Security. Her Journey to Nottingham was never concerted, but occasion'd by the great Consternation She was under at the Kings Sudden Return from Salisbury. She always paid the greatest Respect to King William & Queen Mary; never insisted upon any one Circumstance of Grandeur, more than what was establish'd in Her Family by King Charles II. though after the Revolution, She was Presumptive Heir to the Crown, & after ye Death of Her Sister, was in the Place of Prince of Wales. Upon her Accession to the Throne, the Civil List was not increased. The late Earl of Godolphin, Lord High Treasurer of England, often said, that from Accidents in the Customs, & Lenity in ye Collection it did not arise, one Year with another, to more than Five Hundred Thousand Pounds a Year. She had no Vanity in Her Expences, nor bought any one Jewel in the whole Time of her Reign. She paid out of her Civil List many Pensions granted in former Reigns, which have since been thrown upon the Publick. When a War was necessary to secure Europe against the Power of France, She contributed in one Year, towards ye War, out of her Civil List, One Hundred Thousand Pounds, in Ease of Her Subjects. She granted the Revenue arising from the First Fruits, to augment the Provisions of ye poorer Clergy. She never refus'd her private Charity to proper Objects. Till a few Years before her Death, She never had but Twenty Thousand Pounds a Year for Her Privy Purse. At the latter End of Her Reign, it did not exceed Twenty Six Thousand Pounds a Year; which was much to Her Honour, because it is subject to no Account. And as to Her Robes, it will appear by ye Records in ye Exchequer, that in Nine Years She spent only Thirty Two Thousand & Fifty Pounds, including ye Coronation Expences. She was extreamly well-bred, treated Her chief Ladies & Servants as if they had been Her Equals. Her behavior to all that approached Her was decent, & full of Dignity, & shew'd Condescention, without Art or Meanness.

All this I know to be true.

SARAH MARLBOROUGH. MDCCXXXVIII

Statue of Queen Anne, erected by the Duchess of Marlborough, 1738

Some of the difficulties of reconciling the loves of God and woman show up in the work of Mary Astell. An Anglican, Astell set herself the highest standards of devotion to God and often felt guilty that her strongest passions were still for human beings. Precisely because her fervent friendships were often unreciprocated, Astell decided that they must have been wrong. In one miserable poem, 'I thank thee Lord that I am Friendless too', she argues backwards from her disappointment to God's jealousy which must have caused the friendship to fail.

Mary Astell's published correspondence with the Cambridge Platonist and theologian John Norris begins in 1693. In her second letter, after sixteen pages of dense argument, Astell permits herself to ask about a personal worry: she has been convinced by Norris that God is 'the only proper Object' of love, but must admit to finding it 'more easie to recognize his Right than to secure the Possession'. The problem is that the (female) Creatures are still so much more immediately loveable than the Creator. Astell breaks off to address God as a wife might a jealous husband, nervously insisting on her fidelity: 'No, my fair Delight, I will never be drawn off from the Love of thee by the Charms of any of thy Creatures.' But perhaps – and here Astell wavers – her 'strong Propensity to friendly Love' could lead her to Heaven, 'if it may be kept within the due Bounds of Benevolence'? However, she reminds herself sternly of Norris' instruction to give God all her love. Her confession is full and gloomy:

> I have contracted such a Weakness, I will not say by Nature (for I believe Nature is often very unjustly blam'd for what is owing to *Will* and *Custom*) but by voluntary Habit, that it is very difficult for me to love at all, without something of Desire.

'Desire' here should be read not as simple lust, I think, since Astell mentions it to her mentor with no sense of shame, but as a yearning to enjoy an exclusive friendship, in some sense to possess the beloved woman. Astell is reluctant to abandon her quest for friendship, because her motives are good, yet she is troubled by its elements of greed and emotional investment.

Towards the end of the letter it becomes clear that, as in the earlier poem, it is Astell's disappointments in friendship that have made her question its morality.

> But though I can say without boasting that none ever loved more generously than I have done, yet perhaps never any met with more ungrateful Returns which I can attribute to nothing so much as the Kindness of my best Friend, who saw how apt my Desires were to stray from him, and therefore by these frequent Disappointments would have me learn more Wisdom than to let loose my Heart to that which cannot satisfie.

Her argument is not theological but empirical: her love is not returned, she is not satisfied and, being unwilling to think herself unlovable, she can only attribute this to God's plan and decide that devotion between women 'cannot satisfie'. A husband was commonly referred to as a wife's 'best friend'; here God is presented as a possessive husband who (out of sheer kindness and for her own good, of course) makes sure that his wife gets no pleasure from any source but him.

If her friendship with women were really pious and calm, Astell reasons, she would not feel hurt by unkindness, because her own conscience would be clear. However, she finds herself longing for response and being wounded by ingratitude, swaying rather than standing firm:

> And though I have in some measure rectified this Fault, yet still I find an agreeable Movement in my Soul towards her I love, and a Displeasure and Pain when I meet with Unkindness, which is a strong Indication of somewhat more than pure Benevolence.

'Be pleased therefore', Astell pleads with Norris, 'to oblige me with a Remedy for this Disorder.' His answer in the fourth letter is kind but rather helpless: 'I know no other Way than by long and constant Meditation.'[3]

So far, none of Astell's friends has been presented individually; the disappointments of the last decade have been numerous, the 'her I love' is a general label.[4] But in 1694 Norris asked permission to publish the letters and Astell agreed only on condition that she might dedicate the book to Lady Catherine Jones. There is no mention of Lady Catherine in Astell's papers before that date; she seems to have been a new friend, perhaps met at church in Chelsea where they both lived. In the preface to *Letters Concerning the Love of God* (written in July 1694, only eight months after the miseries of her second letter to Norris), Astell uses the most enthusiastic terms in writing of Lady Catherine, whom, she boasts, 'I love with the greatest Tenderness, for all must love her who have any Esteem for unfeigned Goodness.' This sentence reveals a contradiction within Christian friendship: all must love Lady Jones, with unpossessive admiration, but in fact Astell is claiming a privileged relationship with her, the 'greatest' tenderness. Astell does try to generalise the attraction of holy souls: 'All true Lovers of GOD being like excited Needles, which cleave not only to him their *Magnet*, but even to one another.' Yet why do some – and specifically, two female – needles cleave more closely than others? There is nothing general about Astell's excitement; it is fiercely focused on Lady Catherine, whose piety 'made me every Time I prayed by her, fancy my self in the Neighbourhood of seraphic Flames!' In this preface, Astell shows none of the guilt and anxiety that fills her earlier letter; she is overjoyed finally to have found a friend who is not only as pious as herself, but just as committed to their loving partnership. Astell and Jones were never an exclusive couple, but in Astell's circle of aristocratic patron/disciples, Lady Catherine was her most important lifelong friend. She helped fund Astell's charity school, had several texts dedicated to her and, for the last few years before her friend died of breast cancer, she nursed her in her comfortable home. It seems that the doubts disappeared, the guilt evaporated; after 1695 the 'Creator' Astell praised in her works was not so jealous as to interfere with her love for women.

Published almost a century later, Sarah Weston Young's *Some Particulars, Relating to the Life and Death of Rebecca Scudamore* (1790) tells the story of another religious partnership. Sarah presents herself as a humble protegée, in the social and then religious senses. She gets to know the married Rebecca in 1757, is introduced by her into high society and enjoys her constant company. They sometimes argue over religion, but Rebecca's gentle moderation ends all controversies good-humouredly. The only real bone of contention is that Sarah thinks Rebecca rather too fond (for a Christian) of her husband.

Both women, however, have a secret yen for a more religious life. In 1759 they are together in lodgings in Weymouth when Rebecca, brought low by illness, undergoes a shattering religious experience:

> she would at such seasons frequently continue on her knees from *one to two hours at a time*, in *silent prayer*, when I waited by her side; and tho' it was irksome to my nature,

> and painful to my body, yet I felt the happy effects of it in my spirit.

Agonising visions of hell bring the older woman startling insight into Scripture, which she interprets to her humble friend.

Once the pair return to Bristol, Rebecca's exasperated husband enlists her friends to persuade her out of this religious excess; they make Sarah feel most unwelcome, so she returns to the countryside. Separated from Rebecca for what turns out to be almost seven years, cut off from her beloved friend's elevating influence, Sarah slips back into worldly pleasures. Even when she turns back to God some years later, she is ashamed to contact Rebecca; every time she writes her a letter, she tears it up.

> I afterwards heard, she used to tell her religious acquaintance, that she had a Friend, whom she tenderly loved, that had forsaken her, and was gone into the world, but she was assured in her own mind, she would have her again, and that with an increase of Grace.

Their reunion after seven years is described with an echo of the story of the prodigal son; religious myth is used here to structure the narrative of friendship.

Nothing parts them from now on. Rebecca's impassioned letters, quoted in the memoir, often use religious allusions to characterise their friendship, for example the parable of the wise virgins awaiting Christ as a bridegroom: 'my dear Friend; to our Watch Tower. – methinks some sweet signs of his appearance are already to be seen. – May you soon arrive to the summit of your desires.'[5] The virgins are meant to be concentrating on the bridegroom, but in this passage they seem to meet in the same watch tower; it is together that they will climb to the summit of their desires.

Though belonging to two different churches (Anglican and Presbyterian respectively), Sarah and Rebecca 'became of one heart and of one mind; if possible, in a higher degree than ever before'. Rebecca is always presented as the leader, the influence, the 'happy instrument' of God for 'strengthening' Sarah, but Sarah shows no resentment of these roles. Brought together in religion, they realise that the petty distinctions society draws between women matter not at all. 'Difference in externals, occasion'd not the least degree of difference betwixt us, and why should it amongst any that are candidates for Heaven?' These circumstantial 'externals' include Sarah's marriage and Rebecca's being kicked out of her home by her irreligious and adulterous husband. 'My heart yearn'd over her', Sarah records; she offers Rebecca a home for one happy year until Sarah's family grows too large to allow for a visitor. Then Rebecca goes wandering from lodging to lodging, always keeping in touch through visits and inspirational letters.[6] Even Rebecca's choice not to see any visitors in person for the last two years of her life, dedicating herself wholly to silent prayer, does not damage their friendship. It is Sarah who sits up six nights to help Rebecca when she is dying. Their friendship has a script; they know where they are going.

Even those whose friendships were not built on a spiritual quest could use religious language to justify and raise the status of their feelings. Eliza Frances Robertson, a governess and children's writer, ran a school at Greenwich from 1795 with her beloved friend Charlotte Sharp. When the school ran up debts Robertson came under attack; she was variously accused of fraud, sexual promiscuity, being a man, being a crossdresser and having unnatural feelings for her friend. Undaunted, Robertson leapt into print several times in 1801. *Who Are the Swindlers?* was an initial one-and-sixpenny pamphlet she published to defend herself and to pay for lodgings for Charlotte. The next text, *Dividends of Immense Value,* has a tone of supreme confidence, despite having been written in Huntingdon jail.

> The cavillers at the motives of attachment between my friend Miss Sharpe and self, seem to enter very little into feelings described in holy writ, such as the friendship of Naomi and Ruth ... Our Saviour not only *approved of* an attachment between persons of the same sex, but has himself *consecrated* friendship, by divine example.

Christ's loving bonds with Lazarus and John the Evangelist, as well as the famous biblical tale of devotion between Naomi and Ruth (see p. 141), provide the strongest of precedents for same-sex passions. 'A Poetical Epistle to an Absent Friend' in the same volume is a love poem by Eliza Robertson to 'my Charlotte'; it includes the significant couplet: 'Religion we'll blend with emotions of love,/Refinement of taste our souls will approve.'[7] A Christian society had to 'approve' of such a 'blend' of 'religion' and 'emotions of love'; even a woman with a mud-spattered reputation like Eliza Robertson could tap into this honourable tradition of spiritual friendship.

Mrs Morley and Mrs Freeman

The stormy friendship of Queen Anne and Sarah Churchill, Duchess of Marlborough, has received plenty of attention in biographies and histories. It has often been read in terms of Whig/Tory political influence, or as the exploitation of an infatuated, well-meaning queen by a cold, unscrupulous duchess. Rather than arguing over the rights and wrongs of each detail of this twenty-year partnership, I will focus on just one version of the story, Sarah Churchill's *An Account of the Conduct of the Dowager Duchess of Marlborough* (written between 1702 and 1710, published in 1742), because it was a widely read, controversial publication that concentrated on the women's friendship.

The story begins in childhood, when as miniature ladies-in-waiting Sarah and Anne play together and grow close, mostly because Anne dislikes everyone else around her. With no false modesty, Sarah remembers what a high place she reached in Anne's favour – and all without the help of flattery, 'a Charm, which in Truth her Inclination for me, together with my unwearied Application to serve and amuse her, rendered needless'. Serving and amusing Anne, however, are not always the same thing; Sarah's carefully developed ethic of friendship involves dangerous frankness. For the first few years, we are told, Anne appreciates it, 'promising never to be offended at it, but to love me the better for my Frankness'. As Sarah reports it, the friendship is based on an unwritten code of honour: her unselfish devotion to Anne's true good is to be rewarded by lifelong gratitude and the central place in the princess' heart.

This code of honour reinforces their longing for equality, for some way of evading the barriers of court protocol. Sarah explains that the princess 'grew uneasy to be treated by me with the Form and Ceremony due to her Rank; nor could she bear from me the Sound of Words which implied in them Distance and Superiority'. To counteract the popular assumption that she lured Anne into a position of emotional dependence, Sarah's *Account* presents Anne as the initiator in all moves towards equality. It is Anne who proposes that they write to each other 'as Equals' under 'feigned Names, such as would impart nothing of Distinction of Rank between us' – Anne becoming 'Mrs Morley' and Sarah (because of her frank character) choosing 'Mrs Freeman'. As duchess and princess, their relationship is always under the critical eyes of courtiers; to be most themselves, they have to adopt aliases.

The difference in the friends' personalities becomes clear during the conflict with Mary which begins in 1692. Queen Mary orders her sister to drop Sarah for political reasons, telling her that she knows such a sacrifice is 'hard', but it is one often demanded of royalty. Anne keeps refusing – 'there is no misery that I cannot readily resolve to suffer, rather than the Thoughts of parting with her' – but she makes endless attempts to earn Mary's forgiveness, even when she is being subjected to daily insult and isolation. Sarah, by contrast, loathes the monarchs William and Mary and is secretly scornful of Anne's craven approaches to them, 'for I could not endure to have her do any Thing, that I would not have done in her Place'.[8] The seeds of their estrangement are sprouting.

Anne's earnest letters to Sarah, which Sarah quotes verbatim at every opportunity, use the most conventional of images for devoted love. In May 1692 she is offering to live with dear Mrs Freeman 'on bread and water, between four walls'. If Sarah does bow to royal pressure and leaves court, Anne wails, 'I will shut myself up, and never see the World more, but live where I may be forgotten by human Kind.' After protestations of eternal constancy so plentiful that we begin to doubt it, Anne declares: 'they can never change me'.[9] The possibility she does not consider is that she will change herself.

The couple not only weather the battle with Mary, they are brought closer by it; Anne's devotion to Sarah has been hardened by opposition. When Anne is crowned queen in 1702, Sarah is raised to a position of extraordinary political power. It is in discussing the power she had over Anne that the Duchess of Marlborough is at her least likeable. She alternately glorifies and minimises it – one moment she is the unofficial queen, the next she is the dutiful maid who follows her royal mistress' orders. Convinced that the policies of the Whigs are what Britain needs, Sarah does her best to turn Anne away from the Tory prejudices of her youth. From the very first year of her reign, Anne is uneasy about this political divide, telling her 'I would not have you and your poor, unfortunate, faithful *Morley* differ in Opinion in the least Thing.' But at this stage Sarah has become Anne's right hand – she is Groom of the Stole (in charge of clothes) and Keeper of the Privy Purse (accountant), while her husband leads the army – so it seems that Anne cannot afford to argue.

By 1703, however, Anne's tone is becoming petulant and an element of deceit has crept in; discussing a bill to enforce attendance at Anglican service, Anne admits, 'I never cared to mention any Thing on this Subject to you, because I knew you would not be of my Mind.' Her letter ends, however, with the sad plea 'never let Difference of Opinion hinder us from living together, as we used to do'. Though her letters keep assuring Sarah of her 'most sincere and tender passion', it becomes gradually clear that Anne is holding out against Sarah on many issues and turning instead to Tory advisers who encourage her to ignore Sarah's advice and act as 'Queen indeed'.[10]

This gradual alienation goes beyond the political arena; in fact, what hurts Sarah most is the personal betrayal. When she discovers that her poor relation Abigail Hill Masham, whom she had housed and placed in a position at court, has been supplanting her in Anne's confidence, Sarah's rage is momentous. In the *Account* she presents this development, detail by detail, as a cross between a political conspiracy and the tale of a seduced and discarded mistress. Sarah describes herself (rather out of character) as fondly gullible: 'It was too long before I could bring myself to think [Abigail] other than a true Friend, or forbear rejoicing at any Instance of Favour shown her by the Queen.' She notices Abigail's reserve with her, but attributes it to moodiness; only when Abigail makes a secret marriage to Mr Masham at which Anne is present does Sarah become suspicious, and finally she discovers that Abigail spends 'two Hours every Day in private' with the queen. The manuscripts of Anne's letters show that Sarah went through them in fury at this point, scratching caustic notes on the back, pointing out the hypocrisy of the loving phrases Anne sent to Sarah while she was (as Sarah saw it) conspiring with Abigail.[11]

The *Account* begins to speed up as summary gives way to dramatic encounters. Coming to Anne by the secret passage between their lodgings, Sarah finds proof of the rumours: the sly Abigail, she reports, 'came in with the boldest and gaiest Air possible, but, upon Sight of me, stopped; and immediately, changing her Manner and making a most solemn Courtesy, *Did your Majesty ring?*'. Here the confident walk of a friend is suddenly converted into the deferential curtsey of a maid; Sarah is reading Abigail's status through body language. Sarah picks quarrels about politics, irritating Anne, whose declarations of love are beginning to sound conditional, for example: 'Whenever you will be the same to me as you was five years ago you shall find me the same tender, faithful Morley.'

For three more years, documented in exhausting detail in the Duchess of Marlborough's *Account*, the women exchange accusations, quotes and rebuffs. Their evident love for each other only makes it more painful that they should have to separate because of the wide gulf between their ideas of commitment. To Anne, the best friend is a loving companion who gives advice but does not make life too difficult; in Sarah's opinion, twenty years of devoted service should be rewarded with permanent friendship (and poor relations should show their gratitude by never stealing their benefactors' friends). The encounters of duchess and queen are sometimes wordless with pain:

> I was making my Courtesy to go away, when the Queen, with a great deal of Disorder in her Face, and without speaking one Word, took me by the Hand: And, when thereupon I stooped to kiss her's, she took me up with a very cold Embrace, and then, without one kind Word, let me go.

To keep her overpowering friend at arm's length, Anne has fallen into a royal family habit of learning some phrases in advance and repeating them over and over.[12] At one point they quarrel in church and Sarah hisses to Anne not to answer her, apparently meaning that they should postpone the argument for fear of eavesdroppers – but Anne chooses to take this literally, petulantly refusing to 'answer' on subsequent occasions. These mantric phrases, this retreat into silence, suggest that the queen is literally lost for words to carry on this friendship.

The focus of their dispute has become linguistic, the giving and taking of words. Because Sarah's spoken words are so upsetting to her, Anne starts to refuse to see her, breaking appointments, telling her to put her thoughts in writing. Sarah sends Anne a narrative detailing twenty-six years of faithful service, their former friendship and the artifice of enemies. She even borrows other texts to support her own:

> knowing how great a Respect her Majesty had for the Writings of certain eminent Divines, I added to my Narrative, the Directions given by the Author of the *Whole Duty of Man* with Relation to Friendship; the Directions in the *Common Prayer Book* before the Communion with Regard to Reconciliation.

Sarah's reliance on the published rules of friendship is saddening; she seems to have unlimited faith in her power to turn back the years with words alone. Demanding 'a private hour' in which to clear herself of various charges, Sarah marches into Anne's Kensington home, but Anne turns her face away and speaks robotically, repeating the lines: 'Whatever you have to say, you may put it in Writing' and 'You desired no Answer, and shall have none'. It is their last interview; the process of resignation and banishment from court is over by 1710. The rest of the *Account* is literally a set of accounts, Sarah's pathetic attempt to prove, pound by pound, that she served her friend honestly.

The *Account* suggests that the partnership broke up because it was based on conflicting ideologies. The drama for Sarah was her choice of integrity over flattery. For Anne, what mattered was the necessary limit on friendship: that it must not involve one friend's character swallowing up the other, especially when the other was meant to be running a country. Sarah's husband reported that Anne told him the partnership ended because she could not see with Sarah's eyes, or hear with Sarah's ears.[13] Being true to herself, for each of the women, involved being false to the other.

The partnership was often attacked in print as a matter of bad political influence, but not as a lesbian affair. It was Sarah herself who raised that issue, by casting suspicion on what she saw as Anne's infatuation with Abigail Masham. Sarah's secretary Arthur Maynwaring is the most likely author of 'A New Ballad', which was circulating at court in 1708. It begins by commenting that the queen 'dearly loved/A Dirty Chamber-Maid' called Abigail, and goes on to speculate on what 'sweet Service' Abigail offers her employer and how she takes care of 'some dark Deeds at Night'.[14] When Sarah visited court she showed the queen this ballad, following it up with a letter of 26 July which made the accusation more explicit:

> I remember you said att the same time of all things in this world, you valued most your reputation, which I confess surpris'd me very much, that your Majesty should so soon mention that word after having discover'd so great a passion for such a woman, for sure there can be noe great reputation in a thing so strange & unaccountable, to say noe more of it, nor can I think the having noe inclination for any but one's own sex is enough to maintain such a character as I wish may still bee yours.[15]

Though the phrasing is confused, the implication is clear: in Sarah's opinion, the queen is involved in something 'strange & unaccountable', a great 'passion' for a woman. Although it is just about acceptable according to the codes of romantic friendship to have 'noe inclination for any but one's own sex', Sarah warns, Anne's 'reputation' and 'character' are being destroyed by such a suspicious 'passion' for a lowly Bedchamberwoman.

Soon after came a pamphlet (again, probably by Arthur Maynwaring),*The Rival Dutchess, or Court Incendiary* (1708), an imaginary dialogue between Abigail Hill Masham and Françoise d'Aubigné, Marquise de Maintenon, long-time mistress and second wife to Louis XIV of France. (It is probably this text the Duchess of Marlborough described to Queen Anne as including 'stuff not fit to be mentioned of passions between women'.) Abigail confesses that she was once regarded as a 'modish' (fashionable) court woman, being:

> rather addicted to another Sort of Passion, of having too great a Regard for my own Sex, insomuch that few People thought I would ever have Married; but to free my self from that Aspersion some of our Sex labour under, for being too fond of one another, I was resolv'd to Marry as soon as I cou'd fix to my Advantage or Inclination.

Spinsterhood is identified as a sure sign of lesbianism; the woman who is 'too fond' of her own sex is presumed to have no emotional interest in a husband. To stifle these rumours, Masham explains, she decided to make a marriage of convenience. Having listened to this confession, Madame de Maintenon admits that this 'Female Vice, which is the most detestable in Nature', is common in French convent schools. She cannot quite believe that it has reached England, but Masham assures her 'we are arriv'd to as great Perfection in sinning that Way as you can pretend to'.[16]

The accusations were not directed only at Abigail Masham. The queen herself was attacked, in more private documents. In a letter to Sarah of April or May 1710, Maynwaring refers quite explicitly to the ungrateful Queen's 'shamefull passion' for Abigail. He gloats over Anne's vulnerability to loss and scandal, explaining that she:

> has been lately in a terrible fright, lest this dear Object sh'd have been torn from her, & her own high Character, (which she still thinks it to be) expos'd more than it yet is, to censure both at home & abroad).[17]

These attacks by Sarah and her Whig supporters convince me that she did not think of her own relations with Anne as deviant in any way; if she had, it would have been unbelievably foolhardy of her to raise the issue of lesbianism.[18] Perhaps class is at the root of it; Sarah and Anne were highborn romantic friends, whereas Anne's fondness for a servant must have seemed to Sarah 'unaccountable', and so possibly sexual. There is a certain irony in Sarah accusing the queen and Abigail of having a lesbian affair, when it is the queen and Sarah who have come to be seen as central figures in early lesbian history.

Mrs and Mr Brown

One of the fullest accounts of a long-term partnership between working women is the autobiographical *Narrative of the Life of Mrs. Charlotte Charke* (1755). Charlotte Cibber Charke's crossdressing practices and flirtations with women were looked at in chapter 3 (pp. 99–100), and here I focus on her partnership with an unnamed friend. The *Narrative* mentions how a 'gentlewoman' and fellow actress whom Charlotte has known for years shows her kindly character one evening by lending her stockings to the lead actor, performing herself with a severe stoop in order to make sure her dress covers her bare legs; Charke is both amused and impressed. We know that in 1746 Charke married John Sacheverell, but the *Narrative* makes no reference to her living with him, and she seems to have paired up with her actress friend by 1747. During three years of depressive illness, we are told, Charke is nursed by this unnamed woman, who never complains of 'her Fatigue, which was uninterrupted'. When they leave the troupe to travel together in 1749, she takes the name of 'Mrs Brown' to Charlotte's 'Mr Brown', and shares in the rearing of Charlotte's daughter, Kitty.

Their lives have always been hard, but now survival is almost impossible. 'We had little else to do than to walk out and furnish our keen Stomachs with fresh Air, and come Home and gape at each other for want of a Dinner.' Despite the stress of poverty, their relationship flourishes; though the *Narrative* rarely focuses on it, there are countless unobtrusive references to 'we' or 'my friend' and their wandering life together. Charlotte always speaks tenderly of her partner; she is tactful about Mrs Brown's failings, as when she explains that her friend fell into a ditch because she was 'not the best Horsewoman in the World'. At one point Mrs Brown supports both of them financially with a legacy from her uncle, and Charke notes with gratitude that her friend never loses patience, even when Charke's business ventures go disastrously wrong. Charke explains guiltily:

> I think myself bound in Honour to ask her Pardon, as I really was the Author of many Troubles, from my inconsiderate Folly, which nothing but a sincere Friendship, and an uncommon Easiness of Temper, could have inspired her either to have brooked or to have forgiven.[19]

What troubles Charke here is her own selfishness and bad decisions. Fidelis Morgan quotes this as proof that nothing 'more serious' (sexual) about the relationship was weighing on Charke's conscience.[20] But why should we assume that a woman of Charke's independence from norms of femininity would have felt guilty if her relationship with a woman was one of desire and perhaps sexual expression? Charke's focus on her selfishness shows that she took this relationship more seriously than any other she describes in her book.

Mrs Brown comes across as a quiet woman, dazzled by Charlotte's style and daring. 'I took my Fellow-Sufferer with me', observes Charke on one occasion, 'who was lost in Wonder at so daring an enterprize, to set out, without either Hat or Money, fourscore Miles on Foot.' Here their poverty becomes an adventure, a dramatic farce that they perform for each other. Charke feels most regret about the times she has to lie to keep the show going; to soothe Mrs Brown on one occasion, she tells her that money from a friend is on its way, and 'this pacified the poor Soul, who could scarce see her Way for Tears'. Soon, however, they hit rock bottom, and honesty is necessary. 'We had no Prospect before us, but of dying by inches with Cold and Hunger; and, what aggravated my own Distress, was having unfortunately drawn in my Friend to be a melancholy Partaker of my Sufferings.' This guilt has a good effect on Charke, rousing her into 'an honourable Spirit of Resolution, not to let her perish through my unhappy and mistaken conduct'; she manages to find her partner some food. But after her benefit night at the theatre fails, Charke remembers with pain, 'I was obliged to strip my Friend of the only decent Gown she had, and pledged it to pay the Horse-Hire.' There can be no elaborate role play when the costumes are in hock.

Things ease a little while the couple stay with Charke's daughter in Bath in 1753, but her son-in-law treats them both with scorn, so they pack up again. Mrs Brown is getting a little weary: 'my

Friend, as she had great Cause', admits Charlotte, 'began, though in a tender manner, to reproach me for having left Bath'. Yet she never threatens to go her own way; they have survived too much together. Towards the end of the *Narrative*, Charke describes moving back to London in the winter of 1754, and her usual 'we' becomes 'I'; we are given no clear information about whether the pair are still living together, though neither are we ever told that Mrs Brown has left.[21]

Most critics manage to write about Charke's *Narrative* without referring to this partnership. It is marked by so little gushy sentiment, so few elaborate declarations of fidelity, that it is possible for the heterocentric to miss this quiet documentation of love between women. In fact, the editor of the 1969 edition even manages to misread the reference to Mrs Brown's uncle's legacy, announcing in his introduction that, many years before the story ends, 'Charlotte was rescued by the death of "Mrs Brown," who left her a little legacy.'[22] Through carelessness – or rather, his lack of interest in such things – he truncates one of the most moving accounts we have of a partnership between working women. Other critics insist that it was just an ordinary friendship; Fidelis Morgan points out with great satisfaction that 'in her own, unwitting defence' (from modern suspicions of lesbianism) on one occasion Charke implies that the women were sleeping apart.[23] As many lesbian historians have pointed out, there is a double standard; if a man and a woman acted as loving, interdependent partners for many years, travelling and raising a child together, critics would not light on a hint of separate beds as proof that they were just good friends.

Lillian Faderman sees the Mr and Mrs Brown partnership in Charke's *Narrative* as 'classic "butch/femme"', because Charlotte seems to make the decisions.[24] Yet both Charke and Mrs Brown worked as actresses and they raised a daughter together; their occupations and roles do not seem to have been polarised into anything resembling husband and wife. It is an unexamined commonplace that the history of working-class lesbians (because they sometimes passed as men) is the same as the history of femme-butch roles. Sue-Ellen Case celebrates the role-playing (that is, butch or femme) lesbian who 'relates to her cultural roots',[25] but I am not sure which cultural roots she means. I have found little evidence for such roles in female couples of any class in the seventeenth and eighteenth centuries, however important they were in the 1950s. We come across women who passed as men or crossdressed or adopted a 'mannish' style, but no evidence that they tended to pair up with conventionally feminine women or divided their responsibilities along traditional gender lines. The part-time crossdresser Mary Ann Talbot and her devoted friend have been described by Julie Wheelwright as playing the 'masculine role' of breadwinner and the 'faithful wife' role respectively, whereas in fact they seem to have shared or alternated the bread-winning, and at one stage both did the stereotypically feminine job of taking in laundry.[26] Nor have we any evidence on how such pairs of women related sexually, if they did. To label couples 'butch-femme' without any evidence of their personal styles and sexual activities seems rather meaningless. As recent writings on femme and butch identities point out, each relationship is individual and can appear most misleading from the outside.[27]

Mrs Steele and Mrs Baddeley

The story of the 'Browns' in Charke's *Narrative* shows love transcending poverty; the tale of another theatrical couple makes much more troubling reading. In 1787 Mrs Elizabeth Hughes Steele was broke; she dictated and published a three-volume memoir of her late long-time companion, the famous actress Sophia Snow Baddeley. The critics all slated it, assuming it was written by a man to blackmail Sophia's long list of 'keepers'; the text was forgotten and has received no critical attention. But *The Memoirs of Sophia Baddeley* is one of the most moving, exhaustive (and exhausting) studies of female partnership we have.

The *Memoirs* describe how Elizabeth Hughes and Sophia Snow, both daughters of men employed by the king, meet at school in London. The slightly older Elizabeth marries Mr Steele and has children; Sophia elopes with Mr Baddeley because he has promised to get her on to the stage. After three years Sophia runs away with first one keeper, then another; she is formally separated from Baddeley at the early age of 22. In love with Mr Hanger, her dear 'Gaby' who beats her savagely, she is devastated when he walks out on her; a suicide attempt with laudanum leaves her feeling permanently bilious. At this point, in 1769, Elizabeth steps into the story:

> Our acquaintance was in some measure dropped after her marriage; but I no sooner heard of her distress than I paid

> her a visit, and, on a promise on her part, to attend to her business and give up all thoughts of a person from whom she experienced such unmerited treatment, I extricated her from every difficulty: I paid the greater part of her debts at that time, and the remainder afterwards. I took a house in St. James's Place, made it her home and procured her a carriage. Set so much at her ease, she soon recovered her spirits and was as chearful as before.

Elizabeth does not mention that she has had to desert her family in Oxfordshire to move in with Sophia. In fact, this seems to have been a permanent separation; throughout the story there are no more than a handful of references to her children at boarding school or paying rare visits to her, and she mentions writing to her husband only once. There is no gush, little drama, just an account of facts which reveal Elizabeth's total and helpless devotion to her friend.

However, notice that the terms of the passage quoted above are conditional: in return for the money and management, Sophia has to be a good girl. This tension between loyalty and criticism, giving and demanding, is to dominate their relationship. The memoir shows them living together, staying out all night at parties, saving a girl from the streets, tricking men and other adventures, but ultimately this is a battle of influence: who can drag the other into her way of life?

Sophia knows that Elizabeth wants her to keep to acting and ignore the offers she receives from men, but she is tempted by Lord Molineux's offer of money for sex because she could use it to repay Elizabeth financially; her grateful love pulls her both ways. The cynical landlady Mrs Bell advises her to take the lord's settlement, since Elizabeth is likely to recall the money at any time; what she fails to understand is that Elizabeth wants emotional, not financial, repayment. However, Sophia is a compulsive spender in every sense; she likes change, she likes sex with men, and she cannot extricate herself from the system which invites her to sell herself at such high prices.

The first few times Elizabeth catches her listening to propositions from men, Sophia is meek and repentant. The actress manages to absorb enough of Elizabeth's toughness to refuse Lord Molineux's offer, telling him 'that her own peace, and the influence of her friend (alluding to me) whom he saw present, were objects of dearer concern to her than any consideration his

Lordship had it in his power to offer'. But she finds it harder to resist her old brutal lover Gaby (Hangar), who is drawn back by news of her fame. Elizabeth is incensed:

> Seeing no other mode of estranging her from Mr. Hanger, I availed myself of the house being mine, having defrayed every expence attending it, and assured Mrs. Baddeley that I would not suffer my esteem for her to become subservient to the abuse and perversion of my friendly intentions, and therefore asserting my right of insisting that Mr. Hanger's visits should be discontinued there. Embarrassed and perplexed between the contending passions of love and friendship, Mrs. Baddeley was undetermined.

The emotional blackmail has begun. Both women are skilled at it, but Elizabeth has one disadvantage: she loves Sophia too much to back up her threats. She does plan to move out of their house, and goes as far as renting a place for herself in Chelsea, but Sophia weeps inconsolably; Elizabeth gives in and lets her friend move to Chelsea with her, on the usual conditions of repentance and reformation.[28]

Elizabeth also compromises her principles; she pays Sophia's debts and lets her accept one keeper out of financial necessity, old Lord Melbourne. Soon Sophia is breaking the rules again; weary of the stage, she leaves it and lives entirely off Lord Melbourne. Upset, Elizabeth moves again, this time to Grafton Street; Sophia goes into hysterics, and of course Elizabeth opens her doors to her once more. The real problem is not the keepers, but Sophia's need for young male lovers who pay her nothing. Elizabeth is really frightened when she discovers Sophia's secret affair with Captain Faulkner, because it means that she can no longer trust her friend: 'This gave me more uneasiness than I ever felt before, as I now found Mrs. Baddeley abused my confidence, and was not to be depended on.' Sophia is as apologetic as ever and genuinely tries to please Elizabeth most of the time, but cannot change her desires. Their roles of little girl and chaperone are made even clearer when they go to a masquerade as the Shakespearean characters of Juliet and her Nurse. Sophia's immaturity is a running theme: 'Observe now', Elizabeth tells her, when Sophia is dreaming of marriage to one of her young men, 'how childishly you act, and how easily you are to be led aside.' The irony is that if Sophia were not so easily led, Elizabeth could not have such a great influence over her. Others notice this too; Sophia's lover Thomas Storer asks

Elizabeth contemptuously whether Mrs Baddeley is 'out of leading-strings'.[29]

Elizabeth Steele herself seems to be resolutely uninterested in men; she explains that she had 'temptations' in youth, just like Sophia, but she always resisted them. She repulses men's advances and refuses their money. For example, when the Duke of Ancaster tries to bribe her to let him near Sophia, Elizabeth's private income (from previous business ventures) enables her to throw the cash back. Baddeley asks in exasperation, 'Why did you not take the money and laugh at him?', but Elizabeth has a personal code of sexual and financial independence from men. She battles with Sophia's suitors, losing a tooth to Gaby, threatening others with a horsewhip and grabbing a pistol from a violent Dane who calls her 'fitter for a man, than a woman'.

To escape a creditor on another occasion, Elizabeth returns home from the theatre by cutting her hair and putting on a male actor's costume; Baddeley screams when a 'man' bursts into her room, then is delighted by the disguise. Though Elizabeth never mentions whether her appearance is considered mannish, when they both go to Paris (in the English-style riding habits the Europeans found so androgynous) it is Elizabeth who is taken for a man. The chambermaid promptly falls in love with Mrs Steele, much to the amusement of Sophia, who carries on the joke:

> I never was more embarrassed in my life ... attempting to leave the room, the girl started, took me round the neck, and fell at kissing me with such ardor, that for some time I could not get from her. Mrs. Baddeley laughed so heartily, that she could scarce keep her seat, and the girl began to cry ... Mrs. Baddeley, to keep up the farce, ordered, in her hearing, a room with two beds, though we never slept together on the road.[30]

They do sleep together at home, however. On several occasions Elizabeth takes Sophia by the hand to bring her to bed and away from male visitors. They have passionate night-time arguments, Sophia clinging round Elizabeth's neck and sobbing out confessions of secret affairs she has been having while pretending to be taking naps for her headache. There are a few idyllic moments in this hectic life, for instance when they return from Paris:

> We were now at home, after a ramble of some time, and spent our evening together, talking over the occurences of

> the last month, with a placid satisfaction, that no place but home, with quiet, affords ... We determined to spend a week here, with our birds and our cats, for no one knew of our being in town.

However, 'placid satisfaction' is not enough for Sophia. She takes more male lovers, claiming to need the money. Elizabeth tries refusing to listen to her excuses, but Sophia knows how to put pressure on her: 'If you do not hear me now, I shall not be able to sleep', she complains. On one occasion, Elizabeth reports, 'on my saying I would hear nothing from her, she vowed she would take another bottle of laudanum, which she had in her Pocket'.[31] (This was exactly the same tactic which Sophia used – in vain – to get Gaby back.)

Another bone of contention is money, which is intimately related to the economy of heterosexuality. Elizabeth hates Sophia to live in precarious dependence on men's appreciation of her looks, when she could be earning a secure income by her acting talents. She takes over Sophia's accounts and makes Sophia read them through with her every fortnight, noting the purchases that Elizabeth has marked as wasteful. Sophia, girlish as ever, calls this her 'lesson'. Yet Elizabeth is always the one to compromise:

> I will own that my great regard for her, led me into a compliance with some of her extravagancies, for had I not acquised, we should have been eternally at words; as it was, we were very happy, whilst we lived together.

Sophia is extravagant to the point where she has no will of her own; Elizabeth explains that she 'blamed me for going out and leaving her, saying, that when she was alone, they some way or other always brought things to her, and ever persuaded her to purchase them'. Ultimately Elizabeth always reassures her: 'I told her I would part with all I had, rather than she should be unhappy.'[32]

If Elizabeth's generosity is unlimited, her money is not; debt begins to overshadow the women's lives. Their biggest battle is over some rented diamonds, when Sophia's good-girl mask cracks and she bellows, 'I will not be debarred from *seeing* who I please, and *doing* with them what I please – I will have twenty times the quantity of diamonds I have.' Another departure brings on another suicide threat, another reconciliation. Sophia is getting increasingly fond of Elizabeth and nervous of losing her. In hysterics after a carriage accident, she is sure that she will lose her only comfort. Elizabeth reassures her: 'I never would leave her, while either she or I lived; that I had suffered in my mind, a great deal on her account; but, that as I loved her as my sister, I should never think of living from her.'

But devoted as they are, their future seems more and more uncertain. Elizabeth has to stay in London to deal with debts while Sophia escapes to Ireland and a new keeper, travelling under Steele's name and taking with her Steele's 9-year-old daughter, whom she considers 'part, she was pleased to say, of myself'. Their parting is a wrench: 'I thought Mrs. Baddeley would have broke her heart; she sobbed and cried like a child, and I never thought she loved me till then.'[33] However, the long absence weakens Elizabeth's influence over Sophia's daily decisions. Under financial pressure, Sophia briefly returns to Gaby, but he beats her up and refuses to pay her debts.

The one thing Elizabeth will not do for Sophia is have sex with a man. Their agent, Mr P, thinks Elizabeth's devotion to her debt-ridden friend 'a strange infatuation' but admires her for it. He admires her so much, in fact, that it soon becomes clear that he wants more than business meetings. Elizabeth, realising that 'his determination was to give [Mrs Baddeley] up, and suffer her to be torn to pieces, unless I complied', tries to avoid hearing his proposals. The final straw is Sophia's attempt to make her sleep with Mr P; Elizabeth explodes, telling her:

> I had given her my little fortune, which I had for years worked for, and did not repine; that, I had also forsaken my husband, neglected my family, and given her myself, and would now give up my life, if necessary, to serve her; but to part with my honour, which was dearer to me than life, I would not consent to. I was so angry with her, that I cried. She then begged my pardon, said, she did it merely to try me, and was only in joke.

Elizabeth's 'honour' is not a matter of prudery – after all, she lives with a courtesan – but a sense of her own integrity. To Sophia it is a joke; to Elizabeth it means everything. This resistance to heterosexuality matters more to her than social status; she is quite prepared to give up her ladylike lifestyle, go into 'some way of business' and 'work day and night' to support Sophia's. But Sophia is still dreaming of a rich keeper; she cannot trust herself to a woman for life, no matter what sweet moments they share.

> She took me in her arms, hung round my neck, and cried; and I sympathised with her, and told her, if she would confide in me for her pilot, I would soon steer her into a safe harbour, in which she might lie snug and secure from the dangers of a stormy world. The hair-dresser came, and put an end to our conversation.[34]

The hairdresser, a gentleman caller or another intervention by the male world always seems to interrupt the two women's conversation.

There are no more terrible rows; the pair simply drift unhappily apart. Sophia takes up with a particularly cold keeper called Mr Sayer, by whom she becomes pregnant; she would like Elizabeth to live with them, but Elizabeth cannot bear to be under the roof of someone so hostile to her.[35] When the friends try living apart, both fall sick with depression; long loving visits, and a constant link of money and advice are no substitute for the daily life they once shared. Elizabeth returns from one busines trip to learn that Sophia, heavily pregnant and delirious, has spent two months in a darkened room; 'at intervals she would talk, but it was only of me, and the love she bore me; that she fancied herself a supernatural being, and sometimes a Chinese jar'. For a while Elizabeth acts as saviour again, nursing her friend back to sanity in her house in Chelsea. But soon the gentleman callers return, and Sophia moves beyond Elizabeth's influence. Reduced to being the mistress of an actor, then of his footman, Sophia lets the forces of circumstance drown her; before travelling to Ireland she has a premonition that she will never meet her friend again. After various travels she dies of consumption in Edinburgh, aged 37.

Memoirs of Sophia Baddeley is gripping and overwhelmingly sad. From the start, whichever of the women we sympathise with most, we sense that their union will probably fail, because their personalities and values are so different. After telling their story Elizabeth seems to have had little to live for; a few months after the memoirs were published, the *Gentleman's Magazine* recorded with relish that Steele, in hiding from a capital charge of forgery, had died alone 'in the most extreme agonies and distress'.[36]

Maids and mistresses

Stories of friendships across class lines are usually based on the idealisation of power difference, with the maid gladly devoting all her energy to the mistress's welfare (see pp. 139–42). But two fictions published in the 1720s probe this relationship for its possibilities of mutual emotional dependence and true friendship.

The London butcher's son Daniel Defoe is thought to have produced over 500 pamphlets, journals and full-length books; one of the most memorable is his fictional memoir of a courtesan, *Roxana* (1724). The young heroine has a maid called Amy – her name literally means 'friend' – who is fervently loyal, though not in a passive way. 'Faithful to me, as the Skin to my Back', is how Roxana describes her, in an image of startling physical intimacy. Early on in the story Roxana admits that she cannot pay her maid's wages, but Amy refuses to leave; instead, she uses her organisational resources to get Roxana out of trouble – in this case, by dumping Roxana's children on relatives. Amy lacks Roxana's middle-class hangups about sexual virtue; when their landlord clearly expects some reward for his kindness, Amy tells her mistress bluntly:

> Why look you, Madam, if he would but give you enough to live easie upon, he should lie with me for it with all my Heart ... if I will starve for your sake, I will be a Whore, or any thing, for your sake.

This may sound like the conventional devotion of the humble servant, but Amy is describing a realistic, mutual commitment, a partnership in which both will starve unless at least one of them will be a whore. Roxana, impressed by this 'Excess of Affection', hopes to repay it one day; the irony of her story is that she continually manages not to reward Amy but to drag her deeper into ruin.[37]

Amy is so involved with her mistress that her moods swing wildly to match Roxana's fortunes. When the landlord sets Roxana up financially and comes to dinner, Amy serves merrily: 'it was such an unexpected thing to hear any one talk to her Mistress, that the Wench was besides herself almost'. That night they are intoxicated with relief:

> *Amy* and I went to Bed that Night (for *Amy* lay with me) pretty early, but lay chatting almost all Night about it, and the Girl was so transported, that she got up two or three times in the Night, and danc'd about the Room in her Shift; in short, the Girl was half distracted with the Joy of

> it; a Testimony still of her violent Affection for her Mistress, in which no Servant ever went beyond her.

As soon as Roxana becomes the landlord's mistress, however, she blames her fall on Amy's advice. Looking back from a repentant state many years later, the narrator sees Amy's commitment as a lure: 'I shou'd have repell'd this *Amy*, however faithful and honest to me in other things, as a Viper, and Engine of the Devil.' On one occasion, Roxana strips Amy and puts her in to bed with the landlord – partly to share the pleasure, but partly, she admits, to reduce Amy to her own level.[38] After a brief period of shame Amy gets used to the situation; the two women live together, as respectable as whores can be. Like Rachel and Leah, a biblical story to which Roxana alludes, the maid and mistress share the man and both have children by him.

His death liberates them to travel to France, where their partnership grows less giggly, more equal and stronger. Amy's service involves long-term responsibilities, for example when she travels all the way back to Dover to find an English midwife for Roxana. Soon Roxana is describing her as 'Mistress of the Servants', free to hire and fire, and after a few more years Amy is 'now a Woman of Business, not a Servant, and eat always with us'.[39] The closeness of the two women is erasing the class distinction between them; at this point they are in effect an economic double act, with Roxana earning money as a mistress to rich men, while Amy handles travel, household organisation, and investments.

Their sex lives move in parallel; for instance, Amy has a cheerful affair with the manservant of Roxana's keeper the prince, only because, as she puts it, '*like* Mistress, *like* Maid'. As they face shipwreck during a Channel crossing, Roxana realises how closely they are identified: '*Poor* Amy! *What art thou, that I am not?*' As a friend who has done Amy moral harm, who has taken advantage of Amy's fidelity and her own authority, Roxana is overcome with guilt: she sees herself as the wicked seducer, Amy's 'ruin'. Sexual vocabulary is used about the two women at other points in the story, but more humorously; on one occasion Roxana's keeper finds them in bed together and jokily insists on investigating, arguing, 'How do I know what *Amy* is? It may be Mr. Amy, for ought I know.'[40] In general the erotic charge is not caused by direct desire between the women but by their mirroring of each other, their fusion of personality. Roles are reversed and the servant dominates the employer. The underlying seduction story works ambiguously in terms of class; is Amy luring the genteel Roxana into the lower-class underworld, or is decadent Roxana ruining an innocent maid?

What ultimately breaks up their partnership is Amy's obsessive concern for Roxana's safety, which goes even beyond Roxana's own. When Roxana's long-lost daughter Susan turns up in a position to expose her guilty mother, Amy becomes frantic with stress and offers to murder the girl: 'if I thought she knew one tittle of your History, I wou'd dispatch her if she were my own Daughter a thousand times'. The terms are like those in which Amy first offered to be a whore; she sees no distinction between her life and Roxana's and is ready to offer the equivalent of everything asked of her mistress. But Roxana is sickened by the idea of murder:

> and I, says I in a Rage, as well as I love you, wou'd be the first that shou'd put the Halter about your Neck ... I think it was the first time that ever I was angry with *Amy* in all my Life; and when all was done, tho' she was a devilish Jade in having such a Thought, yet it was all of it the Effect of her Excess of Affection and Fidelity to me.

After this crisis, Roxana's thirty-year affection for Amy draws them even closer together. But when Amy raises the issue again and, on her own behalf, makes a vow to murder the daughter, Roxana throws her out.

Roxana's loss is incalculable. 'I reproach'd myself with my Rashness, in turning away so faithful a Creature, that for so many Years had not only been a Servant, but an Agent; and not only an Agent, but a Friend, and a faithful Friend too.' Her entire chain of support, from 'servant' to 'faithful Friend', has been concentrated in Amy; confused and helpless, Roxana feels as if she has lost her right hand.[41] Amy, Defoe implies, does murder Susan; at this point the story drifts into confusion. Amy and Roxana fall into unspecified disaster in Holland, separate yet identical in their fates, unable to cope without each other. The sheer excess of Amy's passionate devotion to Roxana has shattered the mistress–maid pattern and brought catastrophe on them both.[42]

A briefer but even more startling tale of a partnership across class lines is 'The Unaccountable Wife', a short story within *A Patch-Work Screen for the Ladies* (1723) by Jane Barker. Galesia, the spinster heroine of Barker's trilogy, tells a story of three people she once knew, living in an unusual ménage à trois. The Wife is introduced as a well-born but ugly gentlewoman of limited fortune, whose mother's maid helps her to elope with a handsome young soldier. The couple live peacefully enough, despite all their children dying in infancy, until 'a vile Wretch, her Servant, overturn'd all'. Or so says Galesia – though the narrative leaves several options open. Two alternative versions of each event are offered, with a grammatical ambiguity that allows readers to make up their own minds:

> This Servant, whether she was a Creature of her Master's before she came to her Mistress, is not known; but she became very fruitful, and had every Year a Child; pretending that she was privately married to an Apprentice. Whether the Wife knew the whole of the Matter, or was impos'd upon, is uncertain.

What say does the Servant have in her sexual relationship with the Master? To whom does she 'pretend' about the Apprentice? What does the Wife know, and when, and how? This skeletal narrative raises more questions than it answers.

It is the Wife's unorthodox response on which the story turns. 'Which way soever it was', our disgruntled narrator goes on, the Wife is not only kind to her lowly rival but becomes:

> a perfect Slave to her, and, as if she was the Servant, instead of the Mistress, did all the Household-Work, made the Bed, clean'd the House, wash'd the Dishes; nay, farther than so, got up in the Morning, scour'd the Irons, made the fire, &c. leaving this vile Strumpet in Bed with her Husband; for they lay all Three together every Night.

The cleverness of this passage is that Barker manages to list the ordinary morning duties of an eighteenth-century maid and make them seem extraordinary, a barbaric state of slavery, just by allocating them to a well-born instead of a low-born woman. If this is what it means to be 'a perfect Slave', Barker hints, most Englishwomen are slaves. The juxtaposed details about the bed are also effective; the implication is that the Wife would rather make the bed than stay in it and satisfy her husband's early-morning urges. Barker also makes clear that the Wife knows exactly what is going on and is intimately complicit in it since 'they lay all Three together'.

This role reversal has been interpreted by Janet Todd as the exploitation of a barren 'neurotic' wife by her servant.[43] I read it as a veiled love story between two women whom the Master could not keep apart. The romantic submission of lover to beloved mistress here cuts across the economic submission of servant to employer; when the Mistress loves the Servant, a crack appears in the class hierarchy.

So far the Wife's response has been mute; through her tireless body she has acted out her consent in this swapping of roles. Her friends suspect that she has a low opinion of her 'Imperfections, and Deformity' and is only bearing the humiliation through 'Complaisance, not Choice'. But finally the Master decides he cannot support any more children and plans to discard the Servant; to his surprise, the Wife objects. He calls in a friend (the mother of our narrator Galesia) to use her influence:

> She found the Servant sitting in a handsome Velvet Chair, dress'd up in very good lac'd Linnen, having clean Gloves on her Hands, and the Wife washing the Dishes. This sight put my Mother into such a violent Passion, that she had much ado to refrain from laying Hands on her.

The marriage economy uses gloves, linen, velvet chairs, all the accessories of idleness, as rewards for rich wives. Yet here it is the Servant who is dressed up as the idle doll of patriarchy. What infuriates Galesia's mother to the point of violence, then, is that the maid and the mistress between them are subverting this economy and making its rewards meaningless.

The Wife has been silent up to this point in the story, but when Galesia's mother reproaches her she erupts into speech, announcing that she stands 'Buff in Favour of the Woman'. Buff here means a blow – literally, that she would stand firm enough to resist blows in the Servant's defence – but there is also a hint of the other meaning, buff as bare skin; the Wife has rejected the velvet and linen her marriage earned her, preferring to face life nakedly. She is suddenly eloquent, offering a scathing dissection of the concept of friendship: the maid,

> had been not only a faithful Servant, but the best of Friends, and those that desir'd to remove such a Friend from her deserved not the Name of Friends, neither did she desire they should come into her house.

But in what sense is it the Wife's house, if the Master owns it and she has given up the privileges that go with the wifely role? The Wife is aware of the risks, as she makes clear to Galesia herself, who visits the next day. She tells her:

> we all join'd with her Husband to make her miserable, by removing from her, the only Friend she had in the World; and passionately swore by Him that made her, that if we combin'd to send that Woman away, she would go with her.

'I would try that', Galesia answers sternly, 'were I in your Husband's Place'. When the Master calls her bluff, the Wife promptly sets off with the Servant; leaving the house gives these women a chance to shed their old roles.

The third part of the story takes place in the country, where the Servant has no house of her own but a warm welcome in her beggar father's hovel, where her two children have already been sent. While romantic friends assure each other in lofty poetry that they would be content to share a hovel, this couple actually do it; the transcendant romance of their love is anchored by the gritty realities of their survival. At this point our narrator Galesia loses touch with the Wife's point of view completely. 'Now what this unaccountable Creature thought of this kind of Being, is unknown, or what Measures she and her Companion thought to take, or what Schemes they form'd to themselves, is not conceivable.' From the crowded city, in which everyone kept speculating about her motives and telling her what to do, the Wife has escaped into a momentary silence; her communication with her friend, what they felt or planned, is beyond the reach of the narrative. Her inability (or perhaps refusal) to conceive children within her marriage is matched by her behaving in a manner not 'conceivable' to the narrator.

The respite is brief, however; the neighbours, wanting no further charge on their charity, have the family hauled before a judge. The mob happens to lead them below the window of a rich friend of the Wife's, a 'Lady of Quality', who immediately has her discharged and welcomes her into her house. 'For all which she return'd the Lady but cold Thanks, and begg'd her Ladyship's Assistance to convey her to London along with the other Woman, who, as she said, was the truest Friend in the World.' The Wife has gone beyond the reach of any of her old acquaintances, with their conservative values of respectability and reason. Though they all see the issue as one of her extraordinary loyalty to the Servant, the Wife sees it the other way round; the Servant has proved her commitment by loving the Wife even when what little financial attraction she had is gone.

For a humiliating interlude, the Wife and Servant have to return to their Master in London, but he soon dies. (Helped along by something in his tea? This story leaves so many gaps for fantasy.) The friends, who still believe the Wife was forced by the husband's 'Promises, Flatteries or Threatnings' into playing this perverse game, expect her to come to her senses and accept a genteel life in their homes. They even tell the story to the queen, who offers the Wife a monthly pension if she will only leave her companion. But the Wife, having found love and a family of her own at last, has no difficulty refusing 'the Queen's favour', and spends the rest of her life begging in the streets to support the Servant and her children.[44]

A story like this made explicit the threat which women's love for each other posed to the social order; such rebel women endangered the socially acceptable lifestyles of spinsters and romantic friends like Jane Barker. Though Barker was clearly intrigued by this imaginary relationship, she could only risk including it as an eccentric anecdote within a longer story, and she had to mask its anarchic message by presenting it from the hostile point of view of the Wife's in-laws and acquaintances, as something 'unaccountable'.

This and the preceding chapter can barely scrape the surface of the literature of romantic friendship. The core of this body of literature is poetry: personal lyric poems by women of every class and marital status, though particularly by middle-class spinsters. As well as those whose work has been treated in these two chapters, poets of romantic friendship who deserve to be studied include Sarah Fyge Egerton Field, Elizabeth Thomas, Sarah Dixon, Mary Jones, Elizabeth Carter, Eliza Daye, Mary Chandler, Mary Leapor, Mary Scott, Anne Steele (Theodosia), Eliza Dorothea Cobbe (Lady Tuite), Hannah Brand, Susanna Blamire and Matilda Betham.

The field of romantic friendship fiction has received some attention since the 1970s; such classic novels as Samuel Richardson's *Clarissa* (1747) and Sarah Robinson Scott's *A Description of Millenium Hall* (1762) have been studied for their portrayal of love between women. As well as those fiction writers I have discussed, some others worthy of research are Frances Brooke (who also based poems and a play on romantic friendship),

Harriet Lee, Eliza Fenwick, Anne Hughes, Helen Williams, Frances Burney, Charlote Lennox and Maria Edgeworth. Men who made contributions to this field include William Hayley and (in America) Charles Brockden Brown.

The exploration of this vast body of literature from a lesbian perspective is just beginning.

By permission of the British Library

The Marquise de Merteuil considers seducing Cecile, from Chocherlos de Laclos, Les Liaisons Dangereuses *(1796)*

6 What joys are these?

This chapter is about sex, the particular 'joys' ascribed to lovemaking between women in texts of this period. Lillian Faderman maintains that 'For the most part, English writers seemed not to have been very aware of the possibility of sex without a penis.'[1] But of the texts discussed in this chapter alone which are explicit about sexual possibilites between women, eleven seem to be homegrown British material. I study them side by side with two texts written originally in Latin and five which first appeared in French. Britain and France shared a market for erotica; first published in one country, texts were sometimes translated and published in the other within weeks. Though all these texts have sexually explicit scenes, they cannot all be classed as erotica; some are literary classics. They were probably all written by men, though we cannot know for sure.

Very few of these texts have received any serious attention for their scenes of female eroticism; rather than an exploration of the significant differences between such scenes, critics have focused on just two texts by famous men, Cleland's *Memoirs of a Woman of Pleasure, or, Fanny Hill* and Diderot's *The Nun*. What accounts for this silence? On the one hand, male historians of literature or erotica tend to pass over lesbian moments with the briefest of mentions, out of nervousness or lack of interest; on the other, many feminists have too much contempt for men's erotic texts even to discuss them. Janet Todd assumes that lesbian sex scenes in eighteenth-century literature were incidental, meant only to shock; she sees Diderot's *The Nun* as the only 'serious' treatment of lesbian sexuality in this period.[2] This ignoring of what evidence we have has left us with a de-sexed history. As Martha Vicinus suggests, 'we should not dismiss this material, for such culturally influential male fantasies, derived from both pornography and high art, had a lasting impact upon the public (and, occasionally, the private) image of the lesbian'.[3]

Nor is a study of erotica thankless work; the literature of lesbian sex in this period offers a variety of images of women's desire and the kind of pleasures they could get away with, rather than the unrelieved picture, common in later material, of men punishing and humiliating rebellious women. Though they prove nothing about real women's sexual practices, and though they are all examples of male objectification of women, none of the texts dealt with here are violently pornographic in the twentieth-century sense. In some of these texts sexual desire between women is mocked or shown to be ineffective, in others it has a startling power. Ultimately, whether they offer positive or negative images, these texts are valuable for their explicitness, their saying of what so often went unsaid. For early readers they must have been crucial sources of information about the possibilities of lesbian existence.

One useful way of reading erotica is to study sex as a matter of learning and to trace the struggles between innocence and experience in these stories. The first section of this chapter deals with stories where nothing actually happens, but the language of female friendship is charged with danger. The roles here are clear: the elder woman is the evil seductress; the girl is defended only by her own ignorance about lesbian possibilities, and her 'seducing innocence' lures the seductress on. Next I deal with texts about women who do overtly sexual things together, but in a context of frolicksome exploration. The typical pair is an experienced woman instructing (and being titillated by the ignorance of) a girl who must be prepared for the heterosex that will show her the true meaning of pleasure. In 'The dildo tribe', various meanings of the dildo are explored; texts can use it either as a feeble phallic substitute, or as a way for women to give each other pleasure which is so mysterious and powerful that (in an enduring fantasy) men disguise their penises as dildos. Next I discuss Diderot's novel *The Nun*, focusing on the heroine's struggle to retain her protective ignorance and not to be seduced into knowledge. In the final section I look at a little-known poem, *An Epistle from Signora F_a to a Lady*, in which women's sex with each other is shown as joyful, equal and complete in itself.

Seducing innocence

To show that lesbian desire was not restricted to the 'sub-literary' genres of erotica and bawdy satire, I want to begin with three reputable, classic narratives. Each features a knowing, passionate, sinister adult woman and a girl who comes under her influence but escapes before being seduced.

The middle-aged printer Samuel Richardson's first novel *Pamela* (1740) was one of the century's bestsellers and it has received endless attention from literary critics; however, its scene of same-sex eroticism has rarely been commented on. Having resisted multiple attempts at rape by her employer Squire B., the young serving-maid Pamela has been sent to another of his estates. Squire B.'s housekeeper Mrs Jewkes comes to meet Pamela at an inn on the way; she instantly makes Pamela uneasy because of what the younger woman sees as her ambiguous friendliness. Finding Mrs Jewkes fierce, fat and 40, with 'a hoarse, man-like voice', Pamela places a sinister interpretation on every expression of woman-to-woman affection. She complains, 'The naughty woman came up to me with an air of confidence, and kissed me!' Soon Mrs Jewkes exposes herself by musing aloud, 'Would she not tempt the best lord in the land to run away with her?' Richardson is hinting that the housekeeper not only encourages the squire's lust, blaming it on Pamela's 'tempting' charms, but shares it.

During the journey Pamela continues to read Jewkes' behaviour as a sexual threat: 'every now-and-then she would be staring in my face, in the chariot, and squeezing my hand, saying – "Why, you are very pretty, my silent dear!" And once she offered to kiss me.' At this point Pamela, who has learned how to beat off attacks much more forceful than this, protests aloud that she dislikes this kind of behaviour, since 'it is not like two persons of one sex'. Mrs Jewkes laughs 'very confidently', but backs off. From this point on she restricts herself to teasing Pamela about heterosexual desire, asking her whether she would rather have a kiss from a man than a woman.[4] As Ruth Yeazell has pointed out, Richardson makes Mrs Jewkes serve Squire B.'s plot of heterosexual seduction; she represents the even more repugnant sexual alternative from which Pamela is meant to turn.[5] However, perhaps the most interesting aspect of the encounter is that Pamela, despite the innocence she keeps asserting, knows enough about same-sex desire to refuse a kiss from a woman, to object to the unnaturalness of such 'carriage' (behaviour) between 'two persons of one sex'. In his effort to show Pamela behaving morally, Richardson finds himself in a dilemma; he has to credit his heroine with a kind of knowledge that casts doubts on her innocence.

The innuendo in Pamela's encounter with Mrs Jewkes was noticed by the anonymous author of *Pamela Censured*, a shilling pamphlet published in April 1741. Having reproduced the Jewkes – Pamela meeting in full, the author comments sharply 'There are at present, I am sorry to say it, too many who assume the Characters of Women of Mrs. Jewkes's Cast. I mean Lovers of their own Sex.' Notice that Mrs Jewkes' tastes represent a 'Cast', a definite personality type. The word suggests that she was moulded (cast) that way by God, or that her condition is due to chance (a cast was the result of a throw of dice). Either way, it sounds like a permanent identity based on desiring women. The writer's choice of words also suggests that many others can 'assume the Characters' of lesbians without having been themselves 'cast' that way; is this an early distinction between 'real' lesbians like Mrs Jewkes, and the pseudo-lesbians who imitate them during a passing fashion?

The writer of *Pamela Censured* also notices the girl's unladylike knowledge of lesbianism and makes a barbed comment on it: 'Pamela seems to be acquainted with this, and indeed shows so much Virtue, that she has no Objection to the Male Sex as too many of her own have.'[6] So Pamela loses either way; if she objects to men she is a lesbian, but if she likes men she is a whore. The ideal heroine has somehow to reject lesbians without knowing of their existence, while keeping men at a distance without ever forgetting that she was made to please them.

Pamela's knowledgable rejection of Mrs Jewkes is not typical; most fictional heroines seem ignorant of the potential for sexual desire between women. Their very innocence is what appeals to the knowing seductress and it allows the seduction to reach a critical point without hindrance.

Choderlos de Laclos's *Les Liaisons Dangereuses* (1782) was published in English as early as 1784, as *Dangerous Connections*. While the intricacies of its heterosexual seduction plots have received plenty of critical analysis, little attention has been paid to the hints Laclos gives of the villainous Marchioness de Merteuil's bisexual desires. She is planning to have the teenage Cecile Volanges deflowered by her male partner in crime, the Vicomte de Valmont; her professed motive is to punish an old enemy by making sure his chaperoned bride is no virgin. At the same time, some of the marchioness's references to Cecile carry an erotic charge: 'I am bewitched with this little girl: it is a real passion.' These are common words in the discourse of romantic friendship, but Merteuil's libertine code charges them with sexual danger. The novel offers no frame of innocence for female friendship; at another point in the text, Valmont tells Merteuil the story of three female 'inseparables' who, gossipers hint, only take male lovers to conceal the sexual nature of their own triangular bond.

For a while the marchioness toys with the idea of taking Cecile as a subordinate friend and 'pupil', initiating her into female power: 'I am often tempted to make her my pupil.' The longing for intimacy through shared knowledge works both ways: Cecile, Merteuil reports with pleasure, 'often begs of me to instruct her, with a most seducing innocence'. As in many tales of heterosexual seduction, Laclos apportions some of the blame to the victim; in a sense, he implies, it is the girl's 'seducing innocence' which seduces the seductress. In a letter to her friend Sophie, Laclos has Cecile betray an ambivalent response. What she feels for Merteuil, she tells her friend, is more like her longing for her secret suitor Danceny than her affection for Sophie. 'I sometimes wish she was a man; that is, perhaps because it is not a childish friendship like ours.' What she feels for Madame de Merteuil is sexual, therefore she reasons that she must want Merteuil to be a man, or else, she concludes, this is how adult friends feel about each other. Laclos plays with Cecile's ignorance, allowing lesbian possibilities to titillate the reader.

As the story develops, Merteuil's interest in Cecile goes beyond setting her up to be sexually awakened by a man. To Valmont she admits to being 'almost jealous of whoever that pleasure is reserved for'. Merteuil reports barely controllable physical attraction, for example on the night when she helps the hysterical Cecile into bed: 'I embraced her, she fell back into my arms, and her tears flowed again. Ye gods, how lovely she was! If the Magdalen was thus, she was much more dangerous as a penitent, than as a sinner.'[7] Once again the blame is shifted on to the ignorant girl; as with Mary Magdalene in the gospels, her grief is seen as a whore's trick. As a hater of men, we might ask, why does Merteuil not seduce Cecile herself and educate her as an instrument of revenge on men? The answer must be because Laclos gives his female characters only indirect access to power, through a man's penis; a consummated lesbian seduction would disrupt this book's economy of phallic power.

Franker about same-sex eroticism than either Richardson's or Laclos' novels is an earlier text, Anthony Hamilton's *Memoirs of the Count de Grammont*. The mannish lesbian Mistress Hobart (introduced on pp. 53–4) is a butt of humour throughout this anecdotal history of the Restoration court of Charles II. Three times she tries to seduce a woman; three times she loses her beloved to a man. The first two stories are told briefly. Hobart woos Mistress B_t, who responds affectionately, but 'perceiving that all her

Friendship was not sufficient to repay that of Mistress H[obar]t, she yielded that Conquest' and marries Lord Fallmouth. This suggests that at a certain point Mistress B_t discovers the kind of love Mistress Hobart wants and feels unable – or unwilling – to return it; the polite code of 'yielding' and 'conquest' is here used to poke fun at Mistress Hobart's pretensions to be a suitor. Her next love object is Miss Sarah, the young niece of the governess of the maids of honour. Initially both Miss Sarah and the governess feel honoured by Mistress Hobart's attention, not realising that her motives are seductive. But when the governess hears the ballads that call Mistress Hobart a hermaphrodite, she panics and confides in the rake Lord Rochester (famous for his bisexual tastes, though Hamilton makes no mention of them). Rochester advises that Miss Sarah should be removed from Mistress Hobart at once – and takes a personal interest in the case, going so far as to seduce Sarah himself.[8]

After her first two humiliations Hobart is desperate for love and understandably resentful of male rivals, especially Rochester. When her employer the duchess sends her to protect the silly maid of honour Mistress Temple from the same Lord Rochester, Hobart takes up the task with zeal. Being female gives her a certain advantage, as Mistress Temple will trust her: 'She had already made all the *Advances* to possess herself of her *Confidence* and *Good-Will*, to which Mrs. *T_e*, less suspicious of her than of my Lord *Rochester*, made all imaginable *Returns*.' As their friendship grows, it becomes clear that Hobart is working on Temple's weaknesses, wanting to win her for herself. Miss Temple, Hamilton says, 'was *greedy* of *Praise*, and lov'd all sorts of *Sweet-Meats*, as much as a Girl of nine or ten Years old. *Care* was taken to gratify her *Taste* in both these Respects.' Hobart happens to have a closet stocked with sweetmeats, which 'fitted Mrs. *T_e's Taste* as exactly, as it gratify'd Mrs. *H_t's Inclination* to have something that could allure her'. The language is suggestive; being an immature babydoll, Temple can be tempted with the easiness of lesbian devotion, the sweets of the closet. In case we have missed the point, Hamilton tells us that Temple swallows Hobart's affection and flattery 'as glib as *Sweet-Meats*'.

Having given these initial hints, Hamilton leads up to a detailed seduction scene. After horseriding, the two women come back to the closet for some refreshment. Their conversation is overheard, appropriately enough, by Miss Sarah, spying for her lover Rochester; her cynical reportage makes Hobart's most harmless remarks sound suggestive. Predictably, there is an 'innocent' reason for undressing; hot and sticky, the naive Mistress Temple asks permission to change her underwear:

> which, as one may imagine, was readily granted. *I was going to propose it to you,* said Mrs. H_t, to her, *not but that you are charming as an Angel, in your riding Habit: but there's nothing like a loose Dress, and being at one's Ease, after Fatigue. You can't imagine, dear T_e,* continu'd she, embracing her, *how much you oblige me, by being thus free with me; but above all Things, I am charm'd with your nice Taste for Cleanliness.*

Taking advantage of the physical intimacy allowed among women, Mistress Hobart, 'not to lose Time', begins 'helping her off with her Cloaths'. Temple is 'shy' because of Hobart's higher social position, but Hobart assures her ''twas with the greatest Pleasure she did her that small Office'. Before anything can happen, the chambermaid walks in; here Hamilton cleverly defers the moment of seduction.

Hobart and Temple retire to the bathing closet, where Hobart makes a long speech on the disadvantages of marriage, 'the Baseness of Men in general' and Rochester in particular. She convinces Temple that an obscene poem by Rochester was written to expose her physical defects. Temple, her pride wounded, protests: 'We are all alone, and I have almost a mind to convince you', and strips off again. Mistress Hobart has no objection to this nudity; praising the body highly, she comforts Mistress Temple who is 'weeping like a Child' from injured vanity.[9]

At this point, luck swings in Rochester's direction. Kept informed by Miss Sarah and helped by a fellow rake, he is always one step ahead of Mistress Hobart – who, in any case, is rendered helpless by her sincere feelings for Mistress Temple and her inability to say no to any of her beloved's whims. After several twists of plot, Temple finally hears an explicit denunciation of Hobart:

> Your *Passion* and *fond Desire* for Mrs. *T[empl]e* are known by every Body but herself, for which way soever you imposed upon her Innocence, the World does her the Justice to believe, that she wou'd use you as my *Lady F[allmouth]* did, if the poor Girl knew what Design you have on her ... 'Tis a scandalous thing that all the Maids of Honour should

> pass through your Hands, before they know where-abouts they are.

Confronted with this image of Hobart as a lesbian rake, who (to make matters worse) has been accused of somehow impregnating her own maid, Temple is stupefied. She races home to take off the clothes she borrowed from her friend, 'lest she should be polluted by them'. In the ludicrous final scene, the bewildered Mistress Hobart slips in to hug her friend while she is changing her clothes. Temple panics, seeing in her friend's eyes 'the eager lasciviousness of a *Satyr*', and screams for help. By morning it is all round court that Hobart tried to sexually assault her friend, and only the personal intervention of the duchess saves Hobart's position at court.[10] Without ever directly admitting that women can seduce each other, then, Anthony Hamilton manages to create drama from the possibility.

The veil of ignorance

Denis Diderot's novel *La Religieuse* was written in the 1760s as an elaborate hoax played on a friend, though it was not published until 1796, during a craze for titillating Gothic fiction; it was translated as *The Nun* in 1797. This book has been the subject of many arguments, particularly about whether Diderot's characterisation of the lesbian Mother Superior is sympathetic or hostile. But what I want to explore here is the characterisation of the heroine, Susan, and in particular the question of knowledge. Some critics have noticed the strange variations in Susan's ignorance about same-sex desire, mentioning it as a fault in Diderot's realism. Whether deliberate or not, this inconsistency provides fascinating evidence of eighteenth-century doublethink on issues of sexual deviance.[11]

In many early texts about sex between women, what matters is not what is done but what is thought. No sin has been committed unless the sinner knows what she is doing; this contrasts with tales of heterosexual seduction which emphasise the physical act, the moment of penetration. Ruth Yeazell has explored the paradox of eighteenth-century women's 'modesty', which was meant to be a natural instinct yet had to be carefully taught; women were told to 'guard their modesty', but also that 'true modesty is not conscious of itself and knows nothing of what might violate it'.[12]

I argue that a similar doublethink was necessary for a woman to maintain ignorance about lesbian possibilities, yet recognise the dangers in time to avoid them.

The plot of Diderot's *The Nun* revolves around the desire of the Mother Superior to seduce the young Sister Susan. What she is really seducing her into is knowledge; nothing physical the Superior can do constitutes a sin for Susan as long as Susan's mind stays pure. Only if the Superior can get the young nun to admit to sexual (and specifically lesbian) knowledge, to feel the same shame, will she be able to accomplish the seduction and lure her into the convent's lesbian network. Throughout the novel Susan resists such knowledge – though to what extent she is meant to be conscious of this it is impossible to tell. Diderot allows her no consistency but uses her as a sort of running gag, a puppet who, moment by moment, serves his purpose of mocking the Catholic Church for what he sees as its perverse rules of celibacy and self-punishment.

At times this inconsistency is confusing, as it distorts the internal logic of the novel. For example, in the first convent that Susan joins, she becomes unpopular because she voices criticisms of the regime, specifically 'some imprudent expressions about a suspicious intimacy of some of the favourites'. Yet when a little later her persecutors focus on Susan's own sexuality, she denies all knowledge that there can be any 'suspicious intimacy' between women. Accused of masturbation and 'desires of a strange and extravagant description', and specifically of doing something 'improper' to a young nun, she claims that she simply doesn't 'understand the suspicions to which two women, much less a single woman, may be suspect ... they expressed themselves in terms so obscure, that I never knew what answer was to be made to their charge'. Under pressure, Susan makes her memory go blank.

Her project of forgetting is made more difficult when she transfers to her second convent, at Longchamp, and the Mother Superior chooses her as the latest in a line of 'favourites' (not just 'particular friends' in this case, but sexual partners). Insisting on undressing Susan on the first night, the Superior showers her with 'compliments' and 'caresses' which, Susan explains, 'a little embarrassed me, I know not wherefore, for neither she nor I meant any thing'. Our virtuous narrator keeps insisting that the embrace 'appeared to me, and still appears, innocent'. 'Even now that I reflect upon it,' she insists, 'what meaning could we possibly have?'[13] Though the whole novel is meant to be a memoir written after Susan's escape from the convent in full knowledge of the Superior's sin, the narrator shows no hindsight and the present tense she uses here ('now that I reflect', 'still appears') corresponds to no particular moment of writing. To maximise irony and humour, Diderot creates a heroine with a mind like a sieve; he cannot allow her to remember the knowledge which would make sober sense of her story.

Susan insists that she 'passively suffered' all these erotic encounters with the older woman. But, protected by her apparent innocence, she can act flirtatiously, and sometimes offer kisses and caresses as well as admitting that she enjoys those the Superior demands of her. Becoming aware of her power as the beloved object, she uses it to win pardon for other nuns in exchange for letting the Superior kiss her, or some other 'innocent compliance'. On some level, Diderot hints, she knows what the attraction is: 'Ah! my dear mother,' Susan asks at one point, 'am I happy enough to have any thing which can please you, and which can appease your anger?' And Susan's observations on the Superior – for example, 'she looked like a lover' – show that she is beginning to see a parallel between this fervent friendship and (hetero)sexual roles.

The Superior may have great power in the convent, but she is far from being the cool knowing seductress; she is burdened with knowledge which she longs to share. In some scenes she sounds as though she is trying to come out to the girl, rather than win sexual favours:

> She sighed, she trembled; she seemed as if she had been desirous to communicate to me some secret which she was afraid to reveal. Tears streamed from her eyes, while she said to me, Ah! Sister Susan, you do not love me. – I do not love you, dear Mother! – No. – Tell me then what I must do to prove it. – You must guess that. – I reflect, but nothing occurs to my mind.[14]

It is clear that the Mother Superior does not want simply to tell Susan about lesbian desire; she wants Susan to work it out from her own feelings. To reveal the knowledge to her would not be safe unless they were both implicated, and both had something to lose. But instead of matching her friend's hints, Susan backs off and denies all knowledge.

Unable to ask for the sexual relationship she wants, the Superior goes ahead and takes it – not that Diderot lets his innocent heroine notice. Her naivety in some of the erotic encounters is overstated, to the point of farce. For instance, while Susan is playing the harpsichord, the Superior presses heavily against the back of Susan's chair, sighs and gasps and finally sinks over her; Susan is sure that this shows rare sensitivity to music. Similarly, an encounter involving kissing of bosoms, squeezing all over the body and orgasmic swoons leaves Susan only slightly uneasy, wondering why she feels sleepy in the middle of the afternoon and deciding that perhaps she has caught some disease from the Superior. The French text is fairly explicit, but the English translator of 1797 cuts the crucial two pages; rather than censoring silently, he calls attention to his cut with a double row of asterisks and a defensive footnote. Though he considers Diderot justified in depicting 'the extravagant shapes which the passions assume' in order to show the evil of religious celibacy, he cannot present such passages in English; he says of himself that he:

> hopes he will be excused if he forbears to shock an English reader with details which, though calculated to expose vice, it may, perhaps, be more prudent to conceal from the eye of modesty. The French writers too, in this respect, are permitted a latitude which the English Taste has forbidden.[15]

This is a good example of the English vision of France as the realm of sexual latitude.

After the orgasmic 'fainting' scene, Susan's cheerful innocence becomes more difficult to sustain; she knows that something odd is happening and this causes her, if not shame, then at least some awkwardness. The Superior's previous 'favourite', the fiercely jealous Sister Theresa, asks what Susan and the Superior were doing all afternoon. 'Although my conscience reproached me with nothing, I will yet confess to you, Sir,' the narrator tells her benefactor, 'that I was embarrassed by her question.' It is the question itself which makes the actions seem sinister. But so successful is Sister Susan at forgetting her own suspicions that she can continue her sessions with the Superior, where they intertwine their legs, weep and embrace. Their next fainting attack (as Susan perceives it) is also cut by the English translator; here, the line of asterisks actually suggests something more explicit than the few lines which are cut.

Though she can steal physical intimacies without alarming Susan, what the Superior really seems to want is to share the sexual response and the knowledge. In their next conversation, she asks

Susan if 'certain emotions, certain desires' are what stop her from being content with religious life, but Susan denies that she has any. The Superior mentions marriage, and then sex more generally, but Susan resists every step of the way, insisting that she is 'unacquainted with the language of the senses'. In deft repartee they do battle for Susan's mind:

> It is a delightful language; would you wish to know it? – No, my dear mother, what advantage should I derive from the knowledge? It would dissipate your dissatisfaction. – Perhaps increase it. And besides, what avails that language without an object? – When we speak, it is always to some one; that, doubtless, is better than to confine ourselves to solitary entertainment, though not unaccompanied with pleasure. – I do not at all understand the subject.

Under cover of a discussion of 'language', the two nuns argue over the value of eroticism and who it can be shared with; the Superior's strong hint about the 'solitary enjoyment' of masturbation makes Susan clam up and end the risky debate. Becoming more specific, the Superior asks what Susan thinks of at night, what she daydreams about in her warm bed before getting up; only when she explicitly suggests that in private Susan might sometimes stroke her own beautiful body (a paragraph cut by the English translator) does Susan panic and recognise such an act as sinful. (It is not clear whether it is the nudity or the autoerotic motive that would make this worse than letting the Superior fondle her.) The Superior persists in trying to make Susan take responsibility for her education:

> If you please, my dear child, I will explain more clearly. – No, dear mother, no. I am ignorant, and I prefer that situation, to the acquisition of knowledge that would render me, perhaps, more wretched than I am. I have no desires, nor do I wish to discover such as I cannot gratify. – And why can you not? – And how can I? – How very innocent she is! – True; I am, dear mother, and I would die a thousand deaths rather than cease to be so.[16]

It is here that Susan comes closest to admitting that she knows what it is she is refusing to acknowledge, or at least knows of a secret to do with the language of the senses and female friendship. Diderot shows her ignorance to be deliberate, a barrier to keep out the terror of desires that she must not gratify, to exclude a knowledge that (as long as she obeys the Church) will only make her wretched.

In the final erotic encounter between the two, the Superior comes to Susan's room at night and lies down on her, gasping, with the coverlet between them. This is the only paragraph the translator cuts in this scene; it must have been the traditionally sexual 'missionary position' that disturbed him. With similar logic, Susan is shocked at the idea of breaking a convent rule by letting the Superior into her bed; though, as we have seen, she has allowed frenzied embracing while upright and clothed, she dimly remembers that beds mean sin. Gathering confidence from religious edicts, Susan also mentions her priest's opinion. Though she has told him about the Superior's embraces from the beginning of her stay at the convent, Susan has so far managed not to take his mysterious rebukes seriously. 'In my opinion [the caresses] are innocent, but he considers them in a different light. I don't know how I came to forget his advice; I intended to speak to you on the subject.' This is a good example of Susan's deliberate 'forgetting'. Even within one encounter she is inconsistent and confused; after all her protests at the idea of sharing a bed, once the shivering Superior has been let under the coverlet, Susan is led into suggesting that they take off their nightgowns so that Susan's warmth can get through to the Superior more quickly.

At the heart of Susan's confusion we find conflicting motives. She does not just want to cling to ignorance; she also wants love. Rejected by her mother and consigned to a religious life she hates, Susan seizes every opportunity of intimacy and tenderness that the nuns can offer her. Even when her confessor insists that she must avoid the Superior, Susan finds herself rebelling, asking why she should sacrifice embraces that give the Superior so much pleasure and in which she can still see no fault. Finally she admits that she would miss them herself: 'my natural temper is prone to endearments, and I love to be caressed'.[17]

Although up to this point the Superior has been working to overcome Susan's ignorance, she is also beginning to make use of it. For example, to get into Susan's bed the Superior refers to conventions of female friendship which allow women to sleep together. Then, as crisis looms, the Superior uses Susan's innocence to shield them from discovery. Dissuading her from going to confession, Susan explains, the Superior asks if the priest 'knew more with regard to the innocence of her sentiments and mine, than our own consciences; and whether mine gave me any reproaches. I answered that it did not.' But the priest demands to hear Susan's confession. His attitude is ambivalent too; he wants to enlighten Susan just enough to warn her away from lesbianism, without giving her any ideas she could act on. It torments him (and tortures his syntax) to think that he could be contributing to the rape of her pure mind:

> Without venturing to explain myself more clearly, from a fear of becoming an accomplice of your base Superior, and blasting by the poisoned breath, which, in spite of my care, might issue from my lips, a delicate flower, which is never preserved fresh and without stain till your age but by the particular protection of Providence, I command you to shun your Superior.

Gradually, painfully, Susan is made to open her mind to the possibility of sexual sin between women. She is stubborn about certain things – for instance, she insists that the harpsichord scene was about nothing but music – but admits to a tiny element of wrong in other aspects of the friendship. As she explains to the despairing Superior, the confessor is exaggerating but he has a point: 'Although persons were of the same sex, the manner in which they testified their mutual friendship, might at least be indecent.' Even after this important acknowledgment, however, Susan cannot understand the fuss that the guilt-racked Superior is making: 'whence proceed the pangs of this woman? what crimes can she have committed?'[18]

A burning curiosity keeps bringing Susan closer to the brink of full knowledge. Her new confessor begs her to 'remain ignorant' of his reasons for ordering her to avoid the Superior, because this kind of information would corrupt her, but she is rebellious, telling him 'if I knew the danger, I should be more attentive in shunning it'. Since he will not explain, Susan is driven to eavesdrop on the Superior's despairing confession to him, and at long last she understands the Superior to be an 'abominable woman'.

But this is not the story of a lucky escape. As Susan puts it, with a mixture of relief and horror, 'the veil which hitherto had concealed from me the danger I had undergone, was torn off'.[19] Because the Superior is dying, and because Susan now knows exactly why to avoid her, Susan is safe from direct lesbian seduction – but she will never again be safe from the knowledge. Along with the veil of ignorance, the nun's veil is torn off too; it is no coincidence that at this point in the novel, with no ideals left, Susan escapes from the convent with her priest, is raped by him and left destitute. Those who lose their ignorance, Diderot suggests, lose all the protection it can give.

Foolery from woman to woman

Many of the texts from this period which include sex acts between women present them as playful and ultimately boring or frustrating.[20] Their function is usually to educate or warm up the participants for heterosex, or to add fresh titillation to a conventional heterosexual plot. Much of this erotica takes the form of the so-called 'whores' dialogue', in which a sexually experienced woman tells a girl about sexual techniques. By the late seventeenth century, the women in these dialogues were beginning to act out some of the lessons.

A wealthy lawyer, Nicolas Chorier, was the anonymous author of *The Dialogues of Luisa Sigea*, also known as *Aloisa* and *Satyra Sotadica*, published in Latin at Lyons in 1659 or 1660, which introduced most of the themes that subsequent erotica would explore. His book was available in England in Latin, French (*L'Academie des Dames*), and English (*Tullia and Octavia*) editions by 1684. In five out of the seven dialogues between the 19-year-old wife Tullia and her 15-year-old cousin Octavia in the original, the lesbian content is plentiful. For example, the second dialogue, 'Tribadicon', includes a scene of tribadism which ends only when Tullia screeches that she is dying of pleasure. Octavia is unimpressed by what she experiences as thumping; Tullia explains to her that although sex with women is usually a last resort when men are unavailable or in fear of pregnancy, it is an addictive pleasure, common all over the world, and after disliking it for a long time she herself now prefers it to sex with her husband. In the fifth dialogue, Octavia lies on Tullia, who calls her by the name of her male lover, and Octavia gets Tullia to (as one unimpressed scholar, Roger Thompson, puts it) 'excite her to mutual but non-simultaneous orgasms'. Ros Ballaster has pointed out that this text includes many contradictory ideas about sex between women being unnatural yet worldwide, orgasmic yet unsatisfying, initially a 'torture' to Tullia yet eventually her greatest pleasure. Tullia is presented as the 'real' lesbian, by contrast with the basically heterosexual Octavia, yet we are told that Tullia herself was once reluctantly initiated by her lascivious friend Pomponia.[21] Being the 'real' tribade in any given encounter seems less a matter of identity than of habit and experience.

In English, the Chorier text came to be known as *A Dialogue Between a Married Lady and a Maid*. Its publishing history demonstrates its constant popularity, despite intermittent attempts to censor it. First translated into English in 1684, in 1688 one publisher was fined forty shillings for issuing the *Dialogue*. The text was the subject of another trial in 1707, and it was suppressed in 1745 (when the publisher was sent to Newgate), 1780 and 1798.[22] Unfortunately the sole surviving English edition of 1740 is heavily cut; it seems to have escaped prosecution by leaving out everything except orthodox heterosex – the tribadism, flagellation and orgies have all disappeared. Sex between women is reduced to sisterly explorations; all the women do in this version of the second dialogue is contrast Octavia's tiny premarital vulva with Tullia's giant gap; Octavia gasps, 'I can thrust my whole Hand in almost; how strong it smells!' Manual stimulation, even between men and women, is generally presented as silly and irritating; when Tullia explores Octavia too deeply, she is told, 'O hold Tullia, you tickle me so, that I am not about to endure it; take away that wicked Finger, it hurts me.'[23] Chorier's text is a perfect example of the effects of the education gap; some highly educated women could have read of ecstatic tribadism in the Latin or French versions, while for their sisters who were literate only in English nothing was left but some painful tickling.

Far from building on the woman–woman scenes of Chorier's original, most subsequent erotica (until De Sade and the nineteenth-century writers he influenced) backed away from Chorier's explicitness. Where sex between women turns up in early erotica it is generally kept within firm boundaries; it must not be too graphic, too important or too serious a rival to orthodox intercourse. Sex scenes between women tended not to be mentioned in court cases against these works – not because there was widespread toleration of bisexual and lesbian choices, I think, but because these authors were careful to present sex between women as something trivial which posed no threat to heterosexual institutions.

For all the innuendo and excitement in *Venus dans la Cloître* (1683), for instance, the eroticism between women never reaches any conclusion. This elegant French bestseller of sexual instruction, written by the high churchman Jean Barrin, was translated as *Venus in the Cloister* several times in the late seventeenth century, but its publication in Britain was thwarted by prosecutions in 1725 (for 'obscene libel') and 1745.[24] The book takes the form of a set of dialogues between two nuns, Agnes and Angelica. In the literary tradition of lighthearted eroticism between nuns,[25] it includes evocative descriptions of deep kissing and arousal by self-flagellation (two passages cited in the 1725 trial), but the nuns have little real sexual interest in each other, only a certain tenderness and curiosity. Their main function is to describe what they see, to focus the reader's eye on each titillating detail, each whipped buttock or bared breast.

In the dramatic opening of the first dialogue, Sister Angelica walks in on the younger Sister Agnes, who is half-naked in her cell, doing something 'refreshing'. Angelica offers to help out, in a halfhearted manner – 'my Hand shall now perform that Office which thine did just now so charitably to another part of thy Body' – but it is clear that Agnes would rather talk. 'Good Friends ought to conceal nothing from one another', Angelica tells her, and the pattern is set; they will express their growing friendship, over five dialogues, by revealing and sharing everything that has been concealed: anecdotes, thighs, gossip and tongues.

At times, young Agnes is overwhelmed by her discovery that women can have erotic power over each other:

> For can simple Kisses cause such disorder in the Soul? It is true you are very artful in your Caresses, and all you do is extraordinarily engaging; for you have gained me so much, that I am now yours more than my own.

Barrin does not let it go beyond kisses. The more experienced Angelica does reveal strong desire for her friend, but has no intention of acting on it. She must know about tribadism and about women touching each other because she mentions having read Chorier (an edition called *The Seven Dialogues of Aloisa*), but Barrin has her condemn Chorier for excess and tell Agnes that love and prudence must govern sexual exploration. Each brief erotic encounter peters out, as the reader realises that between women kisses lead only to chat or to more kisses; there is no ultimate destination. Even Angelica's most fevered exclamations – such as 'Let me embrace thee, that our Hearts may talk to each other in the Tumult of our Kisses' – suggest that what she wants from Agnes is not sexual satisfaction (which she gets from the jolly friars), but intimate communication. The true seduction is a verbal one, as Angelica talks away all Agnes's fears and embarrassments: Agnes is made to promise 'to open my self fully to you'. The purpose is educational: a bout of kissing is interrupted by a scholarly dissertation on kissing, while during flagellation Angelica pauses to advise Agnes not to hit too hard.

However, Agnes has to keep reassuring herself of her own normality: as she lets Angelica kiss her bottom, she tells her not to believe 'I would suffer these Fooleries, unless I knew there was nothing criminal in them'. What keeps these 'fooleries' within limits is the nuns' unspoken belief that though women can arouse and to some slight extent pleasure each other, they cannot provide real satisfaction. Phallocentrism shields Agnes' innocence about same-sex possibility; she says pityingly, of a woman who mistook a woman for a man, that 'instead of a Dagger she found only a Scabbard.' The destination of Agnes' erotic journey is sex with the friars.[26]

Some texts do show women desiring each other exclusively. Long before Denis Diderot created the tortured Mother Superior in *The Nun*, he was coyly acknowledging the possibility of passion between women. *Les Bijoux Indiscrets* (1748), which reached English within a year as *The Indiscreet Toys*, plays with the idea of a magical ring which, when pointed at a woman, makes her vulva ('toy') tell its story. In a motif that draws on western men's traditional harem fantasies about the east, Diderot gives this ring to the bored Sultan Mangogul, who explores the secrets of each women in his court in turn.

Only one woman, Fricamona (the first syllables probably echoing 'fricatrice'), desires women. She lives an apparently pious life with 'a troop of young devotees', but the sultan's ring makes her vulva burst into an explicit hymn of praise to her absent female lover Acaris. 'Yes, those are thy eyes, thy smile, thy mouth. Hide not that growing bosom from me – Let me kiss it – I have not sufficiently gazed on it. – Let me kiss it – again. Ah! Let me die on it.' Fricamona is astonished by this passion – 'unknown sentiments have taken possession of my soul', she remarks – but she never condemns herself. These hours of erotic meditation are outdone in sweetness only by 'those which I pass in thy arms', she tells the absent Acaris. Even rivalry does not dash her confidence: 'that Alizali, whom thou prefer'st to me, will not love thee as I do'. (There is no indication of whether Alizali is a male or female rival, nor does it seem to matter.) Sultan Mangogul, a little bewildered, finally stands back to let Acaris enter Fricamona's room, concluding with the simple statement, 'I left them to entertain each other.'

It does not occur to him to compete or intervene. It is interesting, however, that when he tells this curious story to his favourite wife, Mirzoza, she professes utter ignorance about Fricamona's behaviour: 'Either she must be mad, or she is cruelly afflicted with vapours.'[27]

Even when sexual foolery between women is shown to stop before it gets very far, the effect on the participants can be profoundly unsettling. *The History of the Human Heart* (1749) is one of the more imaginative English erotic novels of this era. In one incident, a woman discovers a specifically cunnilingual desire.

The story follows a hero, Camillo, who cannot resist the lure of the vulva; the anonymous author attributes the boy's fixation to something that happened to his mother Florinda when she was six months pregnant with him. Whenever her husband is away, Florinda passes the night with a young kinswoman; in their casual play, a disturbing revelation occurs:

> This Lady was young and frolicksome, and one Night, when undressed for going to Bed, playing some wanton Tricks to make *Florinda* laugh, she discovered a certain Promontory about her, more naturally coveted by a Man than a Woman, but as the latter have sometimes very strange Longings in their Pregnancy, *Florinda*, casting her eyes on that seldom seen Spot, was seized with an irresistible Desire to taste it.

The desire to taste another woman can be conveniently attributed to pregnancy's famous vagaries of appetite; the female body, like charcoal or soap, is just another perverse food, and no blame need attach to Florinda for the whim.

She does struggle with this 'unnatural Idea', but the thwarted desire is so strong that she sickens to the point of death. She tells no one, because she assumes the desire would be impossible to gratify. Understanding her yearning only as a hunger for an object, she cannot imagine tasting what she wants without literally eating it up.

> For though she had heard of Men who had parted with a Slice of their Buttocks to satisfy a lov'd Wife's Longing, yet she could not imagine her young Friend would part with a Bit from a Part so sensible, to gratify her Capricious Taste.

By contrast with the plentiful meat of heterosexual manhood, a woman has only a sensitive little piece. Also, where a husband might be asked to sacrifice his own flesh within the loyal bond of marriage, a mere 'friend' cannot be expected to give so much. Florinda, we are told, 'languished for some time' but was eventually cured by some 'old Woman's Receipt'.[28] The only reported consequence is that her son is born with a precocious interest in women's secret parts. Lesbian desire is raised in this text in coy, metaphorical terms; it must be translated into heterosexual desire to make a plot. Randolph Trumbach uses this single incident as evidence that pregnant women were considered especially likely to seek sex with women, but I have found no other examples of this link.[29]

Probably the best-known story of a girl initiated into pleasure by an older woman is John Cleland's *Fanny Hill, or, Memoirs of a Woman of Pleasure* (1749). It was prosecuted on first publication and again on abridgement in 1750; in 1757 a bookseller was pilloried and in 1780 a publisher convicted.[30] There is no evidence that any of the prosecutors objected to the lesbian scenes in particular. In the context of the many perversions Cleland added for titillating contrast with romantic heterosexual bliss – fellatio, hair fetishism, cunnilingus, whipping, anal sex between men – the element of female bisexuality must have seemed mild to contemporary readers. And indeed Cleland does show that what the prostitutes do with each other is no threat to the brothel's sale of women to men.

A teenage country girl in London, Fanny Hill is lured into Mrs Brown's brothel and put to bed with an older 'tutoress', Miss Phoebe Ayres. The scene begins comically, exploiting the gap between their perspectives; when Phoebe starts kissing her, Fanny, in the usual way of naive heroines, has no objection:

> This was new, this was odd; but imputing it to nothing but pure kindness, which, for aught I knew, it might be the London way to express in that manner, I was determined not to be behind-hand with her and returned her the kiss and embrace with all the fervour that perfect innocence knew.

Similarly, considering men the only source of sexual danger, Fanny is relieved of her fears when Phoebe brings Fanny's hands to her 'pair of breasts that hung loosely down', thus proving that she is a woman. As Phoebe fondles and squeezes Fanny's entire body, Fanny is only 'warmed and surprised'; she cannot recognise this 'strange, and till then unfelt, pleasure' as sexual. Only in retrospect does she see herself as having been tricked by a woman of verbal as well as sexual sophistication: 'The flattering praises she intermingled with these invasions contributed also not a little to bribe my passiveness.'

Despite the tension between what she knows that first night and what she knows when telling the story, between Phoebe as a harmless companion and a sinister seductress, the scene is basically lighthearted. Cleland uses the vocabulary of play: Phoebe 'amused her hands' on Fanny's breasts, then slipped them down to her newly grown pubic hair and 'played and strove to twine in the young tendrils of that moss'. Only when she attempts defloration does the vocabulary become more military, leaping into the present tense for dramatic immediacy: 'but not contented with these outer posts, she now attempts the main spot, and began to twitch, to insinuate, and at length to force an introduction of a finger into the quick itself'. Fanny is 'transported' with strange pleasure, which 'somewhat assuaged the fire' that rages all over her body. At this point, the narrator explains that the reason she made no attempt to stop Phoebe is that she was stupefied by arousal: 'Had she not proceeded by insensible gradations that enflamed me beyond the power of modesty to oppose its resistence to their progress, I should have jumped out of bed and cried out for help.' Only when Phoebe's penetrating finger hurts her does Fanny summon the will to exclaim 'Oh!'[31]

So far, the encounter has paralleled a heterosexual seduction; a man, at this point in a typical eighteenth-century defloration narrative, would encourage the virgin to bear the pain for the sake of future pleasure and would force his way in – exactly what happens to Fanny, in fact, later in the novel. But Phoebe backs off, perhaps because Fanny's virginity is a precious commodity for sale to the highest male bidder, and also because Cleland seems to think that only a penis could break a hymen. Though Fanny receives from Phoebe 'kisses as fierce and salacious as ever I received from the other sex', it is implied that lesbian seduction can never go the whole way.

Phoebe's comments show her acceptance of these limits and her own dissatisfaction with gender roles: 'What a happy man will he be that first makes a woman of you! – Oh! that I were a man for your sake – !' The narrator here pauses to speculate about Phoebe, who finds in initiating new girls 'the gratification of one of those arbitrary tastes for which there is no accounting'. Though her tastes cannot be fully accounted for, she can be rendered less threatening by being explained as bisexual, with a preference for heterosex:

> Not that she hated men or did not even prefer them to her own sex, but when she met with such occasions as this was, a satiety of enjoyments in the common road, perhaps too a secret bias, inclined her to make the most of pleasure wherever she could find it, without distinction of sexes.

In his rush to reassure readers the Phoebe is not a manhating, exclusive lesbian, Cleland here offers four different reasons for her desire for women. Perhaps she is understandably 'sated' with the 'common' heterosex that earns her daily bread and is provoked into so-called situational lesbianism by the 'occasion' of sharing beds with young beauties. Or does she have a 'secret bias' towards women which she keeps secret in case it would spoil her chances or her reputation within the brothel? His last suggestion is that she chooses lovers 'without distinction of sexes'; perhaps Phoebe's lifestyle allows her freely to choose partners of either sex, enjoying a bisexuality similar to that of a male libertine. We are never told for sure, because Cleland cannot afford to let Phoebe move from the margin to the centre of the story.

At any rate, during that first sex scene Phoebe gives up her attempt to deflower Fanny and moves away from the genitals. (Though the clitoris can be directly stimulated during heterosexual encounters elsewhere in the book, the woman lover is not supposed to know too much about this, in case it might prove too effective.) From now on, Fanny is used as a visual and tactile feast in the cause of Phoebe's own satisfaction. 'I must devour with my eyes this springing bosom, – Suffer me to kiss it – I have not seen it enough – Let me kiss it once more.'[32] At a certain point, desire for Fanny is refocused in Phoebe's own body, as a need for Fanny's touch:

> 'Oh! let me view the small, dear, tender cleft! – This is too much. I cannot bear it. I must, I must – '. Here she took my hand and in a transport carried it where you will easily guess ... as soon as she felt it within her, she moved herself to and fro, with so rapid a friction that I presently withdrew it, wet and clammy, when instantly Phoebe grew more composed, after two or three sighs, and heart-fetched Oh's!

> and giving me a kiss that seemed to exhale her soul through her lips, she replaced the bedclothes over us.

What is most unpleasant about this passage is not the choice of such adjectives as 'clammy', but the presentation of Fanny's hand as an inanimate tool; woman–woman eroticism here is reduced to functional, coercive masturbation. Being used in this way leaves Fanny almost untouched; she wakes the next morning unperturbed and 'perfectly gay'. In retrospect the narrator admits that this night with Phoebe gave her 'the first ideas of pollution', and that 'the acquaintance and communication with the bad of our own sex is often as fatal to innocence as all the seductions of the other.' However, her language shows that Phoebe is not a serious threat; the most she can achieve is 'communication' of knowledge or 'pollution' of innocence, never a full seduction.

In subsequent encounters between the two women, Phoebe's tactics are as much verbal as physical. Clearly having no hope of Fanny as an active lover, Phoebe contents herself with warming Fanny up for her heterosexual career by whetting her curiosity. Phoebe's fondlings have taught Fanny how to masturbate her way to 'the critical ecstasy' when she needs to, but Fanny despises these 'vain attempts at digitation', feeling sure they offer only 'a slight satisfaction' compared with the bliss she expects from heterosex. Far from resenting or fearing Phoebe, she confides in her – which effectively neutralises Phoebe as a sexual presence. On one occasion Phoebe takes her to spy on a female–male couple through a crevice in a wall. When arousal distracts Fanny's attention, Phoebe has to calm her down:

> making me stand with my back towards the door, she lifted up my petticoats, and with her busy fingers fell to visit and explore that part of me where now the heat and irritations were so violent that I was perfectly sick and ready to die with desire: that the bare touch of her finger in that critical place had the effect of fire to a train.

Phoebe here sounds almost like a chaperone; ordering Fanny into the right position, examining her condition with 'busy fingers' and applying a temporary solution. Cleland insists that what Phoebe wants is not to satisfy either Fanny or herself, but to finish the lesson.

The irony is that the more information Phoebe gives Fanny, the less she is needed herself; her pupil outgrows and despises her.

After the crevice scene, Fanny is desperate for relief: 'I hugged, I clasped Phoebe, as if she had the wherewithal to relieve me.' This loveless hug is not rewarded; Phoebe makes no attempt to touch Fanny, she simply teases her about her approaching defloration. She still wants to be touched herself, but Fanny has learned to despise everything that is not a penis, seeing the vulva as a negative space:

> now grown more knowing, I missed the main object of my wishes; and finding not even the shadow of what I wanted, where everything was so flat! or so hollow! In the vexation I was in at it, I should have withdrawn my hand, but for fear of disobliging her.

Not being fussy, Phoebe goes ahead and uses the reluctant hand to give herself what Fanny assumes is 'rather the shadow than the substance of any pleasure'. Fanny no longer believes in orgasms without a penis. Her final comment nails the lid on the coffin of lesbian possibilities: 'For my part, I now pined for more solid food, and promised tacitly to myself that I would not be put off much longer with this foolery from woman to woman.'[33] Sure enough, once Fanny has entered heterosexual pornotopia (where a man's ejaculation brings on perfect simultaneous orgasms every time) she shuts her mind to any erotic relations with a woman. Even the group orgies that follow are strictly organised in heterosexual couples. Phoebe, with her strangely lingering taste for such 'foolery from woman to woman', is let slip from Cleland's narrative.

The dildo tribe

For real satisfaction, some (though not all) writers thought that women needed some kind of substitute for a penis. Texts on hermaphrodites could describe them pleasuring each other or more conventionally shaped women with their gigantic clitorises. Another kind of female member, as we have seen in some accounts of female husbands, was a strap-on dildo. Dildos were always good for a laugh in erotic literature, but they had a certain aura of danger as well.

In Lord Rochester's Restoration play *Sodom or the Quintessence of Debauchery* (not published in England until 1707), men turn from women to each other, leaving the frustrated court ladies to use dildos to take the edge off their lust. Queen Cuntigratia sits in the chair of state and has her chief maid of honour service her with a dildo, complaining all the while that it is too short and that 'You frig, as if you were afraid to hurt.' This seems to be just a lazy form of the masturbation in which the whole court indulges; there is no sense of erotic tension between maid and mistress.[34] But other texts in which women from different classes use a dildo together can hint at same-sex desire – at least on the part of the one directing the dildo. Take the case of Tonzenie, one of the libertine heroines of the anonymous *A New Atalantis for the Year One Thousand Seven Hundred and Fifty-Eight*, who learns about her sexuality by reading such texts as Cleland's *Fanny Hill*. Finding her fingers insufficient for satisfaction, she has her French maid Janneton buy her 'one of the middle-sized dildo-tribe'. (These seem to have been widely available, with straps for the jaw as well as the pubis; it was rumoured that a shop in London's Leicester Square sold nothing else.) Janneton, being 'well skilled in such practices', knows how to move it so as to bring her mistress to 'the moment of rapture', at which point she applies 'a warm injection' to mimic a male ejaculation. Sometimes, for greater realism, Janneton will 'artfully gird it to her loins, and act the man with her young mistress'. As in *Fanny Hill*, however, our heroine is determined to move on to the real 'essence', having 'grown too sensible of the inefficacy of all such weak representations'.[35] Janneton may bring her to orgasmic 'rapture', yet this is somehow not a real orgasm.

Janneton's nationality is significant; at this time French servants were in great demand among the wealthy English, as they were considered experts on food, dress and other sophisticated pleasures, but they were also assumed to be naturally fawning and servile and were the targets for xenophobic hostility, especially from middle-class and working-class Londoners.[36] The English often called lesbianism a French vice; according to the logic of this text, only a French maid would be decadent enough to know about same-sex possibilities and servile enough to perform such acts for her mistress.

Janneton's accent is parodied to make her a comic butt. When Tonzenie explains her frustration, for example, Janneton answers sadly, 'I vish me had been one man, your ladyship should not sik so long for de good ting.' She promptly fetches the well-hung footman to give Tonzenie 'de good ting'. But far from retiring discreetly, Janneton takes the stage manager's role in Tonzenie's defloration, plying the tentative footman with champagne and even unbuttoning his breeches. Her symbolic punishment for such presumption is a blow from his penis, which finally 'bolted out with such violence against the French woman's face, that it felled her on her back'. 'Me believe it be Hercules's club', Janneton murmurs respectfully, 'it so knock me down.' Irrepressible, she struggles up and helps with the awkward defloration, advising on the best angle and singing French songs to encourage the couple.

As they lie asleep, we are told, 'Janneton layed her own leachery, provoked by what she had seen, with simple digitation.' Masturbation, presented as second-best sex, is all that is left over for the maid. Tonzenie and the footman are the passive objects of Janneton's bisexual, voyeuristic pleasure; she pulls down the blankets to ogle the sleepers, murmuring, 'Heaven bless de fond pair!' This is a highly ambiguous portrait; is she the abused servant of heterosexuality, left to solitary masturbation, or should we see her as triumphantly running the whole show? It is significant that Janneton outlasts the footman, who soon dies from exhaustion and the aphrodisiacs she kept giving him. She promptly finds Tonzenie another lover, who takes them both abroad.[37]

As well as stories about real dildos we find the enduring fantasy of a penis disguised as a dildo; this seems to combine the titillation of perversion with male satisfaction in outdoing and tricking lesbians whose use of a dildo threatens male power. One example of this is *A Spy on Mother Midnight*, a ninepenny chapbook of 1748, in which the law student Mr F_ goes to a country inn disguised as 'Miss Polly' in order to seduce Miss Maria, the seemingly cold and manhating object of his desire. It shocks and excites him to find that, among themselves, women talk bawdily and swop smutty jokes. Warmed up by one such session with the girls, Miss Maria invites 'Miss Polly' to be her bedfellow and talks of her sexual frustration. Happening to glimpse an 'ivory substitute of virility' among Maria's clothes, 'Miss Polly' is initially shocked, but decides to make use of it. Laughing, he waves it at her, commenting 'here is at least some Kind of Comfort; now, if you get to Bed quickly, I shall use this so artfully, that you shall not know the Difference 'twixt me and Mr._ (naming myself)'. Maria's first emotions are embarrassment and irritation at 'Miss Polly' discovering her secret. But the idea of using the dildo together has a definite appeal: 'we soon came to so good an Understanding as to it's Use, that she expressed great Satisfaction at the Promise I made her, and told me, she would call me Mr._ to help the better to carry on the Deceit'. This can be seen as a useful excuse: invoking the name of her male suitor, Maria can express excitement without admitting to any same-sex desire. Mr. F_ leaps on her in the dark, substituting his penis for the 'poor passive insensible Implement'.

> 'Bless me!' says she, 'What!' She had not Power to ask the Question, but was immediately convinc'd what Sort of a Bedfellow she had got. Great was her Confusion, but not so great as to spoil our Sport; she had gone too far to recede.

Afterwards Miss Maria is furious with him for the deception. Adopting a high moral tone, Mr F_ reminds her that he has given her satisfaction 'in a Manner, I thought, less sinful, and indisputably more natural, than those I presumed she heretofore had Recourse to'.[38] (In this phallocentric world, masturbation with a dildo is evidently a greater crime than fornication with a male stranger.) Mr. F_ stays in petticoats and accomplishes several similar seductions of other women; the irony he fails to notice is that, despite his righteous disapproval of dildos, it is as a woman with a dildo that women welcome him.

Stories of men adopting female disguise in order to seduce women away from a world of women's love may originate with the story of the nymph Callisto in the Latin poet Ovid's *Metamorphoses*, a text circulating in several different English translations throughout the seventeenth and eighteenth centuries. The first point this story makes is that women's love is unreliable, fickle, shallow; Callisto is Diana's favourite nymph only for the moment. Diana's love is as brittle as Callisto's virginity, and closely bound up with it. Lusting after Callisto, Jupiter decides to get close to her by disguising himself as Diana. Callisto greets her mistress warmly, but is soon made uneasy by the fervour in the supposed Diana's kisses, which reveals them to be essentially male. Jupiter rapes her; this does not seduce Callisto into heterosexuality, or change her feelings for her true mistress, but it does leave her deflowered and pregnant. Nine months later, when Diana sees Callisto's shape during a nude bathe, she exiles her in disgust.

The pattern is altered slightly in eighteenth-century variations on this story; it is not pregnancy that causes the rift between women lovers, but the greater satisfaction of heterosex itself. A good example is the story of Theodora and Amaryllis in *A Treatise of Hermaphrodites* (1718), attributed to Giles Jacob. By contrast with the two hermaphroditical females the author has already described (see pp. 47–8), these two respectable Italian maidens, daughters of a courtier and a merchant respectively, are beautiful. (This is a hint that they are not 'real' lesbians and can still be saved.) Both happen to lose their beloved suitors to death; they meet, swap stories and decide never to choose other men – exactly the same excuse for women sharing their lives that was used in reports on the Mary East case (see pp. 70–1). So Amaryllis and Theodora resolve 'to live together as Sisters or inseparable Companions'. But the suggestive vocabulary of their vow 'to use their utmost Artifices for the Relief of each other' hints at the undercurrent of their relationship. Their youth, their luxurious lifestyle, and of course the 'hot inciting Climate' of Italy, all combine to lead the pair into 'the most abominable Pollution'. Jacob ignores the possibility that such polluted desire might be the original motive of their setting up home together; it is reduced to a side effect.

Sex between women is described as a businesslike venture: 'they provided artificial *Penis*'s of the largest Dimensions, and with Ribbins they fasten'd the Root of the Instrument in the same Situation as Nature has plac'd the Substance in Man'. He goes on to describe the method according to the heterosexual model, in which the active partner's ejaculation causes the passive one's orgasm:

> They frequently embrac'd one another by turns, as Man and Woman in the amorous Adventure; and when their Vigour was so much abated, that they were no longer able to struggle, the Female uppermost withdrew, and taking another Instrument in her Hand, she us'd it on her Companion with an Injection of Moisture, which, with the rubbing, occasion'd such a tickling, as to force a discharge of Matter and facilitate the Pleasure.

This becomes their 'daily practice', Jacob explains, and they include a female friend every now and then for variety.

But Theodora has a frustrated suitor, Philensis, who bribes the female friend into telling him all about the women's activities. Effortlessly he disguises himself as a Roman noblewoman, works his way into their friendship and finally into their bed. Overcoming Theodora's initial reluctance to let 'her' make love to her, Philensis swiftly hides the dildo in his pocket while pretending to have strapped it on, and leaps on her. Jacob assures us that Theodora is unaware of the difference, 'till the moment of Ejaculation, which was not usual with the same Instrument in her Embraces with Amaryllis'. (So the only difference felt between woman–woman sex and sex in a mixed couple is that women change equipment at the last minute.) 'Prodigiously surprised', Theodora tries to beat Philensis off. During the ensuing argument, she somehow reinterprets her sensations and 'considering what had happen'd, and experiencing a material Difference between Art and Nature, agreed, on his humble Request, to Marry him'. Yet we know that at the time she felt no 'material difference' between sex with him and with a woman; the author has sacrificed all consistency to produce a happy heterosexual ending.[39]

Not every dildo is presented, as the author of *A Spy on Mother Midnight* would call it, as a 'poor passive insensible Instrument'. *Monsieur Thing's Origin: or, Seignior D—o's Adventures in Britain,* a sixpenny poem about the adventures of a dildo, personified as a French visitor to London, was published in 1722.[40] Apparently it offended one female bookseller so much that she sent constables to suppress its sale by the hawkers.[41] The preface of *Monsieur Thing's Origin* makes clear that, despite the flippant tone of this burlesque, the author has nothing but contempt for dildo-using women who 'can't enjoy the Pleasure design'd, without preferring Art before Nature' and deserve the detestation of their own sex.

The author is gentle enough in his treatment of heterosexual women who, unsatisifed by husbands or languishing in spinsterhood, make use of the ingenious machine which can ejaculate 'Warm Milk, or any other Liquid softer,/Slow as they please, or, if they please, much faster.' He becomes much more hostile in tone when discussing Monsieur Dildo's use by 'two Partners' in a millinery shop. Though they seem innocent, unlike the whores whom the dildo is accustomed to serving, they soon take to humping in a mysterious manner like 'two Cows a playing in the Field'.

> One of these Girls ty'd Monsieur to her Middle,
> To try if she the Secret could unriddle ...
> She acted Man, being in a merry Mood,
> Striving to please her Partner as she cou'd;
> And thus they took it in their turns to please
> Their Lustful Inclinations to appease.

It is interesting that there is no suggestion of fixed roles; the dildo is not an accessory to a masculine identity, but a flexible toy which the women use turn by turn to give each other pleasure.

This is all they need; they are not warming up for heterosex or in any way pining for want of men. Monsieur Dildo is furious when he realises that though his shape is phallic, he is being used as a tool of female power.

> ... Monsieur was almost suffocated
> With that, of all things, that at last he hated.
> So did he leave these Vile and Lustful Elves,
> To run the Frisk together by themselves.[42]

Dehumanised into 'elves' by their unnatural desire, the women have nonetheless escaped to a realm of lighthearted pleasure.

Two orgies

Sexual acts between women in a group are not a common element of early erotica, but there are two very interesting texts – a Latin satire from the first century and a newspaper report from the eighteenth – which are worth putting side by side.

One of the best-known pieces of evidence that women could pleasure each other is the notoriously misogynistic *Sixth Satire* of the Roman writer Juvenal (*ca.* 50 AD–after 127). At the secret women-only ceremonies of the goddess which he describes, Roman ladies and courtesans join in a competition (apparently of tribadic skill) before calling in the men finally to satisfy them. When the former poet laureate John Dryden translated the *Satire* in 1693 (a popular version, reaching six editions in the first half of the eighteenth century), he insisted that the lesbian scenes had no contemporary relevance. Having made this disclaimer, Dryden is able to offer a vivid and fairly explicit translation:

> Where the Rank Matrons, Dancing to the Pipe,
> Gig with their Bums, and are for Action ripe;
> With Musick rais'd, they spread abroad their Hair;
> And toss their Heads like an enamour'd Mare:
> *Laufella* lays her Garland by, and proves
> The mimick Leachery of Manly Loves.
> Rank'd with the Lady, the cheap Sinner lies;
> For here not Blood, but Virtue gives the prize.
> Nothing is feign'd in this Venereal Strife;
> 'Tis downright Lust, and Acted to the Life.[43]

Though he cuts details, Dryden is frank about the meaning of Laufella's actions: she is described as mimicking manly lechery, that is, having sex with a woman.

By contrast, the Irish actor-manager Thomas Sheridan's scholarly prose translation of 1739 aims for the abstract and impersonal, and manages to make the orgy sound like a game of cards. 'The leud Laufella proposes a Prize among the most infamous Strumpets, and in the impure Contention obtains the Victory; but she is all in rapture when Medullina acts her Part.'[44] A vicar's literal version in 1760 is obscure but vivid, making clear at least that this is a sexual matter:

> o how great a desire of copulation is in these minds! what a cry lust tickling them! how great that torrent of old wine over their moist thighs! Laufella challenges the wenches of procurers having placed a crown, and carries off the prizes of the hanging hip.[45]

This last detail of the 'hanging hip' hints more frankly than any other translation at genital rubbing, the literal meaning of tribadism.

By the century's end, it seems, it was no longer acceptable to be so explicit. William Gifford's edition of 1802 disguises the orgy as some kind of wrestling contest: Laufella

> now springs forth, and tries a fall
> With the town prostitutes, and throws them all;
> But yields, herself, to Medullina, known
> For parts and powers, superior to her own.[46]

Despite Gifford's vague references to 'mimic feats' and 'this unnatural game', a reader could scan the whole text without realising that the women are having sex. A slightly later translation, M. Madan's edition of 1813, returns to the abstract vocabulary of Sheridan's 1739 version, probably the only eighteenth-century translation he dares use. Unlike his forebears, however, Madan is honest about his censorship, explaining that the literal sense of a few passages is 'better obscured than explained, especially to young minds'.[47]

The overall move through this period, then, was to bowdlerise and obscure the details of the lesbian orgy in Juvenal's satire; this parallels an overall rise in censorship, as reading changed from an elite to a mass activity. We should remember, however, that bowdlerised translations did not handicap those who could read

Latin – mostly wealthy men, but some women too. Hostile texts could be of great use as sources of information and even enjoyment. Anne Lister, for instance, read and clearly appreciated Juvenal's *Sixth Satire*, mentioning it to test women she suspected were lesbians like herself; her diary for 26 July 1823 comments of a new friend: 'Miss Pickford has read the Sixth Satyr of Juvenal. She understands these matters well enough.'[48]

A very different text describes sex between pairs of women in a group in a somewhat similar way, as an elaborate game or contest. In December 1792, the semi-pornographic *Bon Ton Magazine* reported on a Thursday evening club of 'Female Flagellists' in London's Jermyn Street. The members, the writer explains, are mostly married women who:

> grown weary of wedlock in its accustomed form, and possibly impatient of that cold neglect and indifference which, after a certain term, becomes attendant upon Hymen, determined to excite, by adventitious applications, those extasies which in the earlier period of marriage they had experienced.

Same-sex whipping encounters, then, are shown to be a supplement to heterosexuality, not an alternative; the women are not interested in each other so much as in reviving the pleasure of their honeymoon days.

After wondering coyly whether 'the stimulus exceeds the bounds of conjugal felicity', the *Bon Ton* report goes on to accuse particular women, notably 'the wife of a certain military taylor, and the neglected spouse of a certain military commander', of attending these 'nocturnal carnal orgies'. The fact that both husbands are associated with the army is no coincidence; the point of the gibe is that sexual deviance brings women together across the class spectrum, making a nonsense of the husbands' careful military etiquette. (A similar point is made in Juvenal's satire; the orgy is particularly shameful because well-born ladies are mixing with common prostitutes.) The *Bon Ton* writer clearly feels threatened by this lesbian conspiracy which has infiltrated social levels high and low: 'the practitioners', he complains, 'though numerous now a days, endeavour by every possible means to keep their Propensities, for such we may fairly call them, profoundly secret'.

According to the reporter, the club always has at least twelve attendees. They draw lots for the choice of positions: 'six down, or stooping down, and six up'. The session begins with a lecture by that evening's 'chair-woman' on the history and good effects of flagellation, and then the whipping begins. In its formality and pomposity, the ritual sounds more like the army than a sex club. The six 'patients' lean over, the six 'agents' expose the patients' buttocks and each collects from the leader 'a stout engine of duty'. It is the chairwoman who begins the beating, the others merely watching at first; if anyone begins before her they risk being punished with an unbearable double beating. It is also up to the chairwoman to decide on technique, whether to beat from the thighs up to the buttocks, or directly on to the 'cave of Cupid'. At a certain point, the 'submissive patients' squeal: 'It is too much!' in unison and leap up to discuss their sensations. Rods and roles are now exchanged, and the beaters are beaten.

Since women whipping each other was a staple theme of French erotica for men, and whipping scenes were particularly popular in Gothic and pornographic fiction in the 1790s (especially in the works of the Marquis de Sade), this account should be taken with a large pinch of salt. However, we should not discount the possibility that flagellation was fashionable in the flesh as well as in print, and that this account is based on rumours of a real club of the time. In 1981 Lillian Faderman felt safe in assuming that the *Bon Ton* report was pure fantasy lifted straight from French erotica. Knowing of no examples of SM between women except in the new Samois club in San Francisco, she reassured the lesbian community that 'it is doubtful that a "sexual" act so rarely occuring in our liberated times would have existed in such proportions two centuries ago that clubs were formed especially to practise it'.[49] However, since the coming out of SM dykes in such numbers in the 1980s we have to look again at our history; lesbians 'coming to power' at the end of the eighteenth century might well have formed whipping clubs.

If we begin to take erotica seriously, it offers some fascinating starting points for a history of SM. Rather than a subculture in which clothes, code words, props and techniques all combine to form a sexual style, in eighteenth-century texts these elements are scattered widely. For example, whipping crops up (pun intended!) as a stimulation which anyone could work into a sexual scene, rather than as a taste peculiar to a minority of people. There is no evidence that 'butch–femme' or (in eighteenth-century terms) 'mannish–not mannish' styles had any connection with SM techniques. As we can see in the *Bon Ton* report, whipping could have everything to do with chosen pleasure and bottom/top roles could be swapped with ease.

A thrilling joy, 'till then unknown

Because many of these texts can be seen as treating sex between women as subordinate to heterosex or mocking it for ineffectiveness, historians have often assumed that all such works adopted a similar viewpoint. But some of the texts discussed here show women giving each other great pleasure, without any heterosexual conclusion. In particular, the anonymous three-page poem of 1727, *An Epistle from Signora F_a to a Lady*, is an extraordinary English text, unknown outside a couple of bibliographies. Though it was probably written and published to damage the reputation of the Venetian singer Signora Faustina Bordoni Hasse (1700–81) during her second season in London, at the height of her fame and wealth, the *Epistle* effectively celebrates lesbian relationships in the highest terms.

It takes the form of a letter in rhyming couplets from Faustina to ease the 'tortur'd Mind' of her absent woman lover, who is troubled by 'Jealousy'. Faustina reassures her: 'Unspotted as the Sun, my Love shall rise,/And soon dispell the Fears that cloud your Eyes.' Other women, she insists, may be good at scandal, dress, scholarship, quadrille or dancing, but 'F[austin]a's Glory lies in Loving well.' Like Myra in William King's *The Toast*, but without the savage mockery, Faustina is presented as a glamorous sexual prodigy who experiments with techniques and positions. 'Of Pleasures all the various Modes I know,/Its different Degrees, its Ebb and Flow.' But Faustina does not aspire to a life of promiscuous enjoyment; what she wants is to channel all this experimental energy into one relationship.

> Propitious *Venus* grant me Power to give
> Joy to fair ———, 'tis for her I Live.
> Cease then to let your jealous Fancy rove,
> Nor give me such a cruel Proof of Love.

Yet even as she reassures her lover, Faustina cannot resist boasting a little about the 'rival Beauties' who swarm around her after performances, particularly the contrasting women Thalestris and Chloe. Her explanation of what she is giving up makes her declaration of fidelity even stronger:

To fierce *Thalestris* I disdain to yield,
And gentle *Chloe* ne'er shall gain the Field.
In vain she breathes her Passion in my Ear,
For when you speak I nothing else can hear:
In vain with Transport to my Feet she flew,
All Joys are tastless, but what come thro' you.

This short poem packs in a remarkably detailed account of Faustina's sexual identity and history. She used to be cynical about love, she explains, moving from man to man like a bee between flowers, with all the ethics of a hired mercenary soldier. 'But now I Love', Faustina explains; she has been punished for her exploitation of other people's hearts by being made to fall helplessly in love herself. Returning to the question of this exclusive relationship, she advises her lover to take a look at herself and remember the many qualities she has (youth, beauty, tender loyalty) that will keep Faustina by her side, 'nor fear to see me in another's Arms'.

At this point she recaps the story of their relationship; the lover was the 'first of all the British Fair' to declare support for Faustina, even before she had heard her sing. Their bond was almost telepathic, predating their meeting:

By Sympathy, you felt each Charm, each Grace,
And lov'd my Person, e'er you saw my Face.
Nor was I coy, or difficult to move,
When you reveal'd the Story of your Love ...
I felt a thrilling Joy, 'till then unknown,
And Lov'd with Ardour equal to your own.

Sex, for Faustina, is not separate from love, but a proof of it; sexual fulfilment is the natural culmination of their growing relationship:

Witness the Transports of that happy Day,
When melting in each other's Arms we lay.
With Velvet Kiss your humid Lips I press'd,
And rode triumphant on your panting Breast.

This is no pornotopian dreamland; the bliss of their erotic encounter is scathingly contrasted with the boring reality of heterosex that the lover has been used to and is described as superior even to the lovemaking of Faustina's predecessor on stage, the Italian soprano Margherita Durastanti, who sang in London on and off from 1720–4.

> In Extasy you cry'd, What Joys are these?
> Not *Durestanti*'s self so well cou'd please.
> This is no sleepy Husband's feeble Mite,
> The tasteless Tribute of an ill-spent Night.

The note struck is one of wonder: 'What Joys are these?' the poem asks, what are the surprising and specific delights of a lesbian relationship?

An Epistle ends with a return to the worrying topic of fidelity. Will Faustina, surrounded by admiring fans, be able to resist all offers? All she can promise is that she wants to.

> O did my Power and Will in Concert move!
> And were my Strength but equal to my Love!
> Th' incredulous Philosopher shou'd see
> Perpetual Motion verified in me.

'Perpetual motion', the idea that a machine could find such a perfect harmony with gravitational forces that it would be kept moving without effort for all time, is here used as a powerful image for the kind of relationship these women want: a dynamic one-to-one relationship that is the result of daily choices, and a balance so equal that it lasts forever. Whatever satirical intention the writer of this poem may have had, the effect is utopian.

I do not want to exaggerate either the importance or the positive attitudes of seventeenth- and eighteenth-century accounts of sex between women. They tell us plenty about male fantasies and little about real practices. Yet I have been surprised by the variety of representations, the unsettling power some of these writers ascribe to same-sex desire and actions. Nor does erotica portray only one lesbian social type, the aristocratic libertine; society hostesses and singers are mixed in with soldiers' wives and milliners.

The anecdote in Casanova's *Memoirs* (written before 1798, but not published until the 1820s) of the two nuns he likes to watch in their 'barren' attempts at making love, until finally he leaps in and makes them both almost faint with satisfaction, has often been offered as the paradigm of eighteenth-century men's 'lesbian' erotica.[50] But I have not found any such scene in earlier texts. Even if overall a work tends to subordinate woman–woman to man–woman sex, as in Chorier's *Dialogue* or Cleland's *Fanny Hill*, no man intrudes, Casanova-style, to interrupt the lesbian scene.

(If he does, as I have shown, he often has to disguise his penis as a woman's dildo before it will be acceptable to a woman.) Within a lesbian scene, same-sex practices are usually shown to be very satisfying to at least one of the participants. Even if the younger woman moves on to be deflowered by a man, the older woman is often permanently devoted to pleasure with women. And there are also texts in which both sexual partners seem interested only in women and complete satisfaction needs no penis or phallic substitute. It is unwise to simplify the range of erotica into a single model; as Ros Ballaster has argued, these texts show that:

> female same-sex desire could not be entirely explained away or managed by the attempt to enclose it within a single model of tribadic 'identity'. These materials imply not only the will to contain female same-sex desire within comfortable paradigms of masculine control, orchestration and interpretation of its meaning, but also a continuing difficulty in attaining that end.[51]

Erotica has other uses besides its primary function of arousing men; it provides us with fascinating evidence of some of the many ways desire and sex between women was understood.

By permission of the British Library

A new 'postulant' is initiated into a French lesbian club, from the anonymous La Nouvelle Sapho *(1793)*

7 Communities

We know that men who desired each other had access to a homosexual subculture in cities and large towns across western Europe; it has been assumed that women had no such facilities. Theo van der Meer, for example, concludes that though there were small groups of tribades in 1790s Amsterdam, the rarity of criminal charges against them, together with the lack of recorded reference to their drinking and meeting places, shows that no lesbian subculture existed.[1] Many historians have taken this lack of evidence of pubs and sex houses as proof that lesbianism was not an option or even a concept for most women in this era.[2]

Certainly, I know of no evidence for any network of drinking houses and cruising walks for women parallel to that enjoyed by mollies.[3] However, lesbian culture today does not have the same structures as gay male culture has, so why should we expect them to have been similar in the eighteenth century, long before the liberation movement had brought the two communities together? If we stop looking for exact equivalents to gay male institutions, we can open our eyes to the different ways women-lovers seem to have formed groups and networks in this period.

In this final chapter, I am not so much interested in a distinct subculture – the prefix implying subordination, minority interests and inferiority – as in the representation of lesbian communities, the lesbian culture that permeated British culture, its parties, institutions and homes. I want to study women's groups of all sorts, some tied to a certain city and decade, others more enduring. I begin with two separatist spaces that threatened men – the Roman Catholic convent, often satirised as a den of Sapphic vice, and its secular equivalent, given such a startling erotic charge in Margaret Cavendish's play *The Convent of Pleasure* (1668). Next I look at recorded gossip about networks of lesbian lovers; such a group could be described as a cabal – a word suggesting both a political conspiracy and a tradition of secret knowledge, as in the

Hebrew *caballah*. Because a community stretches over time as well as space, I end this chapter with texts describing lesbianism as a secret cultural tradition invented by Sappho of Lesbos and thriving underground in Britain.

Stories about women-only groups have not so much been ignored by scholars as under-read. Feminist historians often celebrate them as examples of solidarity and sisterhood, ignoring the eroticism that pervades them. Janet Todd, for instance, places both Sarah Scott's *A Description of Millenium Hall* and the 'new Cabal' section of Delarivier Manley's *The New Atalantis* in the 'Political friendship' section of her book on women's friendship and reads them accordingly. The implications are that resistance to heterosexuality is a purely political choice, and that while couples may be romantic, groups are not. Similarly, lesbian historians have generally focused on couples, retelling the great romances such as that of the Ladies of Llangollen. It is significant that in *Surpassing the Love of Men*, Lillian Faderman introduces our history by defining the word lesbian as 'an all-consuming emotional relationship in which two women are devoted to each other above anyone else'.[4] This reduces the rich variety of lesbian culture to its most privileged form, the exclusive pair-bond. So many of us have been left out of such history: celibate women, lesbian friends, women who have more than one lover at a time, and all of us who experience lesbian culture not just as a nation of couples but as many communities.

The nun's smooth tongue

The mysterious walls of the convent, which kept women at least partly free from men's interference in their lives, sent some male writers' imaginations wild.[5] (Similar male fantasies involved sex between women in other 'confined' institutions such as harems, for example in the Baron de Montesquieu's ever-popular novel *Persian Letters*.)[6] The figure of the unchaste nun was always titillating – 'nun', 'abbess' and 'nunnery' were slang for prostitute, madam and brothel – but the ultimate in erotic satire was the lesbian nun. Casually sexualised in Barrin's *Venus in the Cloister* (see pp. 198–200), denounced as a source of evil in Diderot's *The Nun* (see pp. 190–7), the figure of the lesbian nun could be used to expose the Church in a variety of ways.

In Andrew Marvell's 'Upon Appleton House', the luring of a young woman into religious vows stands for a kind of group lesbian seduction. Cromwell's unofficial poet laureate, Marvell probably wrote 'Upon Appleton House' between 1650 and 1652 when he was tutor to Mary Fairfax, though it was not published until 1681; with his other poems it was reprinted several times before the end of the century. Anti-Catholicism filled British literature of this period, but as he had been briefly lured into Roman Catholicism by Jesuits as a student, perhaps Marvell had a personal grudge to express as well. 'Upon Appleton House' has an extraordinary central section which takes the story of General Fairfax's ancestors who built the family home, and reworks it into a parable about a lesbian paradise lost.

The facts are simple enough. On the site of the house was a nunnery, near which lived Isabel Thwaites, who was wooed by William Fairfax. She moved into the convent, which was run by her guardian Lady Anna Langton, and lived there until William seized her from it and married her in 1518. Marvell's version makes no mention of the prioress being Isabel's guardian; instead, the 'subtle Nuns' are presented as false friends who persuade her to join them. One nun in particular plots to lure Isabel in. Her long speech emphasises all the comforts of a house protected from 'those wild Creatures, called Men'; it is not the nuns who are locked in, she explains, but enemies who are locked out. Her descriptions combine biblical and classical allusions to glamorise convent life:

> Here we, in shining Armour white,
> Like *Virgin Amazons* do fight.
> And our chaste *Lamps* we hourly trim,
> Lest the great *Bridegroom* find them dim.

However, it gradually becomes clear that it is not for Jesus the Bridegroom that the nuns work, but to provide themselves with a lifestyle of secret, refined pleasures. Each of them is already a spiritual 'Queen', with all the majesty and status that brings. The imagery is that of the 'oriental' harem:

> Our *Orient* Breaths perfumed are
> With Incense of incessant Pray'r:
> And Holy-water of our Tears
> Most strangely our Complexion clears.
> Not Tears of Grief; but such as those
> With which calm Pleasure overflows.

After an account of the way most of them spend their days, embroidering portraits of saints on to altar cloths, the nun slips in a flattering invitation:

> But much it to our Work would add,
> If here your Hand, your Face, we had:
> By it we would *our Lady* touch;
> Yet thus she you resembles much.
> Some of your Features, as we sow'd,
> Through every *Shrine* should be bestow'd.

The admiring gaze of a whole circle of nuns would touch Isabel, would divide and share her beauty and reproduce it in art. Here Marvell is probably hinting at the idolatrous elements of the Catholic cult of the Virgin Mary. As a powerful, goddess-like woman and a focus of passionate veneration by female supplicants, Mary aroused much resentment in male Protestant writers.

The nun goes on to insist that it would be 'Sacrilege' for Isabel to let a man touch her body, her 'holy Things, for *Heaven* fit'; she comments sharply that William Fairfax would gain more spiritual credit by worshipping Isabel from afar than by demanding her in marriage. Having disposed of this obstacle, the nun continues her flattery, voicing her vision of crowds of angels glorifying Isabel. What she offers the heiress is not just community but the position of honour:

> Here live beloved, and obey'd:
> Each one your Sister, each your Maid.
> And, if our Rule seem strictly penn'd,
> The Rule it self to you shall bend.

She hints that Isabel could quickly be promoted to abbess and that she might inspire the nuns to greater things. What her vocabulary stresses is the sensual intimacy of the nuns' relation to this new saint: 'How soft the Yoke on us would lye,/Might such fair Hands, as yours, it tye!' Her emphasis is on unmarried life not (as the cliché would have it) as a waste of human fruit, but as a preservation of its utmost sweetness:

> Nor is our *Order* yet so nice,
> Delight to banish as a Vice:
> Here Pleasure Piety doth meet,
> One perfecting the other Sweet.
> So through the mortal Fruit we boil
> The Sugar's uncorrupting Oil

Dropping all reference to Christ, the nun describes the sisters' domestic work as a kind of goddess service, an intimate attention to the body of Nature:

> For such indeed are all our Arts,
> Still handling Nature's finest Parts.
> Flow'rs dress the Altars; for the Cloaths
> The Sea-born Amber we compose;
> Balms for the Griev'd we draw; and Pastes
> We mould, as Baits for curious Tastes.

Like several other phrases in this poem, 'curious Tastes' carries a sexual innuendo. At the end of her speech, the nun confronts the possibility coyly, offering Isabel an endless supply of girls to sleep with. She plays with the idea of an innocent sin, pretending to see no sexual meaning in the romantic imagery:

> What need is here of Man? unless
> These as sweet Sins we should confess.
> Each Night among us to your Side
> Appoint a fresh and Virgin bride!

Though she declares that the relationship would be 'chaste', the imagery is sensuous, emphasising both the similarity and the complementarity of two female bodies:

> Where you may lye as chaste in Bed,
> As Pearls together billeted.
> All Night embracing Arm in Arm,
> Like Crystal pure, with Cotton warm.

This is her final argument, and it seems to work. Isabel consents to enter the convent for a trial period. As Marvell puts it grimly, 'The *Nun's* smooth Tongue has suck'd her in': verbal seduction is here presented as spiritual cunnilingus.

Urged on by the poem's narrator, our hero William Fairfax protests at what he sees as his fiancée's condition of captivity. 'Hypocrite Witches', he calls the nuns, and accuses them of working on Isabel's religious feeling for their own secret purposes:

> And yet, how well soever meant,
> With them 'twould soon grow fraudulent;
> For like themselves they alter all,
> And Vice infects the very Wall ...
> I know what Fruit their Gardens yield,
> When they it think by Night conceal'd.

We are reminded of the fruit metaphor the nun used; the convent is not a place for preserving nature's pure sugar, according to Fairfax, but for growing strange fruit to be feasted on in secrecy. Though ostensibly Fairfax is accusing the nuns of wanting Isabel for her 'State' or inheritance, his vocabulary hints at sexual practices that will entrap the 'guiltless' heiress and cause her to 'perish' morally.

Having gone to court and been given permission to seize Isabel, Fairfax attacks the convent. A mock-heroic description of the battle shows the nuns defending themselves with holy water, chains of rosary beads and false relics. Finding the ever-silent Isabel 'weeping at the *Altar*' – not at all relieved to see him, it seems – Fairfax carries her away. The nuns are left guilty and regretful, 'like Gypsys who a Child have stoln' – lesbians and gypsies being considered enemies to the landowning family. Soon, Marvell concludes with satisfaction, the nunnery will be demolished in the Reformation to make way for the dynasty that William and Isabel will found between them.[7]

John Holstun has pointed out that Marvell gives lesbianism a powerful, threatening force in this poem, anchoring it in the solid social institution of the nunnery, but then snatches away that base. By setting the lesbian plot in the poem's distant past and making the triumph of heterosexuality (the Fairfax marriage) coincide with the undeniable historical event of the dissolution of the nunneries, Marvell consigns lesbian community to the unreachable past.[8] 'Upon Appleton House' is a parable of what heterosexists like to see as normal sexual development: young England is shown as wallowing in decadent Catholic pleasures, then, after a struggle, growing up into a modern Protestant nation; on the site of Appleton House, lesbian self-indulgence must give way to heterosexual family values.

The convent of pleasure

To some Roman Catholic women writers such as Jane Barker and Charlotte McCarthy, the convent was not a den of vice but a haven of virtue, and specifically of women-only communal living.[9] Protestants, however, had no parallel space offering a refuge from men. Some women, especially Anglicans, imagined and wrote about 'Protestant nunneries'; two crucial blueprints for such a community, charged with passion between women as well as devotion to God, are Mary Astell's *A Serious Proposal to the Ladies* (1694) and Sarah Scott's *A Description of Millenium Hall* (1762).[10]

The idea of women-only spaces also crops up in more secular literature of this period. The late seventeenth century saw a cluster of plays about the legendary Amazons, while periodical essays and occasional poems of the eighteenth century played with the idea of modern Amazonian projects. Most of these texts mock women for trying to cut themselves off from the patriarchy and show them being undermined by their irresistible desire for men. Struggling with themselves, these Amazons find nothing positive to replace what they are giving up; I have found no text in this period which imagines the Amazon as a lover of women in anything but a sisterly way.[11]

It is all the more startling, then, to find an appreciative and explicitly erotic account of a women-only community, based not on religious but on secular ideals, in a little-known, unperfomed Restoration play. Margaret Cavendish, Duchess of Newcastle was a married Royalist eccentric who combined science, philosophy and fantasy in her prolific writings. *The Convent of Pleasure* was published with other unperformed closet dramas in 1668. In the preface to the collection, Cavendish explained that she wrote for her own pleasure and no malicious critics could put her off, because her words were intended for 'not so much the present as future Ages'.[12] This freedom of spirit, based on wealth and education, allowed Cavendish to create an extraordinarily subversive lesbian romance.

The play opens with the news that Lady Happy has become a fabulously wealthy orphan on the death of her father, and so gentleman are swarming to woo her. But she has decided to cloister herself and a score of fellow noblewomen away from the world, specifically away from men. In the second scene Lady Happy explains frankly to Madam Mediator why she has chosen this life: male admirers make dull company, marriage would curtail her freedom and prostitution would destroy her health.

> L. *Happy*. And since there is so much folly, vanity and falshood in Men, why whould Women trouble and vex themselves for their sake; for retiredness bars the life from nothing else but Men.
> *Mediat.* O yes, for those that incloister themselves, bar themselves from all other worldly Pleasures.
> L. *Happy*. The more Fools they.

Our cheerful heroine explains that she can see no sense in living an ascetic life for religious motives, because why would the gods want humans to deny the senses that the gods themselves gave them? 'If the gods be cruel', she concludes, 'I will serve Nature.' With her group of female friends she intends to enjoy 'all the delights and pleasures that are allowable and lawful'.

Act II opens with Lady Happy's gentleman wooers, furious at the news, planning to visit the convent in disguise. Madam Mediator dashes their hopes by explaining that, unlike a religious convent, this one allows male authorities and servants no access. Lady Happy employs female servants for every task, even women doctors; her house needs no repair and her grounds are large enough to grow food in. It is an entirely self-sufficient women's community. Widows like Madam Mediator are allowed to visit, but not wives; any woman whose life is committed to men is banned from this space. Hearing all this, the suitors become infuriated and indulge in impotent fantasies of burning the convent down or pulling its strong walls apart.[13]

Her friends having assured her that they find this life blissful, Lady Happy tells them of her arrangements for each season. This is a childlike fantasy of total luxury, in which the damask linen napkins are changed between every course of a meal. In winter, for example, Lady Happy decides,

> our Chambers must be hung with Tapestry, and our Beds of Velvet, lined with Sattin, and all things suitable to it, and all the Floor spread over with *Turkie* Carpets, and a Cupboard of Gilt Plate; and all the Wood for Firing to be Cypress and Juniper; and all the lights to be Perfumed Wax.

This sensual paradise is just for women: the fashionable clothes are not meant to impress men, the food is not prepared for guests but for residents, and the comfortable beds (described in great detail) are for women to luxuriate in.

The convent wins fame and attracts a visit from a foreign princess who is described warily by Madam Mediator as 'a Princely brave Woman truly, of a Masculine Presence'. The first thing this mannish visitor does is to beg for Lady Happy's special friendship; having won it, she asks another favour. 'Observing in your several Recreations some of your Ladies do accoustre Themselves in Masculine-Habits, and act Lovers-parts; I desire you will give me leave to be sometimes so accoustred and act the part of your loving

Servant.' Crossdressing and same-sex flirtation, then, are integral parts of the community, even if their pretexts are masques and other theatrical 'Recreations'. Lady Happy is more than content to have this gallant newcomer 'act the part' of her lover in a spirit of 'innocent' theatre.[14]

The convent's members then sit down to watch a play-within-the-play which features women with spendthrift, drunken and violent husbands, women avoiding rapists, women with morning sickness, labour pains, stillbirths and dead children. Its effect is to make the audience more than ever relieved that their lifestyle keeps them safe from all these troubles.

At the beginning of the fourth act, the real drama begins. Lady Happy discovers that she is not just playing with the princess – she is falling in love. Her reactions are psychologically convincing: 'Why', she asks herself, 'may not I love a Woman with the same affection I could a Man?' All she can find to explain the taboo on women's love is that 'Nature is Nature', that is, the reproduction of the species demands opposite-sex mating. (This traditional line of argument may be an echo of the speech Ovid gives to Iphis in the *Metamorphoses*, see pp. 28–9.) Along comes the princess wearing a shepherd's costume to match Lady Happy's shepherdess gown; she asks whether her beloved mistress is avoiding her. Lady Happy tries to explain both her love and her sense of wrongdoing:

> L. *Happy*. Your Presence is more acceptable to me then [sic] the Presence of our Goddess Nature, for which she, I fear will punish me, for loving you more than I ought to love you.
> *Prin*. Can Lovers love too much?
> L. *Happy*. Yes, if they love not well.

Lady Happy is struggling to understand how women can love each other 'too much' and 'not well', but even the principles of the 'Goddess Nature', whom she set out to worship at the beginning of the play, have a less powerful hold on her than this enchanting princess.

The princess refuses to face up to the criminality of their passion; she draws Lady Happy back into the game of 'harmless' platonic love between shepherd and shepherdess:

> *Prin*. Can any Love be more vertuous, innocent and harmless than ours?

L. *Happy*. I hope not.
Prin. Then let us please our selves, as harmless Lovers use to do.
L. *Happy*. How can harmless Lovers please themselves?
Prin. Why very well, as, to discourse, imbrace and kiss, so mingle souls together.

At the word 'kiss', Lady Happy panics; she knows that this is breaking the rules of platonic love. Watch the princess deftly switch into the conventions of female friendship, which (because of the assumption of sexlessness between women) do allow for kissing:

L. *Happy*. But innocent Lovers do not use to kiss.
Prin. Not any act more frequent amongst us Women-kind; nay, it were a sin in friendship, should not we kiss: then let us not prove ourselves Reprobates.
They imbrace and kiss, and hold each other in their Arms.

With a kiss of acknowledged passion between two women who know each other to be women, no wonder this play was never performed, even on the broadminded Restoration stage. The princess underlines the point with a final couplet: 'These my Imbraces though of Femal kind,/May be as fervent as a Masculine mind.'[15]

In a masque-within-the-scene, Lady Happy and the princess court each other as shepherdess and shepherd; in long speeches each praises the other's psychological acuteness and scientific knowledge respectively. In conclusion, Lady Happy tells the princess, 'I can neither deny you my Love nor Person'; it is not clear whether she is speaking in character as the shepherdess, or as herself. After a group dance they are crowned as king and queen of the shepherds; a later masque features them as king and queen of the sea. The point of all these scenes seems to be to reinforce and give a sense of triumphant rightness to the love between the two.

But Margaret Cavendish does not allow the women's love to float free of its moral context; Lady Happy's worries are not over. Once she is alone again, she tries to halt the momentum of the romance by calling on all the deities she has formerly abandoned:

O Nature, O you gods above,
Suffer me not to fall in Love;
O strike me dead here in this place
Rather than fall into disgrace.

Madam Mediator asks what she is so sad about, but Lady Happy cannot risk confiding in her. Without managing to work out a rationale for women's love for each other, Lady Happy seems gradually to come to terms with it; the following stage direction, for the first scene of Act V, shows the couple exchanging tokens of commitment.

> *Enter the* Princess *and the Lady* Happy; *The* Princess *is in a Man's Apparel as going to Dance; they Whisper sometime; then the Lady* Happy *takes a Ribbon from her arm, and gives it to the* Princess, *who gives her another instead of that, and kisses her hand. They go in and come presently out again with all the Company to Dance.*

This harmonious scene is interrupted by Madam Mediator, who enters screaming that there is a man in disguise in the convent. Here Cavendish inserts another significant stage direction: '*They all skip from each other, as afraid of each other; only the* Princess *and the Lady* Happy *stand still together.*' This suggests not just that Lady Happy has no suspicions of her partner, but that they alone have a bond which will endure adversity. When the princess tries to avoid a body search, Madam Mediator tells her: 'you are most to be suspected'. Enter an ambassador, who gives the game away by begging the princess-turned-prince to return to his kingdom, because his loving subjects fear for his welfare. The prince agrees, but will not leave before wedding Lady Happy. We are not shown her reaction; mutely she marries him and after the wedding we see her joking pleasantly with the guests. An interesting scene features Madam Mediator discussing the metamorphosis: she explains that she had suspicions of the so-called princess from the moment she saw 'her' kiss Lady Happy with 'Titillation'; as Mediator explains, 'you know Women's Kisses are unnatural'.[16] She seems to mean that though romantic friends may kiss, passionate 'Women's Kisses' are a sign of deviant desire; does this indicate that what she initially suspected the princess of being was not a man but a lesbian?

Many plays in the Shakespearean tradition feature crossdressed protagonists whose awkward romances are finally resolved by the casting-off of the disguise. Almost invariably, however, the audience knows of the disguise from the start, so scenes of passion that apparently take place between two men or two women are rendered primarily comic. In *The Convent of Pleasure*, by contrast, Cavendish gives no hint of the princess being a man in disguise until the last scene of the fourth act – long after the audience or readers have listened to a woman fall in love with another woman and overcome her qualms about it. In effect, the play is a lesbian romance, made barely acceptable at the last minute by a contrived ending which heterosexualises the plot. What makes it such a satisfying story, despite its conclusion, is that the passion between women is not presented in isolation, but as a logical, delightful consequence of living in a separatist, pleasure-filled community where women can decide what they really want.

New cabals

Both Roman Catholic convents and secular separatist communities, then, could be seen as offering opportunities for lesbian contacts. But some writers also considered the possibility that lesbians could form networks, societies and clubs of their own, that behind the respectable facade of British society women were meeting with the most shocking of intentions.

Delarivier Manley, an Anglo-Dutch woman who maintained herself as a professional writer of drama, journalism and fiction, was best known for her *Secret Memoirs and Manners of Several Persons of Quality of Both Sexes from the New Atalantis, an Island in the Mediteranean* (1709), generally known as *The New Atalantis*. This scandal novel, often mentioned as the favourite reading matter of frivolous fictional heroines, libelled many British celebrities under a thin veil of fiction; a 'key' published later explained who was who. Its section on a 'new Cabal' or conspiracy of women-lovers is a uniquely valuable text, offering a blueprint of a lesbian community that can be read as satirical, utopian or a combination of the two. *The New Atalantis* was, on this and on other sexual themes, too explicit to escape censorship; Manley and her publisher and printer were briefly imprisoned for libel, and the second volume was temporarily suppressed. But despite being condemned as pornographic trash it was enduringly popular, going into seven editions by 1736.

It is the suppressed second volume that includes the sixteen-page section on the 'new Cabal'. Manley's allegorical figures, the goddess Astraea[17] and her guide Intelligence, are surveying English society. After countless tales of incest, infanticide and other disasters, Astraea is relieved to hear the sound of three coachfuls of happy women laughing 'loud and incessantly'. Intelligence mentions the accusations of lesbianism that have been levelled at this cabal – accusations she claims not to believe, but her assertion is undermined by heavy irony. She introduces the group to Astraea as 'a Sect (however innocent in it self) that does not fail from meeting its share of Censure from the World'. This comment ensures that all the 'World's' accusations can be reported without the author having to back them up and risk a very serious libel charge.

Intelligence claims to disbelieve those misogynist censurers who 'pretend to find in these [caballists] the Vices of old *Rome* reviv'd', vices which never existed except in classical poets' fantasies. Yet her coy defence of the typical Cabal relationship is transparent; she lists the suspicious facts:

> Two beautiful Ladies join'd in an Excess of *Amity* (no word is tender enough to express their new Delight) innocently embrace! for how can they be guilty? They vow eternal *Tenderness*, they exclude the Men, and condition that they will always do so. What irregularity can there be in this?[18]

The questions Intelligence puts are not rhetorical; in exactly what ways can women be guilty, she asks the reader, and exactly what irregularity do they indulge in? (In other words, the age-old question, what do lesbians do ... ?)

In case any naive readers are still scratching their heads and wondering how women *can* be guilty, Intelligence explains that 'things may be strain'd a little too far'. It is a matter of degree; even the most apparently harmless romantic friendship can shift in meaning, slip into sensuality. Intelligence describes some of the caballers shrieking at each other in possessive fury, mentioning 'rites' and 'unaccountable intimacies'. Enemies say, reports Intelligence, that this kind of love is no more innocent that that of Socrates for Alcibiades. By making such a bond equivalent to the notorious sexual relationships between men of ancient Greece, Manley taps into British suspicion and horror of sodomy. After we have heard an account of the leading members of the cabal, which is fairly explicit about their sexual partnerships and habits, it is merely comic when Astraea keeps failing to understand. She thinks that if this is really just friendship, it is most edifying, but if there is anything in it 'contrary to Kind' then it is most horrible. If even someone as innocent and well-meaning as Astraea can be brought to realise the danger, Manley shows, then it must be real.[19]

Intelligence goes on to outline the structure of 'the new *Cabal*'. Basically it is an association of loving pairs: 'They vow eternal *Tenderness,* they exclude the Men, and condition that they will always do so.' Though they put up with marriages of convenience, they cannot tolerate the taking of male lovers; when Armida's female 'Favourite' welcomes a male visitor, Armida shrieks at her, 'What happy Wretch is it upon whom you bestow my Rites! to whom do you deliver the Possession of my Kisses and Embraces?' The community is bound together not just by passion but by ethics: as Armida explains to her disloyal lover, by contrast with selfish men, 'our Interest is in mutual *Secresy*, in mutual *Justice*, and in mutual *Constancy*'.[20]

After this introduction to the cabal's principles, Manley returns to the laughing coachfuls of women and gives us more practical details about their meetings. They travel to a '*Bower* of *Bliss*' in the countryside, which is equipped with wine, gardens and bedrooms, as well as mirrors which reflect their embraces. This may sound like the setting for an orgy, but it is also a subversive political conference, and love and conspiracy go hand in hand. 'The Day and hour of their *Rendezvous* is appointed before-hand; they meet, they caress, they swear inviolable Secresy and Amity.' Secrecy is crucial to this carefully closeted group; several times, we are informed, the cabal has been exposed to censure and ridicule when one of its members told her husband about it.

The proceedings are dominated by widows and spinsters, who claim 'a right of *governing,* of *admitting* or *excluding*', because of their vantage point outside heterosexuality. They examine new members carefully, in each case questioning whether the woman's 'Genius' has 'fitted her for the Mysteries of the *Cabal,* as if she may be rendered insensible on the side of *Nature* ... who has the Trick of making them doat on the opposite improving *Sex*'. Heterosexuality may be natural, then, Manley suggests, but a few rare women have the more valuable gift of ignoring nature and turning all their erotic attention on women. If the 'novice' fails the interview by being found to desire men as well as women, she is turned away and all the other members are warned against befriending her or '*initiating* her into the *Mysteries* of their *Indearments*'.[21] The implication is that without their instruction she will never guess how to make love with women.

Any members who have let themselves be seduced by men are exposed and banished from the meeting; the rule of exclusive lesbianism is harsh. Marriage, being considered a loveless matter of convenience, does not seem to count. The caballers regret the social pressures that make it 'almost indispensable' for women to marry at least once; decisions on their own marriages are made communally, 'no such weighty Affair being to be accomplish'd without the mutual consent of the *Society*'. Those who are married are given encouragement in this support group and urged 'to reserve their *Heart,* their tender *Amity* for their Fair Friend'. Perhaps the most utopian aspect of Manley's blueprint is its economy. Money is shared, not quite equally but at least within each couple: 'In this little *Commonwealth* is no *Property;* whatever a *Lady* possesses is, *sans ceremone* [without ceremony], at the service, and for the use of her *Fair Friend.*'[22] Living outwardly conventional lives, then, these women form a secret network of power that works for lesbians against men.

After this general description, Manley has Intelligence mention some of the cabal's members; the initials and pseudonyms in the text itself are explained in the key published soon afterwards. 'Lady L_' (Margaret Sutton, Lady Lexington) and her daughters (Eleonora-Margareta and Bridget) are all called caballers; this shows that the cabal's appeal crosses the generations and perhaps that a lesbian mother has a powerful influence over her daughters. Next is a founder member, the 'Marchioness de Lerma' (Anna Charlotte, Lady Frescheville), who 'fell in Love' with her 'beautiful *Pupil*' Euphelia (Mrs Proud, an attendant of Queen Anne's). This marchioness is the only one who is described as mannish in her style, 'having something so robust in her *Air* and *Mien,* that the other *Sex* wou'd have certainly claim'd her for one of *theirs,* if she had not thought fit to declare herself by her Habit (alone) to be of the *other*'.

The next lesbian type of which we are offered an example is the occasional crossdresser. The 'Marchioness de Sandomire' (Lady Anne Popham), we are told, likes to 'Mask her Diversions in the Habit of the other Sex', as does 'her female Favourite *Ianthe*' (Ann Gerard, Countess Macclesfield, her pseudonymn probably echoing Ovid's story of Iphis and Ianthe; see pp. 28–30). The couple often 'wander through the Gallant Quarter of *Atalantis* in search of Adventures', which consist of picking up prostitutes and escorting them to public gardens and the theatre as well as paying them for sex. It is interesting that the marchioness' long-term bond with Ianthe seems to be strengthened by their joint sexual liaisons with other women. The two ladies, we are told, do not consider these 'little Liberties' as adulterous betrayals of their husbands;

as for the prostitutes, they seem to be open-minded, not failing 'to find their Account in obliging' their clients 'peculiar Taste'.[23] Anxious to deny any link between crossdressing and lesbian desire before the late eighteenth century, Randolph Trumbach misreads this anecdote, claiming: 'The one woman who cross-dresses in Mrs. Manley's novel does so probably as a means of passing unmolested in the prostitutes' quarter.'[24] In fact two women are involved; far from their concern being to pass 'unmolested', they are trying to make sexual contacts with other women.

The one exception to the caballers' rule of exclusive lesbianism is the 'Lady of the Viceroy of Peru' (Lucy Wharton, wife of a Whig minister). Her bisexuality, described as 'a more extensive Taste', takes her on a voyage of sexual exploration described in vocabulary like that of Mlle de Scudéry's allegorical chart of love:[25] 'because she will leave nothing undiscover'd or unattempted in the Map of *Tenderness,* she has encouraged the warbling *Lindamire* (low as is her Rank) to explain to her the *Terra Incognita* of the *Cabal'*. Her low-class lover 'Lindamire' represents Catherine Tofts, the opera singer. The cabal welcomes the 'Lady of the Viceroy', but vainly wishes 'that it were possible to exclude the other Sex, and ingross her wholly to their own'.[26] They can persuade her into neither an exclusive relationship with a woman nor an exclusive dedication to the female sex; she is described as a dazzling creature who cannot be expected to limit herself in these ways. Randolph Trumbach claims that in representations of desire between women up to the late eighteenth century, the participants are usually bisexual; it is interesting to note that in Delarivier Manley's 'new Cabal' bisexuality is a deviation from the lesbian norm.[27]

This pairing of the politician's aristocratic wife and the singer clearly intrigued Manley. In her next scandal novel, the *Memoirs of Europe* (1710), she retells their story, putting woman–woman desire in the context of heterosexual pairing and economic servitude. The portrayal of Lucy Wharton is subtly different this time; she is still charming, but her bisexuality represents not so much an open mind as a manipulative game. As the narrator of *Memoirs of Europe* wanders through the decadent court of eighth-century Constantinople, he spies on a couple drinking wine who look to him like the mythological Ariadne (Lucy Wharton) and Bachus (Sir Richard Temple). There are also two subordinate women: Lydia, Ariadne's confidante and dressmaker (one Mrs Buda, says the published key), and Philomela (a pseudonym for either

Catherine Tofts or Mrs Lindsey), described as a singer valuable not only for her voice but for 'the knack she had in pleasing *Ariadne*'. Sexual power, Manley suggests, is a skill or 'knack' which can be hired. After having 'commanded' Philomela to sing them a love song, Ariadne demands more of her:

> she drew her to her, and kiss'd her Lips, with Eyes swimming in Delight and a peculiar Satisfaction: Let me die, my lovely Girl, said she, if thou hast not all the Deliciousness and Flavour in thy Breath that one can imagine.

Then, without a pause, Ariadne redirects her attention to the man: 'My dear *Bachus*', she invites him, 'try the Pleasure of her moist Kisses.' As Manley describes it, this is not a voluntary erotic moment but a matter of service; for Ariadne a woman's kiss is a commodity to be transferred between powerful women and men.[28]

Ariadne's next comment, however, is more ambiguous; it suggests that she wants to keep the gift herself. 'I cou'd wear away a Life upon her Lips, press me closer, thou enchanting Girl: Not all Mankind can give me such poignant Joys!' What 'mankind' can give her is status, an acceptable lifestyle, a heterosexual framework for more exotic pleasures. Bachus – though not described with any of this admiration – must not be left out; an orgy of four offers him access to women with no male rivals. Manley's narrator explains that he cannot describe this 'very new and out-of-the-way Scene' because Lydia extinguished all the lights and all he could hear was 'tender Sighs and broken Murmurs' until the lights came back on and they all joined in a toast.[29] So women are still allowed to relate sexually to women, but only within the frame of a heterosexual relationship to which they add titillation.

Another woman whose sexuality Manley describes in some detail in *The New Atalantis* is a writer, 'Zara', a code name for Catherine Colyear, Duchess of Portmore and Dorchester. Married to a submissive chevalier, she takes male lovers but finds that they always disappoint her 'Lovesick-romantick Expectations'. Finally, 'disincouraged by the Men, she fell into the Taste of the *Cabal*'. Her 'Favourite' is 'Daphne', a pseudonym for Catharine Trotter (whose play *Agnes de Castro* is discussed on pp. 131–2). Daphne, we are told, hides her sexual sins (with both men and women) behind the 'Mask' of religion. In an interesting passage, Manley describes the difficulties of combining a primary relationship with briefer affairs:

> *Zara* ... had introduc'd her to the *Cabal*, but with infinite Anxiety suffer'd, that any *Lover* should dare to engage where she had fixed her *Heart*: But because narrow Circumstances do not always suffer People to do what they would, *Daphne* was still forc'd to have *Lovers*; tho' if you'll believe her Professions to her *Fair Friend*, they had no part in her Inclinations. In short, they seem'd to live only for each other.

It is difficult to assign gender to the sexual partners in this passage. 'Lovers' in this text usually means male lovers; female lovers tend to be called 'fair friends' or 'favourites'. Yet the syntax implies that it is only when Daphne joins the women-only cabal that she meets these 'Lovers'. A further complication is the tone; the transcendent romance of Zara and Daphne living 'only for each other' is undercut by the sardonic phrase 'if you'll believe her Professions'. The vague explanation of the force of 'narrow Circumstances' can be read as a reference to financial dependence on men, or a feeble excuse on Daphne's part for a side of her 'Inclinations' she cannot admit to Zara. Their story ends sadly; Zara's freedom increases when her husband leaves the country, but by then Daphne has saved her reputation by marrying and retiring into rural religious life. Zara rails against 'the Authority of a *Husband*, who has boldly dar'd to carry his *Wife* into the Country', but most of all she feels betrayed by her hypocritical lover.

Despite the happy laughter with which the caballers are introduced into the story, then, Delarivier Manley makes it clear that their life can be a difficult one. The pressures of the closet, social and economic ties to men, and conflicts over issues of fidelity all take their toll. Financial inequality is sometimes part of the sexual dynamic; certain widows bring themselves to the point of bankruptcy by lavishing 'vast Sums upon their *Inamoretto*'s'.[30] Misunderstandings occur between the caballers who are in the know (having realised that passion between women can be sexual) and women outside the conspiracy. In one case, this is worsened by a class gap, when a rich widow in the cabal, one of a group who share a taste for crossdressers or 'the Representation of *Men* in *Women*', falls 'in Love' with a 'comedian' (actor) playing a breeches part. (Notice the familiar motif of a lady pursuing an actress. This particular story is thought to be based on the passion of Susan Howard, Lady Effingham, for the actress Laetitia Cross.) The widow gives the girl presents, has a portrait painted of her in her androgynous costume and finally brings her to live in her villa. The actress is 'dazzl'd at those Indearments and Advances from a Lady of Fortune' and, being used to fairly bawdy conversation, finds it difficult to behave respectably enough for this genteel setting. When the widow proceeds to 'gentle *squeezes* and *embraces*', the actress apparently does not understand her seductive motive and so responds to the embraces 'with no *New-Cabal-Air*'. Lesbianism is here presented as a set of tones and manners, learned behaviour that the actress fails to get the hang of, or is perhaps resisting. Weary of solitary splendour in the villa, she longs to resume her busy life among theatre folk. Finally realising the trap she is in, she confronts the widow, telling her 'she did not like those *hugs* and *indearments* from her own Sex, they seem'd *un-natural*'. By now the widow has discovered how heterosexually experienced the actress is and she is disgusted, deciding (no doubt with the caballers' advice) that the girl is 'not therefore worthy the Honour of being admitted into their Community'. Gradually they drop each other; the friendship ends bitterly when the widow cuts the face from the 'breeches part' portrait, stamps on it and sends it back with a note full of reproaches. The erotic icon, having proved unsatisfying, must be torn apart. In tears, the actress finally guesses 'the *Reason*' for the widow's fury.[31] The insight comes too late for either of them; the conditions of secrecy under which the caballers function make it almost impossible for them to move outside their own social circle.

In Manley's references to the cabal in *Memoirs of Europe* of the following year, she is careful to describe it as limited in its appeal. Four young ladies, all related to each other, are gossiping about sex. Julia (Elizabeth Godfrey Dunch) explains that she and her cousin Martia (Mary Churchill, Duchess of Montagu, daughter to Queen Anne's beloved Sarah Churchill, Duchess of Marlborough) are lovers as well as conspirators in heterosexual escapades. Men cannot be trusted with a woman's reputation, Julia insists. She describes how she saved Martia from a helpless love for a man,

> then brought her into the *Cabal*, but she had too much Fire for so dull a Commerce; she cou'd not taste the pall'd Delights of her own Sex. I must confess, she made me an

> Apostate to the Religion (her self excepted) whose Votary I am to the highest degree.

Julia seems to be saying that she introduced Martia to the community, but Martia's restless dissatisfaction with lesbian sex was infectious; soon Julia had little sexual interest left in any women, though she retained a flattering lust for her dear Martia. Here, an individual bond between two women can be glamorised, but more general commitment to the lesbian 'Religion' is too threatening and must be mocked for its dullness. Another member of the group, Julia's sister Aurelia (Charlotte Boscawen Godfrey, Countess of Falmouth), is described as a lapsed caballer too, being 'so taken up with managing at Home' and helping her husband in politics that 'she neglects her devoir to the *Sodality*' or fellowship. The superior excitement of sex with men and the demands of heterosexual marriage are offered as the two main reasons why the cabal is losing members. What Julia and Martia still have is a watered-down, private sexual connection. Martia has moved to shabbier lodgings nearer Julia, because, as she explains, 'the distance rob'd me of so much time in going and coming ... time! devoted to nicer Joys!' Their visits are frequent and enjoyable.

> Our Intimacy is so well known, none wonders at the dearness: Our People are sent off. When met, to be sure we pass the Evening together 'till far in the Night; our Women are acquainted with the Pleasure we have in being shut up with one another, and of course deny us to all Company.

The peak of such an evening, however, is the moment when Martia and Julia sneak out of the back door, dressed like prostitutes to preserve their anonymity, go to the theatre and pick up men.[32] Like the women in Juvenal's orgy (see pp. 212–14), their eroticism can only find its fulfilment in heterosexual intercourse. Less than a year after her imprisonment for the shocking accusations in *The New Atalantis*, Manley had reverted to a more traditional message about female sexuality.

Delarivier Manley's accounts of the cabal tell us little or nothing about real women's sexuality; the fact that the women she accused of being members were all connected to the queen or to male Whig politicians suggests that her choice of names was political. What the cabal documents, published in the reign of a female monarch who relied on female favourites, do show is social anxiety about women abusing their power.[33] Manley's mixture of celebration and denigration of the caballers, of satire and utopia, suggests that she was far from sure where her loyalties lay.

Another early eighteenth-century British text, William King's *The Toast* (second edition, 1736), accuses a group of Dublin ladies of being 'tribads'. In a poem about King's famous gift for oratory, Thomas Wharton comments 'What Britons dare to think, he dares to tell.'[34] It is this 'daring to tell' that makes *The Toast* so unusual; King renders explicit the hatred of powerful lesbians that simmers under the surface of many another text.

His (anti-)heroine 'Myra' (whom I discuss in terms of hermaphrodism on pp. 54–7) represents the Duchess of Newburgh. Her lover 'Ali' or 'Al-n' is thought to stand for Lady Allen; she is described with an incongruous cluster of racist slurs, as 'a little Dutch Frow', 'a Jewess and a Dwarf', with 'the Locks of a Negress half mingled with Grey,/And a Carcase ill-moulded of dirty red Clay', so it is clear that as well as fearing lesbians King resents what he sees as foreign, inferior elements in Anglo-Irish society. Ali is always sexually available to Myra, who simply locks up Ali's husband whenever he might get in the way. The lovers wield secret power at the highest level of society; 'Lord Pam' (representing Bishop Hort) is shown as incapable of denouncing Myra as a pervert, because it was her influence that raised him so high in the Church. The women are satirised for their upper-class affectations; for example, when in Ali's mansion in the south Dublin village of Stillorgan her lover hails her with a cry of 'O ma Vie, ma Femme!', a footnote informs us that she speaks 'in *French*, that she might not be understood by her *Irish* Servants'. Myra herself lives in what King grandly calls the '*Androgyne*'s Dome' on Usher Quay in the city.[35]

Reading between the lines of *The Toast*, we find that lesbian sexuality is no novelty in moneyed Dublin, though it does arouse male scorn. Once when a group of gentlemen were drinking toasts to fair ladies after dinner, King tells us, they refused to drink to 'the Dames, who pollute their own Sex', and in short 'the Tribads were all set aside with a Curse'.[36] There is no hint of surprise at or disbelief in these tribadic acts; moreover, such women may be 'set aside' or even cursed, but they are not actively persecuted (except through poetry). According to King, it is well known that the beautiful and virtuous Lady R_sse (probably Grizel Ross, a Dublin beauty) was nearly seduced by Myra and had to break out of the circle of tribades 'at a very critical Juncture'. This is a story, he claims, 'of which nobody is ignorant, who has lived any Time in *Dublin'* – though he seems only to be referring to his particular social set. King is unusual in his insistence that lesbianism is no secret: Myra's behaviour is called the 'Standing jest of [the] Viceroy's Court' in Dublin. When she and Ali appear together they are sneered at because their affair is 'Tattled over Cards and Tea' and 'Fabled in the Comic Play' that same social set watches in the theatre.[37]

A clear source for later British conceptions of lesbian networks is a cluster of late eighteenth-century French texts; these have often been read as reliable history, but their elaborate use of libertine literary conventions may indicate that they are partly or wholly fictional.[38] For example, the secret periodical by (among others) Denis Diderot, entitled *Correspondence Littéraire, Philosophique, et Critique*, mentioned in November 1775 that the actress Raucourt was running Juvenal-style sex parties (see pp. 212–14) in a secret club called 'La Loge des Lesbos' (literally, Lesbian Lodge). Just before the 1789 French Revolution, Pidansat de Mairobert published *Histoire d'une Jeune Fille*, a semi-pornographic work including a description of a club of 'anandrynes' (literally, women without men) under the leadership of a slightly mannish lesbian. This account was so titillating that it was reprinted under such titles as *Anandria, La Jolie T_* (probably tribade) and *La Nouvelle Sapho*, as well as filling letters 9 to 15 of a ten-volume pornographic work published in London entitled *L'Espion Anglais* (The English Spy).[39]

The only account I know of a London lesbian club is in a travel book by Johann Wilhelm von Archenholtz, a German who visited England in the 1780s. In a twentieth-century translation, his report reads as follows:

> There are females who avoid all intimate intercourse with the opposite sex, confining themselves to their own sex. These females are called Lesbians. They have small societies, known as Anandrinic Societies, of which Mrs Y_, formerly a famous London actress, was one of the presidents.[40]

'Mrs Y_' has to be Mary Anne Yates (1728–87), the leading tragedy actress at Drury Lane theatre until her retirement from the stage in 1785. She was unpopular with many for her haughtiness, as well as her bossiness to her husband, and rumours spread about her being mistress to (among others) the Earl of Huntingdon. The young novelist Fanny Burney could never understand why the ladylike writer Frances Brooke was willing to manage the Haymarket opera house in the 1770s with a disreputable woman like Mrs Yates; their devoted friendship mystified her.[41] In combining public fame, financial independence, lack of wifely submission, an unchaste reputation and close female friendship, Mary Anne Yates became the perfect target for accusations of running a lesbian 'cabal'.

Sappho

For the most part lesbians were thought of as connected not over space, in a social network, but over time, as a secret cultural tradition. Those who wrote about this tradition usually traced it back as far as Sappho, a poet of the Greek island of Lesbos in the seventh century BC.

Sappho (or Sapho, the more common form among the French) could be used as a generic name for a lesbian, in titles like *La Nouvelle Sapho* or 'Sapho to Philaensis'. Joan DeJean's otherwise excellent study of French literature about Sappho of Lesbos discounts these connections. She confirms that eighteenth-century French erotic writings about lesbians often used the name Sapho, but insists that this did not touch the scholarly tradition around the real Sappho's poetic fragments; such pornographic texts were merely 'sapphic without being Sapphic'.

> Throughout the eighteenth century, 'Sapho' referred either to a heterosexual poet authorized by an ever more complex tradition of biographical speculation, or to a lesbian heroine whose adventures were either completely fictional or an *à clef* fiction based ... on the lives of contemporary women. Before the late nineteenth century, the two traditions – fictions of Sappho and fictions of the lesbian – were never to intersect.

DeJean pays little attention to parallel texts in English, claiming that they merely mirror French developments of half a century before.[42]

But in fact British texts tell a very different story. Early scholarly works about the poet Sappho of Lesbos often discuss her as Sappho the lesbian or Sappho the bisexual, and seventeenth- and eighteenth-century texts that discuss contemporary lesbians and bisexuals often connect them with their historical foremother, Sappho of Lesbos. Though there were some areas of censorship, some not-sayings that allowed eighteenth-century women writers to model themselves on a chaste Sappho, most British references I have found to the real Sappho at least mention rumours about her sexual deviance.[43] There was, then, a long-standing Sapphic tradition of lesbian culture; this is not a twentieth-century invention.

The main source for Sappho's life-story for early modern writers was the fifteenth epistle of the Latin poet Ovid (43 BC–AD 17), known as 'Sappho to Phaon'. This poem contains several references to Sappho's relationships with women before she fell in love with Phaon the ferryman; these were translated with varying degrees of frankness. In his version of 1680, for example, Sir Carr. Scrope calls the women in Sappho's life her 'dear Companions' and has her tell Phaon vaguely, 'In vain the *Lesbian* Maids claim each a part,/Where thou alone hast ta'ne up all the heart.'[44] In 1712 Alexander Pope is rather more explicit about Sappho's love for the women, whom she addresses as 'Themes of my verse, and objects of my flames.' In one famous line he follows Ovid in pointing out her awareness of deviance: 'No more the Lesbian dames my passion move,/Once the dear objects of my guilty love.'[45] But there is a subtle difference; Ovid refers to Sappho's love for women with the words 'infamen' and 'crimine', suggesting ill fame or the breaking of a criminal law, whereas Pope internalises and Christianises the crime with the word 'guilty'.

According to Germaine Greer and her sister editors of *Kissing the Rod*, there was no fuss made about Sappho's sexuality:

> In the seventeenth century, licentiousness was the same sin whether principally concerned with one's own sex or another; 'guilty love' as in Pope's version of the Ovidian 'Sapho to Phaon' (1712), I.18, was the same whether with a ferryman or 'the Lesbian Dames'.[46]

I find this downplaying of the issue most unconvincing. No seventeenth-century texts I have found give the impression that a heterosexual and a lesbian act are 'the same sin' or have the same moral weight; one is offered as an irresponsible indulgence of a natural passion, the other a perverted deviation from the norm. In Pope's poem, Sappho's passion for Phaon is unfortunate and destructive, but it is only her love for the Lesbian dames that is described as 'guilty'.

Pope's translation, the best known, is one of the few explicit references to 'guilty love' between women to remain in the literary canon, but it is vague about Sappho's partners. The anonymous

Latin and English prose edition of 1746 uses Pope's terminology but gives more of Ovid's details, naming Anactorie, Cydno and Atthis as three of Sappho's women lovers. The editor explains in a footnote that Sappho was 'tax'd with an impure and guilty Love towards the *Lesbian* Ladies her Contemporaries'. Pope's phrase recurs in the translation; the girls are described as 'the Objects of my guilty love' at both the points in the poem where Sappho's feelings for women are mentioned.[47]

Another version, by a schoolmaster, S. Barrett, was published in 1759. Though it is aimed at schoolboys, it does not cut the details of Sappho's interest in particular women. She explains to Phaon that nothing delights her any more,

> Nor all the Lesbian maids I lov'd before:
> Fair Anactoria, Cydno I despise,
> Nor Atthis seems so charming to my eyes.
> With hundreds more, too well belov'd by me:
> Wretch! what was their's now centers all in thee![48]

This last line shows why Ovid's representation of lesbian desire could be reproduced fairly frankly in these texts: the story ends in a helpless conversion to heterosexuality. The 'guilty love' is raised only to be cast down. The poem preaches a particular version of female bisexuality in which a mass of undifferentiated attachments to women are given up for one important, irresistible passion for a man. It is the centrality of Phaon that allows the 'Lesbian dames' to appear on the sidelines without posing a threat.

Sappho's own poetry appeared in fragmentary form in many eighteenth-century publications. Here we can trace a clearer progression of censorship over the century, much like the gradual veiling of the lesbian orgy in Juvenal's *Sixth Satire* (see pp. 212–14). The earliest eighteenth-century edition of Sappho I have found, by Cambridge don Ambrose Phillips, is the frankest. Phillips' translations are far from explicit – they were included in Addison's bland essays on Sappho in *The Spectator* in 1711[49] – but when he came to produce his own two-shilling edition of Sappho a couple of years later, he was remarkably honest about her life. His introduction not only mentions that Sappho was accused of 'Dishonest and Unnatural Pleasure' with her female companions, but calmly argues that she was indeed bisexual: 'It being a constant Tradition that her Amorous Humour was not satisfied with the Addresses of Men; but that she was willing to have her *Mistresses* too, as well as her *Gallants*.' Phillips finds the scholar Anne Dacier amusingly naive, in her late seventeenth-century French edition of Sappho, for standing out against this tradition and insisting on Sappho's innocence (or rather, heterosexuality).

In Sappho's 'Hymn to Venus', there is no indication of the gender of the beloved until the last line, where the participle is feminine; Phillips translates this poem with 'he' for the beloved throughout, a standard practice for this poem until the twentieth century. As for Sappho's other ode, 'Blest as th'Immortal Gods is he', Phillips reproduces quite faithfully the situation of the speaker watching in agony as a lucky man gets to sit beside the speaker's female beloved. He introduces it rather coyly: 'Whatever might have been the Occasion of this Ode, the *English* Reader will enter into the Beauties of it, if he supposes it to have been written in the Person of a *Lover* sitting by his *Mistress*.' The imagined male reader is presumed to have a mental block about lesbian desire, so Phillips urges him to adapt the poem to a familiar situation by supposing it to be spoken by a man to a woman. Lesbianism can only be understood, Phillips advises, by imagining equivalent heterosexual roles. But from Phillips' frank assessment of Sappho's sexuality, the readers already know that 'the Occasion of this Ode' is probably one woman's passion for another. I quote this poem in full because it was the central text for arguments over Sappho's sexual identity:

> Blest as th'immortal Gods is he,
> The Youth who fondly sits by thee,
> And hears and sees thee all the while,
> Softly speak, and sweetly smile.
>
> 'Twas this depriv'd my Soul of Rest,
> And rais'd such Tumults in my Breast;
> For while I gaz'd, in Transport tost,
> My Breath was gone, my Voice was lost:
>
> My Bosom glow'd; the subtle Flame
> Ran quick thro' all my vital Frame;
> O'er my dim Eyes a Darkness hung;
> My Ears with hollow Murmurs rung.
>
> In dewy Damps my Limbs were chill'd,
> My Blood with gentle Horrors thrill'd;
> My feeble Pulse forgot to play;
> I fainted, sunk, and dy'd away.[50]

Notice that Phillips translates this poem with the body language typically ascribed to women, not men; for all the wariness of his introductory note, he makes it read like an expression of passion between women.

A French Protestant philosopher, Pierre Bayle, interprets this poem in a much simpler way. In his entry on Sappho in *An Historical and Critical Dictionary*, which was published in Rotterdam from 1695 and in England in 1710, Bayle explains that 'Blest as th'Immortal Gods is he' is a poem written by Sappho 'to one of her Mistresses'. Despite all the excuses that other editors have made for it, Bayle argues in a long footnote, the ode 'is not in the style of a Friend writing to a Friend: It favours of Love all over, and not of Friendship.' Bayle takes this, along with all the rumours in classical texts that Sappho was a 'tribade', as sufficient evidence to conclude that she was bisexual: 'her Amorous Passion extended even to the Persons of her own Sex, and this is that for which she was most cried down'. He names some of her lovers, and also 'her Female Scholars whom she did, without doubt, initiate in her Mysteries'.[51]

The British were never as comfortable in discussing Sappho's life. More than twenty years after his essays on her in *The Spectator*, Joseph Addison produced his own translation of Sappho's fragments. Less frank about her life than Phillips and Bayle, nevertheless he did go beyond his *Spectator* account in mentioning the charge of bisexuality. (Perhaps a scholarly book aimed at the educational elite could say things which would be unacceptable in a penny newspaper?) In this edition Addison explains that Sappho was known for 'not enduring to confine that Passion to one Person, which, as the Ancients tell us, was too violent in her to be restrain'd even to one Sex'. Bisexuality, promiscuity and excessive sex drive are all conflated here; as a genius, exceptions can be made for Sappho. Addison lists her 'Female Favourites', but quickly reassures us that 'no one seems to have been the Object of her Admiration so much as the lovely Phaon'. Again, Sappho is an acceptable example of lesbian desire, because her life-story ends in heterosexuality. Addison's translations of the poems are fairly frank, however; the second ode, 'Happy as a God is he', is subtitled 'On a *Young Maid* whom she lov'd', and this edition also includes an intense translation of her fragment 'Dire Love, sweet-bitter Bird of Prey!':

The charming Atthis, who so late
To Sappho vow'd her Care;
Now makes Andromeda her Fate,
And leaves me to despair.[52]

After the mid-century, Sappho was censored more heavily. E.B. Greene's edition of 1768 works hard to clean up her reputation. Apart from a vague reference to 'ungovernable passions of all sorts', no mention is made of her interest in women. The translation of the second ode, 'Happy the youth', cunningly alters the emotions experienced on seeing the woman from agonised love to simple envy – the implication being that the female speaker resents the woman's hold over the man, rather than the man's hold over the woman:

I saw Thee, and with envy toss'd,
My voice, my very breath, was lost.
My veins a throbbing ardor prove
The transport of a jealous Love.

This is a deliberate bowdlerisation; the Greek fragment does suggest jealousy, by mentioning that the speaker is greener than grass (the traditional colour of jealousy), but the clear implication is that it is the man she envies so bitterly. Greene's footnote shows his motive for the change: 'I am desirous to understand', he explains, 'that the piece owed its origin to the jealousy of Sappho on finding a rival beauty prefered to herself.' Desiring to be reassured that she is not a lesbian, he alters the words to fit. The same policy sees him through the fragment about the moon watching the speaker languishing in love for an unnamed person; Greene adds the rebuke 'perfidious man' to heterosexualise an ambiguous situation. When he comes to the fragment 'Love, thou sweetly-bitter pow'r', in which all the names are clearly female, he simply lightens the tone:

How I court the charming fair;
How she loads my breast with care!
While my rival in her mind
Rules the place to me assign'd.

Where Addison heard 'despair', Greene expresses only petulance. He explains this fragment, in another carefully guiding footnote, as a poem 'composed upon a favorite companion, who quitted her friendship'.[53] So this is a tiff between women friends, something common to all eras, nothing to worry about.

The British were not the only ones to censor Sappho. The Italian writer Alessandro Verri produced a two-volume fictional biography which was translated into English as *The Adventures of Sappho* in 1789.[54] Falling hopelessly in love with Phaon is the sum total of this Sappho's adventures; she has a faithful maid but not a single female friend. Sappho's ode is included, in the translation by Ambrose Philips that originally began 'Bless'd as the immortal Gods is he', but it has been altered (by Verri or his translator) to read 'Bless'd as the immortal Gods is she,/The maid who fondly sits by thee.' At this point in the story, Verri's determination to clean up Sappho's reputation – even at the cost of a pronoun or two – becomes explicit. In a lengthy footnote, he tells us that this poem, which many 'assert to have been dedicated to a girl by her beloved with inexpressible delirium', is in truth an ode to Phaon, expressing Sappho's jealousy of the girl who sits beside him. The rumours of Sappho's 'unhappy deviation from the natural inclinations', the story that earlier in life she was 'so deeply plunged in dissolute habits' that she was known as a tribade (Verri leaves the word in Greek) – these are nothing but lies spread by 'babbling poets'. Just to be on the safe side, he assures the readers that there were two poetesses in Lesbos at the time who went by the name of Sappho, and it was not 'our' genius but the inferior Sappho who may have suffered from sexual 'deviation'. Verri's next and even shakier argument is that Sappho could not have been a lesbian, because she was so famous; 'it is not probable, that she should become so celebrated, if her habits had been unworthy'. He ends his footnote in a defensive flurry: 'However, be this as it may, her love for her own sex did not, at all events, prevent her from loving ours.'[55] After all the denials, then, he cannot help letting slip that there is some truth in the many stories of her desire for women; his only consolation is her apparent bisexuality, which he offers as much less threatening than exclusive lesbianism.

By the end of the century it seems to have been impossible to translate Sappho explicitly in a respectable publication. The actress and novelist Mary Robinson did not even try; instead, she composed a series of sonnets in which Sappho was able to express her love for Phaon without any of the ambiguities of Sappho's own surviving poetry. For example, Sonnet XXXII, 'Blest as the

Gods!', follows Greene in rewriting Sappho's second ode to express jealousy of the Sicilian maid Phaon is visiting. As Robinson explains tactfully, Ovid's and Pope's portraits of Sappho include flaws 'tending rather to depreciate than to adorn the Grecian poetess'. We have to remember that as a woman writer seeking a role model who was accepted as a genius in poetry, the most lofty of genres, Mary Robinson needed to prove Sappho virtuous, otherwise reputations of all literary women would suffer. (Robinson had a reputation of her own to clean up, being the ousted mistress of the Prince of Wales.) So the introduction to her sonnet sequence declares that all the accusations made about Sappho spring from false translations or lies spread by jealous men. At one point Robinson specifically addresses the lesbian issue, when she admits that Sappho did feel love for her female disciples:

> She loved them to excess, because it was impossible for her to love otherwise; and she expressed her tenderness in all the violence of passion: your surprize at this will cease, when you are acquainted with the extreme sensibility of the Greeks; and discover, that amongst them the most innocent connections often borrow the impassioned language of love.[56]

Mary Robinson was familiar with this argument, because women like her used it to defend the impassioned expressions of their own romantic friendships for each other in the late eighteenth century. Whether or not she really believed her own cleaned-up version of Sappho we cannot tell; it is the only version she is prepared to offer. It is no accident that among early translators of Sappho it tends to be women, such as Anne Dacier and Mary Robinson, who did the censoring. For them there was more at stake: Phillips and Addison could admit Sappho's bisexuality without harming their own reputations, but a literary woman could not be seen to defend something that could damage her own status.

At the same time, alongside the movement of respectable writers towards veiling Sappho, there was a libertine tradition of celebrating her bisexuality. The *Covent-Garden Magazine; or, Amorous Repository* was a London periodical of the early 1770s which mixed bawdy anecdotes and gambling advice with accounts of rape trials. In June 1773 it included a dialogue between the souls of Sappho and the seventeenth-century French courtesan Ninon de L'Enclos. Ninon asks Sappho questions in the coy tone common to discussions of what the index to this magazine calls 'Sapphic passion'. After mentioning Phaon, she probes deeper:

> *Ninon.* It is said that you had another passion, of a more unaccountable Kind. The Lesbian maids can reveal the mystery. For my part I could never form any idea of it.
> *Sappho.* I understand you: I was a hermaphrodite.
> *Ninon.* I cannot say what you were; but you must have been something very different from other women, or you could never have spoke so feelingly of your own sex.
> *Sappho.* That difference consisted only in the warmth of my passions.

Notice that Ninon knows far more than she will admit. Her questions show that she knows Sappho had a 'passion' for the 'Lesbian maids', as demonstrated in her poetry, but she pretends not to know what this means. Sappho's answers are contradictory; at first she states bluntly, 'I was a hermaphrodite' (perhaps meaning that it was 'said' she was a hermaphrodite), then she insists that her lesbian 'difference' was not anatomical but emotional. In the next lines she goes on to explain that real hermaphrodites exist only in 'the regions of romance' and that though she loved women she was a 'mere woman'. In its vagueness, its contradictory mixture of explanations, this piece is clearly influenced by Lucian's dialogue (see pp. 31–3). The question-and-answer format, rather than offering firm theories about Sappho's sexuality, allows every theory to be undermined.

Sappho goes on to tell the story of her emotional development. Her adolescent sensuality focused on other girls:

> When a girl I was exceedingly amorous, and used to twine myself round my companions, and load them with caresses, as if I would have devoured them; and this I did intuitively, even before I was sensible of its cause, it had its effect; nature often unburdened herself in those transports. The younger, and the colder part of my companions, were afraid of me, and supposed I was something more than I should be; but those of similar feelings sympathised with my ardour; they returned my caresses, or were pleased to receive mine.

Far from lesbian sex being depicted as an unnatural, decadent refinement, Sappho here presents it as an instinctive response to the urges of nature. Nor is she unique; although some girls are too young to share her desires, or too sexually 'cold' to understand them, and although rumours of hermaphrodism do cling to these desires, Sappho finds plenty of similar girls to explore her feelings with.

When the anonymous writer comes to give details of lesbian sex, however, he cannot let it sound too good. The description is clearly intended to titillate male readers, but also to reassure them of the ultimate pointlessness of such lovemaking:

> In the height of desire we often undressed ourselves, we pressed our lips and our breasts to each other, and did all that women can, to imitate real enjoyment. We tried every posture, in short, which imagination can invent, till imagination produced – what we would much rather had been the effect of a less refined, but more vigorous impulse.

'Was that all?', Ninon asks; Sappho answers, 'All indeed.' Ninon's implication seems to be that no penetrative intercourse occurred. However, it is clear that Sappho is remembering some kind of orgasmic satisfaction, the thing 'produced' by imagination, the moment that she wishes (probably in retrospect) had been part of a more orthodox heterosexual setting. It is interesting that lovemaking between women, formerly seen as instinctive, is now 'refined' compared to 'vigorous' heterosexual normality. The discourse is unstable; this dialogue sounds as if it was written in a hurry, with contradictory ideas slung in together.

Towards the end, the writer becomes anxious to wipe out the positive associations of lesbian love. Sappho is made to assure Ninon that although her famous ode ('Blest as the Immortal Gods is he') was written to a girl, this was just for lack of a suitable male object. Her protestatation is a jerky, unconvincing chain of clauses:

> Not that I felt all the love and jealousy there described for a girl; but as I was at that time ignorant of any male connection, I addressed it to my favourite female companion, figuring to my self what I would have felt if she had been a man, or I a man.

We already know that Sappho felt intuitive passion for her girl friends – why then this need to project this into a heterosexual relationship she had never experienced? Unlike some translators, this writer does admit that the ode is addressed to a woman, but he tries to take all the emotional force out of it by interpreting it as a fantasy.

Ninon is not just the prompter in this dialogue; her own reactions are interesting. She expresses relief that Sappho is (anatomically) a woman, because:

> to tell you the truth, I always envied you on account of your supposed superiority. Nothing would have pleased me more than to have been able to communicate the delights I have so often received, to clasp a little creature in my arms, and see her expire, as I have so frequently expired – how flattering to pride!

This is an extraordinary fantasy of lesbian desire. What Ninon is describing is not the male longing to possess a 'little creature' and get pleasure from intercourse with her, but what would in the 1950s have been called a 'stone butch' desire to give a woman the utmost in pleasure, to base one's own 'pride' on skill as a 'communicator' of bliss to a female partner.

The end of the dialogue firmly shuts out these possibilities. Sappho assures her friend that 'as soon as I met with a man to my mind, I laid aside such trifling.' Heterosexuality wipes out lesbianism chronologically, both in an individual's life (such as Sappho's) and in the centuries between Sappho and the *Covent-Garden Magazine*; she is presented as a curiosity from antiquity. Ninon claims to be glad to hear that Sappho gave up loving women, 'for it would never have done for me'. As a modern woman she rejects the possibility of lesbian fulfilment; despite her fantasy of giving pleasure to a 'little creature', she insists it would do nothing for her.[57]

So it seems that Sappho of Lesbos had a split reputation among the British, as among the French.[58] Virtuous women writers could cite her as a role model of female genius, yet in other contexts her name was a sign of female sexual deviance. If some texts in this period managed to refer to Sappho in entirely safe, appreciative terms, then, this may not have been because of genuine innocence, but through a careful use of censorship and evasion.

Sapphic and other traditions

We have seen that lesbian culture was often invoked to explain Sappho; conversely, Sappho was often mentioned as the pioneer lesbian. Some seventeenth- and eighteenth-century writers imagined a lesbian tradition originating with Sappho. Others saw lesbianism as a basically modern fashion, but referred to Sappho for comparison. John Holstun suggests that allusions to Sappho's sexuality were meant to tame lesbianism through 'periodization', since the poet of Lesbos was at a safe distance in time; for example, John Donne's poem 'Sapho to Philaenis' (1633) makes lesbian passion sound like 'a vestigial and improper remnant of the past', whereas, Holstun suggests, if the poem had been called something modern like 'Joan to Julia' it might have startled seventeenth-century audiences into acknowledging lesbians in their own culture.[59] There is a certain truth in this; classical or romance names were often used to veil the scandalous content of erotic poems. But Holstun seems to be unaware of the many other references to Sappho's lesbianism in seventeenth- and eighteenth-century texts, in which her name was invoked to describe an undeniably sexual love between women which threatened contemporary society. Beneath the elegant mockery and coy allusions, such writers were issuing a warning that Sappho and Philaenis were around today, as Joan and Julia, or as Anne Damer and Elizabeth Farren (see pp. 145–7). Far from consigning passion between women to the classical or mythic past, some of these writers made it sound like an underground, fast-spreading phenomenon which had raced down the centuries from Sappho of Lesbos to the Sapphists of modern Britain.

Many early modern texts trace lesbian culture from Lesbos through ancient Rome to modern western Europe. The Seigneur de Brantôme's *Lives of Gallant Ladies*, available to anyone in Britain who was literate in French, explains that Sappho invented tribadism and taught it to the manhating women of Lesbos. It soon becomes clear that by 'Dames Lesbiennes' Brantôme means more than the women of the Greek island, since he explains that these 'Lesbiennes' (mostly portrayed as bisexual) can be found in such countries as Italy, Spain, Turkey and France.[60] The idea of a Sapphic tradition does not seem incompatible with the explanation of lesbianism as a matter of big clitorises; for example, in his treatise on marital sex Nicholas Venette insists that 'the lesbian Sappho would never have acquired such indifferent reputation, if this part of hers had been less'.[61] The same point is made by the Comte de Mirabeau in his remarkably liberal chapter on lesbians in *Erotika Biblion* (1783): a mannish body and a tendency to love women combined in Sappho, he explains, to make her the perfect founder of the lesbian tradition.[62] However, generally those writers who alluded to Sappho thought of lesbianism not as a matter of anatomy or nature, but of decadent sexual tastes. In Anne Lister's diaries, for instance, a distinction is drawn between 'Sapphic love', which she sees as artificial, learned, inconsistent behaviour, and her own lifelong, instinctive (and so more forgiveable) passion for women.[63]

The English poet William Walsh, who in 1699 penned 'A Dialogue Concerning Women', used a Sapphic myth of origin in his influential account of lesbian culture. This prose satire contrasts the opinions of two male speakers, Misogynes and Philogynes (a hater and liker of women, respectively). Misogynes sneers at women's lechery, especially the deviant sort:

> *Sapho*, as she was one of the wittiest Women that ever the World bred, so she thought with some Reason, it would be expected she should make some Additions to a *Science* in which all Womankind had been so successful: What does she do then? Not content with our Sex, she begins *Amours* with her own, and teaches us a new Sort of Sin, that was follow'd not only in *Lucian*'s Time, but is practis'd frequently in *Turkey*, at this Day.

Philogynes' answer is not so much shocked as wary. He wants to silence all discussion of this sin, not to protect the reputation of women but to avoid provoking women to retaliate by naming all the famous male bisexual classical writers. 'But not a Word more, I beseech you, of *Sapho*, nor her new Crime', he concludes; 'let *Lucian* be forgotten for putting us in mind of it, and let it be cloister'd up within the Walls of a *Turkish* Seraglio.'[64]

The idea that lesbianism was rife among the sexually-frustrated occupants of harems was common not just in erotica, but in factually based travel books too. The most influential source seems to have been the French baron J.B. Tavernier's accounts of his travels through the Middle East, which were translated into English in 1684. In 'A New Relation of the Inner-Part of the Grand Seignor's Seraglio', Tavernier laments the fact that anal intercourse is common among the male staff of the harem, this desire being 'in a manner naturall to them, though it be against nature'. The women of the harem, rigidly supervised by their elders, follow the men's example in turning to each other:

> Their unvoluntary restraint forces them to the same unseemly Actions among themselves, as the brutish Passions of those Young Men engages them in, whenever they can find the opportunities to commit them. And this presumption has no doubt given occasion to the Fabulous Story, which is related of their being served up with Cucumbers cut into pieces, and not entire, out of a ridiculous fear least they should put them to indecent uses ... But it is not only in the Seraglio, that that abominable Vice reigns, but it is predominant also in the City *Constantinople*, and in all the Provinces of the Empire, and the wicked Example of the Men, who, slighting the natural use of Women-Kind, are mutually inflam'd with a detestable love for one another, unfortunately enclines the Women to imitate them.

It is intriguing that Tavernier sees lesbianism as a direct consequence of male homosexual example, and this is a point he repeats and insists on. If the men are sodomites, the women suffer from '*Gomorrhean* Inflamations'; women are assumed to be mere imitators and followers, who only desire each other in the absence of men.[65]

Later western travellers in Islamic countries heard similar stories and came to the same conclusions. The French naval engineer C.S. Sonnini's *Travels in Upper and Lower Egypt* were translated into English in 1799. He explains that the rich harem women of Egypt, being ignorant and idle, inflamed by the hot climate and neglected by the men (who prefer bestiality and buggery with each other), like to visit each other, undress and exchange clothing. 'This species of metamorphosis', Sonnini comments grimly, 'only serves as a prelude and a pretext to sports less innocent, and of which Sappho passes for having taught and practised the details.'[66]

Most of the texts that invoke Sappho's name credit her with inventing lesbian sexual technique; the reasonable Frenchman Pierre Bayle is the only one to point out that, since Lucian's *Dialogues of the Courtesans* mention the women of Lesbos as being 'very subject to this passion' without reference to Sappho (see pp. 31–2), it is more credible to suppose 'that she found it already Established in her Country than to make her an Inventor of it'.[67] But British writers of the period cling to the idea of Sappho as sole inventor – a myth that makes lesbianism sound like a unique quirk, a secret technique passed along a vulnerable chain from woman to woman, rather than something any woman could discover. By locating lesbianism in one famous, exceptional woman, and endlessly recounting her subjugation to Phaon, these writers attempt to trivialise lesbian culture.

The late 1720s saw a cluster of texts by men who had noticed a frightening increase in lesbian practice. In 1726 the English critic John Dennis clearly felt that heterosexuality was under threat and needed positive promotion. Responding to an attack on the theatre, his essay protests that, if modern plays do (as their accusers say) incite passion between men and women, that is all to the good, since it keeps 'the two Sexes stedfast and firm to the natural Love of each other' in a time of spreading homosexuality. Not only have men wandered from nature, Dennis' pamphlet complains, 'but not a few of the Women too have endeavour'd to make themselves the Center of their own Happiness'. Lesbianism is presented here as selfish and narcissistic, a centring of happiness on the self. The cause of this 'execrable Vice', Dennis explains, is idolatry – so it is no coincidence that the home of lesbianism, since St Paul first reproached the women of Rome for it, has been Italy, that 'Head Quarters' of idolatry (meaning Roman Catholicism).[68] Rather than tracing the development of lesbian culture from Lesbos and Lucian's Greece, then, Dennis starts with the Rome of Juvenal and St Paul, to strengthen his anti-Papist argument. As the centre of Catholicism and as a Mediterranean nation, Italy was often blamed by British Protestant writers as the source of all sexual perversion.[69]

Where lesbianism was understood by western Europeans to be a matter of an overgrown clitoris, it was often located in what they saw as the primitive cultures of India, Asia and Africa. By contrast, those writers who saw it as a secret skill or a decadent vice tended to associate it with the over-civilised nations of Europe. So, for example, Jonathan Swift's hero Gulliver, transported to the land of the noble horselike Houyhnhnms and hideous humanoid Yahoos, finds that the latter have every civilised human vice (avarice, politics, lechery) except homosexuality:

> I expected every Moment that my Master would accuse the *Yahoos* of those unnatural Appetites in both Sexes, so common among us. But Nature it seems hath not been so expert a School-mistress; and these politer Pleasures are entirely the Productions of Art and Reason, on our side of the Globe.[70]

Though Swift's point is to attack lesbianism and homosexuality as vices which stand outside nature, his tone is calmly knowing. These 'politer Pleasures' were evidently old news in the 1720s Anglo-Irish culture which Swift inhabited.

The anonymous author of the sixpenny pamphlet *Plain Reasons for the Growth of Sodomy in England* (1728) would have agreed with Swift in seeing lesbianism as a decadent vice peculiar to the so-called civilised nations. In France, this writer claims, the Italian homosexual 'contagion' has spread and diversified, and even 'the Ladies (in the *Nunneries*) are criminally amorous of each other, in a *Method* too gross for Expression'. He cannot quite believe this is true of the English: 'I must be so partial to my own Country-Women, to affirm, or, at least, hope they claim no Share of this Charge.' But he does admit to doubts; when he sees two English ladies '*Kissing* and *Slopping* each other, in a *lascivious Manner*, and *frequently* repeating it', he is 'shock'd to the last Degree'. Such kisses are a foolish habit which could easily lead to the full horror of lesbian lovemaking.

> I could wish that some among them would seem less Amorous of one another; for tho' Woman *Kissing* Woman, is more suitable to their Natural Softness, and indeed more excusable than the like Practice in the contrary Sex; yet it ought to be done (*if at all*) with Modesty and Moderation, lest Suggestions, which I hope are False, and which to me seem Improbable, should bring such Ladies under Censure; who give themselves too great Liberties with each other: for as the Age encreases in Wickedness, new Vices may arise.[71]

This passage has sometimes been read as an example of eighteenth-century men's disbelief in lesbianism, but the apparent innocence of the passage may show that the author is trying to make passion between women sound inconceivable. If his naivety about these 'new vices' is genuine, it is not typical. Most writers on this subject seem fully aware of the spread of lesbian culture. For example, in *Pretty Doings in a Protestant Nation*, a shilling tract of 1734 attributed to the French priest Father Poussin, the author attacks lesbians by quoting verbatim William Walsh's paragraph about Sappho inventing a new sort of sin.[72]

William King's poem *The Toast* (1736) is full of scornful references to a lesbian cultural tradition stretching from Sappho in Lesbos to Myra of Dublin. So centred is King on Lesbos as the origin of this sexuality that he uses the word 'lesbian' much as we do today, describing 'Lesbian Loves' among women called 'Tribades or Lesbians'. He even offers scholarly etymological explanations for his invented names: 'Myra is a Corruption of Myrrhina a famous Courtesan of Athens, who first practis'd and taught in that City *Sappho's* Manner and the *Lesbian* Gambols.' The implication is that sex between women is a rare skill that must be passed on in an unbroken tradition, perhaps taught within the framework of heterosexual prostitution. King keeps comparing Myra to Sappho herself, for example when he describes her lover Ali as 'To *Myra* most dear! nor so fair in her Sight,/Was *Anacthon* or *Cydno* thus form'd for Delight.' As well as this reference to two of Sappho's legendary list of lovers, we find an allusion to the fires of Mount Aetna (taken from Ovid's 'Sappho to Phaon'). King claims that 'Since the Days of *Sappho*, this Expression hath been familiarly used by all Tribads'; he is claiming that the lesbian folk tradition includes code words. King also implies that modern lesbians have a hierarchy and titles. Valuing sexual skill over physical beauty, the community grants Myra's ugly lover Ali 'the Title of Chief of the *Tribades* or *Lesbians*'.[73]

In the 'Ode to Myra' included in the first edition of *The Toast*, King makes an explicit statement about the lesbian sexuality hidden behind many women's romantic friendships. The speaker assures Myra with transparent sarcasm that he will defend her reputation against all the gossip:

> What if *Sappho* was so naught?
> I'll deny, that thou art taught
> How to pair the Female Doves,
> How to practice *Lesbian* Loves:
> But when little A_n's spread
> In her Grove or on thy Bed,
> I will swear, 'tis Nature's Call,
> 'Tis exalted Friendship all.[74]

Here sex between women is described rather elegantly as 'How to pair the Female Doves'. Doves, famous for the billing and cooing that look to humans like kissing, are symbols of love, usually in its purest form; they are associated with female goddesses such as Venus or Diana.[75] The tendency of female doves to form pairs for life seems to have been well known in this period, and this led to doves being adopted as an image of the chaste commitment of romantic friends. But King presents lesbians as lecherous doves, traitors to the code of innocent friendship. The travel writer Johann von Archenholtz's passage on English women's relationships (see p. 242) echoes this image. In a modern translation, it reads:

> these Lesbians offer up their unclean sacrifices at these places, but their altars are not worthy of the secret groves where Dionne's doves were united in love; all they deserve is a thick veil to obscure them from the sight of men.[76]

Archenholtz seems to be contrasting the pure romantic friendship of Diana's worshippers, symbolised by her votive doves who live in female pairs, with the lowlier sensuality of modern lesbians who are organised in a similar cult. So as well as being traced in a direct line from Sappho, lesbian culture can been seen in this period as a perversion of the Dianic tradition.

In *The Toast*, William King also links Myra to witchcraft – an unusual connection to make at the time, though nowadays feminist scholars often see in the witch-burnings of old a suppression of independent lesbian sexuality. King makes it clear that he is following the classical author Horace in portraying a lesbian witch; he claims that 'all witches ... have that same masculine Appetite'. King shows quite detailed knowledge of the rituals ascribed to witches. For example, he explains that it is said to strengthen a spell if the witch (Myra) gives her imp (Ali) her extra nipple ('Imp's Teat') to suck. So a specific sexual practice such as nipple-sucking takes on demonic significance, building up layers of evil:

> In a Rapture she stroak'd it, and gave it the Teat,
> By the Suction to raise sympathetical Heat.
> Then by *Hecate* she swore, *she was sated with Men*;
> Sung a wanton *Sapphoic*, and stroak'd it agen.

At times King's sarcasm is so high-spirited that it sounds almost as though he is celebrating Myra, as if he has a grudging respect for this powerful lesbian community. At points like these, it helps to remember why Sappho was such a convenient source of allusion for hostile writers: as they saw it, her life proved the ultimate weakness of lesbian connections, because her love for Phaon made her a kind of hostage to heterosexuality. King reminds us of this with an audible sneer:

> As amorous and vicious as the *Greeks* were, yet they accounted this a most infamous Passion. And there seems to have been a peculiar Act of Justice in the punishment of *Sappho*, who killed herself at last for the Love of a Man.[77]

Satan's Harvest Home, a lip-smacking rant about popular vices published in 1749, includes a collage of inconsistent ideas about lesbianism. First the anonymous author reprints the suspicious commentary on women kissing from *Plain Reasons for the Growth of Sodomy in England* (1728), and then repeats William Walsh's much more knowing paragraph of 1699 on Sappho inventing lesbianism. He adds to this passage two crucial phrases that show increased awareness of the spread of lesbian culture: Sappho's sin is now 'call'd the *Flats*' and, we are told, it is not only practised in Turkey but 'in *Twickenham*'. Later in *Satan's Harvest Home*, a passage on 'the Game of Flatts' explains that 'a new and most abominable Vice has got footing among the W_M of Q_y, by some call'd the Game at Flats'.[78] W_M is probably 'Women'; Q_Y sounds like a place name (London's Queensberry, Queensbury, Queensway?). The game of (or at) flats is an interesting slang phrase for lesbian sex. 'Flat' or 'flatt' could mean a 'foolish fellow', and 'flat cock' referred to a woman; other meanings of the word 'flats' included false dice and counterfeit money.[79] So the phrase probably hints at foolish women deceiving each other with something of no real value in a sexual game, as well as the literal contact in tribadism of what the writer sees as women's flat genitals.

By the mid-eighteenth century, knowledge of both Sappho and lesbian desire seems to have been so widespead, and so commonly linked, that derivatives of her name could be used as trigger words in titles. For example, the *London Evening Post* of 11 April 1749 advertises '*The Sapho-an*. An heroic poem of three cantos, in the Ovidian stile, describing the pleasures which the fair sex enjoy with each other ... found among the papers of a lady of quality, a great promoter of Jaconitism.' This attack on an unknown woman's politics via her sexuality purports to be a history of lesbian culture, with special reference to a certain queen of England.[80]

The famous bawdy poem 'An Essay on Woman' by the English MP John Wilkes was circulating in manuscript and pirate editions by the 1760s. Celebrating the sexual licence of 'Pego' (slang for the penis), Wilkes pauses in one footnote to attack those women who will not bow down to it:

> There is a bastard Plant, called Clitoris, much of the same nature, though seldom large; I mean in this country; for at Lesbos it was the formidable Rival of Pego. The Lesbian ladies knew perfectly the Virtues of it, and preferred it to the other Plant.

Wilkes finds this preference most absurd, because the clitoris cannot produce the fertile 'balm' (semen). He ends by saying that 'Sappho, best of all women, knew how to administer this Drug; which pleasing operation was called ———-.'[81] The coy blanks are odd, given that the poem has already mentioned 'fucks', 'pricks', 'clap' and 'cunts'; is there really some word for lesbian sex which Wilkes does not dare print – 'tribady' would be the right number of letters – or is he just pretending to secret knowledge?

After the mid-eighteenth century there seem to be few British texts which comment on the rise of lesbian culture in the abstract. But this does not indicate a decrease in anxiety about or hostility towards the subject. Censorship may have kept the matter out of print to some extent, as the social codes of the late eighteenth century began to stress refinement and sensitivity over frankness; as we have seen, translations of classical texts about lesbian desire tended increasingly to be censored as the century wore on. However, gossip about individual women's relationships flourished in private communications and in published texts behind the safety of initials. If the blunt, general satire of William Walsh's attack on Sappho's 'new Sort of Sin' (1699) is typical of the end of the seventeenth century, then the localised innuendo about an affair between 'Miss. F_n' and 'Mrs. D_r' in the 1794 text *The Whig Club* (see pp. 146–7) suits the end of the eighteenth.

A little-known poem from the late eighteenth century uses both these tactics, mocking Sappho and lesbianism in general, as well as dropping hints about one modern woman in particular. The target, once again, seems to be Anne Damer. *A Sapphic Epistle, from Jack Cavendish to the Honourable and Most Beautiful Mrs. D***** was published as an eighteen-penny pamphlet, possibly in 1782. This rambling, bawdy poem draws together the threads of separatist feminism, romantic friendship and lesbian sex. An introductory footnote charts the persistence of lesbian culture since it was invented by 'Miss Sappho, who was the first young classic maid that bestowed her affections on her own sex'. The anonymous

friends began to make Thrale suspect her own good friends, yet shy away from such knowledge (pp. 146–50). Here I want to trace her dawning awareness of lesbians as a group, almost a secret society, and her elaborate explanations for it.

The context for her first remark on lesbian sexuality is decadent, pre-revolutionary France in 1789. After an argument with her friend and mentor Samuel Johnson, in which he asserted that a child's love for its parents was not a natural instinct at all, Thrale muses on the limits of the natural:

> Nature does get strangely out of Fashion sure enough: One hears of Things now, fit for the Pens of Petronius only, or Juvenal to record and satyrise: The Queen of France is at the Head of a Set of Monsters call'd by each other *Sapphists*, who boast her Example, and deserve to be thrown with the *He* Demons that haunt each other likewise, into Mount Vesuvius. *That* Vice increases hourly in Extent – while expected *Parricides* fright us no longer.[85]

In Hester Thrale's apocalyptic vision, a time of political turmoil brings with it vices of affection, both negative (lack of filial love, leading to patricide) and positive (the love or 'haunting' of one's own sex). What bothers her is how calm people are about it; she wants to call up the reliable fury of classical satirists such as Juvenal to reawaken public outrage at sexual deviance. Lesbians are connected not only to their own cultural tradition (so clearly originating from Sappho that they call themselves Sapphists), but also to the homosexual '*He* Demons' whose sin is exactly parallel. Unlike those eighteenth-century writers who discuss sodomy between men as a horror but tribadism between women as a mere eccentricity, Mrs Thrale has realised the seriousness of the threat Sapphists pose to the status quo, and demands the same capital punishment for them as for male sodomites.

A year later, Hester Thrale's diary comments gloomily on the discovery of another '*unnatural Society* who hold Females in Abhorrence'. Though the example of homosexuality this time is male, she seems more interested in how women can be such monsters; 'There is a strange Propensity now in England for these unspeakable Sins', she complains, giving Anne Damer as an example. Three years later, in January 1704, comes a cry of betrayal:

> Tis my Scourge to think better both of the World & of all the Individuals in it that they deserve: that House of Miss Rathbone's is now supposed to have been but a Cage of unclean Birds, living in a sinful Celibàt. Mercy on us!

Her own social circle is full of devoted female friends who live together in apparently celibate harmony. If one house is revealed to have been 'a sinful Celibàt', what is she to suspect of all the others? Cosy hen parties could really be full of 'unclean Birds'. It is a time of swift punishment, Hester Thrale believes, gloating fearfully over the daily news of guillotinings and massacres in France: 'See how Vengeance does pursue the Guilty!!!'[86]

By the end of the following year Mrs Thrale is seeing lesbianism everywhere in urban Britain. 'Bath is a Cage of these unclean Birds I have a Notion, and London is a Sink for every Sin.' Having attended an Advent sermon in which the preacher claimed that Christianity has wiped out the vices of the ancients, she comes home and begins to reread Juvenal's satires.

> French and English Women are now publicly said to practise Atrocities of which He – Juvenal was ignorant, for he says in His Satire against Men's horrible Propensity for their own Sex – that even Women are more virtuous than they because tho' Flavia does hire herself out to Fellows – She goes home to Bed at last, and lies chastly by the Side of Catulla.

She is referring to Juvenal's second satire, line 49, which can be translated literally as an assertion that certain courtesans do not lick each other.

A teenage prodigy, Thrale's years of education in Latin would have enabled her to read the satires in the original. But in her diary entry she seems to think Juvenal ignorant of lesbian possibilities, which suggests that she read the *Sixth Satire* in an English version that veiled the meaning of the orgy (see pp. 212–14). It strikes Hester Thrale as particularly frightening that women now commit sins that do not even show up in Juvenal's comprehensive catalogues of vice. Contrary to the beliefs of the smug Christian priest who gave that optimistic sermon, she thinks, the world must be worsening day by day.

In yet another footnote, Hester Thrale speculates about the origins of lesbian culture. 'Its odd that ye Roman Women did not borrow that horrible Vice from Greece – it has a Greek name now is call'd Sapphism, but I never did hear of it in Italy.' She does not quite lose herself in scholarship, however, or allow herself to push lesbianism away to 'foreign' cultures. The threat at home is too immediate to be forgotten for more than a few sentences; women Thrale knows, such as Mrs Siddons' sister, have been 'in personal Danger' from lesbian seductresses. She returns to the classics for an assessment of the relative evil of what she sees as the two homosexual roles: 'Gibbon blames Justinian for making no difference between the Guilt of active & passive Paederasty. Justinian was right, were there none of ye 1st the last wd dye away.'[87] With regard to women, we can see in Mrs Thrale's diary a need to blame the 'active' seductress, to identify a few certain 'Female Fiends' for their attempts to prey on innocent young women, rather than a willingness to ask why so many young women she knows would be open to such invitations.

It is often pointed out as a paradox that Hester Thrale was suspicious of lesbians, yet endlessly supportive of romantic friendships among women. But perhaps it was precisely because Thrale was so rooted in the culture of upper-middle-class romantic friendship that, when she heard rumours of Sapphism, she became so obsessed with it. As she began to examine her friends with a suspicious eye, she must have felt danger all around her. Some male writers could afford to be flippant, even tolerant about it; for a woman whose life revolved to a great extent around women friends, the topic of Sapphism was too close to the bone. Hester Thrale's divided mind is utterly typical of her time. Her recorded comments on women's love, swinging from unqualified enthusiasm to prurient suspicion and back again, show the bundle of contradictory attitudes to lesbian culture in Britain during this period.

In *Surpassing the Love of Men* (1981), Lillian Faderman quotes a fragment from the passage about women kissing in *Satan's Harvest Home* (see pp. 258, 261). It does not seem to fit with the mass of evidence she has uncovered about the social acceptability of romantic friendship; Faderman concludes that 'even such slight suspicions as this author voices concerning female same-sex affection are quite rare'.[88] Since Faderman's study was published, many texts have emerged from obscurity or been read with a new eye. Suspicions expressed in seventeenth- and eighteenth-century publications about the eroticism and threat to society posed by attachments between women have turned out to be neither 'slight' nor 'rare'. However much readers of lesbian history may disagree over the interpretation of tones, or the weight given to certain texts rather than others, it can no longer be argued that the lesbian past is one long silence. We have a rich history to argue over, a history in which romantic friendship is not the dominant paradigm but only one part. It is a history which, in its combination of stories of lesbians ignored by society's leaders and lesbians persecuted by them, lesbians celebrated as exceptional women and lesbians silenced as deviants, has much to teach us about survival in our similarly contradictory cultures at the end of the twentieth century.

Notes

Introduction

1. Beatrice Curtis Brown, ed., *The Letters and Diplomatic Instructions of Queen Anne*, Cassell, 1968, pp. 97, 98, 104, 67, 103, 198, 204.
2. Sarah Churchill, Duchess of Marlborough, letter of 1709, in *Private Correspondence*, 2 vols, Henry Colburn, 1838, vol. I, p. 235.
3. Duchess of Marlborough to Queen Anne, 26 July 1708, in Edward Gregg, *Queen Anne*, Ark Paperbacks, 1984, pp. 275–6.
4. Eve Kosofsky Sedgwick, *Epistemology of the Closet*, Hemel Hempstead, Harvester Wheatsheaf, 1991, p. 52.
5. Entire theories rest on the *OED* dates. For example, André Lardinois claims that the British must have been particularly slow to become aware of lesbian culture, because they used the term 'lesbianism' only from 1870 onwards, by contrast with the French and Dutch who were using the words 'lesbienne' and 'sapfisch' respectively from the 1840s; see 'Lesbian Sappho and Sappho of Lesbos', in Jan Bremmer, ed., *From Sappho to De Sade: Moments in the History of Sexuality*, Routledge, 1989, pp. 15–35 (n. 2 p. 31).
6. Judith C. Brown, *Immodest Acts: the Life of a Lesbian Nun in Renaissance Italy*, New York, Oxford University Press, 1986, p. 17, n. 54 pp. 171–3; George E. Haggerty, '"Romantic Friendship" and Patriarchal Narrative in Sarah Scott's *Millenium Hall*', *Genders*, no. 13, spring 1992, pp. 108–22 (n. 19 p. 120).
7. Brown, *Immodest Acts*, p. 173.
8. *No Priest but Love: the Journals of Anne Lister from 1824–1826*, ed. Helena Whitbread, Otley, West Yorkshire, Smith Settle, 1992, p. 31. Whitbread published an earlier selection (1817–24) under the title *I Know My Own Heart: the Diaries of Anne Lister (1791–1840)*, Virago, 1988.
9. For example, John Holstun, '"Will You Rent Our Ancient Love Asunder?": Lesbian Elegy in Donne, Marvell, and Milton', *English Literary History*, vol. 54, no. 4, winter 1987, pp. 835–67: 'Even when there are occasional references to lesbian acts, there are none to "the lesbian" considered as a social type or a distinct mode of human personality' (p. 836).
10. William King, 'Ode to Myra' in *The Toast*, 1st edn, 2 books, Dublin, 1732, pp. 84–5.

11. King, *The Toast*, 2nd edn, 4 books, London, 1736, p. 53. Unless otherwise specified, this is the edition used.
12. Floyer Sydenham, *The Banquet: a Dialogue of Plato Concerning Love. The First Part*, W. Sandby, 1762, p. 53, quoted in Louis Crompton, *Byron and Greek Love: Homophobia in 19th-Century England*, Faber & Faber, 1985, p. 90.
13. *Covent-Garden Magazine; or, Amorous Repository*, June 1773, index.
14. Hester Lynch Thrale Piozzi, *Thraliana: the Diary of Mrs. Hester Lynch Thrale (Later Mrs. Piozzi), 1776–1809*, ed. Katherine C. Balderston, 2 vols (continuous numbering), 2nd edn, Oxford, Clarendon, 1951, pp. 740, 770, n. 3 p. 949.
15. The *OED* gives only one entry for 'tribade' from 1601 and one from 1890; it dates 'tribadism' and 'tribady', in the general sense of sex between women, to 1811. Martha Vicinus claims that 'tribade' was used in England only in the sixteenth and early seventeenth centuries, but I have found it in English-language texts published in 1725, 1736, 1745, 1766 and 1789; see Vicinus, '"They Wonder to Which Sex I Belong": the Historical Roots of the Modern Lesbian Identity', *Feminist Studies*, vol. 18, no. 3, fall 1992, pp. 467–97 (p. 477).
16. Dr James Parsons, *A Mechanical and Critical Enquiry into the Nature of Hermaphrodites*, J. Walthoe, 1741, p. 14: tribades 'may be capable, perhaps, of that Action from whence the Name arose, whether they perform it or not'.
17. The Christian writer Tertullian refered to 'frictrix' (one who rubs) in the third century. Edmond Huguet's *Dictionnaire de la Langue Francaise du Seizième Siècle*, Paris, Didier, 1950, explains that in sixteenth-century French 'fricarelle' was a specific word for the kind of sex-by-rubbing (friction, frigging) enjoyed by 'tribades' or 'fricatrices'. 'Fricatrice' seems to have dropped out of French by the nineteenth century, or at least out of the dictionaries. The *OED* defines it as 'a lewd woman', giving examples from English of the seventeenth to nineteenth centuries.
18. Randle Cotgrave's *A Dictionarie of the French and English Tongues*, 1601, repr. Menston, The Scolar Press Ltd, 1968, defines 'ribaude/ribaulde' as a whore, the feminine of 'ribaud/ribauld', a rogue or male user of whores. The writers Nicholas Venette (*Tableau de l'amour conjugal*, trans. as *The Mysteries of Conjugal Love Reveal'd*, 2nd edn, 1707, p. 455) and Samuel Tissot (*Onanism* [1766], New York, Garland, 1985) offer 'ribande [sic]' and 'ribaude' respectively as French variations on the Greek work 'tribade'. In fact 'ribaude' seems to have derived from another root meaning the same thing, rubbing; see Oscar Bloch and W. von Wartburg, *Dictionnaire Etymologique*, Paris, Presses Universitaires de France, 1964. This word was rare in French by the nineteenth century; it gave us the English adjective 'ribald', meaning coarse or obscene.
19. The *OED* traces 'hermaphrodite' in English from the fourteenth century and gives as one of its meanings 'an effeminate man or virile

woman', though the list of examples (from the late 1500s to the early 1700s) only covers male effeminacy.

20. Randolph Trumbach, 'London's Sapphists: from Three Sexes to Four Genders in the Making of Modern Culture', in Julia Epstein and Kristina Straub, eds, *Body Guards: the Cultural Politics of Gender Ambiguity*, Routledge, 1991, pp. 112–41 (p. 117).
21. King, *The Toast*, p. 2.
22. Honoré Gabriel Riquetti, Comte de Mirabeau, *The Secret History of the Court of Berlin*, trans. John Slachne, Dublin, 1789, p. 239.
23. Anon, *Pamela Censured* [1741], intro. by Charles Batten Jr., Augustan Reprint no. 175, Los Angeles, William Andrews Clark Memorial Library, University of California, 1976, p. 51.
24. King, *The Toast*, pp. 100–1.
25. Anon, *Satan's Harvest Home* [1749], New York, Garland, 1985, pp. 18, 60.
26. Anon, *The Adulteress*, S. Bladon, 1773, pp. 25–6.
27. Eric Partridge, *A Dictionary of Slang and Unconventional English* [1937], ed. Paul Beale, Routledge & Kegan Paul, 1984, entry for 'Tom'.
28. Trumbach, 'London's Sapphists', p. 113.
29. Joannes Benedictus Sinibaldus, *Geneanthropeiae* [Rome, 1642], trans. 'Erotodidascalus' (Richard Head), as *Rare Verities: the Cabinet of Venus Unlocked, and Her Secrets Laid Open*, P. Briggs, 1687, p. 50.
30. Thomas Gibson, *The Anatomy of Humane Bodies Epitomized*, T. Flesher, 1682, p. 159, and John Marten, *A Treatise of All the Degrees and Symptoms of the Venereal Disease, in Both Sexes*, 6th edn, S. Crouch, 1708, p. 374.
31. Giovanni P.S. Bianchi, *The True History and Adventures of Catherine Vizzani*, trans. John Cleland, for W. Reeve & C. Sympson, 1755, p. 61.
32. Delarivier Manley, *The New Atalantis* [1709] in *The Novels of Mary de la Riviere Manley*, ed. Patricia Koster, 2 vols, Gainesville, Fla., Scholars' Facsimiles and Reprints, 1971, p. 578.
33. Robert James, *A Medicinal Dictionary*, 3 vols, T. Osborne, 1745, vol. III, entry for 'Tribades'.
34. Jonathan Swift, *Gulliver's Travels. A Facsimile Reproduction of a Large-Paper Copy of the First Edition (1726)*, intro. by Colin McKelvie, Delmar, New York, Scholars' Facsimiles and Reprints, 1976, book IV, ch. 7, pp. 115–16.
35. Henry Fielding, *The Female Husband* [1746] *and Other Writings*, ed. Claude E. Jones, English Reprints Series no. 17, Liverpool, Liverpool University Press, 1960, pp. 51, 30.
36. King, *The Toast*, p. 49.
37. William Walsh, 'A Dialogue Concerning Women' [1699], in *The Works of Celebrated Authors, of Whose Writings There are but Small Remains*, 2 vols, J. & R. Tonson & S. Draper, 1750, vol. II, pp. 151–209 (pp. 168, 196–7).
38. Anon, *Plain Reasons for the Growth of Sodomy in England*, A. Dodd & E. Nutt, 1728, p. 16.

39. James, *A Medicinal Dictionary*, vol. III, 'Tribades'.
40. Jane Sharp, *The Midwives Book* [1671], Garland, 1985, pp. 44–5.
41. Anon, *Monsieur Thing's Origin; or, Seignior D—o's Adventures in Britain*, R. Tomson, 1722, p. 19.
42. Denis Diderot, *La Religieuse* [1796], trans. as *The Nun*, Dublin, G. Smith, 1797, p. 188.
43. Thrale Piozzi, *Thraliana*, p. 949.
44. John Cleland, *Fanny Hill, or, Memoirs of a Woman of Pleasure* [1749], Penguin, 1985, p. 50.
45. Manley, *The New Atalantis*, p. 582.
46. Ovid, Epistle XV, 'Sappho to Phaon', trans. Alexander Pope [1712], repr. in *Ten Epistles of Ovid*, ed. Reverend William Fitzthomas, C. & R. Baldwin, 1807, pp. 248, 264.
47. Not that much agreement has been reached on the word lesbian during the debates of the past three decades or so. Definitions vary from a continuum of supportive and loving bonds between women, through an exclusive emotional devotion to one woman, to desire for and sex with women as the criteria. One good survey of the arguments is Bonnie Zimmerman's 'What Has Never Been: an Overview of Lesbian Feminist Criticism', in Elaine Showalter, ed., *The New Feminist Criticism*, New York, Pantheon Books, 1985, pp. 200–24 (pp. 204–8).
48. Bonnie Zimmerman, 'Is "Chloe Liked Olivia" a Lesbian Plot?', *Women's Studies International Forum*, vol. 6, no. 2, 1983, pp. 169–76 (p. 174).
49. Lillian Faderman, 'Who Hid Lesbian History?', in Margaret Cruikshank, ed., *Lesbian Studies: Present and Future*, New York, Feminist Press, 1982, pp. 115–21 (pp. 115–16).
50. For example, Lillian Faderman (in *Surpassing the Love of Men: Romantic Friendship and Love between Women from the Renaissance to the Present* [1981], Women's Press, 1985) ignores or explains away as marriages of convenience the relationships with men chosen by such women as Mary Wortley Montagu and Mary Wollstonecraft. She does not call a single woman 'bisexual' between Mary Frith in the sixteenth century and Kate Millett in the 1970s.
51. A clear explanation of lesbianism as 'the silent sin' is offered by Brown, *Immodest Acts*, pp. 19–20.
52. Examples are too numerous to list; a rare exception is Rictor Norton's informed chapter on lesbians in *Mother Clap's Molly House: the Gay Subculture in England, 1700–1830*, Gay Men's Press, 1992.
53. See Rosemary Auchmuty, Sheila Jeffreys and Elaine Miller, 'Lesbian History and Gay Studies: Keeping a Feminist Perspective', *Women's History Review*, vol. 1, no. 1, 1992, pp. 89–108.
54. Elaine Hobby estimates that, though there were 200 women publishing in the earlier period 1649–88, they contributed only 1 per cent of the published texts; *Virtue of Necessity: English Women's Writing 1649–88*, Virago, 1988, p. 6.

55. See Janet Todd, *The Sign of Angellica: Women, Writing and Fiction, 1660–1800*, Virago, 1989, p. 115.
56. See Katherine Kendall, 'From Lesbian Heroine to Devoted Wife: or, What the Stage Would Allow', in Monika Kehoe, ed., *Historical, Literary, and Erotic Aspects of Lesbianism*, New York, Harrington Park Press, 1986, pp. 9–22 (pp. 19–20).
57. Janice Raymond, *A Passion for Friends: Towards a Philosophy of Female Affection*, Women's Press, 1986, p. 11.
58. David Cressy, 'Levels of Illiteracy in England 1530–1730' [1977], in Harvey J. Graff, ed., *Literacy and Social Development in the West: a Reader*, Cambridge, Cambridge University Press, 1981, pp. 105–24 (p. 112); Roger Schofield, 'Dimensions of Illiteracy in England 1750–1850' [1973], in Graff, pp. 201–13.
59. R.A. Houston, *Scottish Literacy and the Scottish Identity: Illiteracy and Society in Scotland and Northern England 1600–1800*, Cambridge, Cambridge University Press, 1985, pp. 60, 62; Ian Watt, *The Rise of the Novel* [1957], Hogarth, 1987, p. 39.
60. R.A. Houston, *Scottish Literacy*, pp. 66, 195.
61. Watt, *Rise of the Novel*, p. 42.
62. Donald Thomas, *A Long Time Burning: the History of Literary Censorship in England*, Routledge & Kegan Paul, 1969, p. 116.
63. Faderman, *Surpassing*, n. 17, p. 436.
64. Since the writings of the Marquis de Sade were not translated into English until the nineteenth century, I have been spared the decision of whether or not to include his bloodthirsty tribades.
65. Paul Kaufman, *Libraries and Their Users*, Library Association, 1969, p. 172.
66. Noel Perrin, *Dr. Bowdler's Legacy: a History of Expurgated Books in England and America*, Macmillan, 1970, pp. 5, 19–21, 30, 46, 53.
67. Erasmus Darwin, *A Plan for the Conduct of Female Education in Boarding Schools*, Derby, J. Johnson, 1797, p. 35.
68. Peter Wagner, *Eros Revived: Erotica of the Enlightenment in England and America*, Paladin Grafton Books, 1990, pp. 108–19.
69. For example, Henry Fielding, *Covent-Garden Journal*, 11 February 1752.
70. Quoted in Roy Porter, 'Mixed Feelings: the Enlightenment and Sexuality in Eighteenth-Century Britain', in Paul-Gabriel Boucé, ed., *Sexuality in Eighteenth-Century Britain*, Manchester, Manchester University Press, 1982, pp. 1–27 (p. 11).
71. *Critical Review*, early 1760, review of Elizabeth Nihell's book on midwifery, vol. IX, p. 196.
72. *Critical Review*, early 1762, vol. XIII, pp. 304–5.
73. Sedgwick, *Epistemology*, p. 8.
74. Ruthann Robson, *Lesbian (Out)law: Survival under the Rule of Law*, Ithaca, NY, Firebrand Books, 1992, pp. 34–41; Polly Morris, 'Sodomy and Male Honor: the Case of Somerset, 1740–1850', in Kent Gerard and Gert Hekma, eds, *The Pursuit of Sodomy in Early Modern Europe*, New York, Haworth, 1987, pp. 383–406 (p. 386, n. 9 p. 401).

75. Robbie Smith, 'Lesbians before Lesbianism? Female Same-Sex Desire in Early Modern England', at the 'Lesbian Desires' session of the London Renaissance Seminar, 1993. Alan Bray has a similar argument about the British not recognising male homosexuality at home unless they could link it to foreign countries and Catholicism; see *Homosexuality in Renaissance England* [1982], Gay Men's Press, 1988, p. 75.
76. Randolph Trumbach, 'The Birth of the Queen: Sodomy and the Emergence of Gender Equality in Modern Culture, 1660–1750', in Martin Bauml Duberman, Martha Vicinus and George Chauncey Jr, eds, *Hidden from History: Reclaiming the Gay and Lesbian Past,* [1989], Penguin, 1991, pp. 129–40 (p. 139); 'Gender and the Homosexual Role in Modern Western Culture: the 18th and 19th Centuries Compared', in Denis Altman and others, *Homosexuality, Which Homosexuality? Essays from the International Scientific Conference on Lesbian and Gay Studies,* Gay Men's Press, 1989, pp. 149–69 (pp. 150, 158–9, 161).
77. Trumbach, 'London's Sapphists', pp. 112–15, 128.
78. Rudolph M. Dekker and Lotte C. van de Pol, *The Tradition of Female Transvestism in Early Modern Europe,* Macmillan, 1989, p. 57.
79. Dekker and van de Pol, *Tradition of Female Transvestism,* pp. 57–8, 69–70.
80. Martha Vicinus, 'Sexuality and Power: a Review of Current Work in the History of Sexuality', *Feminist Studies,* vol. 8, no. 1, spring 1982, pp. 133–56 (p. 148).
81. Vicinus, 'Sexuality and Power', p. 147; '"They Wonder to Which Sex I Belong"', p. 470.
82. Elaine Hobby, 'Katherine Philips: Seventeenth-Century Lesbian Poet', in Elaine Hobby and Chris White, eds,*What Lesbians Do in Books,* Women's Press, 1991, pp. 183–204.
83. Haggerty, '"Romantic friendship"'.
84. Lisa Moore, '"Something More Tender Still than Friendship": Romantic Friendship in Early-Nineteenth-Century England', *Feminist Studies,* vol. 18, no. 3, fall 1992, pp. 499–520.

1 Female hermaphrodites

1. Michel Foucault, introduction to *Herculine Barbin: Being the Recently Discovered Memoirs of a Nineteenth-Century French Hermaphrodite,* trans. Richard McDougall, Brighton, Harvester, 1980.
2. Anne Rosalind Jones and Peter Stallybrass, 'Fetishizing Gender: Constructing the Hermaphrodite in Renaissance Europe', in Julia Epstein and Kristina Straub, eds, *Body Guards: the Cultural Politics of Gender Ambiguity,* Routledge, 1991, pp. 80–111.
3. Lynne Friedli, 'Women Who Dressed as Men', *Trouble and Strife,* no. 6, summer 1985, pp. 24–9.

4. Michel Foucault, *The History of Sexuality*, vol. I, trans. Robert Hurley, Harmondsworth, Penguin, 1981, esp. pp. 37–9, 43–4.
5. Robert James, *A Medicinal Dictionary*, 3 vols, T. Osborne, 1745, vol. III, entry for 'Tribades': 'in other Women it hardly exceeds the Bulk of a Nail'.
6. *Ovid's Metamorphoses in Latin and English*, trans. Garth, Dryden and others [1717, 1732], repr. New York, Garland, 1976, pp. 322–4.
7. Hester Lynch Thrale Piozzi, *Thraliana: the Diary of Mrs. Hester Lynch Thrale (Later Mrs. Piozzi), 1776–1809*, ed. Katherine C. Balderston, 2 vols (continuous numbering), 2nd edn, Oxford, Clarendon, 1951, p. 356.
8. George Arnauld, *A Dissertation on Hermaphrodites*, in M. Jourdan de Pellerin, *A Treatise on Venereal Maladies*, Andrew Millar, 1750, pp. 441–3.
9. Martial, 'To Bassa', in *The Epigrams of Martial in Twelve Books*, trans. James Elphinston, 1782, p. 302.
10. 'A Dialogue Between Cleonarium and Laeana [sic]', fifth in *The Dialogues of the Courtizans*, in *Lucian's Works, Translated from the Greek*, trans. Ferrand Spence, 4 vols, W. Benbridge and others, 1684–5, vol. IV, pp. 304–6.
11. *Miss Marianne Woods and Miss Jane Pirie Against Dame Helen Cumming Gordon*, New York, Arno, 1975, 'Speeches of the Judges', p. 94. For a thought-provoking study of the case, see Lillian Faderman, *Scotch Verdict: Miss Pirie and Miss Woods V. Dame Cumming Gordon*, New York, William Morrow, 1983.
12. Judith C. Brown, *Immodest Acts: the Life of a Lesbian Nun in Renaissance Italy*, New York, Oxford University Press, 1986, p. 12.
13. Nathaniel Wanley, *The Wonders of the Little World; or, a General History of Man*, 1678, book 1, ch. 33, pp. 52–4.
14. Jane Sharp, *The Midwives Book* [1671], Garland, 1985, pp. 43–4.
15. Sharp, *Midwives Book*, pp. 45–7.
16. Barbara Bush, *Slave Women in Caribbean Society, 1650–1838*, James Currey, 1990, pp. 14–15.
17. Judith Brown (*Immodest Acts*, p. 173) makes this point about Sinistrari's backwards reasoning; see also Lillian Faderman, *Surpassing the Love of Men* [1981], Women's Press, 1985, p. 36.
18. Sharp, *Midwives Book*, p. 46.
19. Donald Thomas, *A Long Time Burning: the History of Literary Censorship in England*, Routledge & Kegan Paul, 1969, p. 22.
20. Joannes Benedictus Sinibaldus, *Geneathropeiae* [Rome, 1642], trans. 'Erotodidascalus' (Richard Head) as *Rare Verities: the Cabinet of Venus Unlocked, and Her Secrets Laid Open*, P. Briggs, 1687, pp. 13, 50.
21. Faderman, *Scotch Verdict*, p. 65.
22. See Brown, *Immodest Acts*, pp. 18–19, and Faderman, *Surpassing*, pp. 35–6.
23. Another important writer of Latin treatises aimed at the medical profession was Martin Schurig, whose *Spermatologia* (Frankfurt, 1720) mentions women changing into men and whose *Muliebra*

(Dresden/Leipzig, 1729) discusses tribades. I have not been able to locate any English translations of Schurig.

24. Nicholas Venette, *Tableau de l'amour conjugal*, trans. as *The Mysteries of Conjugal Love Reveal'd*, 2nd edn, 1707, pp. 15, 55–6.
25. Venette, *Conjugal Love*, pp. 453–67.
26. Venette, *Conjugal Love*, pp. 462–3, 458, 464.
27. Venette, *Conjugal Love*, pp. 466–7, 470.
28. Thomas Gibson, *The Anatomy of Humane Bodies Epitomized*, T. Flesher, 1682, p. 159.
29. John Marten, *A Treatise of All the Degrees and Symptoms of the Venereal Disease, in Both Sexes*, 6th edn, S. Crouch, 1708, p. 374.
30. Marten, *Venereal Disease*, pp. 374–6.
31. Richard Carr, *Dr. Carr's Medicinal Epistles upon Several Occasions*, trans. John Quincy, for William Newton & J. Phillips, 1714, Epistle 16, 'Concerning the Two *Nuns* Reported to Have Changed their Sex', pp. 142–50.
32. Peter Wagner, *Eros Revived: Erotica of the Enlightenment in England and America*, Paladin Grafton Books, 1990, pp. 16–17.
33. Plautus, *Persa* (The Persian Woman), ch. 2.
34. Anon, *The Supplement to the Onania* [after 1725?], New York, Garland, 1986, pp. 155–66.
35. *Supplement*, pp. 164–5.
36. Oscar Paul Gilbert, *Women in Men's Guise*, trans. J. Lewis May, Bodley Head, 1932, pp. 136–7.
37. Anon, *Aristotle's Book of Problems* [30th edn, 1776], Garland, 1986, p. 72.
38. Seventeenth edition of *Supplement*, pp. 319–20, quoted in Wagner, *Eros Revived*, p. 18.
39. *Supplement*, pp. 152–3.
40. *Supplement*, pp. 154, 165.
41. The E.N. letter was summarised in the anonymous *Ladies' Dispensatory; or, Every Woman her Own Physician*, 1740, p. 10. Lillian Faderman (*Surpassing*, p. 27) cites that summary as an example of authors not seeing lesbianism as distinct from masturbation, but in the original text in the *Supplement* it is clear that the story is treated as a matter of penetrative tribadism between women, not just masturbation. Randolph Trumbach makes the same mistake, reading the E.N. letter as a matter of 'mutual masturbation' rather than tribadic intercourse; see 'London's Sapphists: from Three Sexes to Four Genders in the Making of Modern Culture', in Julia Epstein and Kristina Straub, eds, *Body Guards: the Cultural Politics of Gender Ambiguity*, Routledge, 1991, pp. 112–41 (p. 118). The anonymous author of *The Ladies Physical Directory*, 1742, devoted most of his preface to a scathing attack on *Ladies' Dispensatory* for reprinting such an 'odious Piece' about 'the Fair Sex'.
42. Giles Jacob, *A Treatise of Hermaphrodites* (published with John Henry Meibomius, *A Treatise of the Use of Flogging at Venereal Affairs*), E. Curll, 1718, pp. 17, iii–iv, ii.

43. Jacob, *Hermaphrodites*, p. 18.
44. Jacob, *Hermaphrodites*, pp. 21–3.
45. Jacob, *Hermaphrodites*, pp. 46, 50, 54–5.
46. Dr. John Quincy, *Lexicon Physico-Medicum: or, a New Physical Dictionary*, Andrew Bell and others, 1719, p. 197.
47. Ephraim Chambers, *Cyclopaedia, or, an Universal Dictionary of Arts and Sciences*, 2nd edn, 2 vols, D. Midwinter and others, 1738, vol. I, entries for 'Clitoris' and 'Hermaphrodite'.
48. Dr James Parsons, *A Mechanical and Critical Enquiry into the Nature of Hermaphrodites*, J. Walthoe, 1741, vii, pp. 14, 10–11.
49. Parsons, *Hermaphrodites*, p. 22. This idea of contraception as a motive also crops up in Jacob, *Hermaphrodites*, p. 17.
50. James, *Medicinal Dictionary*, vol. III, entry for 'Tribades'.
51. For the facts of Hendrikje Verschuur's life, see Theo van der Meer, 'The Persecutions of Sodomites in Eighteenth-Century Amsterdam: Changing Perceptions of Sodomy', in Kent Gerard and Gert Hekma, eds, *The Pursuit of Sodomy in Early Modern Europe*, New York, Haworth, 1987, pp. 263–307 (p. 281).
52. James, *Medicinal Dictionary*, vol. III, entry for 'Tribades'.
53. Foucault, *Sexuality*, p. 44.
54. Arnauld, *Hermaphrodites*, pp. 440–3, 450.
55. Samuel Tissot, *Onanism* [trans. 1766], New York, Garland, 1985, pp. 45–7.
56. Trumbach, 'London's Sapphists', pp. 120–1.
57. Edward Gibbon, *Memoirs of My Life* [1796], ed. Betty Radice, Penguin, 1984, p. 45.
58. Anthony Hamilton, *Memoirs of the Life of Count de Grammont*, trans. Boyer, 1714, p. 234.
59. Hamilton, *Count de Grammont*, pp. 234–5, 259, 261.
60. See Ivan Bloch, *A History of English Sexual Morals*, trans. W.H. Forstern, Francis Aldor, 1936, p. 528.
61. William King, *The Toast*, 2nd edn, 4 books, 1736, pp. 97, 100, 2, 110.
62. King, *The Toast*, lix, pp. 110, 165–6.
63. King, *The Toast*, pp. 118, 116, 177–8, 194, 196.
64. Lillian Faderman, *Surpassing the Love of Men* [1981], Women's Press, 1985, p. 46.
65. Behn, 'To the Fair Clarinda, Who Made Love to Me, Imagined More than Woman', in Sandra M. Gilbert and Susan Gubar, eds, *The Norton Anthology of Literature by Women*, New York, Norton, 1985, p. 94.
66. Another reading of the poem, concentrating on its playful refusal to give the beloved a fixed identity, is offered by Ros Ballaster in *Seductive Forms: Women's Amatory Fiction from 1684–1740*, Oxford, Clarendon, 1992, pp. 75–6.

2 Female husbands

1. Julie Wheelwright, *Amazons and Military Maids: Women Who Dressed as Men in the Pursuit of Life, Liberty and Happiness*, Pandora, 1989; Dianne Dugaw, *Warrior Women and Popular Balladry, 1650–1850*, Cambridge, Cambridge University Press, 1989. See also Lillian Faderman, *Surpassing the Love of Men* [1981], Women's Press, 1985, pp. 47–61. On the other hand, certain essays, notably Lynne Friedli's 'Women Who Dressed as Men', *Trouble and Strife*, no. 6, summer 1985, pp. 24–9, do give female husbands a central place in the history of sexuality.
2. Mary Elizabeth Perry, 'The "Nefarious Sin" in Early Modern Seville', in Kent Gerard and Gert Hekma, eds, *The Pursuit of Sodomy in Early Modern Europe*, New York, Haworth, 1987, pp. 67–89 (p. 79).
3. Dirk Jaap Noordam, 'Sodomy in the Dutch Republic, 1600–1725', in Gerard and Hekma, *The Pursuit of Sodomy*, pp. 207–28 (pp. 212–13).
4. Lynne Friedli, '"Passing Women" - a Study of Gender Boundaries in the Eighteenth Century', in G.S. Rousseau and Roy Porter, eds, *Sexual Underworlds of the Enlightenment*, Manchester, Manchester University Press, 1987, pp. 234–60.
5. Anne Rosalind Jones and Peter Stallybrass, 'Fetishizing Gender: Constructing the Hermaphrodite in Renaissance Europe', in Julia Epstein and Kristina Straub, eds, *Body Guards: the Cultural Politics of Gender Ambiguity*, Routledge, 1991, pp. 80–111 (pp. 89–90).
6. Rudolph M. Dekker and Lotte C. van de Pol, *The Tradition of Female Transvestism in Early Modern Europe*, Macmillan, 1989, pp. 74, 80.
7. Randolph Trumbach, 'London's Sapphists: from Three Sexes to Four Genders in the Making of Modern Culture', in Epstein and Straub, eds, *Body Guards*, pp. 112–41 (p. 115).
8. Dekker and van de Pol, *Female Transvestism*, pp. 55, 57.
9. Caeia March's *The Hide and Seek Files*, Women's Press, 1988, is a very convincing fiction about one such twentieth-century working-class couple who are never exposed.
10. Nathaniel Wanley, *The Wonders of the Little World; or, a General History of Man*, 1678, book 1, ch. 33, pp. 52–4 (p. 52).
11. A.G. Busbequius, *Travels into Turkey*, J. Robinson & W. Payne, 1744, pp. 146–7.
12. J.B. Tavernier, Baron of Aubonne, *Collections of Travels Through Turkey into Persia and the East-Indies*, 2 vols, Moses Pitt, 1684, vol. II, pp. 86–7.
13. Anon, *Satan's Harvest Home* [1749], New York, Garland, 1985, p. 61.
14. Anthony à Wood, *The Life and Times of Anthony à Wood*, Wishart, 1932, entry for 10 July 1694.
15. Wood, entry for 14 June 1683.
16. Greater London Record Office, MJ/SR/2344, New Prison list, cited in Trumbach, 'London's Sapphists', n. 13 p. 137.

17. Mary Turner, 'Two Entries from the Marriage Register of Taxal, Cheshire', *Local Population Studies*, no. 21, autumn 1978, p. 64.
18. John Southerden Burn, *The Fleet Registers*, Rivingtons and others, 1833, pp. 50, 49, 61.
19. *London Chronicle, or, Universal Evening Post*, 9 June 1759, vol. V, p. 448.
20. *London Chronicle*, 2 February 1760, vol. VII, p. 117.
21. *London Chronicle*, 24 March 1760, vol. VII, p. 291.
22. *London Chronicle*, 5–8 April 1760, vol. VII, p. 338.
23. *London Chronicle*, 17 February 1764, vol. XV, p. 161.
24. *Gentleman's Magazine*, 28 June 1773, and *Annual Register*, 1773, p. 111.
25. *Gentleman's Magazine*, 5 July 1777, and *Annual Register*, 1777, pp. 91–2.
26. Andrew Knapp and William Baldwin, *The Newgate Calendar*, 1810, vol. III, p. 395.
27. R.S. Kirby, *Kirby's Wonderful and Eccentric Museum*, 6 vols, Kirby, 1820, vol. III, pp. 414–8.
28. Paraphrased in Bram Stoker, *Famous Imposters*, Sidgwick & Jackson, 1910, pp. 241–6 (p. 246).
29. Henry Fielding, *Ovid's Art of Love* [1747], reprinted as *The Lovers Assistant* [1760], ed. Claude E. Jones, Augustan Reprint no. 89, William Andrews Clark Memorial Library, University of California, 1961, p. 14.
30. Sheridan Baker, 'Henry Fielding's *The Female Husband*', *Publications of the Modern Language Association (PMLA)*, vol. LXXIV, June 1959, pp. 213–24 (p. 224).
31. Terry Castle, 'Matters Not Fit To Be Mentioned: Fielding's *The Female Husband*', *English Literary History*, vol 49, no. 3, fall 1982, pp. 602–23 (p. 608).
32. Henry Fielding, *The Female Husband* [1746] *and Other Writings*, ed. Claude E. Jones, English Reprints Series no. 17, Liverpool, Liverpool University Press, 1960, pp. 30–1.
33. Castle, 'Matters Not Fit to be Mentioned', p. 613.
34. Fielding, *Female Husband*, pp. 32–3, 37.
35. Fielding, *Female Husband*, pp. 37–40.
36. Fielding, *Female Husband*, pp. 42–3, 47–9, 46.
37. Baker, 'Fielding's *The Female Husband*', p. 220.
38. Brigitte Eriksson, 'A Lesbian Execution in German, 1721: the Trial Records', in Salvatore J. Licata and Robert P. Petersen, eds, *The Gay Past*, New York, Harrington Park Press, 1985, pp. 27–40.
39. Fielding, *Female Husband*, pp. 50–1.
40. Roger Lonsdale, 'New Attributions to John Cleland', *Review of English Studies*, vol. XXX, no. 119, August 1979, pp. 268–90 (p. 277).
41. Giovanni Bianchi, *The True History and Adventures of Catherine Vizzani*, trans. John Cleland, for W. Reeve & C. Sympson, 1755, e.g. pp. 2–3.
42. *Catherine Vizzani*, pp. 3–4.

43. *Catherine Vizzani*, pp. 6–7, 13–14.
44. *Catherine Vizzani*, pp. 8, 11, 38.
45. *Catherine Vizzani*, pp. 19, 35.
46. *Catherine Vizzani*, pp. 21–2, 29–30, 34–5, 37.
47. *Catherine Vizzani*, pp. 35, 41, 43–4, 15.
48. *Catherine Vizzani*, pp. 9, 51–2, 54–5.
49. *Catherine Vizzani*, pp. 61, 63, 65.
50. Noordam, 'Sodomy in the Dutch Republic, 1600–1725', pp. 212–13; Theo van der Meer, 'The Persecutions of Sodomites in Eighteenth-Century Amsterdam: Changing Perceptions of Sodomy', in Gerard and Hekma, *Female Transvestism*, pp. 263–307 (pp. 281–3).
51. Dekker and van de Pol, *Female Transvestism*, pp. 69–70, 102.

3 The breeches part

1. Terry Castle, 'Matters Not Fit To Be Mentioned: Fielding's *The Female Husband*', *English Literary History*, vol. 49, no. 3, fall 1982, pp. 602–23 (p. 616).
2. Quoted in Pat Rogers, 'The Breeches Part', in Paul-Gabriel Boucé, ed., *Sexuality in Eighteenth-Century Britain*, Manchester, Manchester University Press, 1982, pp. 244–58 (p. 250).
3. Kristina Straub, 'The Guilty Pleasures of Female Theatrical Cross-Dressing and the Autobiography of Charlotte Charke', in Julia Epstein and Kristina Straub, eds, *Body Guards: the Cultural Politics of Gender Ambiguity*, Routledge, 1991, pp. 142–66 (pp. 144–50).
4. Laurence Senelick, 'The Evolution of the Male Impersonator in the Nineteenth-Century Popular Stage', *Essays in Theatre*, vol. I, no. I, 1982, pp. 31–44 (p. 32).
5. Jacqueline Pearson, *The Prostituted Muse: Images of Women and Women Dramatists 1642–1737*, Hemel Hempstead, Harvester Wheatsheaf, 1988, pp. 109, 40.
6. *The Recruiting Officer* [1706] in *The Works of George Farquhar*, ed. Shirley Strum Kenny, 2 vols, Oxford, Clarendon, 1988, vol. II, pp. 1–129 (p. 102).
7. Randolph Trumbach, 'London's Sapphists: from Three Sexes to Four Genders in the Making of Modern Culture', in Epstein and Straub, eds, *Body Guards*, pp. 112–41 (pp. 121–2).
8. *Freethinker*, 1719, no. 108.
9. Quoted in Terry Castle, *Masquerade and Civilisation: the Carnivalesque in Eighteenth-Century English Culture and Fiction*, Methuen, 1986, p. 46.
10. Marjorie Garber, *Vested Interests: Cross-dressing and Cultural Anxiety*, Routledge, 1992, pp. 44–5.
11. Julie Wheelwright, *Amazons and Military Maids: Women Who Dressed as Men in the Pursuit of Life, Liberty and Happiness*, Pandora, 1989, pp. 12, 60.

12. Peter Anthony Motteux, ed., *Gentleman's Journal*, April 1692, pp. 22–3 (p. 23).
13. Anon, *The Female Soldier or the Surprising Life and Adventurs of Hannah Snell* [1750], intro. by Dianne Dugaw, Augustan Reprint no. 257, Los Angeles, William Andrews Clark Memorial Library, 1989, pp. 6–10, 20, 24–5, 28.
14. *The Female Soldier*, pp. 20, 24–5, 28.
15. Wheelwright, *Amazons and Military Maids*, p. 58.
16. *The Female Soldier*, pp. 32–3.
17. Anon, *The Life and Adventures of Mrs Christian Davies, the British Amazon*, 2 parts, 2nd edn, Richard Montagu, 1741, part I, pp. 2, 6, 19–20, and 'To the Reader'.
18. Wheelwright, *Amazons and Military Maids*, pp. 59–60.
19. *Christian Davies*, part I, pp. 27–8, 32.
20. *Christian Davies*, part I, pp. 65, 69, 36–7; part II, p. 29.
21. Later versions of Bonny and Read are summarised in Rictor Norton, *Mother Clap's Molly House: The Gay Subculture in England, 1700–1830*, Gay Men's Press, 1992, pp. 243–7, n. 27 p. 282. A play of 1934, *Mary Read*, starred Flora Robson as the pirate.
22. Daniel Defoe (attrib), *A General History of the Pyrates* [1724], ed. Manuel Schenhorn, J.M. Dent & Sons, 1972, vol. I, pp. 153–65 (pp. 156–7).
23. Maureen Duffy draws on Charke's *Narrative* to give ancestry to the male-identified bar dykes in *The Microcosm* (1966). Pat Rogers (in 'The Breeches Part', p.252) ascribes to Charke 'a lesbianism which might be described as part-cultural, in that Charke seeks a more active and dynamic role outside bed as well as in it'. (Rogers clearly has some secret source of evidence on Charke's activities in bed.) By contrast, Fidelis Morgan, assuming that Charke would have shared her own sense of lesbian love as a moral and psychological 'fault', argues fiercely for Charke's exclusive heterosexuality in *The Well-Known Troublemaker: a Life of Charlotte Charke*, Faber & Faber, 1988, pp. 200–6 (p. 204). Kristina Straub's excellent essay 'The Guilty Pleasures of Female Theatrical Cross-Dressing and the Autobiography of Charlotte Charke' shows how Charke plays with sexual identities and veers between presenting herself as a harmlessly crossdressed actress and a guilty female husband.
24. Charlotte Cibber Charke, *A Narrative of the Life of Mrs Charlotte Charke* [1755], intro. by Leonard R.N. Ashley, Gainesville, Fla, Scholars' Facsimiles and Reprints, 1969, pp. 13, 23, 17–18, 41, 21–2, 44.
25. Charke, *Narrative*, pp. 272, 51–4, 75–7, 90, 139.
26. Charke, *Narrative*, pp. 76, 91–2, 144.
27. Charke, *Narrative*, pp. 107, 92, 98–9, 164, 106–9, 112.
28. Lynne Friedli, '"Passing Women": a Study of Gender Boundaries in the Eighteenth Century', in G.S. Rousseau and Roy Porter, eds, *Sexual Underworlds of the Enlightenment*, Manchester, Manchester University Press, 1987, pp. 234–60, p. 242.
29. Charke, *Narrative*, pp. 24, 17.

30. Lillian Faderman, *Surpassing the Love of Men* [1981], Women's Press, 1985, pp. 55, 58.
31. Lynne Friedli, 'Women Who Dressed as Men', *Trouble and Strife*, no. 6, summer 1985, p. 25.
32. Maria Edgeworth, *Belinda* [1801], Pandora, 1986, pp. 39, 48, 209, 34–5.
33. Edgeworth, *Belinda*, pp. 34, 36–7, 39.
34. Edgeworth, *Belinda*, pp. 37–8, 44, 47–8, 55.
35. Lisa Moore discusses Harriot Freke in '"Something More Tender Still than Friendship": Romantic Friendship in Early-Nineteenth-Century England', *Feminist Studies*, vol. 18, no. 3, fall 1992, pp. 499–520 (pp. 503–10); she points out that though Harriot is presented as a stereotypical male buffoon in this scene, she is allowed to act as a suitor; the friendship she offers women is linked to dangerous duels and riots throughout the novel.
36. Edgeworth, *Belinda*, pp. 183, 200, 207, 204, 210–11, 208.
37. Edgeworth, *Belinda*, pp. 228–32, 284.
38. Aphra Behn, *The False Count* [1682] in *Five Plays*, intro. by Maureen Duffy, Methuen, 1990, act II, scene ii, p. 321.
39. Samuel Richardson, *The History of Sir Charles Grandison* [1753–4], ed. Jocelyn Harris, 3 parts, Oxford University Press, 1972, part I, pp. 42–3, 57–8.
40. Richardson, *Charles Grandison*, part I, pp. 58, 69, 62, 42–3, 62.
41. One source for this character could be the classicist Miss Bennet in Henry Fielding's *Amelia* (1752).
42. Charlotte Lennox, *Euphemia* [4 vols, 1790], Scholars' Facsimiles and Reprints, vol. 435, New York, Delmar, 1989, vol. II, pp. 159, 164–5, 162.
43. Elizabeth Mavor, *The Ladies of Llangollen: a Study in Romantic Friendship* [1971], Penguin, 1973, pp. 74–5.

4 A sincere and tender passion

1. Lillian Faderman, *Surpassing the Love of Men,* [1981], Women's Press, 1985, e.g. p. 20 and part III B, ch. 3.
2. Chris White, '"Poets and Lovers Evermore": Interpreting Female Love in the Poetry and Journals of Michael Field', *Textual Practice*, vol. 4, no. 2, summer 1990, pp. 197–212 (p. 205).
3. Elizabeth Mavor, *The Ladies of Llangollen: a Study in Romantic Friendship* [1971], Penguin, 1973, xvii.
4. Bonnie Zimmerman, 'Is "Chloe Liked Olivia" a Lesbian Plot?', *Women's Studies International Forum*, vol. 6, no. 2, 1983, pp. 169–76 (p. 171).
5. Jean Hagstrum, *Sex and Sensibility: Ideal and Erotic Love from Milton to Mozart,* University of Chicago Press, 1980, pp. 203, 228–34.

6. Germaine Greer and others, eds, *Kissing the Rod: an Anthology of Seventeenth-Century Women's Verse*, Virago, 1988, p. 188.
7. Examples include Nina Auerbach, *Communities of Women: an Idea in Fiction*, Harvard University Press, 1978, pp. 156–7, n. 8 p. 200; Janet Todd, *Women's Friendship in Literature*, New York, Columbia University Press, 1980, pp. 319–20, 327, 342, 360, 413; Tess Cosslett, *Woman to Woman: Female Friendship in Victorian Fiction*, Brighton, Harvester, 1988, p. 7.
8. Lynne Friedli, 'Women Who Dressed as Men', *Trouble and Strife*, no. 6, summer 1985, pp. 24–9 (p. 29).
9. Myriam Everard, 'Lesbian History: a History of Change and Disparity', in Monika Kehoe, ed., *Historical, Literary and Erotic Aspects of Lesbianism*, New York, Harrington Park Press, 1986, pp. 123–37.
10. Mary Granville Pendarves (later Delany) to Ann Granville, 25 November 1727, in *The Autobiography and Correspondence of Mary Granville, Mrs Delany*, ed. Lady Llanover, 3 vols, Richard Bentley, 1861, vol. I, p. 148.
11. Virginia Woolf, *A Room of One's Own* [1928], Grafton Books, 1977, ch. 5, pp. 77–8.
12. D.J. Enright and David Rawlinson, eds, *The Oxford Book of Friendship*, Oxford, Oxford University Press, 1991, ch. 4.
13. An excellent close reading of lesbian eroticism in these poems is offered by Ann Messenger in *His and Hers: Essays in Restoration and Eighteenth-Century Literature*, Lexington, Kentucky, the University Press of Kentucky, 1986, pp. 29–36. Messenger reprints 'Cloris Charmes Dissolved by Eudora' in her appendix, pp. 230–4.
14. Katherine Philips, *The Collected Works*, ed. Patrick Thomas, Stump Cross, Essex, Stump Cross Books, 1990, vol. I, *The Poems*. See also Harriette Andreadis, 'The Sapphic-Platonics of Katherine Philips, 1632–1664', *SIGNS*, vol. XV, no. 1, autumn 1989, pp. 34–60. Faderman (*Surpassing*, pp. 68–71) reads Philips' love for women as loftier than heterosexuality; by contrast Elaine Hobby ('Katherine Philips: Seventeenth-Century Lesbian Poet', in Elaine Hobby and Chris White, eds, *What Lesbians Do in Books*, Women's Press, 1991, pp. 183–204) detects a closet, almost sado-masochistic lesbian desire. Ros Ballaster, in her groundbreaking essay '"The Vices of Old Rome Revived"' (in Suzanne Raitt, ed., *Volcanoes and Pearl-Divers: Lesbian Feminist Studies*, Onlywomen, forthcoming) suggests we concentrate not on the autobiographical 'truth' behind the conventions, but on how writers like Philips exploited those conventions to create a 'different' economy of desire.
15. Jane Barker, *Poetical Recreations*, 1688, part I.
16. Aphra Behn, *The Works*, ed. Montague Summers, 6 vols, William Heinemann, 1915, vol. VI, p. 389.
17. Beryl Rowland, *Animals with Human Faces: a Guide to Animal Symbolism*, George Allen & Unwin, 1974, p. 127.
18. Anne Finch, Countess of Winchilsea, *The Wellesley Manuscript Poems*, ed. Jean M. Ellis D'Allessandro, Florence, 1988, p. 122.

19. Elizabeth Rowe, *Miscellaneous Works*, 2 vols, Hett & Dodsley, 1739, vol. I, pp. 11–13. In the poem that follows this one, 'To the Author of the foregoing Pastoral. By Mr. Prior', Matthew Prior assures the author that, if she is Sylvia, he will praise Aminta in every second verse, 'and love himself submit to friendship's laws'.
20. Donna Landry, *The Muses of Resistance: Laboring-Class Women's Poetry in Britain, 1739–1796*, Cambridge, Cambridge University Press, 1990, p. 195.
21. Elizabeth Hands, 'An Epistle', in *The Death of Amnon ... and Other Poetical Pieces*, Coventry, the author, 1789, pp. 91–2.
22. Anna Seward, *The Poetical Works*, ed. Walter Scott, 3 vols, Edinburgh, John Ballantyne and others, 1810, 'Llangollen Vale', vol. III, pp. 70–80 (p. 80).
23. Seward, vol. III, p. 131. Faderman gives a thoughtful account of Seward's poetry and emotional life in *Surpassing*, pp. 132–8.
24. One interesting essay that looks at stereotypes of the old maid in eighteenth-century novels, and concludes that women writers were rather more sympathetic than men, is limited by the author's assumption of universal heterosexuality: Jean B. Kern, 'The Old Maid, or "to Grow Old, and Be Poor, and Laughed at"', in Mary Anne Schofield and Cecilia Macheski, eds, *Fetter'd or Free? British Women Novelists, 1670–1815*, Athens, Ohio University Press, 1986, pp. 210–15. Janet Todd traces the praise of single life from its militant early statements to the more wary comments of mid-century women writers, though she interprets it as making the best of a bad lot; see *The Sign of Angellica: Women, Writing and Fiction, 1660–1800*, Virago, 1989, pp. 29, 115, 210.
25. Laurence Stone, *The Family, Sex and Marriage in England, 1500–1800*, Weidenfeld & Nicolson, 1977, pp. 43–7, 386.
26. Elizabeth Davis (Betsy Cadwaladyr), *An Autobiography of Elizabeth Davis, a Balaclava Nurse*, ed. Jane Williams, 1857, repr. Cardiff, Honno, 1987, p. 68. This seems to have been the first published autobiography of a working-class woman.
27. In Barker, *Poetical Recreations*, part II.
28. Rowland, *Animals with Human Faces*, p. 9.
29. Ruth Perry, *The Celebrated Mary Astell: an Early English Feminist*, Chicago, University of Chicago Press, 1986, pp. 136–48.
30. Mary Astell, *A Serious Proposal to the Ladies for the Advancement of Their True and Greatest Interest ... by a Lover of Her Sex* [1694], in *The First English Feminist: 'Reflections upon Marriage' and Other Writings*, ed. and intro. by Bridget Hill, Aldershot, Gower/Maurice Temple Smith, 1986, pp. 169, 141, 179.
31. Astell, *Reflections upon Marriage* [1700], in *The First English Feminist*, preface and pp. 93–4, 130.
32. As Janice Raymond has shown, bonds between spinsters are often read as a matter of love 'by default', but instead we can understand the absence of men as removing 'barriers to female friendship'; see

A Passion for Friends: Towards a Philosophy of Female Affection, Women's Press, 1986, p. 125.

33. Anon, 'Cloe to Artimesa', in Roger Lonsdale, ed., *Eighteenth-Century Women Poets: an Oxford Anthology*, Oxford, Oxford University Press, 1989, pp. 83–4.
34. Barker, *A Patch-work Screen for the Ladies*, E. Curll & T. Payne, 1723, pp. 64, 79, 80, 88–9, 90, 95.
35. Faderman claims that 'both of these women decided very consciously not to marry men' (*Surpassing*, p. 126), but there is considerable evidence that Talbot had an unhappy six-year romance with George Berkeley which she kept secret from her friend; see T.C. Duncan Eaves and Ben D. Kimpel, *Samuel Richardson, a Biography*, Oxford, Clarendon, 1971, pp. 361–2.
36. See Jane Spencer, *The Rise of the Woman Novelist*, Oxford, Basil Blackwell, 1986, though she exaggerates the taming of Sarah Fielding.
37. Sarah Scott, *A Description of Millenium Hall* [1762], Virago/Penguin, 1986, p. 115.
38. Mary Chandler, *The Description of Bath*, 1755, p. 26.
39. Priscilla Pointon (later Pickering?), 'The Maid's Resolution', in *Poems on Several Occasions*, Birmingham, the author, 1770, pp. 16–17.
40. William Hayley, *A Philosophical, Historical, and Moral Essay on Old Maids by a Friend to the Sisterhood*, 3 vols, T. Cadell, 1785, vol. I, pp. 12–13, 230–5, 241–50.
41. Charlotte Lennox, *Sophia*, 2 vols, James Fletcher, 1762, vol. I, p. 157.
42. George Elers, *Memoirs*, ed. Lord Monson and George Leveson Gower, William Heinemann, 1903, p. 29.
43. Todd, *Women's Friendship*, p. 132.
44. Behn, *Works*, vol. VI, pp. 393–4; 'To my Lady Morland', vol. VI, pp. 175–77.
45. Catharine Trotter (later Cockburn), *Olinda's Adventures: or the Amours of a Young Lady* [1693, 1718], intro. by Robert Adams Day, Augustan Reprint no. 138, Los Angeles, William Andrews Clark Memorial Library, University of California, 1969, p. 149.
46. On the Trotter–Piers letters see Kendall (sic), ed., *Love and Thunder: Plays by Women in the Age of Queen Anne*, Methuen, 1988, pp. 64–5.
47. Catharine Trotter, *Agnes de Castro* [1696], in *The Plays of Mary Pix and Catharine Trotter*, ed. Edna L. Steeves, 2 vols, New York, Garland, 1982, vol. II, pp. 3, 5, 6.
48. Trotter, *Agnes de Castro*, pp. 6, 7, 20.
49. Kathryn Kendall, 'From Lesbian Heroine to Devoted Wife', in Kehoe, ed., *Aspects of Lesbianism*, pp. 9–22 (p. 16).
50. Edna L. Steeves, introduction to Trotter, *Agnes de Castro*, xxvii.
51. Catharine Trotter, *The Unhappy Penitent*, William Turner & John Nutt, 1701, pp. 2, 13–14, 16–20, 35–7, 40.
52. Mary Pix, *The Double Distress* [1701], in *The Plays of Mary Pix and Catharine Trotter*, ed. Edna L. Steeves, 2 vols, New York, Garland, 1982, vol. I, p. 11.

53. Mary Pix, *Queen Catharine* [1698], in *The Plays of Mary Pix and Catharine Trotter*, vol. I, pp. 14, 2–3, 36, 52.
54. See Todd on this motif, *Women's Friendship*, pp. 353–4.
55. Sarah Fielding, *Familiar Letters Between the Principal Characters in David Simple, and Some Others*, 2 vols, the author, 1747, vol. I, pp. 322–8 (letter 17).
56. Sarah Fielding, *The Governess* [1749], Pandora, 1987, pp. 44–52.
57. Eve Kosofsky Sedgwick, *Between Men: English Literature and Male Homosocial Desire*, New York, Guildford, Columbia University Press, 1985.
58. Anon, 'To Mrs. B. from a Lady who had a desire to see her, and who complains on the ingratitude of her fugitive Lover', from *Lycidas* (1688), pp. 172–5, repr. in Greer and others, *Kissing the Rod*, pp. 266–7.
59. By contrast, Janet Todd reads *Mary* psychoanalytically, as the failure of friendship between two girls who are unconsciously seeking to revenge themselves on the mothers who failed them; *Women's Friendship*, pp. 191–207.
60. Mary Wollstonecraft, *Mary, a Fiction* [1788], ed. Gary Kelly, Oxford, Oxford University Press, 1976, pp. 5, 23, 18–19, 27, 30.
61. Wollstonecraft, *Mary*, pp. 35, 49, 61, 68.
62. Hester Mulso Chapone, *Works*, 2 vols, Dublin, W. Colles, 1786, vol. I, pp. 55–6, 64–5. A similar conclusion about age and rank is reached in the anonymous conduct book, *The Polite Lady*, T. Carnan & F. Newbery, 1775, pp. 57, 60.
63. Warnings against corrupt servants are found in, for example, Dr. D.T. de Bienville, *Nymphomania*, trans. Edward Sloane Wilmot [1775], repr. with Samuel Tissot's *Onanism* [1766], New York, Garland, 1985.
64. Mary Wollstonecraft, *Vindication of the Rights of Woman* [2nd edn, 1792] in *The Works*, ed. Janet Todd and Marilyn Butler, 7 vols, William Pickering, 1989, vol. V, p. 197.
65. Fielding, *The Governess*, pp. 39, 123.
66. Mary Collier, *The Woman's Labour* [1739], repr. with Stephen Duck, *The Thresher's Labour* [1736], intro. by Moira Fergusson, publication no. 230, Augustan Reprint Society, Los Angeles, William Andrews Clark Memorial Library, University of California, 1985, p. 13.
67. Ann Yearsley, 'Address to Friendship', in *Poems, on Several Occasions* [1785], 4th edn, G. & J. Robinson, 1786, p. 66; for her split from More, see the prefatory 'Narrative'.
68. Charlotte MacCarthy, *The Fair Moralist*, the author, 1745, p. 28.
69. *The Book of Ruth*, in *The Holy Bible*, Cambridge, 1668.
70. Charlotte Lennox, *Henrietta*, 2 vols, Andrew Millar, 1758, vol. II, pp. 5–6.
71. Jacqueline Pearson, *The Prostituted Muse: Images of Women and Women Dramatists 1642–1737*, Hemel Hempstead, Harvester Wheatsheaf, 1988, p. 237.

72. Samuel Johnson, *The History of Rasselas, Prince of Abyssinia* [1759], in *Shorter Novels of the Eighteenth Century*, New York, Everyman, 1930, pp. 31, 63–8, 82, 74.
73. Faderman, *Surpassing*, pp. 84, 153.
74. Horace Walpole, letters to Horace Mann, 3 May 1749, and to George Montagu, 26 July 1755, in *Correspondence*, ed. W.S. Lewis and others, Oxford University Press, 1960, vol. XX, p. 53, and vol. IX, p. 171 and n. 8.
75. Martha Vicinus, '"They Wonder to Which Sex I Belong": the Historical Roots of the Modern Lesbian Identity', *Feminist Studies*, vol. 18, no. 3, fall 1992, pp. 467–97 (p. 479). For rumours from the 1770s onwards of Marie Antoinette's affairs with women, see Terry Castle, 'Marie Antoinette Obsession', *Representations*, no. 38, spring 1992, pp. 1–38 (pp. 17–18).
76. According to Marie-Jo Bonnet, French texts from the 1770s onwards comment on the fashion of tribadism/Sapphism among women of all classes, but especially among 'artistes' such as actresses and opera singers; see *Un Choix Sans Equivoque: recherches historiques sur les relations amoureuses entre les femmes, XVie–XXe siècle*, Paris, Denoêl, 1981, pp. 11, 65, 113–14.
77. Sir Herbert Croft, *The Abbey of Kilhampton; or, Monumental Records for the Year 1980* [sic], G. Kearsley, 1780, p. 2.
78. Hester Lynch Thrale Piozzi, *Thraliana: the Diary of Mrs. Hester Lynch Thrale (Later Mrs. Piozzi), 1776–1809*, ed. Katherine C. Balderston, 2 vols (continuous numbering), 2nd edn, Oxford, Clarendon, 1951, 9 December 1795.
79. The Devonshire triangle has inspired several furiously partisan accounts for and against Elizabeth; more useful as a source for lesbian history are the passionate letters of the two women, in Lord Bessborough's edition of 1956.
80. E.J. Burford, *Wits, Wenches and Wantons: London's Low Life: Covent Garden in the Eighteenth Century*, Robert Hale, 1986, p. 178. He gives no source for his claim.
81. Thrale Piozzi, *Thraliana*, pp. 770.
82. Charles Pigott (attrib), *The Whig Club, or a Sketch of the Manners of the Age*, the author, 1794, pp. 55, 60–1.
83. Thrale Piozzi, *Thraliana*, p. 949.
84. The Damer papers are in the W.S. Lewis collection at Farmington, Conn., USA.
85. Joseph Farington, *The Farington Diary*, ed. James Greig, 8 vols, Hutchinson & Co., no date, vol. I, pp. 233–4.
86. Thrale Piozzi, *Thraliana*, pp. 850–1.
87. Hester Lynch Thrale Piozzi, *The Intimate Letters of Hester Piozzi and Penelope Pennington, 1788–1821*, ed. Oswald C. Knapp, John Lane, 1914, pp. 56, 61.
88. Thrale Piozzi, *Thraliana*, p. 868
89. Thrale Piozzi, *Intimate Letters*, pp. 107, 169.
90. Thrale Piozzi, *Thraliana*, p. 927.

91. Faderman, *Surpassing*, p. 125.
92. Randolph Trumbach, 'London's Sapphists: from Three Sexes to Four Genders in the Making of Modern Culture', in Julia Epstein and Kristina Straub, eds, *Body Guards: the Cultural Politics of Gender Ambiguity*, Routledge, 1991, pp. 112–41 (p. 133).
93. Liz Stanley, 'Epistemological Issues in Researching Lesbian History: The Case of Romantic Friendship', in Hilary Hinds, Ann Phoenix and Jackie Stacey, eds *Working Out: New Directions for Women's Studies*, Falmer Press, 1992, pp. 161–72 (p. 163).
94. Martha Vicinus, '"They Wonder to Which Sex I Belong"', pp. 467–97 (p. 483).

5 The truest friends

1. Evans and Cheevers wrote of their shared life in *This is a Short Relation*, 1662 (expanded into *A True Account*, 1663) and *A Brief Discovery*, 1663. With Sarah Davy and Hester Biddle, they are briefly discussed in Elaine Hobby, 'Katherine Philips: Seventeenth-Century Lesbian Poet', in Hobby and Chris White, eds, *What Lesbians Do in Books*, Women's Press, 1991, pp. 183–204 (pp. 184–6).
2. Theophilia Townsend and others, *A Testimony Concerning the Life and Death of Jane Whitehead*, 1676, p. 5.
3. Mary Astell and John Norris, *Letters Concerning the Love of God*, Norris, 1695, letters 3 and 4.
4. Here I differ from Bridget Hill, who in the biographical introduction to *The First English Feminist: 'Reflections upon Marriage' and Other Writings*, Aldershot, Gower/Maurice Temple Smith, 1986, assumes that Letter 3 refers to a troubled friendship with Lady Catherine Jones.
5. Sarah Weston Young, *Some Particulars, Relating to the Life and Death of Rebecca Scudamore*, Bristol, 1790, pp. 7, 5, 8, 19, 21, 30.
6. Young, *Rebecca Scudamore*, pp. 20, 45, 47.
7. Eliza Frances Robertson, *Dividends of Immense Value*, 1801, pp. 5–6, 34.
8. Sarah Churchill, Duchess of Marlborough (assisted by N. Hooke), *An Account of the Conduct of the Dowager Duchess of Marlborough, from Her First Coming to Court, to the Year 1710*, George Hawkins, 1742, pp. 10–12, 14–15, 48, 59, 120.
9. *The Letters and Diplomatic Instructions of Queen Anne*, ed. Beatrice Curtis Brown, Dassell, 1968, p. 56; *Account*, pp. 79, 69.
10. Churchill, *Account*, pp. 131, 56–7, 76, 137–9, 141, 148, 161, 211.
11. Churchill, *Account*, pp. 216, 219, 220–3.
12. Churchill, *Account*, p. 224; Anne, *Letters*, p. 225; Churchill, *Account*, pp. 244–9.
13. Churchill, *Account*, pp. 262, 268, 279–85, 267.

14. Arthur Maynwaring (attrib.), 'A New Ballad to the Tune of Fair Rosamond' [1708], in *Poems on Affairs of State: Augustan Satirical Verse, 1660–1717*, 7 vols, vol. VII, ed. Frank H. Ellis, New Haven, Conn., Yale University Press, 1975, p. 309.
15. Quoted in Edward Gregg, *Queen Anne*, Ark Paperbacks, 1984, pp. 275–6.
16. Arthur Maynwaring (attrib.), *The Rival Dutchess, or Court Incendiary*, 1708, p. 8.
17. Arthur Maynwaring, letter to Sarah Churchill, 30 April or May 1710, British Library Additional MS 61461.f.27.
18. Though Ros Ballaster (in 'The Vices of Old Rome Revived', in Suzanne Raitt, ed., *Volcanoes and Pearl-Divers: Lesbian Feminist Studies*, Onlywomen, forthcoming) suggests that Sarah attacked the sexuality of the Abigail–Anne relationship precisely to 'turn the tables on rumours' about her own passionate bond with the queen.
19. Charlotte Cibber Charke, *A Narrative of the Life of Mrs. Charlotte Charke* [2nd edn, 1755], Gainesville, Fla, Scholars' Facsimiles and Reprints, 1969, pp. 185, 192, 197, 203, 230–1, 244.
20. Fidelis Morgan, *The Well-Known Trouble Maker: a Life of Charlotte Charke*, Faber & Faber, 1988, p. 204.
21. Charke, *Narrative*, pp. 231–13, 236–7, 240, 261, 267.
22. Leonard R.N. Ashley, introduction to Charke, *Narrative*, xxi.
23. Morgan, *Well-Known Trouble Maker*, p. 205.
24. Lillian Faderman, *Surpassing the Love of Men* [1981], Women's Press, 1985, p. 58.
25. Sue-Ellen Case, 'Toward a Butch-Femme Aesthetic', in Lynda Hart, ed., *Making a Spectacle: Feminist Essays on Contemporary Women's Theatre*, University of Michigan Press, 1989, pp. 282–99 (p. 283).
26. Julie Wheelwright, *Amazons and Military Maids: Women Who Dressed as Men in the Pursuit of Life, Liberty and Happiness*, Pandora, 1989, p. 57; Mary Anne Talbot's life is told in R.S. Kirby, *Kirby's Wonderful and Eccentric Museum*, 6 vols, Kirby, 1820, vol. II, pp. 160–225 (p. 217).
27. See Joan Nestle's daring and readable *A Restricted Country: Essays and Short Stories*, Sheba Feminist Publishers, 1988, especially 'Esther's Story', 'Butch–Femme Relationships: Sexual Courage in the 1950s' and 'A Change of Life'.
28. Elizabeth Hughes Steele, *The Memoirs of Mrs. Sophia Baddeley, Late of Drury-Lane Theatre*, 3 vols, Dublin, Colles and others, 1787, vol. I, pp. 19–22, 27, 40–1, 42.
29. Steele, *Sophia Baddeley*, vol. I, pp. 65–6, 219, 84, 97, 223; vol. II, pp. 77, 122.
30. Steele, *Sophia Baddeley*, vol. I, pp. 194, 214–18, 101; vol. III, pp. 10, 188–9; vol. I, pp. 140–1.
31. Steele, *Sophia Baddeley*, vol. I, pp. 150, 163, 158; vol. II, pp. 26, 13.
32. Steele, *Sophia Baddeley*, vol. I, pp. 210, 183, 206, 241, 244.
33. Steele, *Sophia Baddeley*, vol. II, pp. 62–5, 139, 231, 227, 231.
34. Steele, *Sophia Baddeley*, vol. III, pp. 106, 113, 117, 88, 90.

35. A similar situation arose for the courtesan Margaret Leeson. When an old keeper of hers tried to stop her from consorting with a beloved 'Lady of fashion', she defied him; even when he cut off her annuity, she refused to break with her friend. *Memoirs of Mrs. Margaret Leeson, Written by Herself*, Dublin, the author, 1795 (vols 1, 2) and 1797 (vol. 3), vol. I, pp. 120–2.
36. *Gentleman's Magazine*, 1787, p. 1033.
37. Daniel Defoe, *Roxana* [1724], ed. Jane Jack, Oxford, Oxford University Press, 1981, pp. 25, 16, 28.
38. An interesting essay by Terry Castle casts Amy as Roxana's 'phantom mother'; she reads the putting-to-bed scene as Roxana's attempt to place Amy as the mother in the Freudian 'primal scene', while Roxana gets to play the passive, observing child; '"*Amy*, Who Knew My Disease": a Psychosexual Pattern in Defoe's *Roxana*', *English Literary History*, vol. 46, no. 1, spring 1979, pp. 81–96 (pp. 81–2).
39. Defoe, *Roxana*, pp. 31–2, 38–9, 47–8, 77, 196, 245.
40. Defoe, *Roxana*, pp. 83, 126, 186–7.
41. Defoe, *Roxana*, pp. 197, 270–1, 317, 318.
42. Terry Castle sees their relationship in wholly negative terms, and blames the final disasters on 'the heroine's deep-seated transference onto Amy ('"*Amy*, Who Knew My Disease"', p. 91).
43. Janet Todd, ed., *Women's Friendship in Literature*, New York, Columbia University Press, 1980, p. 326.
44. Jane Barker, 'The Unaccountable Wife', in *A Patch-Work Screen for the Ladies*, 1723, pp. 97–105. The novel was republished by Garland Publishing, 1973; the story is reprinted in full in Moira Ferguson, ed., *First Feminists: British Women Writers 1578–1799*, Bloomington, Ind., Indiana University Press, 1985, pp. 175–9.

6 What joys are these?

1. Lillian Faderman, *Surpassing the Love of Men* [1981], Women's Press, 1985, p. 27.
2. Janet Todd, ed., *Women's Friendship in Literature*, New York, Columbia University Press, 1980, p. 320.
3. Martha Vicinus, '"They Wonder to Which Sex I Belong": The Historical Roots of the Modern Lesbian Identity', in *Feminist Studies*, vol. 18, no. 3, fall 1992, pp. 467–97 (p. 476).
4. Samuel Richardson, *Pamela* [1740], 2 vols, Dent, 1986, vol. I, pp. 91, 97 (letter 32).
5. Ruth Bernard Yeazell, *Fictions of Modesty: Women and Courtship in the English Novel*, Chicago, University of Chicago Press, 1991, pp. 269–70.
6. *Pamela Censured* [1741], Augustan Reprint no. 175, Los Angeles, William Andrews Clark Memorial Library, University of California, 1976, pp. 50–1.

7. Pierre Choderlos de Laclos, *Dangerous Connections*, 4 vols, T. Hookham, 1784, letter 20, vol. I, p. 88; letter 79, vol. II, pp. 144–5; letter 38, vol. I, pp. 179–80; letter 55, vol. II, pp. 22–3; letter 63, vol. II, p. 56.
8. Anthony Hamilton, *Memoirs of the Life of Count de Grammont* [1713], trans. Boyer, 1714, pp. 234–5.
9. Hamilton, *Grammont*, pp. 237–44, 246, 251.
10. Hamilton, *Grammont*, pp. 259–62, 264.
11. A relevant essay on *The Nun* which I have not been able to find is Eve Kosofsky Sedgwick, 'Privilege of Unknowing', *Genders*, no. 1, spring 1988, pp. 102–24.
12. Yeazell, *Fictions of Modesty*, p. 5.
13. Denis Diderot, *La Religieuse* [1796], trans. as *The Nun*, Dublin, G. Smith, 1797, pp. 45, 78, 92, 79, 129.
14. Diderot, *The Nun*, pp. 132, 137, 142.
15. Diderot, *The Nun*, pp. 138, 168–9, n. p. 142.
16. Diderot, *The Nun*, pp. 142–4, 146–9.
17. Diderot, *The Nun*, pp. 152–3, 129, 162–3, 172.
18. Diderot, *The Nun*, pp. 164, 166–7, 183, 172, 174, 179.
19. Diderot, *The Nun*, pp. 183–4, 188.
20. For similar texts in French libertine literature from Brantôme to Casanova, see Faderman, *Surpassing*, pp. 23–7.
21. Roger Thompson, *Unfit for Modest Ears: a Study of Pornographic, Obscene and Bawdy Works Written or Published in England in the Second Half of the Seventeenth Century*, Macmillan, 1979, pp. 29–30; Ros Ballaster, '"The Vices of Old Rome Revived": Representations of Female Same-Sex Desire in Seventeenth- and Eighteenth-Century England', in Suzanne Raitt, ed., *Volcanoes and Pearl-Divers: Lesbian Feminist Studies*, Onlywomen, forthcoming.
22. David Foxon, *Libertine Literature in England 1660–1745*, Book Collecter, 1964, pp. 11, 17; Donald Thomas, *A Long Time Burning: the History of Literary Censorship in England*, Routledge & Kegan Paul, 1969, pp. 77, 115, 120.
23. Nicholas Chorier, *A Dialogue Between a Married Lady and a Maid*, 1740, pp. 12, 15, 14.
24. Thomas, *A Long Time Burning*, pp. 80–3, and Foxon, *Libertine Literature*, pp. 16, 45.
25. See Faderman, *Surpassing*, n. 16 p. 421.
26. Jean Barrin, *Venus dans la cloître* [1683], trans. Robert Samber as *Venus in the Cloister*, 2nd edn, E. Curll, 1725, pp. 7, 2, 9, 4, 10, 118, 22, 24, 170.
27. Denis Diderot, *Les Bijoux Indiscrets* [1748], trans. as *Les Bijoux Indiscrets, or, the Indiscreet Toys*, 2 vols, 'Tobago' [London], 1749, vol. II, pp. 97–100.
28. Anon, *The History of the Human Heart: or, the Adventures of a Young Gentleman*, J. Freeman, 1749, pp. 20–1.
29. Randolph Trumbach, 'London's Sapphists: from Three Sexes to Four Genders in the Making of Modern Culture', in Julia Epstein

and Kristina Straub, eds, *Body Guards: The Cultural Politics of Gender Ambiguity*, Routledge, 1991, pp. 112–41 (p. 118).
30. Thomas, *A Long Time Burning*, pp. 84–5, 115.
31. John Cleland, *Fanny Hill, or, Memoirs of a Woman of Pleasure* [1749], Penguin, 1985, pp. 48–9.
32. Cleland, *Fanny Hill*, pp. 49–50. This line may be a direct echo of Diderot, *Les Bijoux Indiscrets, or, the Indiscreet Toys* [1749], vol. II, p. 99 (see p. 200).
33. Cleland, *Fanny Hill*, pp. 50–1, 61–4, 69, 71.
34. Lord John Wilmot, 2nd Earl of Rochester, *Sodom* (attrib.) [Antwerp, 1684], repr. Paris, Verlag von H. Welter, 1904, act II, scene iii, p. 20.
35. Anon, *A New Atalantis for the Year One Thousand Seven Hundred and Fifty-Eight*, 2nd edn, M. Thrush, 1758, pp. 52–3.
36. J. Jean Hecht, *Continental and Colonial Servants in Eighteenth-Century England*, Smith College Studies in History vol. XL, Northampton, Mass., Department of History of Smith College, 1954, pp. 8–9, 12, 31–2.
37. *A New Atalantis*, pp. 54, 57–8, 60–1, 64, 66–7, 69.
38. Anon, *A Spy on Mother Midnight*, E. Penn, 1748, pp. 32–4.
39. Giles Jacob (attrib.), *A Treatise of Hermaphrodites*, E. Curll, 1718, pp. 40–5.
40. Lord Rochester's similar poem, 'Signior Dildo', had been circulating since the 1670s.
41. *Daily Journal*, 9 June 1722.
42. Anon, *Monsieur Thing's Origin; or, Seignior D—o's Adventures in Britain*, R. Tomson, 1722, pp. 4, 12, 18–19.
43. Juvenal, *The Satires ... Translated into English Verse*, trans. Dryden and others, Jacob Tonson, 1693, Satire VI, p. 106.
44. Juvenal, *The Satires*, trans. T. Sheridan, for D. Browne, 1739, Satire VI, p. 159.
45. Juvenal, *The Satires ... with the Original Text*, trans. John Stirling, for J. Fuller, 1760, Satire VI, p. 86.
46. Juvenal, *The Satires ... translated into English Verse*, trans. William Gifford, for G. & W. Nicol & R. Evans, 1802, p. 198.
47. Juvenal, *A New and Literal Translation of Juvenal and Persius*, trans. M. Madan, 2 vols, Oxford, 1813, Satire VI and p. 5.
48. Anne Lister, *I Know My Own Heart: the Diaries [1817–24] of Anne Lister (1791–1840)*, ed. Helena Whitbread, Virago, 1988, 6 July 1823.
49. Faderman, *Surpassing*, p. 40, n. 4 p. 420.
50. Faderman, *Surpassing*, pp. 26–7.
51. Ballaster, '"The Vices of Old Rome Revived"'.

7 Communities

1. Theo van der Meer, 'The Persecutions of Sodomites', in Kent Gerard and Gert Hekma, eds, *The Pursuit of Sodomy in Early Modern Europe*, New York, Haworth, 1987, p. 292.

2. Judith C. Brown, *Immodest Acts: the Life of a Lesbian Nun in Renaissance Italy*, New York, Oxford University Press, 1986, p. 173; Julie Wheelwright, *Amazons and Military Maids: Women Who Dressed as Men in the Pursuit of Life, Liberty and Happiness*, Pandora, 1989, pp. 59–60.
3. E.J. Burford mentions pubs open to lesbians as well as lesbian brothels, but does not name his sources; *Wits, Wenchers, and Wantons: London's Low Life: Covent Garden in the Eighteenth Century*, Robert Hale, 1986, pp. 92, 166, and *Royal St James's: Being a Story of Kings, Clubmen and Courtesans*, Robert Hale, 1988, p. 235.
4. Lillian Faderman, *Surpassing the Love of Men* [1981], Women's Press, 1985, p. 19.
5. See Janice Raymond, *A Passion for Friends: Towards a Philosophy of Female Affection*, Women's Press, 1986, ch. 2, 'Varieties of Female Friendship: The Nun as Loose Woman'.
6. Charles-Louis de Secondat, Baron de Montesquieu, *Lettres Persanes* [1721], trans. as *Persian Letters* by J. Ozell, 2 vols, J. Tonson, 1722, Letters IV and CXXXIX.
7. Andrew Marvell, 'Appleton House', in *The Works of Andrew Marvell Esq.*, 2 vols, E. Curll, 1726, vol. I, pp. 5–35 (pp. 9–15).
8. John Holstun, '"Will You Rent Our Ancient Love Asunder?": Lesbian Elegy in Donne, Marvell, and Milton', *English Literary History*, vol. 54, no. 4, winter 1987, pp. 835–67 (pp. 847–52).
9. See for example 'The Anchorite', in Jane Barker's *Poetical Recreations*, 1688, and her story 'The Heroik Cavalier; or, the Resolute Nun', in *A Patch-work Screen for the Ladies*, E. Curll & T. Payne, 1723, pp. 18–27, and also Charlotte MacCarthy's *The Fair Moralist*, the author, 1745, p. 67.
10. For a detailed but unanalytical survey of this tradition see Bridget Hill, 'A Refuge from Men: the Idea of a Protestant Nunnery', *Past and Present*, no. 117, November 1987, pp. 107–30. The idea is also discussed in Samuel Richardson, *The History of Sir Charles Grandison* [1753–4], ed. Jocelyn Harris, 3 parts, Oxford University Press, 1972, part II, pp. 355–6, n. p. 496. A more thoughtful account of the texts by Astell and Scott is found in Barbara Brandon Schnorrenberg, 'A Paradise like Eve's: Three Eighteenth-Century English Female Utopias', *Women's Studies*, vol. 9, no. 3, 1982, pp. 263–73.
11. Thomas D'Urfey, *A Common-Wealth of Women*, 1686; *Spectator*, nos. 433–4, 17 and 18 July 1712; Samuel Johnson, *Idler*, no. 87, 15 December 1759, in *The Idler and The Adventurer*, ed. W.J. Bate and others, Yale University Press, 1963; Anna Williams, 'The Nunnery' [1766] in Roger Lonsdale, ed., *Eighteenth-Century Women Poets: an Oxford Anthology*, Oxford, Oxford University Press, 1989, pp. 242–4.
12. Margaret Cavendish, Duchess of Newcastle, *Plays, Never Before Printed*, 1668, 'To the Readers'.
13. Cavendish, *The Convent of Pleasure*, in *Plays, Never Before Printed*, pp. 3–6, 11–12, 16 and act II scene iv.

14. Cavendish, *The Convent*, pp. 14–16, 22–3. A good account of this play's focus on theatre is Sophie Tomlinson, '"My Brain the Stage": Margaret Cavendish and the Fantasy of Female Performance', in Clare Brant and Diane Purkiss, eds, *Women, Texts and Histories 1575–1760*, Routledge, 1992, pp. 134–63 (pp. 152–8).
15. Cavendish, *The Convent*, pp. 32–3.
16. Cavendish, *The Convent*, pp. 37, 40, 45–8.
17. There may be no link, but it is worth noting that Aphra Behn's literary name was the Incomparable Astrea.
18. Delarivier Manley, *The New Atalantis* [1709], in *The Novels of Mary de la Riviere Manley*, ed. Patricia Koster, 2 vols, Gainesville, Fla, Scholars' Facsimiles and Reprints, 1971, vol. I, pp. 575–6.
19. Manley, *The New Atalantis*, pp. 576–8, 590.
20. Manley, *The New Atalantis*, pp. 575–7.
21. Manley, *The New Atalantis*, pp. 578–81.
22. Manley, *The New Atalantis*, pp. 579, 589.
23. Manley, *The New Atalantis*, pp. 578, 580–1. An interesting contrast is found in Eliza Haywood, *The History of Jemmy and Jenny Jessamy*, 1753, p. 51, when the eccentric Lady Fisk goes to Covent Garden in men's clothes, picks up a prostutite and is 'severely beaten by her on the discovery of her sex'.
24. Randolph Trumbach, 'London's Sapphists: from Three Sexes to Four Genders in the Making of Modern Culture', in Julia Epstein and Kristina Straub, eds, *Body Guards: the Cultural Politics of Gender Ambiguity*, Routledge, 1991, pp. 112–41 (p. 128).
25. Madeleine de Scudéry (1607–91) describes a 'Carte de Tendre' (map of tenderness) in her heroic romance *Clélie*, 10 vols, 1654–60.
26. Manley, *The New Atalantis*, p. 582.
27. Trumbach, 'London's Sapphists,' p. 128.
28. See Ros Ballaster, *Seductive Forms: Women's Amatory Fiction from 1684 to 1740*, Oxford, Clarendon, p. 141.
29. Manley, *Memoirs of Europe* (1710), in *Novels*, vol. II, pp. 300–1.
30. Manley, *The New Atalantis*, pp. 582–9.
31. Manley, *The New Atalantis*, pp. 738–41.
32. Manley, *Memoirs of Europe*, in *Novels*, vol. II, pp. 717–18.
33. For a subtle analysis of Manley's writings on the cabal, see Ros Ballaster, '"The Vices of Old Rome Revived": Representations of Female Same-Sex Desire in Seventeenth- and Eighteenth-Century England', in Suzanne Raitt, ed., *Volcanoes and Pearl-Divers: Lesbian Feminist Studies*, Onlywomen, forthcoming.
34. Thomas Wharton, quoted in Ivan Bloch, *A History of English Sexual Morals*, trans. W.H. Forstern, for Francis Aldor, 1936, p. 526.
35. William King, *The Toast*, 2nd edn, 4 books, 1736, pp. 52–3, 109, 86–7, 110, 177.
36. King, *The Toast*, 1736, p. 49.
37. King, *The Toast*, 1st edn, 2 books, Dublin, 1732, pp. 87, 83; 1736, p. 118.

38. Marie-Jo Bonnet, *Un Choix Sans Equivoque: recherches historiques sur les relations amoureuses entre les femmes, XVie–XXe siècle,* Paris, Denoêl, 1981, pp. 120, 144.
39. Bonnet, *Choix Sans Equivoque,* pp. 107–9.
40. J.N. von Archenholtz, *England und Italien,* Leipzig, 1787, vol. I, pp. 269–70, translated and quoted in Bloch, *English Sexual Morals,* p. 425. I have been unable to find this passage in the English translations of Archenholtz printed in the late eighteenth century.
41. Frances Burney, *The Early Journals and Letters of Fanny Burney,* ed. Lars E. Troide, Oxford, Clarendon, 1988, vol. II, pp. 55–6. For more mockery of Yates, see Sir Herbert Croft, *The Abbey of Kilhampton; or, Monumental Records for the Year 1980* [sic], G. Kearsley, 1780, p. 99. The Brooke–Yates friendship is described in Lorraine McMullen, *An Odd Attempt in a Woman: the Literary Life of Frances Brooke,* Vancouver, University of British Columbia Press, 1983, pp. 154–7, 191.
42. Joan DeJean, *Fictions of Sappho, 1546–1937,* University of Chicago Press, 1989, pp. 120, 5.
43. One account of Sappho's texts and reception in the seventeenth century is Elizabeth D. Harvey, 'Ventriloquizing Sappho: Ovid, Donne, and the Erotics of the Feminine Voice', *Criticism,* vol. 31, no. 2, 1989, pp. 115–38.
44. Ovid, Epistle XV, 'Sappho to Phaon', trans. Sir Carr. Scrope in *Ovid's Epistles, Translated by Several Hands,* Jacob Tonson, 1680, p. 2.
45. Ovid, Epistle XV, 'Sappho to Phaon', trans. Alexander Pope [1712], repr. in *Ten Epistles of Ovid,* ed. Reverend William Fitzthomas, C. & R. Baldwin, 1807, pp. 248, 264.
46. Germaine Greer and others, eds, *Kissing the Rod: an Anthology of Seventeenth-Century Women's Verse,* Virago, 1988, p. 265.
47. Ovid, Epistle XV, 'Sappho to Phaon', in *The Epistles of Ovid,* Joseph Davidson, 1746, n. 3 pp. 164–5, pp. 167, 179.
48. Ovid, Epistle XV, 'Sappho to Phaon', trans. by S. Barrett, in *Ovid's Epistles translated into English Verse,* J. Richardson, 1759, p. 230.
49. Sappho, odes trans. A. Phillips, in *Spectator* nos. 223 (15 November 1711) and 229 (22 November 1711), with biographical comment by J. Addison.
50. Sappho, odes trans. with a life by A. Phillips, in *The Works of Anacreon and Sappho,* E. Curll & A. Bettesworth, 1713, pp. 65, 74–5.
51. Pierre Bayle, *An Historical and Critical Dictionary,* 4 vols, C. Harper and others, 1710, vol. IV, p. 2671.
52. Sappho, odes trans. with a life by Joseph Addison, in *The Works of Anacreon,* John Watts, 1735, pp. 251–2, 263, 271.
53. Sappho, odes trans. with a life by E.B. Greene, in *The Works of Anacreon and Sappho,* J. Ridley, 1768, pp. 130, 144–5, 165, 167.
54. John Nott's *Sappho. After a Greek Romance,* Cuthall & Martin, 1803, seems to be an uncredited translation of Verri's text.
55. Alessandro Verri, *Le Avventure di Saffo .../The Adventures of Sappho, Poetess of Mitylene* [dual-language edition], 2 vols, T. Cadell, 1789

(amended in Cambridge University Library copy to 1792), vol. II, pp. 211–19.

56. Mary Robinson, *Sappho and Phaon*, the author, 1796, pp. 70, 18, 22, 26, 28.
57. Anon, 'Dialogue Between Sappho and Ninon de L'Enclos, in the Shades', *Covent-Garden Magazine; or, Amorous Repository*, June 1773, pp. 255–6.
58. Bonnet, *Choix Sans Equivoque*, p. 32.
59. John Holstun, '"Will You Rent Our Ancient Love Asunder?"', pp. 837–47, esp. 846.
60. Pierre de Bourdeille, Seigneur de Brantôme, *Oeuvres*, 15 vols, 1779, *Vies des Dames Galantes*, vol. III, pp. 219–26.
61. Nicholas Venette, *Tableau de L'Amour Conjugal*, trans. as *The Mysteries of Conjugal Love Reveal'd*, 2nd edn, 1707, p. 15.
62. Honoré Gabriel Riquetti, Comte de Mirabeau, *Erotika Biblion*, Rome [actually Neuchâtel or Paris?], 1783, 'L'Anandryne', pp. 83–100 (pp. 91–2).
63. Anne Lister, *I Know My Own Heart: the Diaries [1817–24] of Anne Lister (1791–1840)*, ed. Helena Whitbread, Virago, 1988, p. 273, and *No Priest but Love: the Journals of Anne Lister from 1824–1826*, ed. Whitbread, Otley, West Yorkshire, Smith Settle, 1992, pp. 49, 50, n. p.56.
64. William Walsh, 'A Dialogue Concerning Women' [1699], in *The Works of Celebrated Authors, of Whose Writings There Are but Small Remains*, 2 vols, J. & R. Tonson & S. Draper, 1750, vol. II, pp. 151–209 (pp. 168, 196–7).
65. J.B. Tavernier, Baron of Aubonne, *Collections of Travels Through Turkey into Persia and the East-Indies*, 2 vols, Moses Pitt, 1684, vol. II, pp. 20, 86–7.
66. C.S. Sonnini, *Travels in Upper and Lower Egypt*, trans. Henry Hunter, 3 vols, John Stockdale, 1799, vol. I, p. 258.
67. Bayle, *Historical and Critical Dictionary*, p. 2671.
68. John Dennis, 'The Stage Defended' [1726] in *The Critical Works*, ed. Edward Niles Hooker, 2 vols, Baltimore, Md., Johns Hopkins Press, 1943, vol. II, pp. 300–21 (pp. 314–5).
69. For a survey of British texts that link male sodomy to Italy, see Alan Bray, *Homosexuality in Renaissance England*, Gay Men's Press, 1988, pp. 19–21 and 75, and Louis Crompton, *Byron and Greek Love*, Faber & Faber, 1985, pp. 52–6.
70. Jonathan Swift, *Gulliver's Travels. A Facsimile Reproduction of a Large-Paper Copy of the First Edition (1726)*, intro. by Colin McKelvie, Delmar, New York, Scholars' Facsimiles and Reprints, 1976, book IV, ch. 7, pp. 115–16.
71. Anon, *Plain Reasons for the Growth of Sodomy in England*, A. Dodd & E. Nutt, 1728, p. 16.
72. Father Poussin (attrib.), *Pretty Doings in a Protestant Nation*, J. Roberts & others, 1734, pp. 23–4.
73. King, *The Toast*, 1736, pp. 15, 53, 50, 109, 103, 53.

74. King, *The Toast*, 1732, 'Ode to Myra', pp.84–5.
75. Beryl Rowland, *Birds with Human Souls: a Guide to Bird Symbolism*, Knoxville, Tenn., University of Tennessee Press, 1978, pp. 42, 44.
76. Archenholtz, *England und Italien*, trans. and quoted in Bloch, *English Sexual Morals*, p. 425.
77. King, *The Toast*, 1736, pp. 100, 97, 107, 110.
78. Anon, *Satan's Harvest Home* [1749], New York, Garland, 1985, pp. 18, 53–4, 60.
79. Captain Francis Grosse, *A Classical Dictionary of the Vulgar Tongue* [1785], Routledge and Kegan Paul, 1963, p. 147; Eric Partridge, *A Dictionary of Slang and Unconventional English* [1937], ed. Paul Beale, Routledge & Kegan Paul, 1984, entry for 'flat'.
80. See Peter Wagner, 'The Discourse on Sex – or Sex as Discourse: Eighteenth-Century Medical and Paramedical Erotica', in G.S. Rousseau and Roy Porter, eds, *Sexual Underworlds of the Enlightenment*, Manchester, Manchester University Press, 1987, pp. 46–68 (p. 59). I have not been able to consult the only known copy of *The Sappho-an*, which is in the Institute of Sex Research, Indiana, USA.
81. John Wilkes, 'An Essay on Woman' [1760s?] in *The Infamous Essay on Woman, or, John Wilkes Seated Between Vice and Virtue*, ed. Adrian Hamilton, André Deutsch, 1972, p. 215 (p. 14 of the facsimile).
82. Anon, *A Sapphic Epistle, from Jack Cavendish to the Honourable and Most Beautiful Mrs. D*****, no date, p. 5. The date suggested by Randolph Trumbach ('London's Sapphists', p. 131), 1782, would make sense, since the poem mentions Anne Damer's trip to Italy after her husband's death (she went in 1777) but makes no reference to her relationship with Elizabeth Farren (which developed from the mid-1880s onwards).
83. *A Sapphic Epistle*, pp. 5–6, 10–13.
84. *A Sapphic Epistle*, pp. 14, 20, 23.
85. Hester Lynch Thrale Piozzi, *Thraliana: The Diary of Mrs. Hester Lynch Thrale (Later Mrs. Piozzi), 1776–1809*, ed. Katherine C. Balderston, 2 vols, 2nd edn, Oxford, Clarendon, 1951, 1 April 1789, vol. II, p. 740.
86. Thrale Piozzi, *Thraliana*, 17 June 1790, vol. II, p. 770; 25 January 1794, vol. II, p. 868.
87. Thrale Piozzi, *Thraliana*, 9 December 1795, vol. II, p. 949.
88. Faderman, *Surpassing*, p. 76.

Select bibliography

The date of first publication, where it differs from the edition consulted, is shown in square brackets. Unless otherwise stated the place of publication is London.

Adburgham, Alison, *Women in Print: Writing Women and Women's Magazines from the Restoration to the Accession of Victoria*, George Allen & Unwin, 1972

Alger, William R., *The Friendships of Women*, Boston, Roberts Brothers, 1868

Altman, Denis and others, *Homosexuality, Which Homosexuality? Essays from the International Scientific Conference on Lesbian and Gay Studies*, Gay Men's Press, 1989

Anne, *The Letters and Diplomatic Instructions of Queen Anne*, ed. Beatrice Curtis Brown, Cassell, 1968

Anon, *The Adulteress* (a modernisation of Juvenal's *Sixth Satire*), S. Bladon, 1773

Anon, 'The Counterfeit Bridegroom', *ca.* 1720, British Library 816.m.19.(21)

Anon, *Critical Review*, review of Elizabeth Nihell's book on midwifery, early 1760, vol. IX, p. 196

Anon, 'Dialogue Between Sappho and Ninon de L'Enclos, in the Shades', *Covent-Garden Magazine; or, Amorous Repository*, June 1773, pp. 255–6

Anon, *An Epistle from Signora F_a to a Lady*, 'Venice' [London], 1727

Anon, 'Extraordinary Female Affection' [on the Ladies of Llangollen], *General Evening Post*, 24 July 1790

Anon, 'Female Flagellists. A Club, in Jermyn Street', *Bon Ton Magazine; or, Microscope of Fashion and Folly*, December 1792, pp. 378–80

Anon, 'The Female Husband, a New Song', Madden collection of ballads in Cambridge University Library, vol. 4, no. 606

Anon, *The Female Soldier*, Richard Walker, 1750 (187-page version)

Anon, *The Female Soldier or the Surprising Life and Adventurs of Hannah Snell* [1750], Augustan Reprint no. 257, Los Angeles, William Andrews Clark Memorial Library, University of California, 1989 (46-page version)

Anon, *Gentleman's Magazine*, reports of female husbands, 28 June 1773, 5 July 1777; Mary East case: July, August and October 1766

Anon, *The History of the Human Heart: or, the Adventures of a Young Gentleman*, J. Freeman, 1749

Anon, *The Life and Adventures of Mrs. Christian Davies, the British Amazon*, 2nd edn, Richard Montagu, 1741

Anon, *London Chronicle, or, Universal Evening Post*, reports of female husbands, 9 June 1759, vol. V, p. 448; 2 February 1760, vol. VII, p. 117; 24 March 1760, vol. VII, p. 291; 5–8 April 1760, vol. VII, p. 338; 17 February 1764, vol. XV, p. 161

Anon, *Monsieur Thing's Origin; or, Seignior D—o's Adventures in Britain*, R. Tomson, 1722

Anon, *A New Atalantis for the Year One Thousand Seven Hundred and Fifty-Eight*, 2nd edn, M. Thrush, 1758

Anon, *Onania* [8th edn, 1723] and *A Supplement to the Onania* [after 1725?], New York, Garland, 1986

Anon, *Pamela Censured* [1741], intro. by Charles Batten Jr, Augustan Reprint no. 175, Los Angeles, William Andrews Clark Memorial Library, University of California, 1976

Anon, *Plain Reasons for the Growth of Sodomy in England*, A. Dodd & E. Nutt, 1728

Anon, *A Sapphic Epistle, from Jack Cavendish to the Honourable and Most Beautiful Mrs. D****, no date [1782?]

Anon, *Satan's Harvest Home* [1749], (with *Hell upon Earth*) New York, Garland, 1985

Anon, *A Spy on Mother Midnight*, E. Penn, 1748

Arnauld, George, *A Dissertation on Hermaphrodites*, in M. Jourdan de Pellerin, *A Treatise on Venereal Maladies*, Andrew Millar, 1750

Astell, Mary, *A Serious Proposal to the Ladies* [1694], in *The First English Feminist: 'Reflections upon Marriage' and Other Writings*, ed. Bridget Hill, Aldershot, Gower/Maurice Temple Smith, 1986

Astell, Mary and John Norris, *Letters Concerning the Love of God*, John Norris, 1695

Baker, Sheridan, 'Henry Fielding's *The Female Husband*', *Publications of the Modern Language Association*, vol. LXXIV, June 1959, pp. 213–24

Ballaster, Ros, *Seductive Forms: Women's Amatory Fiction from 1684 to 1740*, Oxford, Clarendon, 1992

Ballaster, Ros, '"The Vices of Old Rome Revived": Representations of Female Same-Sex Desire in Seventeenth- and Eighteenth-Century England' (draft), in Suzanne Raitt, ed., *Volcanoes and Pearl-Divers: Lesbian Feminist Studies*, Onlywomen, forthcoming

Barbin, Herculine, *Herculine Barbin: Being the Recently Discovered Memoirs of a Nineteenth-Century French Hermaphrodite*, intro. by Michel Foucault, trans. Richard McDougall, Brighton, Harvester, 1980

Barker, Jane, *A Patch-work Screen for the Ladies*, E. Curll & T. Payne, 1723

Barker, Jane, *Poetical Recreations*, 1688

Barrin, Jean, *Venus dans la Cloître* [1683], trans. Robert Samber as *Venus in the Cloister*, 2nd edn, E. Curll, 1725

Bayle, Pierre, *An Historical and Critical Dictionary*, 4 vols, C. Harper and others, 1710, vol. IV entry for 'Sappho', p. 2671

Behn, Aphra, *The False Count* [1682], in *Five Plays*, intro. by Maureen Duffy, Methuen, 1990

Behn, Aphra, 'To my Lady Morland' [1684], and 'To Mrs Harsenet' [a later version, 1692], in *The Works*, ed. Montague Summers, 6 vols, William Heinemann, 1915, vol. VI, pp. 175–7, 393–4

Behn, Aphra, 'To the Fair Clarinda, Who Made Love to Me, Imagined More than Woman' [1688], in *The Norton Anthology of Literature by Women*, ed. S.M. Gilbert and Susan Gubar, New York, Norton, 1985; p. 94

Behn, Aphra, 'Verses design'd by Mrs. A. Behn to be sent to a fair Lady, that desir'd she would absent herself to cure her Love. Left unfinish'd', in *The Works*, vol. VI, p. 389

Bell, G.H., ed., *The Hamwood Papers of the Ladies of Llangollen and Caroline Hamilton*, Macmillan, 1930

Bianchi, Giovanni P.S., *The True History and Adventures of Catherine Vizzani*, trans. John Cleland, for W. Reeve & C. Sympson, 1755

Bloch, Ivan, *A History of English Sexual Morals*, trans. W.H. Forstern, for Francis Aldor, 1936

Bonnet, Marie-Jo, *Un Choix Sans Equivoque: Recherches Historiques sur les Relations Amoureuses entre les Femmes, XVie–XXe Siècle* [An Unequivocal Choice: Historical Research into Love Relationships between Women from the Fifteenth to the Twentieth Centuries], Paris, Denoêl, 1981

Boucé, Paul-Gabriel, ed., *Sexuality in Eighteenth-Century Britain*, Manchester, Manchester University Press, 1982

Brantôme, Pierre de Bourdeille, Seigneur de, *Vies des Dames Galantes*, in *Oeuvres*, 15 vols, 1779

Bray, Alan, *Homosexuality in Renaissance England* [1982], Gay Men's Press, 1988

Bremmer, Jan, ed., *From Sappho to De Sade: Moments in the History of Sexuality*, Routledge, 1989

Brown, Judith C., *Immodest Acts: the Life of a Lesbian Nun in Renaissance Italy*, New York, Oxford University Press, 1986

Burn, John Southerden, *The Fleet Registers*, Rivingtons and others, 1833

Busbequius, A.G., sixteenth-century travel account, trans. as *Travels into Turkey*, J. Robinson & W. Payne, 1744

Bush, Barbara, *Slave Women in Carribbean Society, 1650–1838*, James Currey, 1990

Carr, Richard, *Dr. Carr's Medicinal Epistles upon Several Occasions*, trans. John Quincy, for William Newton & J. Phillips, 1714, Epistle 16, 'Concerning the two *Nuns* Reported to Have Changed their Sex', pp. 142–50 (repr. entire in Anon, *The Supplement to the Onania*, pp. 155–62)

Carter, Elizabeth, *Letters from Mrs Elizabeth Carter to Mrs Montagu, Between the Years 1755 and 1800*, ed. Montagu Pennington, 3 vols, F.C. & J. Rivington, 1817

Carter, Elizabeth and Catherine Talbot, *A Series of Letters ... 1741 to 1770*, ed. Montagu Pennington, 4 vols, 1809

Castle, Terry, '"*Amy*, Who Knew My Disease": A Psychosexual Pattern in Defoe's *Roxana*', *English Literary History*, vol. 46, no. 1, spring 1979, pp. 81–96

Castle, Terry, 'Matters Not Fit to Be Mentioned: Fielding's *The Female Husband*', *English Literary History*, vol. 49, no. 3, fall 1982, pp. 602–23

Castle, Terry, *Masquerade and Civilisation: the Carnivalesque in Eighteenth-Century English Culture and Fiction*, Methuen, 1986
Castle, Terry, 'Marie Antoinette Obsession', *Representations*, no. 38, spring 1992, pp. 1–38 (pp. 17–18)
Chapone, Hester Mulso, *The Works of Mrs Chapone*, 2 vols, Dublin, W. Colles, 1786
Charke, Charlotte Cibber, *A Narrative of the Life of Mrs. Charlotte Charke* [2nd edn, 1755], Gainesville, Fla, Scholars' Facsimiles and Reprints, 1969
Chorier, Nicholas, *Satyra Sotadica* [1659/60], trans. as *A Dialogue Between a Married Lady and a Maid*, 1740
Cleland, John, *Fanny Hill, or, Memoirs of a Woman of Pleasure* [1749], Penguin, 1985
Coward, D.A., 'Attitudes to Homosexuality in Eighteenth Century France', *Journal of European Studies*, vol. 10, part 4, December 1980, pp. 231–55
Croft, Sir Herbert, *The Abbey of Kilhampton; or, Monumental Records for the Year 1980* [sic], G. Kearsley, 1780
Crompton, Louis, *Byron and Greek Love: Homophobia in 19th-Century England*, Faber & Faber, 1985
Cruikshank, Margaret, ed., *Lesbian Studies: Present and Future*, New York, Feminist Press, 1982
Dabydeen, David, ed., *The Black Presence in English Literature*, Manchester, Manchester University Press, 1985
Davis, Elizabeth (Betsy Cadwaladyr), *An Autobiography of Elizabeth Davis, a Balaclava Nurse* [ed. Jane Williams, 1857], repr. Cardiff, Honno, 1987
Defoe, Daniel (attrib), *A General History of the Pyrates* [1724], ed. Manuel Schenhorn, J.M. Dent & Sons, 1972
Defoe, Daniel, *Roxana* [1724], ed. Jane Jack, Oxford, Oxford University Press, 1981
DeJean, Joan, *Fictions of Sappho, 1546–1937*, University of Chicago Press, 1989
Dekker, Rudolph M. and Lotte C. van de Pol, *The Tradition of Female Transvestism in Early Modern Europe*, Macmillan, 1989
Dennis, John, 'The Stage Defended' [1726] in *The Critical Works*, ed. Edward Niles Hooker, 2 vols, Baltimore, Md., Johns Hopkins Press, 1943, vol. II, pp. 300–21
Diderot, Denis, *Les Bijoux Indiscrets* [1748], trans. as *Les Bijoux Indiscrets, or, The Indiscreet Toys*, 2 vols, 'Tobago' [London], 1749
Diderot, Denis, *La Religieuse* [written from 1760, publ. 1796], trans. as *The Nun*, Dublin, G. Smith, 1797
Dugaw, Dianne, *Warrior Women and Popular Balladry, 1650–1850*, Cambridge, Cambridge University Press, 1989
Edgeworth, Maria, *Belinda* [1801], Pandora, 1986
Epstein, Julia and Kristina Straub, eds, *Body Guards: the Cultural Politics of Gender Ambiguity*, Routledge, 1991
Eriksson, Brigitte, 'A Lesbian Execution in German, 1721: The Trial Records', in Licata and Petersen, pp. 27–40
Everard, Myriam, 'Lesbian History: a History of Change and Disparity', in Kehoe, pp. 123–37

Faderman, Lillian, *Surpassing the Love of Men: Romantic Friendship and Love Between Women from the Renaissance to the Present* [1981], Women's Press, 1985

Faderman, Lillian, *Scotch Verdict: Miss Pirie and Miss Woods V. Dame Cumming Gordon*, New York, William Morrow, 1983

Ferguson, Moira, ed., *First Feminists: British Women Writers 1578–1799*, Bloomington, Ind., Indiana University Press, 1985

Fielding, Henry, *The Female Husband* [1746] *and Other Writings*, ed. Claude E. Jones, English Reprints Series no. 17, Liverpool, Liverpool University Press, 1960

Fielding, Sarah, *Familiar Letters*, 2 vols, the author, 1747

Fielding, Sarah, *The Governess* [1749], Pandora, 1987

Foster, Jeannette H., *Sex Variant Women in Literature* [1956], 4th edn, Tallahassee, Fla., Naiad Press, 1985

Foucault, Michel, *The History of Sexuality* [vol. I, 1976], trans. Robert Hurley, Harmondsworth, Penguin, 1981

Foxon, David, *Libertine Literature in England 1660–1745*, Book Collector, 1964

Friedli, Lynne, 'Women Who Dressed as Men', *Trouble and Strife*, no. 6, summer 1985, pp. 24–9

Friedli, Lynne, '"Passing Women": a Study of Gender Boundaries in the Eighteenth Century', in Rousseau and Porter, pp. 234–60

Fryer, Peter, *Staying Power: the History of Black People in Britain*, Pluto, 1984

Gagen, Jean, *The New Woman: Her Emergence in English Drama, 1600–1730*, New York, Twayne Publishers, 1954

Garber, Marjorie, *Vested Interests: Cross-dressing and Cultural Anxiety*, Routledge, 1992

Gerard, Kent and Gert Hekma, *The Pursuit of Sodomy in Early Modern Europe*, New York, Haworth, 1987

Gibson, Thomas, *The Anatomy of Humane Bodies Epitomized*, T. Flesher, 1682

Grahn, Judy, *Another Mother Tongue: Gay Words, Gay Worlds*, Boston, Beacon Press, 1984

Greer, Germaine and others, eds, *Kissing the Rod: an Anthology of Seventeenth-Century Women's Verse*, Virago, 1988

Haggerty, George E., '"Romantic Friendship" and Patriarchal Narrative in Sarah Scott's *Millenium Hall*', *Genders*, no. 13, spring 1992, pp. 108–22

Hamilton, Count Anthony, *Memoirs of the Life of Count de Grammont* [1713], trans. Boyer, 1714

Hands, Elizabeth, *The Death of Amno ... and Other Poetical Pieces*, Coventry, the author, 1789

Harvey, Elizabeth D., 'Ventriloquizing Sappho: Ovid, Donne, and the Erotics of the Feminine Voice', *Criticism*, vol. 31, no. 2, 1989, pp. 115–38

Haywood, Eliza, *The British Recluse: or, the Secret History of Cleomira, Suppose'd Dead*, 2nd edn, D. Brown and others, 1722

Haywood, Eliza, *The History of Jenny and Jemmy Jessamy*, 1753

Hennegen, Alison, 'Lesbians in Literature', *Gay Left*, no. 9, 1979, pp. 20–5
Hobby, Elaine, *Virtue of Necessity: English Women's Writing 1649–88*, Virago, 1988
Hobby, Elaine, 'Katherine Philips: Seventeenth-Century Lesbian Poet', in Elaine Hobby and Chris White, eds, *What Lesbians Do in Books*, Women's Press, 1991, pp. 183–204
Holstun, John, '"Will You Rent Our Ancient Love Asunder?": Lesbian Elegy in Donne, Marvell, and Milton', *English Literary History*, vol. 54, no. 4, winter 1987, pp. 835–67
Jacob, Giles (attrib.), *A Treatise of Hermaphrodites*, with John Henry Meibomius, *A Treatise of the Use of Flogging at Venereal Affairs*, E. Curll, 1718
James, Robert, *A Medicinal Dictionary*, 3 vols, T. Osborne, 1745, vol. III, entry for 'Tribades'
Jones, Anne Rosalind and Peter Stallybrass, 'Fetishizing Gender: Constructing the Hermaphrodite in Renaissance Europe', in Epstein and Straub, pp. 80–111
Jones, Vivien, ed., *Women in the Eighteenth Century: Constructions of Femininity*, Routledge, 1990
Juvenal, *The Satires ... Translated into English Verse*, trans. by Dryden and others, Jacob Tonson, 1693
Juvenal, *The Satires*, trans. T. Sheridan, for D. Browne, 1739
Juvenal, *The Satires ... with the Original Text*, trans. John Stirling, for J. Fuller, 1760
Juvenal, *The Satires ... Translated into English Verse*, trans. William Gifford, for G. & W. Nicol & R. Evans, 1802
Juvenal, *A New and Literal Translation of Juvenal and Persius*, trans. M. Madan, 2 vols, Oxford, 1813
Kearney, Patrick J., *The Private Case: an Annotated Bibliography of the Private Case Erotica Collection in the British (Museum) Library*, Jay Landesman, 1981
Kehoe, Monika, ed., *Historical, Literary and Erotic Aspects of Lesbianism*, New York, Harrington Park Press, 1986
Kendall, Kathryn, 'From Lesbian Heroine to Devoted Wife: or, What the Stage Would Allow', in Kehoe, pp. 9–22
King, William, *The Toast*, 1st edn, 2 books, Dublin, 1732; 2nd edn, 4 books, 1736
Kirby, R.S., *Kirby's Wonderful and Eccentric Museum*, 6 vols, Kirby, 1820
Laclos, Pierre-Ambroise-François Choderlos de, *Les Liaisons dangereuses* [1782], trans. as *Dangerous Connections*, 4 vols, T. Hookham, 1784
Landry, Donna, *The Muses of Resistance: Laboring-Class Women's Poetry in Britain, 1739–1796*, Cambridge, Cambridge University Press, 1990
Lardinois, André, 'Lesbian Sappho and Sappho of Lesbos', in Bremmer, pp. 15–35
Lennox, Charlotte, *Sophia*, 2 vols, James Fletcher, 1762
Lennox, Charlotte, *Euphemia* [1790], Scholars' Facsimiles and Reprints, vol. 435, Delmar, New York, 1989

Licata, Salvatore J. and Robert P. Petersen, eds, *The Gay Past*, New York, Harrington Park Press, 1985

Lister, Anne, *I Know My Own Heart: the Diaries [1817–24] of Anne Lister (1791–1840)*, ed. Helena Whitbread, Virago, 1988

Lister, Anne, *No Priest but Love: the Journals of Anne Lister from 1824–1826*, ed. Helena Whitbread, Otley, West Yorkshire, Smith Settle, 1992

Lonsdale, Roger, ed., *Eighteenth-Century Women Poets: an Oxford Anthology*, Oxford, Oxford University Press, 1989

Lucian, 'A Dialogue between Cleonarium and Laeana [sic]', fifth in *The Dialogues of the Courtizans*, in *Lucian's Works, Translated from the Greek*, Ferrand Spence, 4 vols, W. Benbridge and others, 1684–5, vol. IV, pp. 304–6.

MacCarthy, Charlotte, *The Fair Moralist* and *Occasional Poems*, the author, 1745

Maccubbin, Robert Purks, ed., *'Tis Nature's Fault: Unauthorized Sexuality During the Enlightenment*, Cambridge, Cambridge University Press, 1987

Manley, Delarivier, *The New Atalantis* [1709] and *Memoirs of Europe* [1710], in *The Novels of Mary de la Riviere Manley*, ed. Patricia Koster, 2 vols, Gainesville, Fla, Scholars' Facsimiles and Reprints, 1971

Marlborough, Sarah Churchill, Duchess of (assisted by N. Hooke) *An Account of the Conduct of the Dowager Duchess of Marlborough, from Her First Coming to Court, to the Year 1710*, George Hawkins, 1742

Marlborough, Sarah Churchill, Duchess of, *Private Correspondence*, 2 vols, Henry Colburn, 1838

Marten, John, *A Treatise of all the Degrees and Symptoms of the Venereal Disease, in Both Sexes*, 6th edn, S. Crouch, 1708

Martial, 'To Bassa', in *The Epigrams of Martial in Twelve Books*, trans. James Elphinston, 1782, p. 302

Marvell, Andrew, 'Appleton House', in *The Works of Andrew Marvell Esq.*, 2 vols, E. Curll, 1726, vol. I, pp. 5–35

Mavor, Elizabeth, *The Ladies of Llangollen: a Study in Romantic Friendship* [1971], Penguin, 1973

Maynwaring, Arthur (attrib.), 'A New Ballad to the Tune of Fair Rosamond' [1708], in *Poems on Affairs of State: Augustan Satirical Verse, 1660–1717*, 7 vols, ed. Frank H. Ellis, vol. VII, New Haven, Conn., Yale University Press, 1975, p. 309

Maynwaring, Arthur (attrib.), *The Rival Dutchess, or Court Incendiary*, 1708

Maynwaring, Arthur, letter to Sarah Churchill, Duchess of Marlborough, 30 April or May 1710, British Library Additional MS 61461.f.27

Messenger, Ann, *His and Hers: Essays in Restoration and Eighteenth-Century Literature*, Lexington, Ken., University Press of Kentucky, 1986

Mills, Jane, *Womanwords: a Vocabulary of Culture and Patriarchal Society*, Virago, 1991

Mirabeau, Honoré Gabriel Riquetti, Comte de, *The Secret History of the Court of Berlin*, trans. John Slachne, Dublin, 1789

Montesquieu, Charles-Louis de Secondat, Baron de, *Lettres Persanes* [1721], trans. J. Ozell as *Persian Letters*, 2 vols, J. Tonson, 1722, letters IV and CXXXIX

Moore, Lisa, '"Something More Tender Still Than Friendship": Romantic Friendship in Early-Nineteenth-Century England', *Feminist Studies*, vol. 18, no. 3, fall 1992, pp. 499–520

Newcastle, Margaret Cavendish, Duchess of, *The Convent of Pleasure*, in *Plays, Never Before Printed*, 1668

Norton, Rictor, *Mother Clap's Molly House: the Gay Subculture in England, 1700–1830*, Gay Men's Press, 1992

Ovid, Epistle XV, 'Sappho to Phaon', trans. Sir Carr. Scrope in *Ovid's Epistles, Translated Several Hands*, Jacob Tonson, 1680

Ovid, Epistle XV, 'Sappho to Phaon', trans. by Alexander Pope [1712], repr. in *Ten Epistles of Ovid*, ed. Reverend William Fitzthomas, C. & R. Baldwin, 1807

Ovid, Epistle XV, 'Sappho to Phaon', in *The Epistles of Ovid*, Joseph Davidson, 1746

Ovid, Epistle XV, 'Sappho to Phaon', trans. S. Barrett, in *Ovid's Epistles Translated into English Verse*, J. Richardson, 1759

Parsons, Dr James, *A Mechanical and Critical Enquiry into the Nature of Hermaphrodites*, J. Walthoe, 1741

Partridge, Eric, *A Dictionary of Slang and Unconventional English* [1937], ed. Paul Beale, Routledge & Kegan Paul, 1984

Pearson, Jacqueline, *The Prostituted Muse: Images of Women and Women Dramatists 1642–1737*, Hemel Hempstead, Harvester Wheatsheaf, 1988

Perrin, Noel, *Dr. Bowdler's Legacy: a History of Expurgated Books in England and America*, Macmillan, 1970

Perry, Ruth, *The Celebrated Mary Astell: an Early English Feminist*, Chicago, University of Chicago Press, 1986

Philips, Katherine, *The Collected Works*, ed. Patrick Thomas, Stump Cross, Essex, Stump Cross Books, 1990, vol. I: *The Poems*

Pigott, Charles (attrib.), *The Whig Club, or a Sketch of the Manners of the Age*, the author, 1794

Pix, Mary, *Queen Catharine, or, The Ruines of Love* [1698] and *The Double Distress* [1701], in *The Plays of Mary Pix and Catharine Trotter*, ed. Edna L. Steeves, New York, Garland, 1982, vol. I

Porter, Roy, 'Mixed Feelings: the Enlightenment and Sexuality in Eighteenth-Century Britain', in Boucé, pp. 1–27

Poussin, Father (attrib.), *Pretty Doings in a Protestant Nation Being a View of the Present State of Fornication, Whorecraft, and Adultery, in Great-Britain*, J. Roberts and others, 1734

Quincy, Dr John, *Lexicon Physico-Medicum: or, a New Physical Dictionary*, Andrew Bell and others, 1719

Raymond, Janice, *A Passion for Friends: Towards a Philosophy of Female Affection*, Women's Press, 1986

Richardson, Samuel, *Pamela* [1740], 2 vols, Dent, 1986, vol. I

Robinson, Mary, *Sappho and Phaon*, the author, 1796

Robson, Ruthann, *Lesbian (Out)law: Survival Under the Rule of Law*, Ithaca, NY, Firebrand Books, 1992

Rochester, John Wilmot, 2nd Earl of (attrib.), *Sodom* [Antwerp, 1684], repr. Paris, Verlag von H. Welter, 1904

Rogers, Pat, 'The Breeches Part', in Boucé, pp. 244–58

Rousseau, G.S., 'The Pursuit of Homosexuality in the Eighteenth Century: "Utterly Confused Category" and/or Rich Repository?', in Maccubbin, pp. 132–68

Rousseau, G.S., and Roy Porter, eds, *Sexual Underworlds of the Enlightenment,* Manchester, Manchester University Press, 1987

Rowe, Elizabeth Singer, *Miscellaneous Works*, Hett & Dodsley, 1739

Rowland, Beryl, *Animals with Human Faces: a Guide to Animal Symbolism*, George Allen & Unwin, 1974

Rowland, Beryl, *Birds with Human Souls: a Guide to Bird Symbolism*, Knoxville, Tenn., University of Tennessee Press, 1978

Sappho, odes trans. A. Phillips, *Spectator*, nos. 223 (15 November 1711) and 229 (22 November 1711), with biographical comment by J. Addison

Sappho, odes trans. with a life by A. Phillips, in *The Works of Anacreon and Sappho*, E. Curll & A. Bettesworth, 1713, pp. 65, 74–5

Sappho, odes trans. with a life by Joseph Addison, in *The Works of Anacreon*, John Watts, 1735, pp. 251–2, 263, 271

Sappho, odes trans. with a life (by E.B. Greene), in *The Works of Anacreon and Sappho*, J. Ridley, 1768, pp. 130, 144–5, 165, 167

Schofield, Mary Anne and Cecilia Macheski, eds, *Fetter'd or Free? British Women Novelists, 1670–1815*, Athens, Ohio University Press, 1986

Scott, Sarah Robinson, *A Description of Millenium Hall* [1762], Virago, 1986

Sedgwick, Eve Kosofsky, *Epistemology of the Closet*, Hemel Hempstead, Harvester Wheatsheaf, 1991

Senelick, Laurence, 'The Evolution of the Male Impersonator in the Nineteenth-Century Popular Stage', *Essays in Theatre*, vol. I, no. 1, 1982, pp. 31–44

Seward, Anna, *The Poetical Works*, ed. Walter Scott, 3 vols, Edinburgh, John Ballantyne and others, 1810

Sharp, Jane, *The Midwives Book* [1671], Garland, 1985

Shepherd, Simon, *Amazons and Warrior Women: Varieties of Feminism in Seventeenth-Century Drama*, Brighton, Harvester, 1981

Sinibaldus, Joannes Benedictus, *Geneanthropeiae* [Rome, 1642], trans. 'Erotodidascalus' [Richard Head] as *Rare Verities: the Cabinet of Venus Unlocked, and Her Secrets Laid Open*, P. Briggs, 1687

Smith, Hilda L., *Reason's Disciples: Seventeenth-Century English Feminists*, Urbana, Ill., University of Illinois Press, 1982

Sonnini, C.S., *Travels in Upper and Lower Egypt*, trans. Henry Hunter, 3 vols, John Stockdale, 1799

Stanley, Liz, 'Epistemological Issues in Researching Lesbian History: the Case of Romantic Friendship,' in Hilary Hinds and others, eds, *Working Out: New Directions for Women's Studies*, Falmer, 1992, pp. 161–72

Steele, Elizabeth Hughes, *The Memoirs of Mrs. Sophia Baddeley*, 3 vols, Dublin, Colles and others, 1787

Stone, Laurence *The Family, Sex and Marriage in England, 1500–1800*, Weidenfeld & Nicolson, 1977

Tavernier, J.B., Baron of Aubonne, *Collections of Travels through Turkey into Persia and the East-Indies*, 2 vols, Moses Pitt, 1684

Thomas, Donald, *A Long Time Burning: the History of Literary Censorship in England*, Routledge & Kegan Paul, 1969

Thompson, Roger, *Unfit for Modest Ears: a Study of Pornographic, Obscene and Bawdy Works Written or Published in England in the Second Half of the Seventeenth Century*, Macmillan, 1979

Thrale Piozzi, Hester Lynch, *The Intimate Letters of Hester Piozzi and Penelope Pennington, 1788–1821*, ed. Oswald C. Knapp, John Lane, 1914

Thrale Piozzi, Hester Lynch, *Thraliana: The Diary of Mrs. Hester Lynch Thrale (Later Mrs. Piozzi), 1776–1809*, ed. Katherine C. Balderston, 2 vols, 2nd edn, Oxford, Clarendon, 1951

Tissot, Samuel Auguste David, *Onanism; or, a Treatise upon the Disorders Produced by Masturbation* [trans. 1766], New York, Garland, 1985

Todd, Janet, *Women's Friendship in Literature*, New York, Columbia University Press, 1980

Todd, Janet, ed., *A Dictionary of British and American Women Writers 1660–1800*, Methuen, 1987

Todd, Janet, *The Sign of Angellica: Women, Writing and Fiction, 1660–1800*, Virago, 1989

Trumbach, Randolph, 'London's Sapphists: from Three Sexes to Four Genders in the Making of Modern Culture', in Epstein and Straub, pp. 112–41

Turner, Mary, 'Two Entries from the Marriage Register of Taxal, Cheshire', *Local Population Studies*, no. 21, autumn 1978, p. 64

Venette, Nicholas, *Tableau de L'Amour Conjugal*, trans. as *The Mysteries of Conjugal Love Reveal'd*, 2nd edn, 1707

Verri, Alessandro, *Le Avventure di Saffo ... /The Adventures of Sappho, Poetess of Mitylene* (dual-language edition), 2 vols, T. Cadell, 1789

Vicinus, Martha, 'Sexuality and Power: a Review of Current Work in the History of Sexuality', *Feminist Studies*, vol. 8, no. 1, spring 1982, pp. 133–56

Vicinus, Martha, Martin Bauml Duberman and George Chauncey Jr., eds, *Hidden from History: Reclaiming the Gay and Lesbian Past*, Penguin, 1991

Vicinus, Martha, '"They Wonder to Which Sex I Belong": the Historical Roots of the Modern Lesbian Identity', in *Feminist Studies*, vol. 18, no. 3, fall 1992, pp. 467–97 (a revision of her paper in Altman and others, pp. 171–98)

Wagner, Peter, 'The Discourse on Sex – or Sex as Discourse: Eighteenth-Century Medical and Paramedical Erotica', in Rousseau and Porter, pp. 46–68

Wagner, Peter, *Eros Revived: Erotica of the Enlightenment in England and America*, Paladin Grafton Books, 1990

Walpole, Horace, *Correspondence*, ed. W.S. Lewis and others, Oxford University Press, 1960

Walsh, William, 'A Dialogue Concerning Women' [1699], in *The Works of Celebrated Authors, of Whose Writings There Are but Small Remains*, 2 vols, J. & R. Tonson & S. Draper, 1750

Wanley, Nathaniel, *The Wonders of the Little World; or, a General History of Man*, 1678

Wheelwright, Julie, *Amazons and Military Maids: Women Who Dressed as Men in the Pursuit of Life, Liberty and Happiness*, Pandora, 1989

White, Cynthia, *Women's Magazines 1693–1968*, Michael Joseph, 1970

Wilkes, John, 'An Essay on Woman' [1760s?], in *The Infamous Essay on Woman, or, John Wilkes Seated Between Vice and Virtue*, ed. Adrian Hamilton, André Deutsch, 1972

Winchilsea, Anne Finch, Countess of, *Selected Poems*, ed. Katharine M. Rogers, New York, Ungar, 1979

Winchilsea, Anne Finch, Countess of, *The Wellesley Manuscript Poems*, ed. Jean M. Ellis D'Alessandro, Florence, 1988

Wiseman, Jane, *Antiochus the Great: or, the Fatal Relapse*, William Turner & Richard Bassett, 1702

Wollstonecraft, Mary, *Mary* [1788], ed. Gary Kelly, Oxford, Oxford University Press, 1976

Yearsley, Ann, *Poems, on Several Occasions* [1784], 4th edn, G.G.J. & J. Robinson, 1786

Young, Sarah Weston, *Some Particulars, Relating to the Life and Death of Rebecca Scudamore*, Bristol, 1790

Index